INTERNATIONAL ORGANIZATIONS

A Comparative Approach

Werner J. Feld
and Robert S. Jordan
with Leon Hurwitz

PRAEGER SPECIAL STUDIES • PRAEGER SCIENTIFIC

Library of Congress Cataloging in Publication Data

Feld, Werner J.
   International organizations.

   Includes index.
   1. International agencies. I. Jordan, Robert S.,
1929–   II. Hurwitz, Leon.   III. Title.
JX1995.F36   1983   341.2   82-22313
ISBN 0-03-059621-1
ISBN 0-03-059622-X (pbk.)

Published in 1983 by Praeger Publishers
CBS Educational and Professional Publishing
a Division of CBS Inc.
521 Fifth Avenue, New York, New York 10175 U.S.A.

3456789 052 987654321

Printed in the United States of America
on acid-free paper

This book is dedicated to our many students, some of whom have gone on to careers in diplomacy or in international administration. We hope that they and those other students who will read this book can appreciate the sentiment by Barbara Ward that follows:

. . . the two worlds of man, the biosphere of his inheritance and the technosphere of his creation, are out of balance, indeed, potentially in deep conflict. And man is in the middle. This is the hinge of history at which we stand. The door of the future opening onto a crisis more sudden, more global, more inescapable, more bewildering than any ever encountered by the human species. And one which will take decisive shape within the life span of children who are already born. No problem is insoluble in the creation of a balanced and conserving planet, save humanity itself. Can it reach in time the vision of joint survival? Can its inescapable physical interdependence, the chief new insight of our century, induce that vision? We do not know. We have the duty to hope.

Barbara Ward, *Only One Earth*.

Preface

This textbook on international organizations represents an attempt by the authors to convey a sense of the role and functions of IGOs and INGOs as they exist today. References to the past are intended to provide a sense of the trend—or evolution—of how IGOs or INGOs came to play the role that they do, but such references are not designed to supplant published works on the histories of any specific international organizations. Thus, references to peace keeping by the United Nations are not as great as references to INGOs, to the economic activities of IGOs, or to regional IGOs, because in our opinion the range of non-peacekeeping activities by the United Nations and other international organizations outweigh multilateral peace-keeping activities. The highly nationalistic state of contemporary world politics simply does not provide the occasion for the United Nations to fulfill earlier expectations concerning dispute settlement and conflict resolution. By the same token, the fact that there has not been a major war in Europe for over a generation, although taken for granted by persons born since World War II, is very significant, and this is reflected in the proliferation of IGO activities involving the major—and to a lesser extent, the minor—states of Western Europe. Thus, references in the text to these activities are more numerous than in many other textbooks discussing international organizations. Finally, we attempt to reveal the broad range and variety of international activities as such—whether inter-governmental or non-governmental—because it is often overlooked by students residing in a country where international organizations have very little direct impact on their daily lives. In most of the rest of the world, international organizations play a very important role in the way in which states are able to advance the welfare of their citizens.

We wish to acknowledge the assistance of Muriel Murphy of the Department of Political Science, Carolyn Mangiaracina and Donna Myers of the Graduate School of the University of New Orleans, for their help in preparing the manuscript for publication. Mr. Anthony Judge, of the Union of International Associations, provided valuable advice and data in the preparation of certain charts and graphs. Ronald Meltzer of the State University of New York at Buffalo, and Michael Schechter of Michigan State University provided generously of their time to review the manuscript in draft and to provide advice on its suitability for classroom use. We would also like to express our appreciation to Betsy Brown, Political Science Editor for Praeger Publishers, for her patience and excellent counsel, as well as to Susan Goodman for her efficiency in supervising the production of this book.

New Orleans
November, 1982

Contents

4   DECISION-MAKING PROCESSES AND
POLICY-MAKING SCOPE

LIST OF TABLES

LIST OF FIGURES

LIST OF ACRONYMS

AFL-CIO	American Federation of Labor-Congress of Industrial Organizations
AMC	American Mining Congress
ANCOM	Andean Common Market
ASEAN	Association of Southeast Asian Nations
BENELUX	Belgium, The Netherlands, Luxembourg
BIS	Bank for International Settlements
BTO	Brussels Treaty Organization
CACM	Central American Common Market
CAM	Central American Market
CAP	Common Agricultural Policy
CARICOM	Caribbean Community and Common Market
CD	Committee on Disarmament
COMECON/CMEA	Council for Mutual Economic Assistance
COMSAT	Communication Satellite Corporation
COSPAR	Committee on Space Research
CPR/COREPER	Committee of Permanent Representatives
CTC	Center on Transnational Corporations
DG	Directorate-General
DPC	Defense Planning Committee
EAC	East African Community
EACSO	East African Common Services Organization
EAGGF	European Agricultural Guidance and Guarantee Fund
EC	European Communities
ECA	U.N. Economic Commission for Africa
ECLA	U.N. Economic Commission for Latin America
ECOSOC	U.N. Economic and Social Council
ECOWAS	Economic Community of West African States
ECSC	European Coal and Steel Community
ECU	European Currency Unit
EDC	European Defense Community
EEC	European Economic Community
EFTA	European Free Trade Association
EIB	European Investment Bank
EMCF	European Monetary Cooperation Fund
EMF	European Monetary Fund

EMS	European Monetary System
ENDC	Eighteen Nation Disarmament Committee
EP	European Parliament
EPC	European Political Cooperation
ERDF	European Regional Development Fund
EURATOM	European Atomic Energy Community
FAO	Food and Agriculture Organization
FCCD	Fund for Cooperation, Compensation, and Development
FFH/AD	FAO Freedom from Hunger Campaign/Action for Development
FICSA	Federation of International Civil Servants Associations
GATT	General Agreement on Tariffs and Trade
GDR	German Democratic Republic
GNP	Gross National Product
IACHR	Inter-American Commission on Human Rights
IAEA	International Atomic Energy Agency
IATA	International Air Transport Association
IBRD	International Bank for Reconstruction and Development
ICAs	International Commodity Agreements
ICAO	International Civil Aviation Organization
ICDA	International Coalition for Development Action
ICSU	International Council of Scientific Unions
IDA	International Development Association
IDB	Inter-American Development Bank
IFAD	International Fund for Agricultural Development
IFC	International Finance Corporation
IGO	Intergovernmental Organization
IGY	International Geophysical Year
ILO	International Labor Organization
IMF	International Monetary Fund
IMO	Inter-Governmental Maritime Organization
INFCE	International Nuclear Fuel Cycle Evaluation
INGO	International Non-Governmental Organization
INTERPOL	International Criminal Police Organization

IOC	Intergovernmental Oceanographic Commission
IPRA	International Peace Research Association
ISA	International Seabed Authority
ISPAs	International Scientific and Professional Associations
ITU	International Telecommunication Union
IVC	Index of Voting Cohesion
IVL	Index of Voting Likeness
LAFTA	Latin American Free Trade Association
LAIA	Latin American Integration Association
LDCs	Less Developed Countries
MEP	Member, European Parliament
MNC	Multinational Corporation
MNE	Multinational Enterprise
NATO	North Atlantic Treaty Organization
NGO	Non-Governmental Organization
NICs	Newly Industrialized Countries
NIEO	New International Economic Order
NORAD	North American Defense Command
NPT	Nuclear Non-Proliferation Treaty
NTBs	Non-Tariff Trade Barriers
OAS	Organization of American States
OAU	Organization for African Unity
OCAM	African and Malagasy Common Organization
OECD	Organization for Economic Cooperation and Development
OEEC	Organization for European Economic Cooperation
ONUC	U.N. Congo Force
OPEC	Organization of Petroleum Exporting Countries
PLO	Palestine Liberation Organization
PPE	European Peoples Party
PRC	People's Republic of China
PRDCYT	Regional Scientific and Technological Development Program
PTVAs	Professional, Technical, and Voluntary Associations

SCOPE	Scientific Committee on Problems of the Environment
SCOR	Scientific Committee on Oceanic Research
SDRs	Special Drawing Rights
SEATO	Southeast Asia Treaty Organization
SELA	Latin American Economic System
SPIDs	Sectoral Programs of Industrial Development
STABEX	Commodity Export Earnings Stabilization Scheme
TAB	Trade and Development Board
TCDC	U.N. Conference on Technical Cooperation among Developing Countries
TNC	Transnational Corporation
UK	United Kingdom
UNCLOS	U.N. Conference on the Law-of-the-Sea
UNCTAD	U.N. Conference on Trade and Development
UNDOF	U.N. Disengagement Observer Force
UNDP	U.N. Development Program
UNEF	U.N. Emergency Force
UNEP	U.N. Environment Program
UNESCO	U.N. Educational, Scientific, and Cultural Organization
UNFICYP	U.N. Peace-Keeping Force in Cyprus
UNFPA	U.N. Fund for Population Activities
UNHCR	U.N. High Commissioner for Refugees
UNICEF	U.N. Childrens Fund
UNIDO	U.N. Industrial Development Organization
UNIFIL	U.N. Interim Force in Lebanon
UNITAR	U.N. Institute for Training and Research
UNMOGIP	U.N. Military Observer Group in India and Pakistan
UNRWA	U.N. Relief and Works Agency
UNTSO	U.N. Truce Supervision Organization in Palestine
UNU	U.N. University
UPU	Universal Postal Union
USDA	U.S. Department of Agriculture
USSR	Union of Soviet Socialist Republics
WCAARD	World Conference on Agrarian Reform and Rural Development
WFC	World Food Council

WHO	World Health Organization
WIPO	World Intellectual Property Organization
WMO	World Meteorological Organization
WTO	Warsaw Treaty Organization

Introduction: An Overview

BRIEF HISTORICAL BACKGROUND

It is commonplace to date the beginning of the contemporary system of sovereign territorial states from the end of the Thirty-Years War in 1648, concluded by the Peace of Westphalia. During the seventeenth and the greater part of the eighteenth centuries, interactions between states in Europe were determined primarily by the interests of dynastic rulers who reigned as absolute monarchs over such states as France, Russia, Austria, and Prussia. Their concerns were prestige, military power, and territorial security, and therefore many of their interactions dealt with the formation of military or dynastic alliances. But as the agrarian economies of Western Europe began to respond to the impact of the Industrial Revolution, international economic relations assumed greater importance. Consequently, by the nineteenth century interstate relations increasingly embraced matters of commerce and trade in manufactured goods.[1]

This growth of manufacturing capacity in the rising industrial states of Western Europe and North America altered rapidly traditional distribution and consumption patterns throughout the world. With rapid industrialization came revolutionary improvements in the facilities of travel, transportation, and communication within and between states. These improvements offered opportunities but also generated new problems for governments.

The sheer complexity of all of this led governments to seek new forms of interstate cooperation that resulted, by the nineteenth and early twentieth centuries, in what used to be known generally as international organizations, but which we now call intergovernmental organizations (IGOs) since their members are sovereign nation states. Some of the earlier IGOs, many of which are examined in this text, had limited purposes both in time and in function—for example, perhaps providing nothing more than secretariat support for a meeting of heads of government or their representatives, as was the case for the periodic gatherings that grew out of the Congress of Vienna in 1815, and which became known as the "Congress System." Other IGOs were somewhat more elaborate, such as the Zollverein, which was a customs union of Germanic states set up in 1819 with Prussia as a leader. Still others, created near the end of the nineteenth century and more permanent, were the Universal Postal Union (UPU) and the International Telegraphic Union (ITU).

It is in the past half-century that IGOs have proliferated, some possessing extensive and intricate bureaucratic structures. The League of Nations, created in 1919 after World War I, and the United Nations, established in 1945 after World War II, are of course primary examples of attempts at creating IGOs based on what were hoped would be universal concepts that would provide the normative basis, as well as operational guidelines, to regulate the problems of conflict between or among states. But the European Communities (EC), the North Atlantic Treaty Organization (NATO), and the Organization of American States (OAS) are also important examples of the proliferation of regional IGOs dedicated to resolving tensions and conflict situations generated by both military/security, and economic conditions.

As the IGOs proliferated, another kind of international organization composed of nongovernmental organizations (INGOs) interested in the promotion of a variety of goals in the international arena also grew by leaps and bounds. These organizations, known as international NGOs or INGOs for short, play increasingly important roles in international politics and cannot be ignored in a study of international organizations.

APPROACHES TO THE STUDY OF INTERNATIONAL ORGANIZATION

As in the study of international relations in general, a number of approaches can be taken in the study of the academic field known as "international organization." Although, as just noted, both IGOs and INGOs make up this field of study, our text focuses more on IGOs because the current configuration of global politics continues to rest on the notion of territorial sovereignty which, when combined with ideological formulations, becomes the driving force of nationalism.

One of the possible ways of studying international organization is the historical approach, which is especially important because, as has been implied, international organization (used in its collective sense) has a clearly defined history marked by institutional successes and failures. But, as Inis Claude aptly remarks, "the advantages of learning from history are offset by the perils of being blinded by history."[2] Nevertheless, it is generally accepted that our contemporary world can be better understood, and future trends more clearly perceived and assessed, if we possess some familiarity with the past. In particular, the pages that follow reflect our belief that the future of international organization may indeed be more successfully perceived if the experiences of the last century in particular, are kept in mind.

Another well-recognized approach to the study of international organization consists of the analysis of the international legal norms and treaties underlying the establishment of particular IGOs, and of the competencies that the bureaucracies and other organs of these organizations possess both in the international arena and vis-a-vis their respective member-states. While legal analysis and codification has a definite place in the understanding and evaluation of particular IGOs, they provide only partial insights into the actual political dimensions that define the effectiveness of contemporary global or regional IGOs.[3]

Another approach is the structural-functional analysis of institutions created by particular IGOs. In a broad sense, as one scholar suggests, functions refer to "what must be done," while structures refer to how what must be done is to be done.[4] Structure means a pattern—that is, observable uniformity—of institutional actions and operations. A main purpose of function in a very abstract sense is the maintenance of the larger or transcendent unit within which the structure is embedded.[5] This approach therefore focuses on both the formal (that is, legal) and informal (that is, political) manner in which the pertinent institutional bureaucracies perform their assigned functions.

This form of analysis can also provide an understanding as to how these institutional bureaucracies function in the context of international politics, and how far the expectations of the states founding IGOs are being fulfilled. The analysis must take into account how demands (inputs) by the various constituencies of IGOs are being processed, what the end product(s) of the function performance process is/are (output), how feedbacks are monitored by the IGO to determine how well it fulfills its purpose, and how satisfactorily the interests of member-states are being promoted and safeguarded.[6] In this connection, it should be emphasized again that INGOs are becoming increasingly salient actors in the field of international organization, both in their own right and as interacting agents with governments at the national level and with IGOs at the international level.

Another useful approach to the study of the IGOs (and to a lesser degree INGOs) is decision-making analysis. International bureaucracies, with their intergovernmental political organs, have various competencies for decision making conferred upon them by their governing charters or statutes. The nature and consequences of these competencies varies from IGO to IGO; in some cases decisions may be directly binding on the member-states as well as on the international bureaucracy; in a few cases decisions can affect directly persons residing in the member-states as, for example, under certain circumstances in the EC. In more cases, however, the decisions are nonbinding or nonself-enforcing, with compliance or noncompliance dependent on the governments of the member-states' perceptions of how their respective national interests can best be served.

Another aspect of IGO decision making is its locus. In our complex world, the effect of decisions made by an IGO may well depend on whether a particular decision can be taken exclusively with the institutional apparatus of the IGO or whether national organs of the member-states need participate in the decision-making process. What then is the impact of the participating member-states on IGO decision making, and which functional areas of the national governments have the greatest influence on the international decision-making process? What kind of interplay between IGO institutions and national governments as well as their respective bureaucracies, exists with respect to the international decision-making process and what effect does this have on the functions to be performed by the IGO? What are the domestic policy-making dynamics in national governments that explain the governments' voting behavior in IGOs? We intend to analyze and discuss these important questions.

So far we have concentrated on the analysis of the circumstances surrounding and influencing the decisions to be taken. Another aspect of decision-making analysis, often considered the core of such an analysis, is the inquiry into the motivations, attitudes, and behavior of those decision-makers who give particular decisions their shape, scope, and direction. Seen from this perspective, decision making refers to the act of choosing among available alternatives.[7] But this simple statement conceals the difficulty of such analysis. Problems abound and include the sufficiency of information available to decision makers, uncertainty about alternatives and their consequences, and the manifold pressures exerted on policy makers to accommodate domestic interest groups and foreign governments. These problems make it very difficult for a decision maker to reach a rational decision—one directed toward the attainment of a clearly-defined goal that would reflect the highest preference. This preference would be based on the assumption that, for the choice of alternatives, comprehensive, relevant information would be available and is used; that the consequences of all alternative courses could be fully established; and that the selected preferred alternative would possess the highest utility in reaching the goal desired.

Social scientists must assume, nevertheless, that in all human relations, the rational elements that go into a decision will tend to predominate over the irrational.[8] These elements must be discovered rather than taken for granted, and their discovery requires an assessment of the various influences bearing on every decision made. They include the social and economic backgrounds of the decision makers; their personal goals, interests, and aspirations; their prior commitments; and the specific motivations that may stem from the bureaucratic position they hold.

Despite the many factors that affect the making of IGO (and INGO) decisions, and the recognition that international action involves not only a single decision to be analyzed but also a continuum of interrelated decisions, the decision-making approach to the study of IGOs can provide significant insights into the dynamics of IGO activities and the bureaucratic and political processes used to obtain national and international objectives. Indeed, movement in the international arena flows from hundreds of decisions made not only in IGOs, but also in INGOs and in national institutions and enterprises around the world.

In summary, while our basic commitment in this textbook is to a comparative analysis, we employ both the structural-functional and decision-making approaches as appropriate, focusing, however, more on relevant formal and informal circumstances of decision making than on the idiosyncratic attributes of decision makers with respect to particular decisions. The historical and legal approaches will be utilized whenever they contribute directly to our knowledge of those IGOs discussed in the text.

THE COMPARATIVE APPROACH

All international organization textbooks discuss a variety of IGOs and suggest appropriate classifications or categories thereof, with the treatment of the organizations sometimes done chronologically but mostly broken down according to broad issue areas. Occasionally, in the case of economic IGOs, they are addressed according to function.[9] The larger IGOs, especially the U.N. system and its specialized and affiliated agencies, are also examined in historical terms.

In contrast, our text pursues a comparative approach. We believe that the comparative analysis and assessment of the wide variety of IGOs that exist today can give students a better understanding of this rapidly-growing global phenomenon, and can generate a greater and deeper interest in a subject matter that is intimately intertwined with the dynamics of world and domestic politics. The purpose of the study of national politics on a comparative basis is to stimulate in the student an interest in discovering the commonalities and differences that exist in the United States and elsewhere. A similar interest may be evoked when the student of international organization can see the commonalities and differences that explain why IGOs are established, how they perform their tasks, and to what extent they achieve the objectives for which the organization and its supporting bureaucracy were created in the first place. Finally, by looking at IGOs comparatively, the student can gain an overall perspective about the capabilities and constraints, the successes and failures of IGOs—a perspective that can be obtained only with difficulty if IGOs are studied in consecutive order, either chronologically, by issue-area, by function, or by geographic region.

Of course, the comparative approach has its difficulties as well. Criteria must be identified against which specific IGOs can be compared, and indicators may have to be developed that will aid in the evaluation of organizational features and operational trends. Variables relevant for the explanation of the successes or failures of IGOs need to be determined. But in spite of these possible problem areas, we are convinced that the comparative undertaking is useful and will contribute to our knowledge about international organization as a major field of academic inquiry.

Illustrative cases are presented, beginning with Chapter 2, to provide the student with selected concrete examples and explanations of IGO (and INGO) activities and behavior.

SUMMARY OF CONTENTS

No textbook dealing with international organization in a collective sense can limit itself to an analysis only of the United Nations and its specialized and affiliated agencies, even if one were to accept the premise that there exists an incipient "world organization" that might lead eventually to some form, or forms, of world government. On the contrary, we are impressed with the pluralism of the world community, its decentralized nature, and its resistance to system and order either in theory or in practice. Yet it is not entirely accurate to characterize what goes on in world politics as reflective of an essentially chaotic "state of nature" (to recall Thomas Hobbes); nonetheless there are very few normative, constitutional, legal, functional, or power/political levers that can be pulled by one or more decision makers that can effectively and systematically determine the course of human history. We hope that the cases that form an important part of this text will mirror this diverse, pluralistic, largely unmanageable and hence ungovernable political, social, cultural, and economic world in which we live.

It will also be noted quickly by the student that, in contrast to many textbooks, our book does not focus primarily on security or conflict issues. It is true as is discussed in Chapter 1 that the primary motivation for the evolution of some major IGOs arose out of the increasingly destructive nature of interstate conflict. But we must resist the temptation to posit the pursuit of peace as an antidote to the pursuit of war as a primary rationale for the proliferations of IGOs. In fact, the unilateral resort to force as a means to achieve national goals rests upon such a melange of domestic and international conditions that if we made conflict itself the centerpiece of the book we could commit the academic crime of oversimplification. At the same time, if we have used the case studies judicially, we hope to have avoided the other academic crime of rendering simplicity unnecessarily complex.

Chapter 1 discusses some of the conceptualizations on the role and function of IGOs as a general background for what follows in succeeding chapters. Chapter 2 examines in detail the creation of IGOs, and discusses the problems of IGO genesis and continuity in seven illustrative cases. This leads directly in Chapter 3 to an examination of the institutional and bureaucratic aspects of IGOs, with the cases stressing the issue of task performance through the internal structures of the organizations, without neglecting their history and overall character. The actual process by which IGOs engage in decision making and in policy making are then taken up in Chapter 4, with the cases focusing on the modalities used as well as on the imponderables of multinational leadership in decision making. This chapter also affords us the opportunity to reveal how principles of democracy have been universalized through the parliamentary practices of IGOs. Finally, we seek to determine the reasons for and consequences of breakdowns in IGO decision-making processes and the decline of task performance.

Chapter 5 discusses aspects of political analysis that earlier textbooks ran the risk of oversimplifying—the interactions of domestic politics and the pursuit of foreign policy goals on the behavior of IGOs. Indeed, we consider the interface between IGO decision making and the pursuit of the national interests of the member-states as providing salient explanations for the quality of task performance by IGOs. This interface is affected by the formation of various coalitions among member governments, IGO and national bureaucrats, and parliamentarians and their impact on organizational effectiveness and output implementation. The cases in this chapter are more likely to leave us with a sense of uncertainty (rather than a sense of certainty) that multinational and multilevel decision making can be fully comprehended, thus requiring careful evaluation in order to make explicit the policy directions of IGO member-states and to reveal how IGOs are used for promoting their national interests.

Chapter 6 focuses on an increasingly important aspect of both domestic and international life—the role of INGOs and their domestic counterparts. Even though other IGOs could be included in this chapter, the interaction of INGOs with the United Nations system, including the specialized and affiliated agencies, furnishes a sufficient body of information for us to grasp the significance of this growing form of international activity. Finally, Chapter 7 provides us with an opportunity to understand, through the various forms of sustained and institutionalized multinational cooperation afforded by international regimes, how it might be possible to view interdependence and resultant regime formation as a strengthening and positive force in the life of states, rather than as a means of exploitation of some states by others, or of prolonging dependency.[10] A short concluding Chapter 8 dwells on the quality of IGO task performance in past, present, and future and suggests that international organizations have a long way to go before they can meet the high and well-justified aspirations of the world community.

The reader should note that we have expanded the footnotes from the usual citation of sources to a listing of important references for further reading and elucidation. We believe that these references, being made specific to a particular part in the text, are much more useful than our simply providing a catalogue of suggested readings at the end of each chapter. The various appendixes at the end of the text are also designed to help the reader obtain a better understanding of the often complex materials presented in the book.

NOTES

1. For a good historical overview, see Paul Reuter, *International Institutions* (London: George Allen and Unwin, 1958).

2. Inis Claude, *Swords into Plowshares*, 3rd ed. rev., (New York: Random House, 1964), p. 5.

3. For an elaboration of this approach, see Stephen M. Schwebel, *The Effectiveness of International Decisions* (Dobbs Ferry, N.Y.: Oceana, 1971).

4. Marion J. Levy, Jr., *The Structure of Society* (Princeton, N.J.: Princeton University Press, 1952), p. 64.

5. Ibid., pp. 57–62.

6. For an elaboration of the functional approach to the study of IGOs, see Thomas George Weiss, *International Bureaucracy* (Lexington, Mass.: D. C. Heath, 1975).

7. See James E. Doughtery and Robert L. Pfaltzgraff, Jr., *Contending Theories of International Relations* (Philadelphia: Lippincott, 1971), p. 312.

8. Ibid., pp. 316–17.

9. See A. J. R. Groom and Paul Taylor, eds., *Functionalism: Theory and Practice in International Relations* (New York: Crane, Russak, 1975).

10. See, for example, Ernst B. Haas, *The Web of Interdependence: The United States and International Organizations* (Englewood Cliffs, N.J.: Prentice-Hall, 1970).

Chapter 1

Changing Conceptualizations

Although the subject of international organization has been studied intensively for decades, it has only been fairly recently that careful distinctions began to be made between international organizations whose constituent members were nation-states and those composed of private citizens organized in the manner of interest groups. The former, as already mentioned in the Introduction, are known as intergovernmental organizations (IGOs). The latter are termed international nongovernmental organizations (INGOs), examples of which are the International Chamber of Commerce and the World Confederation of Labor. In some instances mixed governmental-nongovernmental units have been formed, such as, for example, the Communication Satellite Corporation (COMSAT).

The number of IGOs and INGOs has grown tremendously since World War II. The total of IGOs operating in 1977 was about 308; their number may reach 380 by 1985.[1] This proliferation of IGOs should not be surprising when one considers that the number of states has more than tripled since World War II, largely as a consequence of decolonization. The number of nation-states, as measured by the membership of the United Nations, now exceeds 155.

The growth of INGOs has been even more spectacular. In 1972 a total of 2470 INGOs was listed by the Union of International Associations; that number was estimated by the Union to go possibly as high as 10,815 by the year 2000.[2] But it should be noted that not all INGOs are still actively pursuing their general objectives. But even the dormant INGOs may retain their institutional structures and so can be reactivated to pursue either the same or different objectives. Chapter 6 will deal in greater detail with different aspects of INGO operations.

Concomitant with their growth, IGOs and INGOs have become increasingly significant elements in world politics. We are well acquainted with some of the larger IGOs such as the United Nations, the North Atlantic Treaty Organization (NATO), the Organization of American States (OAS) and more recently, the Organization of Petroleum Exporting Countries (OPEC). But there are also many smaller IGOs, which have various impacts on what happens in the international arena. Likewise, INGOs can affect the behavior of states although the power of individual INGOs is generally relatively limited as we will see in Chapter 6.

THE NATURE OF IGOs

Basically, IGOs are set up by three or more states to fulfill common purposes or to attain common objectives.[3] In most instances, they constitute the framework for political and military alliances or economic cooperation schemes. IGOs possess a number of particular features that we will examine briefly:

1. The purposes and objectives pursued by IGOs reflect common or converging national interests of the member-states and, therefore, are normally long-range in nature.

2. The achievement of IGO goals is theoretically carried out with the equal participation of all states although in practice, this is often not the case. The process of achieving IGO goals is best described as a round-table operation. This is in contrast to normal one-on-one diplomacy under bilateral treaties through which two states may also pursue common purposes but for which the basis is trade-offs of advantages and disadvantages between the participating governments.

3. The most distinguishing feature of an IGO is its institutional framework. This framework may be very simple and consist of nothing more than a lightly staffed secretariat; or it may be complex and comprehensive, approximating the legislative, executive, and judicial branches of a national government. In most instances, however, the legislative functions are quite limited. Representatives of the member-states of the IGO normally meet in an annual plenary conference at which general policy is laid down. Decisions usually require a two-thirds majority and in special circumstances, unanimity. A council (usually composed of the permanent representatives of the member governments) is frequently entrusted with supervising the day-to-day executive functions of the IGO. It meets more frequently than the conference and almost always decides questions by unanimous vote. The performance of judicial functions is normally carried out by selected international tribunals, such as the International Court of Justice, which is a principal organ of the United Nations, but to which other IGOs may also assign jurisdictional competencies. Or a special court may be established, such as the Court of Justice of the European Communities. We will examine in detail the variations in institutions and their functions in Chapter 3.

4. IGOs are always established by a multilateral international treaty. This treaty is often called a convention, a charter, or a constitution. It stipulates the competencies

of the intergovernmental or bureaucratic organs of the IGO, the interrelations among them, and sets up the basic norms and operational principles of the organization.

5. IGOs are considered to have "international legal personality," which means that, under international law, they can act in some ways similarly to a state: some, that is, the United Nations, have standing to sue or may be sued in the International Court of Justice. They can conclude international treaties in their own name and diplomatic missions from their own member states, as well as from other states or from INGOs, can be accredited to them.

CLASSIFICATION OF IGOs

IGOs may be classified into several categories. The most general classifications are derived from their geographic or functional scope. Their geographic spread may be global, as is that of the United Nations and its specialized and affiliated agencies, or it may extend only to a particular region, such as Western Europe, Southeast Asia, or Central America. Examples are the European Communities (EC) covering most of Western Europe (except Sweden, Norway, Austria, Switzerland, and the Iberian Peninsula), the Association of Southeast Asian Nations (ASEAN), or The Central American Common Market (CACM). Global IGOs are sometimes referred to as universal in the literature.

Functional scope refers to the function or functions an IGO is designated to perform. These may be: the enhancement of the member-states' security, adding collective military strength to their political power; the advancement of their economic performance in order to raise the economic well-being of their people; the improvement of their scientific and technological capabilities as well as technical cooperation.[4] In some cases IGOs are assigned more than one function. The main functions of the United Nations embrace security, economic, social, and cultural responsibilities on a global basis. These are laid out in Article I of the U.N. Charter. The Organization of American States (OAS) is a regional organization composed of most of the states in the Western hemisphere with the same range of basic functions.

Figure 1.1 provides a matrix showing possible combinations of functions. Perhaps the largest number of IGOs falls in category II that would include the whole array of the specialized and affiliated agencies of the United Nations. But the number of IGOs in category I also is significant, considering the high level of interest of states in both economic and security regional organizations.

There are several IGOs in category III: the Organization of African Unity (OAU) and the OAS are examples. But obviously only one global, multifunctional IGO exists at present: the United Nations.

Other possible functional categories are the scope of an IGO's compe-

FIGURE 1.1

Classification of IGOs

	By Scope		
		Geographic Scope	
Functional Scope		Regional	Global
Monofunctional		I	II
Multifunctional		III	IV

	By Competence and Function				
Competence			Function		
	Security	Economic	Political	Social	Cultural
General	NATO OAS UN	EEC ANCOM	Arab League		UNESCO
Limited	OAU	ECSC	Council of Europe	OAS	OAS

	By Integration
Low	
	Alliance without institutional framework
	Intergovernmental relationship with institutional framework
	Independent IGO decision making
	Supranational organization
	World government
High	

tence, and its degree of integration (also shown in Figure 1.1). The competence may either be general or limited. For example, the European Coal and Steel Community (ECSC) is a regional IGO of the EC with a competence that is limited to the coal and steel sectors of its member-states. On the other hand, the European Economic Community (EEC) of the EC, also a regional IGO, has a nearly general competence in all the economic sectors of the member-states, including agriculture, excepting coal and steel.

In terms of degree of integration, IGOs may be judged as being either very loosely integrated with a minimum of institutional structure and a minimum of powers conferred upon them by their member-states, or as falling at the other end of the integration spectrum. The highest level of integration exists when an IGO approaches supranational status. The term "supranational" means that the member-states of the IGO have transferred to the organs of the organization some of the powers of decision making and implementation usually exercised only by sovereign states. The organs or institutions of the IGO may have been given the authority to issue certain legal rules that are binding upon the populations of the member-states without requiring having been endorsed with the force of law through national legislative procedures. A supranational IGO, then, is the nearest international unit of governance to a state, which is the primary national unit of governance.

The most useful classification scheme for purposes of comparative analysis may be to focus on the prime organizational tasks to be carried out by IGOs. These tasks are what we would call the "management of cooperation," taking into account the skills employed in the coordination of organizational activities and in the achievement of necessary political compromises. Most economic IGOs clearly are task oriented because they are propelled by a community of economic interests. Security IGOs, for which conflict resolution through the coordination of cooperation by political compromise may be more difficult, usually also may experience greater disharmony over defining the tasks to be performed by the IGO. Political IGOs such as the Council of Europe, along with military alliances, are subject to this difficulty. Conflict resolution is the foremost task of the United Nations, the OAS, and the OAU as is clearly indicated by their constituent treaties. However, these IGOs and especially the United Nations, also perform economic coordinating tasks, and these indeed are the main missions for many of the U.N. specialized and affiliated agencies.

Attempts have been made to introduce organization theory into explaining and perhaps predicting the behavior of IGOs, but so far these efforts have not been very comprehensive.[5] Nevertheless, an evaluation of task performance by individual IGOs provides an important criterion for comparative analysis and assessment. Such evaluation would include: the degree of need satisfaction achieved as related to the attainment of the purposes for which the IGO was created; judgments on the capacity of the IGO to solve functional problems; examination of the quality of the IGO's executive leadership and its ability to maintain institutional effectiveness, as well as to shape the IGO's overall functional environment.

The degree of success of an IGO's task performance depends to a large extent on the effectiveness of the IGO's international bureaucracy. To make judgments on the civil servants composing the bureaucracy requires evaluations of bureaucratic autonomy and morale, of the existence of strong or weak organizational ideologies, and of the prospects for needed institutional change, reinforcement, or perhaps merely survival.

Another important aspect of comparing IGOs' task performances is their ability to develop policies and implement them. Success in this area depends on the IGO's autonomy and the confidence of member governments in the IGO's political leadership. But even more important are the perceptions of member governments as to how closely policies developed by the IGO will match their respective national interests. Hence, member governments may encourage or discourage policy development by the IGO in accordance with their judgments regarding national benefits and costs. If the development by an IGO of particular policies is viewed as useful by member governments, or if an IGO has acquired such a high measure of autonomy in a specific (usually functional) policy area that it can go ahead with policy formulation without the specific blessing of the member governments, then its implementation success will depend on how well flows of constituency demands and supports are continually processed into policy outputs. In turn, the IGO's capacity to influence the behavior of governmental (and nongovernmental) actors and its actual exercise of this influence will be enhanced. Task performance evaluation must also take into account policy outcomes, especially how far these outcomes differ from policy intent and what the unintended direct or indirect effects of these policies have been.

Finally, the saliency to the member-states of issues that are the potential objects of IGO policies is a significant variable for policy development and successful task performance. This is particularly the case when policy implementation requires action by the member-states of the organization. A good example here is the implementation of the EEC's Common Agricultural Policy (CAP). The greater the saliency of the issues to the member-states, the greater are the chances that member-states will want to exercise control over IGO policy development or perhaps assume policy formulation themselves. Such circumstances might lead to the redefinition of IGO goals by the member governments, the reduction of IGO autonomy, the request for changes in IGO operational or bureaucratic modes (such as the restructuring effort in the United Nations), and maybe the need for the renewed justification of the IGO's existence.[6]

According to Anthony Judge, a number of IGOs (and INGOs) may also be usefully characterized according to the peculiarities in their structure.[7] One such category could be the intergovernmental profit-making corporation; it could include the various regional development banks such as the Asian Development Bank (ADB), and the International Finance Corporation (IFC) component of the World Bank group. Other characteristics of IGOs may refer to their mode of action. Examples are the Permanent Court of Arbitration whose sole purpose is to provide the means for the settlement of international disputes through arbitration; the Bank for International Settlements (BIS), which concentrates on facilitating bank clearings across national boundaries; and, because of their focus on consultation and negotiation, the so-called Group of 77 and the Non-Aligned Movement, which together embrace almost all of the nearly 125 Third World states.

In our view, task performance and the evaluation of its quality provide the most significant criteria against which to compare IGOs and perhaps even large INGOs. Figure 1.2 offers a graphic overview of basic tasks to be performed and a number of variables that may explain high or low success of task performances in individual IGOs. A note of caution is in order here.

FIGURE 1.2

Organizational Tasks and Evaluation

Task Performance	Management Evaluation	
	High Success	Low Success
Cooperation	I	II
Conflict resolution	III	IV

Explanatory Variables for IGO Management Evaluation

Degree of need satisfaction
Quality of IGO policy development, implementation, and outcomes
Issue saliency for member-states
Executive leadership quality
Management and problem-solving skills of IGO executives and administrators
Nature and capabilities of civil servants (IGO and national and seconded to the organization)

It is easier to set up the comparative criteria than to develop, at times, the empirical evidence regarding particular variables. In other words, we may observe the results of IGO activities and policy outcomes, but do not have sufficiently precise evidence to attribute particular results or outcomes to specific actions or operations. Nevertheless, the illustrative cases provide indications that suggest the influence and effects of certain variables.

IGOs: PATTERNS OF GROWTH

In the beginning of this chapter we pointed to the remarkable growth of IGOs. Table 1.1 shows the pattern of growth since 1815, relating it to the expansion of the number of states since that time and providing information on the mean number of states per IGO and the mean number of IGO membership per state.

From an inspection of this table, it is clear that the growth of IGOs has been steady and that by 1964 the mean number of states per IGO had reached 22.7 per IGO and the mean number of shared memberships 14.3. It is evident that an international network-building process has occurred during the last 100 years among states, and furthermore it is obvious that many states belong to a number of IGOs, either global or regional. (For further illustration, see Appendix A, "Membership of the United Nations and Its Specialized and Related Agencies"). We will examine the implications of this network-building process later, after we have discussed the general growth pattern of INGOs.

TABLE 1.1: Growth of IGOs

Period	Number of IGOs	Number of Memberships	Mean Number of Nations per IGO	Mean Number of IGO Memberships per Nation	Number of Nations
1815–19	1	5	5.0	0.2	23
1820–24	1	5	5.0	0.2	23
1825–29	1	5	5.0	0.2	25
1830–34	1	5	5.0	0.2	28
1835–39	2	18	9.0	0.6	31
1840–44	2	18	9.0	0.5	35
1845–49	2	18	9.0	0.5	38
1850–54	2	18	9.0	0.5	40
1855–59	3	24	8.0	0.6	42
1860–64	3	21	7.0	0.5	44
1865–69	6	54	9.0	1.4	39
1869–74	7	65	9.3	1.9	34
1875–79	9	106	11.8	3.1	34
1880–84	11	136	12.4	3.9	35
1885–89	17	203	11.9	5.3	38

1890–94	21	267	12.7	7.0	38
1895–99	23	299	13.0	7.3	41
1900–04	30	412	13.7	9.6	43
1905–09	44	639	14.5	14.2	45
1910–14	49	753	15.4	16.7	45
1915–19	53	826	15.6	16.2	51
1920–24	72	1336	18.6	21.2	63
1925–29	83	1528	18.4	23.5	65
1930–34	87	1639	18.8	24.8	66
1935–39	86	1697	19.7	25.3	67
1940–44	82	1560	19.0	24.0	65
1945–49	123	2284	18.6	30.5	75
1950–54	144	2684	18.6	32.7	82
1955–59	168	3338	19.9	37.1	90
1960–64	195	4436	22.7	36.4	122
1965–77	292	6432	24.6	38.2	195

Source: *Yearbook of International Organizations*, 1972–73, 14th ed. (Brussels, Belgium: Union of International Associations), p. 885, and 1981, 19th ed. Table 4.

Returning to Table 1.1, it is interesting to note certain spurts in the creation of IGOs. A noticeable acceleration took place during the 1905–09 period that may have been caused by increasing economic transactions across national boundaries (which needed regulation), and by technological developments (which required coordination). However, it was clearly the periods immediately following World Wars I and II that witnessed the greatest proliferation of new IGOs. Various means for the settlement of disputes through conflict resolution measures, for better organizational tools and management techniques to enhance international cooperation, and for border-crossing defensive arrangements, were put in place to prevent a repetition of the destructive havoc of life and property that were the result of the two world wars. Figure 1.3 provides a graphic presentation of the IGO trend of growth.

In terms of number of IGO memberships, France ranks first, being a member in 131 IGOs, followed by the United Kingdom (124) and The Netherlands (118). The United States holds 102 IGO memberships and ranks as number seven. All this can be seen on Table 1.2 that also suggests that

TABLE 1.2: States Belonging to the Greatest Number of IGOs in 1970

State	Number of IGO Memberships	Rank Order
France	131	1
United Kingdom	124	2
Netherlands	118	3
Italy	111	4
Belgium	110	5
Germany, Federal Republic of	108	6
United States	102	7
Denmark	99	8
Sweden	97	9
Spain	93	10
Norway	92	11
Austria	90	12
Argentina	89	13
Brazil	87	15.5
Canada	87	15.5
Japan	87	15.5
Mexico	87	15.5
Switzerland	83	18
India	82	19
Chile	81	20

Source: Harold K. Jacobson, *Networks of Interdependence* (New York: Alfred A. Knopf, 1979) p. 54.

FIGURE 1.3

Growth Pattern of International NGOs Compared with IGOs, 1860–1970

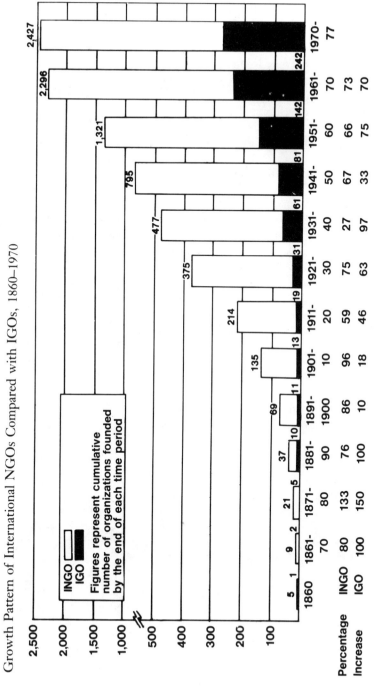

Source. Werner J. Feld, Nongovernmental Forces and World Politics (New York: Praeger, 1972), p. 177.

19

as of 1970, few developing states are among those states occupying the first 20 places among all IGO members.

As far as a breakdown by constituents of members of the main global IGOs is concerned, Table 1.3 indicates that the European share of the League of Nations' membership in 1934 was 48 percent. In 1976 this percentage in the United Nations had fallen to 21 percent, with the overwhelming majority being mostly the developing states of Africa, Asia, and the Americas. The trend in favor of these states has continued.

HISTORICAL FLASHBACKS

The first IGO on Table 1.1 is the Congress of Vienna that attempted to institutionalize regular consultations among the great powers of that era. It was convened in 1815 to lay the diplomatic foundations for a new European order amid the ruins left by the Napoleonic Wars. Although four major conferences were held between 1815 and 1822, severe differences in policies and objectives among the Great Powers made it clear that the time had not arrived for institutionalized collaboration and management in Europe. Nevertheless, the leaders of the major states involved had constituted themselves as the Concert of Europe, which met sporadically to deal with pressing political issues.

The Rhine Commission

The Congress of Vienna established a subordinate organization, the Rhine Commission, whose purpose was to regulate traffic and trade along the Rhine

TABLE 1.3: Membership in the League of Nations in 1934 and in the United Nations in 1976

Region	1934 League of Nations		1976 United Nations	
	Number	Percentage	Number	Percentage
Africa	3	5	49	33
Asia	6	10	33	23
Oceania	2	4	5	3
Americas	19	33	29	20
Europe	28	48	31	21
Total	58	100	147	100

Source: Harold K. Jacobson, *Networks of Interdependence* (New York: Alfred A. Knopf, 1979) p. 48.

River. The members of this Commission were the littoral states of the Rhine, each of which had one vote. The Commission was given considerable powers to amend its own rules and to act as a court of appeals for the decisions of local courts regarding river problems or issues. Similar commissions were established later for the Danube, Elbe, Douro, and Po rivers.

Public International Unions

While the various river commissions dealt at times with politically sensitive issues, another type of IGO sprang up in the middle of the nineteenth century that was concerned primarily with nonpolitical, technical matters. These IGOs were known as public international unions, and the most important of these were the International Telegraphic Union (1865) (ITU), the Universal Postal Union (1874) (UPU), and the International Union of Railway Freight Transportation (1890). Other IGOs of a very nonpolitical nature established during that period dealt with such diverse fields as agriculture, health, standards of weights and measurements, patents and copyrights, and narcotics and drugs. Some of these IGOs had elaborate institutional frameworks: for example, the Universal Postal Union had a Congress of Plenipotentiaries that met every five years, a Conference of Delegates of Administrations, and a Permanent International Bureau. The Conference had amendment powers and frequently used majority voting.

The Zollverein

The first attempt at economic integration in Europe came with the establishment of the German Zollverein in 1834. This organization was a loosely joined customs union and lasted until 1867. Initially, only 18 of the 38 German states—kingdoms, duchies, and free cities—participated, but by 1867, almost all states had become members. Prussia was the moving spirit and overall manager of the Zollverein. The General Congress was the chief organ; decisions were made by unanimity.

The League of Nations

The first major effort to organize a global security IGO for the peaceful settlement of disputes through mechanisms for conflict resolution was the creation of the League of Nations. It was established in 1919 by the victorious nations of World War I led by President Woodrow Wilson, but the United States did not join. The principle underlying the League of Nations was the notion of collective security, under which all member-states of this IGO were obligated to come to the aid of a member-state that was the victim of military aggression.

The United Nations

The creation of the United Nations in 1945 is the culmination of the global IGO. It represents not only a single IGO, derived from the precedent of the League (although the International Labor Organization [ILO] was associated with it) but also a whole family of global IGOs that includes the ILO as well as the (United Nations) Educational, Scientific, and Cultural Organization (UNESCO), the World Health Organization (WHO), the Food and Agriculture Organization (FAO) and many others (see Table 1.4). Indeed, over the years there has been a continuing proliferation of United Nations specialized and affiliated agencies, many of which were created to deal with the problems of Third World development. Details of the U.N. structure will be examined in Chapter 2, and the assessment of various U.N. activities will follow in subsequent chapters.

Regional IGOs

The rapid increase of regional IGOs follow the conclusion of World War II when economic cooperation schemes were seen as providing solutions for the ravages of the war in Western Europe, and led to the establishment of the European Communities (EC) and the European Free Trade Association (EFTA). The Benelux Convention, in fact, was signed already in 1944 but did not come into force until 1948. The Council for Mutual Economic Assistance, better known as COMECON or CMEA was the Soviet bloc response to the EC.

Many regional economic IGOs were also set up in the Third World, but the rationale there was to accelerate the development process. In spite of many failures, this rationale has continued to provide the major justification for creating new regional IGOs or expanding their functions.

A number of regional security IGOs also sprang up following World War II. However, their establishment was primarily in response to the bipolar competition known as the Cold War that had evolved between the two superpowers and that had global ramifications. Hence, by the 1950s NATO and the Warsaw Treaty Organization (WTO) had come into being and continue to this day. Security IGOs that were set up by the United States in Southeast Asia and in the Middle East to contain the Soviet Union and the People's Republic of China (PRC)—CENTO and SEATO—have since disappeared.[8]

THE NATURE OF INGOs

In the early pages of this chapter we commented briefly on the rapid rise in the number of INGOs and provided estimates of how many of these organ-

TABLE 1.4: Associated Agencies and Institutes of the United Nations

The specialized Agencies, listed chronologically according to date of entry into force of respective agreements with the United States:

International Labor Organization
International Institute of Labor Studies
International Occupational Safety and Health Information Center
International Center for Advanced Technical and Vocational Training
Food and Agriculture Organization of the United Nations
U.N. Educational, Scientific, and Cultural Organization
    International Institute for Educational Planning
World Health Organization
    International Agency for Research on Cancer
International Bank for Reconstruction and Development
    International Monetary Fund
    International Finance Corporation
    International Development Association
International Civil Aviation Association
Universal Postal Union
International Telecommunication Union
    International Frequency Registration Board
    International Telegraph and Telephone Consultative Committee
    International Radio Consultative Committee
World Meteorological Organization
Inter-Governmental Maritime Organization

Other Members of U.N. Family:

Office of the U.N. High Commissioner for Refugees
International Narcotics Control Board
U.N. Children's Fund
U.N. Conference on Trade and Development
International Trade Center UNCTAD/GATT
U.N. Development Programs
U.N. Industrial Development Organization
U.N. Institute for Training and Research
U.N. Research Institute for Social Development
World Food Program

Source: *Yearbook of International Organizations, 1972–73*, 14th ed. (Brussels, Belgium: Union of International Associations), p. 855.

izations might be operating by the year 2000. Naturally, such estimates are risky and the reliability of such predictions depends on many circumstances, including how an INGO is defined.

The variety of objectives pursued by INGOs is extensive. We have already mentioned the International Chamber of Commerce, representing business and trade interests and the World Confederation of Labour, consisting mainly of Catholic unions and promoting their goals. Other examples are the International Union of Architects, the International Federation of Teachers, and the Afro-Asian People's Solidarity Organization coordinating the struggle of its members against imperialism, and the African Football Confederation. Fields in which INGOs are active are listed in Table 1.5.

The Union of International Associations has set up a number of criteria for defining INGOs covering aims, membership, governance, and financing. The aims must be genuinely international in character and manifest the intention to engage in activities in at least three states; the membership must be drawn from individuals or collective entities of at least three states and must be open to any appropriately qualified individual or entity in the organization's area of operations; the constitution must provide for a permanent headquarters and make provisions for the members to periodically elect the governing body and officers; the headquarters and the officers should be rotated among the various member-states at designated intervals; the voting procedure must be structured in such a way as to prevent control of the organization by any one national group; and substantial financial contributions to the budget must come from at least three states. As a consequence many international societies and unions in North America are excluded since their funds are usually derived wholly from U.S. members. Furthermore, no attempt must be made to make profits for direct distribution to the members of the INGOs, but this does not mean that members may not be helped to increase their profits or better their economic organization through the activities of the INGOs.[9]

A resolution by the U.N. Economic and Social Council (ECOSOC) in 1968 (No. 1296–XLIV) appears to broaden the above criteria. It defines an INGO as follows: "Any international organization which is *not* established by intergovernmental agreements shall be considered as a nongovernmental organization . . ., including organizations which accept members designated by government authorities, provided that such membership does not interfere with the free expression of views of the organization." Kjell Skjelsbaek has expanded the definition of INGOs even further by considering the representation of members from only two states to be sufficient if at least one of the representatives is not a governmental official.[10]

Why is it important to worry about these differences in definition? The reason is that they change somewhat the nature of INGOs, they affect their ability to interact with such U.N. bodies as ECOSOC (depending on whether they are recognized by these bodies as legitimate INGOs), and they have an effect on what entities are construed as INGOs in statistical comparisons.

INGOs carry out a variety of border-crossing activities to attain their goals in the pursuit of the interests for which they have been created. These activities create relationships of the INGOs with both governmental and nongovernmental entities and actors; such relations have been labelled transnational in contrast to traditional international relations, which are generally understood to apply only to activities and contacts between governmental actors.

The objectives of transnational INGO initiatives can be broken down into three groups: 1) to promote their own interests in the international and national arenas; 2) to promote, modify, or oppose the goals of the United Nations, its specialized agencies and affiliates, and regional IGOs, and; 3) to support, modify, or oppose the goals of national governments.

The objectives under groups 2 and 3 are likely to be functions of the specific objectives in the first category, but this is not necessarily the case when it comes to general, often ideological goals. It is also quite conceivable that a particular INGO will support specific IGO goals, but oppose national goals of a particular government. Therefore, IGOs and national governments may perceive an individual INGO as either friendly or hostile, and these perceptions may differ from case to case.

The capability of INGOs to mount effective transnational initiatives depends on the strength and distribution of their membership, their organizational effectiveness and financial resources, and their institutionalized and informal contacts with governmental and IGO agencies. Some of the criteria for evaluation discussed earlier with respect to IGOs may also be applicable to INGO assessment. These issues will be examined further in Chapter 6.

CLASSIFICATION OF INGOs

The functional breakdown of INGOs provided in Table 1.5 shows that in 1976 health and medical groups led the field in numbers, followed closely by commerce and industry INGOs and significantly less numerous, by science INGOs. Political, legal, and administration groups were smallest in number.

Two features of Table 1.5 should be noted. First, in 1976 the criteria for inclusion in the INGO statistics were broadened and this allowed the addition of borderline cases. Apparently the arguments put forth by scholars such as Professor Skjelsbaëk for expanding the INGO description have been effective. Second, a relatively large number of INGOs, close to 30 percent of the total, are defunct or dormant. It is interesting to find that, according to figures for 1970/71, a high ratio of groups pursuing interests involving politics such as international relations, law, and administration fall in the defunct or dormant category, while the percentage of defunct or inactive economic and health groups is relatively small.

The *Yearbook of International Organizations* (1978) identifies other classi-

TABLE 1.5: INGOs 1909–77

Year	1909	1951	1954	1956	1958	1960	1962	1964	1966	1968	1970	1972	1976	Defunct Dormant 1970–7
Bibliography, documentation, press	19	–	29	26	33	34	41	54	58	69	63	72	77	31
Religion, ethics	21	–	79	70	79	87	86	87	93	103	109	112	129	62
Social sciences, humanistic studies	10	–	38	57	55	57	57	67	80	90	95	104	133	35
International relations	12	–	83	61	71	92	99	106	111	125	127	144	132	102
Politics	3	–	12	13	14	17	15	14	15	22	22	27	30	30
Law, administration	13	–	31	28	30	37	42	45	48	54	54	58	45	29
Social welfare	10	–	52	52	53	56	64	70	76	88	95	104	120	51
Professions, employers	2	–	56	67	67	73	76	78	93	105	112	119	132	34
Trade Unions	1	–	49	48	49	54	54	59	63	70	70	70	67	22
Economics, finance	3	–	14	15	16	26	30	33	35	40	45	47	56	15
Commerce, industry	5	–	116	123	134	163	160	168	211	233	239	251	273	34
Agriculture	5	–	32	27	34	46	55	64	76	83	83	88	105	26

	1	2	3	4	5	6	7	8	9	10	11	12	13	14
Transport, travel	5	–	28	40	43	57	57	63	72	76	82	89	93	15
Technology	8	–	34	36	50	60	63	70	83	102	113	133	147	28
Science	21	–	81	69	77	83	92	118	137	152	174	184	190	53
Health, medicine	16	–	101	100	104	123	133	150	173	214	225	256	306	37
Education, youth	10	–	54	56	62	68	71	83	91	105	106	116	134	35
Arts, literature, radio, cinema, TV	6	–	41	34	34	57	57	65	70	75	80	80	93	27
Sport, recreation	6	–	67	51	55	65	72	76	90	93	99	110	119	18
A-Section NGOs	176	832	997	973	1060	1253	1324	1570	1675	1899	1993	2173	2401	
EEC/EFTA INGOs	–	–	–	–	–	–	216	233	245	273	288	283	285*	
National NGOs with U.N. consultative status	–	–	11	12	13	13	12	15	15	16	15	14	14	
Total INGOs	176	832	1008	985	1073	1268	1552	1718	1935	2188	2296	2470	2700	
Defunct/Dormant	–	–	–	–	–	–	–	–	707	741	742	938	1067	676

* estimated

Source: Adopted from *Yearbook of International Organizations*, 13th and 18th eds. (Brussels, Belgium: Union of International Association).

fications that are only indirectly related to the general functional purposes of Table 1.5 although all ultimately seek to promote specific causes.[11] One such category is characterized by its hybrid nature; this means that they are mixtures of IGOs and INGOs. Some INGOs have government-related memberships; examples are Interpol—The International Criminal Police Organization—and the International Union of Official Travel Organizations. Other INGOs have special status in international law: the best known is the International Committee of the Red Cross, recognized by the Geneva Convention.

We should note that political parties may also develop into transnational organizations. Examples are the European Peoples Party, the European Christian Democratic Union, and the Socialist International, all of which are INGOs with a special relationship to a number of national governments and the first two also to the European Communities, a regional IGO. Opposition bodies to established governments are also considered to be INGOs, such as the World Anti-Communist League and the Palestine Liberation Organization (PLO).

While, as we have seen, INGOs are basically nonprofit-making entities, many transnational activities with powerful effects on international politics and decision making are carried out by another type of INGO: the profit-oriented multinational enterprise (MNE), now more frequently referred to as the transnational corporation (TNC). Although it would be tempting to include TNCs in our comparative analysis of the field of international organization, because they contribute in interesting and important ways to the web of economic and political interdependence, their nature and structure are quite different from IGOs and INGOs. This seriously hampers meaningful comparison. Moreover, a vast literature exists on TNCs that would have to be considered carefully if we were to make TNCs part of our analytical efforts. Hence, TNCs will generally be omitted from our study, except where references to them might offer special insights.

In the same way as with IGOs, it is useful to distinguish between global or universal INGOs and regional organizations. INGOs often have sprung up or are related to regional IGOs. The number of European INGOs expanded rapidly after the establishment of the three IGOs comprising the European Communities (EC), especially the EEC. However, regional INGOs also exist and operate outside the context of regional IGOs. We will discuss their growth and geographic distribution later in this chapter.

Finally, INGOs can be classified in terms of their task performance. Since most INGOs pursue particular interests, their foremost task is the attainment of specific goals for the promotion of their interests. Successful goal attainment requires the design of appropriate strategies and the effective execution and implementation of the strategies devised. In turn, the competent performance of these tasks depends on the management of cooperation among members of the INGO, including the careful coordination of aspirations and the achievement of necessary compromises. In some cases, this will require expertise in conflict resolution. For some INGOs whose primary concern is the maintenance of peace or the arbitration of disputes, conflict resolution is likely to be the central task, although the management of co-operation might be equally important.

INGO GROWTH PATTERN AND DISTRIBUTION

International NGOs as delineated above are generally assumed to date back to 1846 when the World's Evangelical Alliance was founded.[12] The dramatic growth of INGOs from 1860 to 1970 is illustrated in Figure 1.3. The number of INGOs founded increased sharply in the period immediately following major wars (for example, the Russo-Japanese War and World Wars I and II) and decreased during periods of rising international conflict and wars, such as the time spans from 1911–20 and from 1931–40. This suggests that in-ternational strife and turmoil impede the growth of INGOs.[13] In contrast, the settlement of devastating wars, coupled with the bitter memories of their misery and deprivation, seems to stimulate the formation of INGOs reflecting a revived spirit of border-crossing cooperation.

It is interesting to note that a very similar situation prevailed in the growth pattern of IGOs since 1860, also shown in Figure 1.3. Expanding international cooperation after World Wars I and II is clearly evidenced by the sharp increases in the founding of IGOs during the periods from 1921 to 1930 and from 1941 to 1960. Equally visible is the distinct drop in increases between 1931 and 1940.[14]

From Table 1.5 we learn that between 1954 and 1976 the number of INGOs nearly tripled and that most of the functional categories shared in this rise. However, there are some notable exceptions based primarily on the nature of the groups. For example, the number of trade unions increased only by about 15 percent while sports and recreation groups increased by about 90 percent. Some groups, such as agriculture and transport, nearly quintupled.

Table 1.6 furnishes growth data by continents on the basis of national representation in INGOs from 1960 to 1977. The largest representation came from Europe, followed by North and South America; however, the highest growth rates in national representation are found in Africa and Asia, where national representation nearly tripled and doubled respectively. These in-creases reflect rising participation of the Third World states in INGOs. Nevertheless, in net numbers of representation, the European states and the other Western-oriented industrial states predominate, as can be seen from Table 1.7, with France, the United Kingdom, and the Federal Republic of Germany holding top honors. Europe's predominance is also seen in the

TABLE 1.7: Twenty Top-Ranking Countries by National Representation in International Organizations, 1960–77

Organizations reporting	1960 Number 1165	1966 Number 1596	1966 Percentage Increase 37.0	1977 Number 2112	1977 Percentage Increase 32.3
1 France	976	1268	29.9	1590	25.4
2 United Kingdom	818	1129	19.6	1575	39.5
3 Germany FR	1070	1200	12.1	1515	26.3
4 Belgium	1031	1162	12.7	1448	24.6
5 Italy	1033	1141	10.5	1442	26.4
6 Netherlands	1044	1158	10.9	1415	22.2
7 Switzerland	796	1078	35.4	1345	24.8
8 Sweden	814	921	13.1	1271	27.5
9 Denmark	775	929	19.9	1245	34.0
10 United States	671	915	36.4	1212	32.5
11 Spain	697	840	20.5	1183	40.8
12 Austria	708	963	36.0	1177	22.2
13 Norway	602	830	37.9	1108	33.5
14 Canada	535	757	41.5	1070	41.3
15 Finland	548	770	40.5	1070	39.0
16 Japan	454	689	51.8	963	39.8
17 Australia	424	615	45.0	919	49.4
18 Brazil	458	607	32.5	835	37.6
19 Argentina	430	646	50.2	818	26.6
20 India	432	588	36.1	813	38.3
21 Israel	402	597	48.5	810	35.7

Source: Yearbook of International Organizations, 16th ed. (1978), Table 5.

TABLE 1.6: National Representation in INGOs by Continent, 1960–77

	1960	1966	1977
Organizations Reporting	1165	1596	2112
Continents:			
Africa	2267	5343	8603
America	5874	8694	12688
Asia	3899	6025	9346
Europe	14409	19863	26628
Pacific	793	1186	1961

Source: Yearbook of International Organizations, 1981 16th. ed.

location of INGO headquarters and secondary offices as is evidenced in Table 1.8. However, from 1954 to 1976 African and Asian states have become increasingly popular for locations of headquarters, whereas Europe and the Americas show small declines.

INTERNATIONAL ORGANIZATION AND INTERDEPENDENCE

Our discussion of the growth and geographic distribution pattern of IGOs and INGOs is a clear indication that the web of international and transnational contacts and relationships between governments and nongovernmental actors has grown immensely and has become more closeknit. It is fair to assume that as a result of this development, the number of border-crossing interactions such as diplomatic intercourse, trade, employment shifts, and various lobbying efforts has also increased, but it will require further investigation to determine the full meaning of these interactions. Do they signify increased creation of interdependence among states, with varying effects on the international system as it often seems fashionable to assert? Or are these border-crossing activities merely a reflection of an expanding world population trying to manage its affairs within an increasingly complex political, economic, and social environment? To answer these questions, we need to explore briefly the nature and effects of interdependence, a term that during the last decade has become an "in" concept and has generated a vast literature.[15]

It would exceed the scope of this text to evaluate critically this literature in its totality. What we plan to do here is to present a description and definitions of interdependence and to examine its effects on national governments. In addition, we will examine the role IGOs and INGOs might play within the operational context of interdependence.

TABLE 1.8:   Location of International Headquarters and Secondary Offices by Continent, 1850–1976

Year	Africa HQ	Africa Sec	America (N) HQ	America (N) Sec	America (S/C) HQ	America (S/C) Sec	Asia HQ	Asia Sec	Pacific HQ	Pacific Sec	Europe HQ	Europe Sec
1850											6	
1870			2								32	
1880	1		7								59	
1890	1		11		1						104	
1895	1		17		2		2				186	
1905	1		18		3		2				270	
1912	1		15		3		1				417	
1921	1	–	19	–	2	–	2	–	–	–	297	–
1926	–	–	24	–	3	–	1	–	–	–	369	–
1930	1	–	26	–	5	–	4	–	–	–	669	–
1951	10	–	12	–	25	–	12	–	1	–	772	–
1954	13	11	145	36	37	30	19	29	5	6	971	117
1958	10	21	133	155	47	69	27	67	2	8	1036	306
1960	12	29	158	164	56	110	35	91	3	13	1203	376
1962	25	40	170	79	58	94	42	77	4	14	1469	363
1964	39	64	192	85	77	106	56	82	3	14	1627	326
1966	50	64	231	62	107	97	71	87	7	16	1986	281
1968	73	81	277	65	143	103	98	105	19	14	2320	316
1970	77	85	288	74	147	116	100	108	17	16	2348	332
1972	87	95	299	88	152	123	116	110	10	18	2523	362
1976	117	78	283	157	148	99	121	96	17	10	1990	446

Source: Yearbook of International Organizations, 18th ed. (1978), Table 8.

The basis for global and regional interdependence is the differential distribution of needs, aspirations, and capabilities of states, their people, and other international actors including such IGOs as the European Communities. William Coplin and Michael O'Leary describe interdependence as the existence of conditions in which the perceived needs of some individual groups in one state are satisfied by the resources or capabilities that exist in at least one other state. Thus patterns of transnational interdependence are a product of the interface between needs and capabilities across national boundaries.[16]

Interdependence is manifested by flows of people, civilian and military goods and services, capital, and information across national boundaries in response to needs in one or more states and in accordance with the capabilities of others. These flows are often referred to as transactional flows and can be quantitatively measured. Depending on their particular interests, a variety of governmental groups and national NGOs, such as particular bureaucracies or economic pressure groups, may be involved in these flows. The existence of similar needs may lead to formal and informal coalitions among states, among states and IGOs, and among governmental and nongovernmental actors. Complementary capabilities may also produce alliances. On the other hand, the unequal distribution of capabilities may conjur up perceptions of dependence and indeed actual dependency by less favored states on economically and politically more powerful states. Similar capabilities coupled with unequal resources may sharpen economic competition in international trade and in the search for sources of raw materials. The competition between the United States and Japan is one example; that between the United States and the European Economic Community is another.

From the foregoing discussion it is evident that the different capabilities possessed by governmental and nongovernmental actors play a crucial role not only for present and future interdependence relationships in regional and global contexts, but also for the successful pursuit of the satisfaction of needs and aspirations of individual actors. Such capabilities as military forces, economic and financial means, and industrial and technological proficiency can be translated into international power and influence, while their absence may signal serious vulnerability. Hence, small states usually must be more modest in their policy aspirations than the big powers because they have control over more limited resources, although the skillful exploitation of a larger state's weaknesses may compensate for the limitations in resources. If the hostilities in Vietnam have proved anything, it is that even the greatest military power on earth, the United States, does not possess unlimited resources and/or sufficient means to achieve everything, especially in the face of internal dissension and increasing domestic political pressures against an unpopular, protracted war.

Given that the conditions exist that can produce interdependence, what actually triggers such a relationship and what are the effects on and consequences for states and their governments involved in interdependence relationships?[17] A broad notion of interdependence has been put forth by Oran Young, who defines it as "the extent to which events occurring in any given part or within any given component of a world system affect (either physically or perceptually) events taking place in each of the other parts or component units of the system."[18] When directed primarily to economics, interdependence is present when there is an increased sensitivity to external economic developments.[19] According to Robert Keohane and Joseph Nye, sensitivity "involves degrees of responsiveness within a policy framework—how quickly do changes in one country bring costly changes in another, and how great are the costly effects?"[20] The problems of the oil price increases beginning in 1973 for Western Europe, Japan, and the United States come to mind.

A second dimension of interdependence is "vulnerability," that "rests on the relative availability and costliness of the alternatives that various actors face."[21] In other words, vulnerability reflects a state's or an IGO's or a private actor's varying inability to accept and cope with the economic, political, and social costs imposed by external events, even if policies have been or will be changed. The different effects of the actions of OPEC upon consumer states in both the industrially advanced states and in the Third World constitutes a good example of varying degrees of vulnerability.

The emphasis on vulnerability is also a criterion in Kenneth Waltz's definition of interdependence that focuses on the cost of disentanglement from an interdependent relationship.[22] For Waltz then, a country or an IGO may be affected by what another actor does or may be sensitive to border-crossing actions of other actors, but it would not necessarily be interdependent unless there is a definitive cost for extracting itself from the interdependence relationship and here the economic and other capabilities of different actors are likely to be decisive.

What are the consequences for participants of an interdependence relationship? Keohane and Nye observe that such relationships may produce benefits, but costs are also incurred because interdependence restricts the autonomy of the participants in this relationship. Whether the benefits exceed the costs depends on the values of the actors as well as on the nature of the relationship.[23] Obviously, it is very rare that in terms of benefits and costs a truly reciprocal, symmetric relationship exists anywhere. Indeed, it is the asymmetries in interdependence caused by differing economic, political, and perhaps military capabilities of the actors that are the normal circumstances in their relationships and that provide sources of influence for governmental and nongovernmental actors in their dealings with each other.

As already pointed out, it is the inequality of capabilities within interdependence relationships that at times evokes fears of dependence on the part of governmental and nongovernmental actors. Unequal capabilities among states, instead of producing perceptions of reciprocal dependence that might induce governments to treat the actions of other governments or IGOs as though they were events within their own borders and might be seen within the context of converging, if not identical, interests, are more likely to lead to suspicion, envy, and tensions.[24] Hence, governmental leaders may feel called upon to resort to national means and solutions as a countervailing force against the real or imagined threat of dependence on other states or private entities. Such actions harm the prospects of useful collaboration among states and are likely to undermine, if not destroy, the benefits that interdependence networks may produce. Perceptions of this dependence have aggravated all the other problems that many leaders of the developing states have faced in their priority task of nation building and their consequent preoccupation with sovereignty and autonomy of choice.

While these leaders may perceive various degrees of dependence and restrictions on their autonomy, there is also a reverse dependence on certain developing states on the part of some industrial states. This dependency stems from the need for certain raw materials, especially petroleum, and a number of nonfuel strategic raw materials such as bauxite, manganese, tungsten, and zinc, among others. However, the interdependence pattern that flows from minerals dependence is subject to modification as new technologies are developed, substitutes for minerals in short supplies are found, and industrial needs change. The possible accessibility of the manganese and other mineral resources on the seabed threatens to alter this dependency relationship. Also, problems of debt management have underscored the high degree of interdependence between the Western banking system and the Third World.

During recent years, United States foreign policy regarded growing interdependence as not only inevitable but also desirable in producing consensus and restraining unacceptable conduct by foreign governments. It was viewed as a positive value in the expanding relationship between industrially advanced and developing states. Indeed, during the mid-1970's the State Department promoted the notion of purposefully pursuing a strategy of interdependence, and that included the deliberate support of larger entities such as the European Communities and COMECON.[25] In United States-Soviet relations, interdependence was pursued as a pragmatic mechanism by both sides as an alternative to unwanted confrontation and unattainable friendship, and in response to a perceived political imperative.

Former Secretary of State Henry Kissinger articulated this strategy in a speech in Boston on March 11, 1976:

> . . . The interdependence of nations—the indivisibility of our security and our prosperity—can accelerate our common progress or our common decline.

Therefore, just as we must seek to move beyond a balance of power in East-West relations, so must we transcend tests of strength and build a true world community.

We do so in our self-interest, for today's web of economic relationships links the destinies of all mankind. The price and supply of energy, the conditions of trade, the expansion of world food production, the technological bases for economic development, the protection of the world's environment, the rules of law governing the world's oceans and outer space—these are concerns that affect all nations and can be satisfactorily addressed only in a framework of international cooperation.[26]

However, the views of the former secretary are not shared in all quarters. Many Third World representatives as well as a number of Western intellectuals look at interdependence as creating undesirable dependence, and some think it is a code word for economic bondage.[27] They see a widening economic gap between affluent and poor societies. For these observers, the process of interdependence escalates tensions over the restrictions of national or societal autonomy, threatens the achievement of national economic, social, and political objectives, and may produce violent nationalist and interstate conflict.

Is interdependence increasing or declining? After engaging in a very careful and thoughtful study based on statistical data ranging from 1880 to the present Richard Rosecrance and five collaborators came to the following conclusions:

. . . The pattern of contemporary interdependence is much more mixed than many have believed. The amplitude of economic change has increased, and the response of one economy to another has become more unpredictable. Relationships no longer appear to be stable across time. Interdependence may be becoming unstable.[28]

Rosecrance et al. state that data from recent years indicate a gradual and progressive detachment of individual national policies from the general trend toward interdependence. Since their study concentrates on the advanced industrial states, perhaps this conclusion may not be generally applicable to all states. Moreover, they acknowledge that the decline in the relationship among the industrialized states may have led to a more intimate relationship of these states with outside states—the oil producers, the Third World, and the communist bloc.[29] But whatever the thrust and the outcome of these developments, we agree that continuing linear increases in interdependence may not occur only among the industrially-advanced states, but also with the remainder of the world where, in fact, interdependence may be actively resisted. Much will depend on the future organization and structure of economic, political, or military cooperation among states and nongovernmental actors, and it is here where IGOs and INGOs can play an important role.

It seems to us that the mere increase in the number of IGOs and INGOs, and the resulting proliferation of border-crossing contacts and relations, by itself has little effect on the intensification of regional and global interdependence. Only when IGOs and INGOs become involved in the management of existing interdependencies or in the purposeful creation of new interdependencies can we speak of their positive contribution. This brings us back to our discussion of IGO and INGO organizational tasks, which include the management of cooperation through coordination measures, the achievement of compromise, the selection of appropriate goal-attaining strategies, and the resolution of conflicts. The effective execution of all these tasks can produce or maintain beneficial interdependence relationships, accomplish a more adequate distribution of costs, resolve perceptions of dependency, and initiate new interdependence arrangements that maximally promote the interests of all participants.

It is in Europe where we find the best examples of regional interdependence enhancement through the management of cooperation by IGOs and INGOs. The European Economic Community (EEC), the Organization for Economic Cooperation and Development (OECD), COMECON, and NATO are cases in point. However, there have also been management failures. An example is the attempt at renationalization of the EEC's Common Agricultural Policy (CAP) that has been at least partially successful.

Another instance of less than successful management of cooperation is the inability of the OECD to obtain the collaboration of its member-states in the full coordination of their economic policies in spite of the annual economic summit meetings of the largest OECD states. In Eastern Europe, the desire for maximum national autonomy, especially by Poland and Romania, has caused difficulties for economic policy, and the efforts at coordination by the COMECON institution, have in fact impeded the creation of greater bloc interdependence.

Security IGOs in Europe also have encountered problems in the management of cooperation. Although the NATO states committed themselves in 1977 to increase their defense expenditures annually by 3 percent in real money considering the impact of inflation, most of the members are not meeting this commitment.

Selected INGOs in Western Europe also have contributed to the enhancement of interdependence, especially in the economic sector. A large number of regional business and agricultural interest groups have been established at the Brussels headquarters of the European Communities, and have assisted the EC institutions in their cooperation management tasks. However, the effectiveness of these INGOs has been spotty and have depended very much on the objectives of national interest groups that often were more attuned to the promotion of their more parochial national rather than broader regional interests.

The management of cooperation has been much more difficult and much less successful in the Third World. The main reasons have been differing perceptions of benefits and costs that might be derived from the enhancement of regional interdependence by regional IGOs, as well as by the lower management skills of many IGO civil servants. Few INGOs directly related to IGO objectives have been formed in the Third World, and whatever influence they might have been able to exert has been minimal.[30]

Globally, the United Nations, with its many specialized and affiliated agencies, conferences and other units has the potential of increasing economic and political interdependence. Although the initial inspiration for the creation of the United Nations was the peaceful settlement of disputes, the relative ineffectiveness of the U.N. apparatus for this purpose and the consequent inability to manage the needed cooperation suggest that the organization has been limited in its ability to provide or to enhance the kind of interdependence that would impose compelling constraints on states to refrain from the use of force. Clearly, the avoidance of conflict has not been due to the existence of the United Nations, but to international systemic elements such as the nuclear balance of terror among the superpowers.

In the economic and political sectors, North-South issues have become a major preoccupation of the United Nations, and, theoretically at least, the effective management of cooperation, including the application of planning, programming, and budgetary tools, could have made contributions to the enhanced and beneficial interdependence of the member-states. But while on lower, mostly technical levels, some positive interdependence arrangements have been engineered (for example, increased opportunities for loans for Third World development or preferential treatment of Third World imports), the great issues of the North-South dialogue such as the implementation of the New International Economic Order (NIEO) have not been resolved.[31] The United Nations has become the most important forum for the Third World, as embodied in the work of the Group of 77, to promote this ambitious scheme and the U.N. civil service in general is highly supportive, but in terms of benefit and cost perceptions, wide gaps exist between North and South and therefore, successful cooperation between the contending groups of U.N. member-states has been impossible to achieve.

The ability of universal INGOs to contribute effectively to enhanced interdependence has also been minor. Although many INGOs have official consultative status with a number of U.N. bodies (described in Chapter 6), their influence with U.N. officials is generally very limited. In fact, from the perspective of contributing to interdependence, informal actions of powerful INGOs such as the International Chamber of Commerce or the International Confederation of Free Trade Unions (ICFTU) on states are likely to be more important than official consultations with the United Nations.

The foregoing discussion of interdependence underscores the role IGOs and INGOs can play in the process of redressing the asymmetries of the capabilities that national governments and nongovernmental actors have at their disposal. This process depends on the quality with which IGOs perform (or are allowed to perform) their assigned tasks and on the skills with which they use their organizational tools. A comparative analysis as to how these tasks are performed will give us greater insight into how IGOs and the various clusters of INGOs participate in the international system than would a sequential study of individual IGOs and INGOs. In addition, it may aid us in making a reliable assessment of the impact that these organizations might have on continuity or change in the global political system and subsystems.

INTERNATIONAL ORGANIZATIONS AND INTERNATIONAL REGIMES

Before embarking on our comparative analysis, it is important to comment briefly on the conceptual distinction in the field of international organization between particular IGOs on the one hand and international regimes on the other. Both deal basically with the management of cooperation for various purposes, but they differ in a number of aspects.

The term "international regime" is of relatively recent vintage (early 1970s) and also has become an "in" concept. It applies to arrangements involving mostly governmental actors but affecting also the nongovernmental in a wide variety of issue areas, including fisheries conservation, international food production and distribution, international trade issues, telecommunications policy, and meteorological coordination across national boundaries. In some cases, regimes may be formal, as was the case with the Bretton Woods monetary arrangement, which was based on an interstate agreement. Or they may be informal where the regime may be merely implicit from the actions of the states involved.[32] They may be global, as are the Bretton Woods arrangements and the fisheries conservation regimes, or they may be regional. An example of the latter is the European Monetary System (EMS), which is primarily an informal regime because it lacks a formal and specific interstate accord for its operation although the EEC Treaty provides overall legitimacy.

Definitions for international regimes vary. According to Keohane and Nye, they refer to regulations and control of transnational and interstate relations by governments through the creation or acceptance of procedures, rules, and institutions for certain kinds of activity.[33] Ernst B. Haas defines regimes as "norms, rules, and procedures agreed to in order to regulate an issue area."[34] The most comprehensive concept of an international regime comes from Oran Young. He regards them as social institutions governing the actions of those interested in "specifiable" activities (or meaningful sets of activities). As such, they are recognized patterns of practice around which expectations converge.[35] Young views regimes as structures that may be more-or-less formally articulated and may or may not be accompanied by explicit organizational arrangements, although the core of every regime is "a collection of rights and rules."[36] He also asserts that in formal terms "the members of international regimes are always sovereign states, though the parties carrying out the actions governed by international regimes are often private entities (for example, fishing companies, banks or private airlines)."[37] The number of regime members may vary from a very few to several hundred if the nongovernmental participants are included. Finally, the various actions of states flowing from any given regime will often shape further the regime's contents, especially if clearcut goals are kept in mind.

From this discussion, it emerges that international regimes are goal-oriented enterprises whose participating members seek benefits through explicit or tacit authoritative allocations of values, that is, the conservation of fish or the profits from deep-seabed mining. Nongovernmental actors, including multinational corporations, are often participants and it is in fact conceivable that the latter may be at times the instigators or proponents for the creation of regimes. In any event, they are likely to participate assiduously in the negotiations and bargaining that may lead up to the formation of international regimes, as the many sessions of the Law-of-the-Sea Conference have clearly demonstrated.

While, then, both IGO's and international regimes are designed to pursue goals in the international arena and both may be based on international accords that set up institutions, assign rights and obligations, and provide for particular procedures, the issues and issue areas addressed by regimes appear to be more narrow and lack the comprehensive nature of most IGO concerns. Regime structures also are more fluid and are more subject to evolutionary developments than are IGOs. As Keohane and Nye point out, correctly in our view, IGOs "in the broad sense of networks, norms, and institutions" may include the norms associated with specific international regimes, but they belong to a broader category than regimes because they encompass patterns of elite networks and (if relevant) a range of formal institutions.[38] Interactions and relations between IGOs and international regimes, including the effects of INGO activities, will be discussed and illustrated through the illustrative cases that follow each of the subsequent chapters.

NOTES

1. Union of International Associations, *Yearbook of International Organizations* 1978 (17th ed.), Brussels, 1979 Supplement, Statistical Summary Tables 1 and 7.

2. Ibid., Tables 7 and 8.

3. This is part of the conventional definition. Michael Wallace and J. David Singer argue that bilaterally-created IGOs should not be excluded; otherwise an organization such as the North American Defense Command (NORAD), composed of the United States and Canada, would be excluded. See their "Intergovernmental Organizations in the Global System, 1815–1964: A Quantitative Description," *International Organization* 24 (Spring 1970): 239–87.

4. See also Ephraim Been-Baruch "An Examination of Several Classifications of Organizations," *International Review of History and Political Science* 17 (May 1980): 1–19. A useful compendium of IGOs is contained in Arthur S. Banks and William Overstreet, eds., *The Political Handbook of the World* (New York: McGraw-Hill, 1981).

5. See Leon Gordenker and Paul R. Saunders, "Organization Theory and International Organizations," in *International Organization*, ed. Paul Taylor and A. J. R. Groom (London: Francis Parker, 1978), pp. 84–110, and the works cited therein.

6. Much of the preceding discussion leans heavily on the excellent analysis by Lawrence S. Finkelstein, "International Organizations and Change," *International Studies Quarterly* 18 (December 1974): 485–519. See also Robert W. Cox, "The Executive Head," *International Organization* 22 (Spring 1968): 205–30.

7. Anthony J. N. Judge "International Institutions: Diversity, Borderline Cases, Functional Substitutes and Possible Alternatives," in Taylor and Groom, op. cit., pp. 28–83.

8. For an elaboration on the concept and uses of regionalism, see Richard A. Falk and Saul H. Mendlovitz, eds., *Regional Politics and World Order* (San Francisco: W. H. Freeman, 1973).

9. Cf. *Yearbook of International Organizations* (1978) regarding types of organization included.

10. Kjell Skjelsbaëk, "The Growth of Intergovernmental Organizations in the Twentieth Century," *International Organization* 25 (Summer 1971): 420–42.

11. For these categories see *Yearbook of International Organizations* 1978 Supplements, An Overview.

12. According to Lyman C. White, *International Non-Governmental Organizations* (New York: Greenwood Press, 1968), p. 279, fn. 5, the first international NGO was founded in 1855 and was the World Alliance of the YMCAs. White contends that the Evangelical Alliance was not a truly international NGO because "its so-called members . . . were mere subscribers to its publications, without any voting rights." Others believe that the Rosicrucian Order founded in 1674 was the first international NGO. Cf. Kjell Skjelsbaëk, "The Growth of International Nongovernmental Organization in the Twentieth Century," *International Organization* 25 (Summer 1971): p. 424.

13. Ibid., p. 425.

14. We should note that J. David Singer and Michael Wallace in "Intergovernmental Organization and the Preservation of Peace, 1816–1864: Some Bivariate Relationships," *International Organization* 24 (Summer 1970): 520–47, use slightly different data for IGOs founded from those used in Figure 1.3. These disparities, perhaps due to definitional differences, do not, however, affect the general growth trend.

15. See, for example, Robert O. Keohane and Joseph S. Nye, *Power and Interdependence: World Politics in Transition* (Boston: Little Brown, 1977) and Richard Rosecrance et al., "Wither Interdependence," *International Organization* 31 (Summer 1977): 425–71.

16. William D. Coplin and Michael K. O'Leary, "A Policy Analysis Framework for Research, Education and Policy-Making in International Relations," delivered to the 1974 International Studies Association Convention, St. Louis, Missouri. See also Robert S. Jordan, "The Role of Actors in Global Issues," in *Global Issues*, eds. James E. Harf and B. Thomas Trout (Columbus, Ohio: Consortium for International Studies in Education, in press)

17. Edward L. Morse, "Transnational Economic Processes," *International Organization* 25 (Summer 1971): 373–97. See also Guy F. Erb and Valeriana Kallab, eds., *Beyond Dependency: The Developing World Speaks Out* (Washington, D.C.: Overseas Development Council, 1975).

18. Oran R. Young, "Interdependence in World Politics," *International Journal* 24 (Autumn 1969): p. 726.

19. Richard N. Cooper *The Economics of Interdependence* (New York: McGraw Hill, 1968), pp. 3–8.

20. Keohane and Nye, op. cit., p. 12.

21. Ibid., p. 13.

22. Kenneth F. Waltz, "The Myth of Interdependence," in *The International Corporation*, ed. Charles P. Kindelberger (Cambridge, Mass.: The M.I.T. Press, 1970), pp. 205–23.

23. Keohane and Nye, op. cit., pp. 9–11.

24. An extensive literature on the issue of Third World dependency has evolved during the last few years. For example, the entire issue of *International Organization* 32 (Winter 1978) is devoted to dependency and dependence with five articles focusing on theoretical aspects and four dealing with regional problems. See also Richard B. Fagan, "Studying Latin American Politics: Some Implications of a Dependence Approach," *Latin American Research Review* 12 (1977): 3–26; Robert R. Kaufman, Harry I. Chermotsky, and Daniel S. Geller, "A Preliminary Test of the Theory of Dependence," *Comparative Politics* 7 (April 1975): 303–30; Benjamin Cohen, *The Question of Imperialism* (New York: Basic Books, 1973), which is a critical analysis of dependency theory; and Thomas Moran, *Multinational Corporations and the Politics of Dependence* (Princeton, N.J.: Princeton University Press, 1974).

25. United States Department of State, *Toward a Strategy of Interdependence*, Bureau of Public Affairs, no. 17, July 1975.

26. United States Department of State, Bureau of Public Affairs, Washington D.C., P.R. 121, March 11, 1976.

27. See Hayward R. Alker, Lincoln P. Bloomfield, Nazli Choucri, *Analyzing Global Interdependence*, vol. 2 (Cambridge, Mass.: Center for International Studies, M.I.T. 1974), p. 3.

28. Rosecrance, op. cit., p. 441.

29. Ibid., p. 442.

30. See W. Andrew Axline, "Underdevelopment, Dependence, and Integration: The Politics of Regionalism in the Third World," *International Organization* 31 (Winter 1977): 83–105.

31. See Robert S. Jordan, "Why an NIEO: The View from the Third World," in *The Emerging International Economic Order: Dynamic Processes, Constraints, and Opportunities*, eds. Harold Jacobson and Dusan Sidjanski (Beverly Hills, Calif.: Sage, 1982).

32. See Keohane and Nye, op. cit., p. 20.

33. Ibid., p. 5.

34. Ernst B. Haas, "Why Collaborate?, Issue Linkage and International Regimes," *World Politics* 32 (April 1980): 357–405.

35. Oran R. Young, "International Regimes: Problem of Concept Formations," *World Politics* 32 (April 1980): 331–56.

36. Ibid., p. 333.

37. Ibid.

38. Keohane and Nye, op. cit., p. 55.

Chapter 2

The Creation of Intergovernmental Organizations

MOTIVATIONS

What motivates nation-states to establish IGOs? This question has not been discussed systematically in the literature, although answers to this question may well provide significant clues as to the durability of and prospective changes in the role of IGOs.[1]

In Chapter 1 we pointed out that the pursuit of particular interests by governments gave rise to the establishment of IGOs. These interests are the enhancement of a state's security and, beyond that, the hoped-for assurance that conflict does not become excessively destructive. Another set of interests may be advancing the level of national economic development, raising the economic and social well-being of a state's citizens, managing economic interdependence in the world, and, in conjunction with national policy, participating in and perhaps in some cases controlling the exploration, marketing, and pricing of raw materials. Another important interest pursued through the creation of IGOs may be enhancing the national political power of states by building coalitions. The attainment of this interest may also be achieved through membership in security and/or economic-oriented IGOs. Finally, a major set of interests can be served by utilizing IGOs in the search for solutions to problems arising from the spread of scientific knowledge and the accompanying technologies; for example, the spread of pollution of the global environment, nuclear proliferation, and extraordinary advances in worldwide transportation and communications. Appropriate solutions may be various kinds of border-crossing cooperation to enhance the technological capabilities of individual states. Figure 2.1 illustrates the technological motivations for the establishment of IGOs.

While the preceding list of states' interests reflects indeed a variety of

FIGURE 2.1

Technological Motivations for the Establishment of IGOs

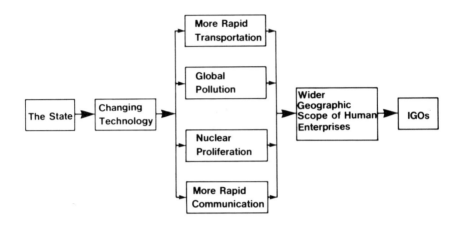

Source: Adapted from Chadwick Alger and David Hoovler, *You and Your Community in the World* (Columbus, Ohio: Consortium for International Studies Education, 1978), p.64.

motivations for the establishment of IGOs, a determination must be made as to under what conditions a government will resort to the instrument of an IGO to satisfy these and other interests. It is fair to assume that, normally, a government will seek national (unilateral) means to meet its security, political, economic, scientific, and technological needs because, if it does decide to become involved in setting up an IGO for whatever purpose or to join an existing IGO, its independence and freedom of action will be impaired to some degree, even if the management authority conferred upon the IGO is very low. Moreover, the relations with other member-states of the IGO impose differing and often unforeseeable restraints on the actions and behavior of all the participating governments.

The governmental decision whether to organize multilaterally for the pursuit and satisfaction of particular interests depends to a large extent on a state's resources and capabilities. If these are perceived to be sufficient to ensure the successful implementation of appropriate domestic and foreign policies, then establishing or joining an IGO may not be desirable. If, on the other hand, the resources and capabilities to implement national policies are not regarded as adequate and therefore IGOs would appear to offer a more likely path to assuring the satisfaction of what nevertheless would be perceived as important national interests, then a state may be inclined to encourage the performance of the necessary tasks multilaterally. These are basically the circumstances forming the background for what John Ruggie calls a state's "propensity for international organization."[2]

Ruggie's conceptualizations are of significance for our comparative study. His premise is that each state is willing to accept and therefore to engage to some extent in some form of international organizational or multilateral activity. He makes the useful distinction between institutionalized arrangements for joint and perhaps binding decision making, as reflected by various alliance systems and economic arrangements, and the informal coordination of states' unilateral behavior coupled with the systematic exchange of information, such as, for example, the annual economic summit meetings of the Organization for Economic Cooperation and Development's (OECD) "Big Seven" industrial democracies. In this case, the freedom for national domestic policy formulation is hardly affected, although foreign-policy independence may be constrained somewhat, depending on the specific issue involved. An example, however, would be the subsequently unsuccessful attempt by the United States at the 1982 Versailles economic summit to steer the other governments into a stronger anti-Soviet economic posture. According to Ruggie, the capabilities of a state include the extent of knowledge regarding cause/effect relations that underlie problems, the solutions of which may require IGO involvement. Lack or inadequacy of such knowledge could reduce a state's capabilities.[3]

The general loss of independence or the loss of control over a state's own activities resulting from the accumulation of collective constraints caused by the creation of, or participation in, IGOs is termed by Ruggie as "interdependence" costs. We should note that our definition of interdependence put forth in Chapter 1 is more limited than that used by Ruggie.[4] Nonetheless, several propositions formulated by Ruggie seem to characterize well the basic decision of governments to set up or to join IGOs for the enhancement of national interests in various interest and policy areas:

1. The propensity for international organization is determined by the interplay between the need to become dependent upon others for the performance of specific tasks, and the general desire to keep such dependence to the minimum level necessary.

2. There exists an inverse relationship between the ratio of international to national task performance and the total level of national resources a state possesses.[5] In other words, from the perspective of the state, the greater the resources it commands, the lower will be the number and scope of tasks it assigns to IGOs for performance, with more of its resources assigned to national task performance.

3. The propensity for international organization decreases over time, as national capabilities increase and become sufficient to perform a given task.[6] (This proposition is not actually relevant for the motivations that lead to the creation of an IGO, but will be important for our discussion in later chapters regarding the durability, decline, or complete demise of IGOs).

4. A process of encapsulation built into the international performance of any given task tends toward limiting further commitments to, or further increases in, the scope or capacity of the collective arrangements.[7]

To return to the motivations for the creation of IGOs, it is our contention that the successful pursuit of important national interests in various policy sectors generates propensities toward creating or participating in intergovernmental, multilateral organizations if the national capabilities and resources are perceived as being insufficient to attain the desired goals through purely national policies and instruments. Figure 2.2 illustrates these national capabilities and resources and IGO involvement.

When viewed in this way, it is no small wonder that the newer, and most vulnerable politically and economically, states are also the most supportive of IGOs. Membership in IGOs broadens their range of national options—they can "shop," for instance, among various international technical cooperation programs (in addition to the various bilateral aid programs) to

FIGURE 2.2

Capabilities and Resources and the Enhancement of National Interests

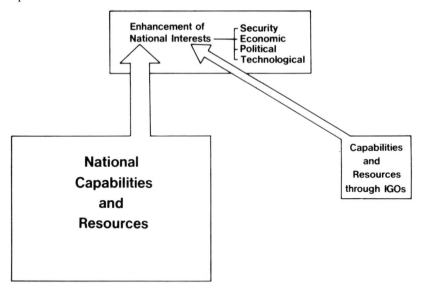

get the best "deal." The least desirable situation that a new state can find itself in is to be neglected by the IGO community. Without IGO membership, its foreign policy has often no place to go other than to justify its internal politics and its prospects for escaping from grinding poverty and eternal indebtedness would be nil.

We must also keep in mind that the motivations underlying the creation of and participation in an IGO continue to influence the degree of participation in subsequent years. Trade-off of advantages and costs among member-states may strengthen the IGO; the buildup of national capabilities either through participation in the IGO or for other reasons may lead to a declining interest in the IGO or perhaps to the complete withdrawal of a member-state. In the latter case, the outcome for the IGO may be its demise, although this rarely occurs. Hence, the interaction between indigenous capabilities and the strengthening of national capabilities through IGO participation, are likely to exert a significant influence on an IGO's course of action.

There is another theoretical dimension that may affect the motivations for the creation of IGOs, especially in regard to military alliances, and that is the public goods approach to the study of alliances.[8] The term "public goods," coined by economists, refers to a good that exhibits properties of nonappropriability of benefits and indivisibility with respect to consumption opportunities. If it is a pure public good, the provider is completely unable to appropriate the benefits derived from the good, and one man's or state's consumption of the good does not detract from another's consumption. The classical case of a pure public good is common military defense among allies. A unit of defense is hypothesized to render full defense service to all citizens of the alliance member-states regardless in which of the allied states they reside. Hence, all states of the alliance benefit irrespective of the size of the contribution they may make to the common defense; and, indeed, a state might be a free rider in the alliance and contribute nothing, or may even receive the benefits without joining. In NATO, for example, Iceland has no armed forces and Spain has benefited from NATO before it became a member in 1982.[9]

However, there is some doubt whether the totality of defense is a pure public good. While the hoped-for deterrence effects of nuclear defense or of the various early-warning systems devised by the superpowers on behalf of themselves and/or their respective allies are such that no individual citizen as such can be excluded from their benefits and no individual's consumption of these presumed benefits necessarily detracts from another's consumption, for other forms of defense, characteristics of a pure public good may be lacking. For example, retaliation may be withheld or may be carried out in such a way as to benefit one ally more than another. For conventional weapons, a defensive line around one strategic town might reduce the amount of protection that other towns can receive.[10] Whatever the particular ratio of pure to impure public goods in a military alliance, many states, especially smaller ones, may perceive that as a consequence of the applicability of the public goods concept, they may enjoy financial advantages through their alliance membership since such a step may lower their national defense expenditures.

The public goods concept may also be applied to other issue areas such as international pollution control efforts and large-scale climate modification. The effects of successful multilateral efforts with respect to these problems would benefit all states located in a particular region or provide worldwide benefits, and therefore could either trigger or reinforce propensities of states for creating or joining appropriate IGOs.

SCOPE AND STRUCTURE OF NEW IGOs

To translate the propensity of states for international organization into the establishment of a particular IGO requires bargaining-out the scope and structural dimensions of the new organization. This can be a complex and drawn-out process that can tax severely the endurance and creativity of the negotiators, who usually must operate under fairly strict directions from their governments. They must mesh their governments' nationalistic desire for maximum autonomy with the assurance that the prospective IGO can perform optimally and effectively the tasks for which it is being created.

One of the main questions to be settled in the bargaining process between the prospective member-states is the extent of the institutional framework and the degree of decision-making authority to be conferred upon the IGO. Ideally, this authority should be commensurate with the performance of tasks expected of the IGO and involves the determination of such issues as the latitude of power to be granted to the IGO's executive head, or whether task management decisions by the regional institutions should be made by unanimity or by majority vote; perhaps either a qualified majority or weighted votes would be required. IGO task performance may also require the formulation of appropriate national policies and often national supervision over multilateral policy implementation because these can be highly sensitive matters affecting the member-state autonomy and hence likely to produce interdependence costs. Will these costs exceed the benefits anticipated from the IGO or should perhaps the multilateral commitment be made more modest? Only the very best judgments of the political leaders of the governments involved and their negotiators can produce the necessary fine tuning of the IGO's scope and institutional structure to achieve a sound balance of benefits and costs.

When bargaining-out the proper institutional framework and decision-making procedures, the prospective IGO member government must keep in mind the obligations (that is, costs) it is willing to assume and the rights it intends to exercise (that is, benefits) as a consequence of membership. An important obligation beyond accepting a general limitation of its freedom of action in both foreign and, to a smaller degree, domestic affairs is the financial contribution to the IGO's operations. This includes expenditures for the construction and maintenance of physical facilities as well as salaries for necessary international civil servants. The size of the contribution usually depends on the economic prowess of the IGO member including the size of its Gross National Product (GNP) or is a reflection of the political benefits the state anticipates receiving. In a few cases IGOs have been given limited taxing power (as was done for the European Coal and Steel Community) or have been granted their own financial resources in the form of import duties collected by the member governments or by the allocation of a percentage of the added-value taxes of the member-states. The European Communities now enjoy such revenue-raising resources. During the last few years, the United Nations also has attempted to generate its own resources through some kind of direct taxation of the member-states, but the realization of this idea remains very doubtful at this writing.[11] Meanwhile, Table 2.1 shows the largest contributors to the U.N. expenditures for 1946 and 1980–1982.

Among the rights of IGO member-states is the right of full participation in the decision-making process as stipulated in the underlying international treaty or convention. This also includes, of course, the right of denial of consent on a particular issue. However, rights may not be equally distributed among IGO members; the veto right in the U.N. Security Council is accorded

TABLE 2.1: U.N. Members States with Largest Assessments, 1946 and 1980–82 (Per Cent)

Member States	1946 Assessment	Member States	1980–82 Assessment
1. USA	39.89	1. USA	25.00
2. UK	11.98	2. USSR	11.10
3. China	6.30	3. Japan	9.58
4. France	6.30	4. Germany, Federal Republic of	8.31
5. USSR	6.62	5. France	6.26
6. India	4.09	6. UK	4.46
7. Canada	3.35	7. Italy	3.45
8. Australia	2.00	8. Canada	3.28
9. Argentina	1.94	9. Australia	1.83
10. Brazil	1.94	10. Spain	1.70
Total	84.41	Total	74.97

Source: Reports of the U.N. Committee on Contributions.

in the charter only to the five permanent Council members.[12] Weighing the vote of member-states in such bodies as the EC Council of Ministers, where a qualified majority is required for a favorable decision, also affects an IGO member's power to deny consent on a particular matter.[13]

Another important right of a member government is to deny or to delay accession to the IGO of new member-states. The expansion of IGO membership could impair the task performance potential of the original organization, reduce the anticipated benefits for the charter members of the IGO, or increase materially the interdependence costs. An interesting example is the United Kingdom's protracted accession to the EC.[14] Generally, under international law, the consent of all member-states is necessary before IGO membership can be enlarged. Nevertheless, an appropriate specific provision concerning new members (or withdrawal of members) in the treaty setting up a new IGO can avoid problems in the future.

As already pointed out, states participate in the creation of IGOs in anticipation of specific benefits. These may not always be made explicit in the constituent treaties, but there is an implied expectation that the ratio of benefit to cost is not completely unreasonable. This is an issue that has surfaced in nearly all economic IGOs from the EC to the Central American Common Market to the now-defunct East African Community. It can develop into a major problem in all IGOs, leading to serious disputes and in some cases to the complete disarray of the IGO. The cost-benefit ratio should be very carefully considered when the contractual details of an IGO are negotiated by the prospective members.

Finally, in negotiations to create a new IGO, there must be a carefully-drawn division of functions between national and IGO institutions. This is a difficult task because national institutions have acquired over time a legitimizing power and authority that cannot be modified easily. Interest-group constituencies have built up around national ministries or parliamentary bodies have buttressed the power of these institutions. These constituencies are often opposed to changes that might result in new (and competing) centers of power. In most cases, loyalties have grown up around the national institutions endowing them with symbolic as well as political legitimacy. Hence, unless the national institutions are willing to accept a reduction in the scope and nature of their competencies, or can be persuaded over time to do so, the multilateral decision-making authority of the IGO institutions is likely to be rather limited, at least at the beginning. These circumstances must be recognized by the founders of new IGOs. History has shown, especially in the evolution of the EC, that the initial conferral of broad decision-making competencies on the IGO institutions suffers gradual erosion under the pressure of national political and bureaucratic forces. The incremental acquisition or diminution of decision-making authority is one measure as to whether an

IGO possesses the political and administrative rigor to carry out its legal mandate.

The foregoing has been a brief survey of major items and variables that must be considered carefully in the creation of a new IGO. In spite of apparent commonalities and convergences of interests of the prospective member-states, and in spite of the clear propensity of these states to use IGOs for the pursuit of their particular interests, it is clear that negotiating a treaty for the creation of the appropriate IGO is a highly complex undertaking which must be approached with prudence, care, judgment, and foresight to ensure future success. To illustrate the complexity of this enterprise and to spotlight some of the pertinent motivations (political, economic, security, technological, and so on) leading to the establishment of an IGO, we will briefly review the birth of the United Nations, NATO, the ECSC and EEC, COMECON, the Central American Common Market (CACM), OAU, and the International Civil Aviation Organization (ICAO).

ILLUSTRATIVE CASES

The Origins of the United Nations

The basic motivation for the establishment of the United Nations as well as for its predecessor, the League of Nations, was to avoid the extraordinary loss of life and destruction caused by two world wars. The United States' failure to join the League, which most likely contributed to that organization's ineffectiveness to maintain international peace during the 1930s, may well have been an additional stimulus for the United States becoming a charter member of the United Nations.

If the goal of settling international disputes peacefully could be attained, it obviously would enhance the security of all states. It became obvious to President Franklin D. Roosevelt during World War II that even the most powerful state on earth might not be able to assure the security of its citizens and the integrity of its territory without resorting to some kind of international organization.[15] The need for such a peace-keeping IGO was inferentially recognized as early as 1941 in the famous Atlantic Charter drafted by President Roosevelt and Prime Minister Churchill. This document aimed at the creation of a permanent IGO that would provide for the disarmament of aggressor states "pending the establishment of a wider and permanent system of general security."[16]

Following serious deliberations by the U.S. State Department's Advisory Committee on Post-War Foreign Policy and consultations between the president and congressional leaders, proposals were drafted for a permanent

IGO for the maintenance of peace and security that became the basis for discussion during the Dumbarton Oaks meeting near Washington, D.C. in the late summer of 1944. While the United States and Great Britain had already agreed to seek the establishment of such an organization a year earlier, the Soviet Union, initially unsure about such a development, and the Republic of China added their informal consent in the fall of 1943.[17]

During the Dumbarton Oaks discussions, the question was raised as to whether economic and social matters should be included within the scope of the projected organization. Although the original position of the Soviet Union had been that the organization should be exclusively devoted to security matters and that it should not be concerned with the promotion of international cooperation regarding economic and social problems, the position of the United States and Britain finally prevailed. However, the Soviet delegation did not display the same interest in the economic and social aspects of the new organization's work as in the political and security.[18] And indeed, according to the Dumbarton Oaks agreements, the new IGO's primary function was to be the maintenance of international peace and security, although it was to seek also international cooperation in the solution of international economic, social, and often humanitarian problems.[19]

During the Yalta Conference in February 1945 another function was assigned to the prospective IGO: the establishment of a trusteeship system to replace the League of Nations system of mandates, which had become a means to improve the economic well-being of the populations of the colonial territories of the defeated states. This was viewed as an assumption by the United Nations of a serious responsibility.[20] However, by the end of the 1960s most colonies had become independent states and indeed had themselves become members of the organization.[21] Only the United States retains a strategic trusteeship over a few islands in the Western Pacific.

During the early 1940s it was very difficult for the prospective member governments of the United Nations to foresee the economic configuration of the post-war period. The warring nations of Europe, Japan, and China had many of their industries destroyed and physical facilities, especially in the cities, had been obliterated by bombings and artillery fire. Hence, the economic outlook in these areas was bleak. Decolonization was seen by only a few, at that time, as an inevitable process to begin soon after the end of the war. As it turned out, the principles that were to be the foundation of the United Nations were to promote this process, especially the concept inherited from the League of Nations embodied in the phrase "national self-government and political independence."

But the newly-independent states soon found themselves after independence confronted with enormous economic, social, and political problems. Even though the United States emerged from World War II the economically most powerful state, it had neither the resources nor the capabilities to deal with these issues by itself or on a bilateral basis with all the needy states. As a consequence, in contrast to the security-oriented genesis of the League of Nations, there was no alternative for the U.N. member-states but to turn to multilateral means to deal with the various tasks that had to be performed.[22] Obviously, then, the motivations for the creation of the United Nations were very pervasive. Indeed, it could be argued that the successful solution of economic and social problems in different areas of the world could make a major contribution to the assurance of peace.

Having acknowledged that powerful motivations existed worldwide for the establishment and enlargement of the United Nations, let us now briefly review the negotiating process regarding the obligations and rights of the member-states and the institutional framework and decision-making procedures. As we pointed out earlier in this chapter, the propensity to organize internationally is circumscribed by the desire of states for the maximum retention of their independence and freedom of action as well as by their concern for holding down interdependence costs.

These concerns were clearly reflected in the initial phases of the endeavor for the creation of the United Nations. In paragraph 4 of the Declaration of Four Nations on General Security, signed by the foreign ministers of the Soviet Union, Great Britain, and the United States as well as by the ambassador of the Republic of China in late 1943, the signatories declared that a general organization for the maintenance of international peace and security had to be based on "the principle of sovereign equality of all peace-loving states and open to membership by all such states, large and small."[23] The principle of the "sovereign equality" of all U.N. member-states did indeed become a key provision of the U.N. Charter and is embodied in Article 2, paragraph 1.

This principle signifies that the usual powers of government are left to the U.N. member-states and that the U.N. organs and institutions have only those functions and powers specifically conferred upon them. Hence, except for the explicitly stipulated powers of the Security Council (enforcement action such as the imposition of a boycott under Chapter VII of the U.N. Charter), no organ of the United Nations can obligate any U.N. member to any substantial action in its relations with other states except with its consent. Nor, according to Article 2, paragraph 7, can the U.N. organization intervene in any matter that is "essentially" within the domestic jurisdiction of a state. This provision reflects the special concerns of the U.S. negotiators and in particular their congressional members to make it clear that there would be no U.N. interference in U.S. domestic affairs.[24]

An exception to the principle of sovereign equality had been bargained-out during the Yalta Conference for the five permanent members of the Security Council. We should note that the United States, Great Britain, and the Soviet Union were already in agreement before Yalta that some kind of veto should be given to the permanent members of the Council (that is, the "Big Powers") on decisions regarding nonprocedural (substantive) matters of peace and security. What was done at the Yalta Conference was to find an acceptable formula for the voting procedure and this formula required that on substantive questions it was necessary that the majority of seven favorable votes (now nine) include the affirmative votes of the permanent members.[25] On procedural matters nine votes are needed for a favorable decision and the veto does not apply. When efforts are made to settle a dispute by pacific means (Chapter VI of the U.N. Charter), a party to the dispute shall abstain from voting. The Soviet Union was initially opposed to this provision, but finally accepted it at Yalta.

The agreement on the voting procedure in the Security Council reflected the perception of the current and future distribution of power following World War II. This power distribution accounts also for another exception to the principle of sovereign equality: admission of two socialist republics (the Ukraine and Byelorussia) to full membership in the United Nations although neither of these republics are sovereign states under international law because they are part of the Soviet Union and controlled by that government. The admission of these two "states" was the result of various trade-offs between the Soviet Union, the United States, and Britain during the Yalta Conference.[26]

When in 1945 the final version of the U.N. Charter was negotiated in San Francisco, 50 states participated and the smaller states were able to influence effectively the final shape of the General Assembly and the Economic and Social Council (ECOSOC), whose functions and powers were extended and clarified. In these efforts they were supported by the United States, which was especially sensitive to the interests of the Latin American delegations. The San Francisco Conference was a huge affair, attended by 282 delegates who were advised by more that 1,500 specialists and staff members.[27]

To return again to the relationship between maintaining the principle of sovereignty and the need to organize internationally, it is instructive to cite the comments of Senator Arthur Vandenberg regarding the issue of sovereignty, made during the U.S. Senate debate on the Charter: "These things [sovereignty] we toiled in San Francisco to preserve. We can effectively cooperate for peace without the loss of these things. To cooperate is not to lose our sovereignty."[28]

Obviously, in legal terms the United States and the four other permanent members of the Security Council did not suffer any impairment of their sovereignty. But how much sovereignty did the other U.N. member-states lose by accepting the obligation to permit the Security Council to act on their behalf and bind them by its decisions (Articles 24 and 25)? In terms of infringement of a state's national interests, the loss was most likely minor because if a national government wanted to disobey a decision of the Security Council in the event that it perceived vital interests were at stake, it could do so with impunity since the United Nations was not, in fact, given the means (police or armed forces) to compel compliance except in specific and unique circumstances. Indeed, as Inis Claude notes, "the Charter left no room for doubt that San Francisco had launched a project for cooperation among independent states rather than for consolidation of the nations under a kind of super-sovereign."[29] This project for cooperation, however, is very extensive, consisting of a vast complex of international machinery including an ever-expanding Secretariat and a Court of Justice, carried over from the League and so far proven rather ineffective. The United Nation's territorial and substantive scope is, however, very broad, and its structure is characterized by decentralization and specialization. Its institutions and operations require skilled management to perform their assigned tasks, a subject to which we return in subsequent chapters.

The secretary-general plays a most significant role in the operation of the United Nations. He possesses four categories of powers: 1) express powers under Article 99; 2) implied powers under Article 99; 3) other political powers and functions under the U.N. Charter and under the Rules of Procedures and Resolutions of the General Assembly and the councils; and 4) function as mediator, adviser, and so on. Although Article 7 of the Charter refers to the Secretariat and not to the secretary-general in naming the principle organs, Articles 97 and 101 underline that the Secretariat is composed of the secretary-general and a secretariat recruited by the secretary-general, who is alone responsible for the work of the Secretariat. Logically, therefore, the office of the secretary-general can be viewed as a "principal organ" within the meaning and scope of the U.N. Charter. Figure 2.3 displays the structure of the United Nations.

By creating this vast and complex organizational framework, the San Francisco Conference met the perceived needs of the participating states for international cooperation and for a perhaps purposefully somewhat ambiguous blueprint for global order, while at the same time satisfying national ambitions and interests. The smaller states accepted the principle of great power leadership because it was the only way to enhance their own interests in peace, security, and economic welfare. Most likely few participants in the San Francisco Conference realized that the unity of the Big Powers was to be broken before the end of the decade.

The Origins of the North Atlantic Treaty Organization (NATO)

The basic motivation for the creation of NATO was clearly the enhancement of the security of individual charter members and the states that subsequently joined. Resources and capabilities of even the most powerful of the allies, the United States, were perceived as insufficient to forego resorting to mul-

FIGURE 2.3

The Structure of the United Nations

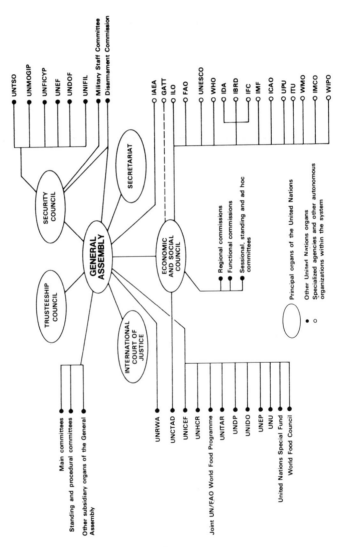

Source: U.N. Department of Information.

tinational means to meet the threat of aggression in Europe by a militarily powerful Soviet Union.

The threat began with attempts of a communist take-over in Greece, increased with the communist coup and seizure of governmental power in Czechoslovakia in 1948, and continued with heavy political pressure to establish pro-Soviet influence in Norway and Finland, efforts by indigenous communist parties to disrupt the economic reconstruction of Western Europe, and the blockade of Western road and rail access to Berlin in the fall of 1948.[30]

In Western Europe the first organizational arrangements for the enhancement of security after the end of World War II were made by Great Britain and France by signing the Dunkirk Treaty in March 1947. However, this treaty was directed primarily toward providing mutual aid in the event of a renewal of German aggression. It also aimed at economic cooperation and, therefore, a longer-range goal was to bring in the Benelux states (Belgium, The Netherlands, and Luxembourg) and perhaps later other West European nations. Alarmed by the expansion and consolidation of Soviet influence in Eastern Europe and the Balkans, the British government in January 1948 called for a "Western Union," which was followed up by preliminary negotiations with the Benelux states along with France aiming chiefly at a military alliance, but also seeking greater economic, social, and cultural cooperation. A treaty to this effect was signed in Brussels on March 17, 1948. This so-called Brussels Treaty made reference to Article 51 of the U.N. Charter, which authorized collective self-defense and stipulated that in the event of an armed attack on one of the signatories the other parties to the treaty would come to the aid of the victim of aggression. The treaty mentioned Germany as a potential aggressor; the Soviet Union was not named as such but was evidently very much on the mind of the alliance partners.[31]

The principal policy organ of what came to be called the Brussels Treaty Organization (BTO) was the Consultative Council, which consisted of the foreign ministers of the five member-states and that met several times. Between meetings, policy was determined by a permanent commission located in London and administration matters were handled by a Secretariat, also set up in London. A unified defense force was established in Fontainbleau, France, under Field Marshal Montgomery, but in fact he had very few troops to command.[32]

To the British government it soon became clear, however, that the BTO would not be sufficiently strong to deal with joint pressures, although Washington had promised to aid that organization in a way yet to be specified.[33] Ernest Bevin, British Foreign Secretary, was particularly concerned about Norway becoming subservient to Soviet wishes that might result in the collapse of the whole of Scandinavia and that "in turn prejudiced our chance of calling any halt to the relentless advance of Russia into Western Europe."[34]

Mr. Bevin perceived two threats: an extension of the Soviet Union's sphere to the Atlantic, and a political threat to destroy all the efforts made (with U.S. approval) to build up a Western Union. He therefore strongly recommended to the United States a regional Atlantic pact in which all states directly threatened by a Soviet move to the Atlantic could participate, and these were to include the United States, Britain, Canada, Ireland, Iceland, Norway, Denmark, Portugal, France, the Benelux states, and Spain when it had again a democratic form of government.[35] For the Mediterranean, he envisaged a separate system, with Italy playing a major role.

The United States response to the British proposal was given promptly by General George C. Marshall, then secretary of state. He suggested that joint discussions on the establishment of an Atlantic security system were to be undertaken at once. The initial discussions began in Washington on March 22, 1948, and revealed a number of uncertainties in the British proposals regarding prospective membership and the geographic area to which the system was to apply. There seemed to be an increasing need to include Italy, Greece, and perhaps Turkey, in the membership list but the acceptability of the Western zones of Germany as a member seemed at that time doubtful because it had been the enemy of most of the prospective members during World War II, terminated only three years earlier.[36]

For the U.S. government to join any kind of alliance raised fundamental questions. First, the United States had at that time potential capabilities and resources that might have been perceived by policy makers and the public as adequate for a successful defense of its territory and people. On the other hand, doubt may have been cast on such a judgment by the enormous advances in military technology that had been made by 1948 and could be expected to go even further in the years to come and by the extraordinary destructiveness of nuclear warfare as was seen in the Nagasaki and Hiroshima attacks. Second, George Washington's warning against entangling alliances was known to every American and was often reiterated in political oratory. With 1948 being an election year and the political power divided between a Democratic president and a Republican Congress, this was a most difficult time to move beyond Washington's warning into the uncharted territory of peacetime international politics.

The initial reaction of Secretary Marshall to the British proposal was somewhat negative. He considered U.S. participation in a military guarantee as impossible; U.S. aid would have to be confined to supplying material assistance to the members of the West European security pact. Two of the most able and senior officers in the State Department supported this view.[37] On the other hand, the directors of the Office of European Affairs and of the Division of West European Affairs, John Hickerson and Theodore Achilles, strongly advocated a North Atlantic Treaty and alliance.

During the spring of 1948 the State Department, reacting to the Soviet coup in Czechoslovakia and the continued pressure on Norway, began to commit itself to the treaty; in April the National Security Council approved a State Department recommendation that the president announce U.S. preparedness to negotiate a collective defense agreement with the Brussels Treaty members and Norway, Denmark, Sweden, Iceland, and Italy. Pending the conclusion of such an agreement, the United States would regard an armed attack against any member of the Brussels Treaty as an armed attack against itself.[38]

Since ratification of this proposed agreement was to require Senate approval and it was a Democratic president who needed consent from a Republican-controlled Senate, a bipartisan approach was essential. The means used was senatorial advice to the president in the form of a resolution introduced by Senator Vandenberg, the Republican Chairman of the Senate Foreign Relations Committee, which was adopted by the Senate in an overwhelming vote on June 11, 1948. The resolution advocated progressive development of regional and other collective arrangements for individual and collective self-defense in accordance with the U.N. Charter and specifically referred to the right of collective self-defense under Article 51 of the U.N. Charter. It also approved U.S. association with such arrangements "as are based on continuous and effective self-help and mutual aid, and as it affects national security."[39]

The so-called Vandenberg Resolution opened the way to negotiation for a North Atlantic Treaty that included regular meetings with the Senate Foreign Relations Committee and its staff to discuss actual treaty language. These discussions were important because there were arguments over various specific provisions, particularly those with respect to the nature of the commitment, geographic coverage, and duration, and which other governments should be invited to become members of the prospective security IGO.[40] The basic differences were due to the fact that the Western Europeans, especially the French, wanted as binding and as long a commitment as possible and the Americans, while agreeing in principle, were constrained by what the Administration believed Senator Vandenberg would accept.[41]

Disparities of views between the United States and other prospective alliance members about the substance of the treaty under consideration were not surprising, in view of the large gap in the capabilities and resources of the individual states involved in the negotiations. France wanted to accept an Atlantic security pact only if unity of command of the armed forces of the allies were to be achieved at once, and U.S. military personnel and supplies were to be moved to France immediately. For Norway, the matter was also urgent because of Soviet pressure for a pact similar to the Soviet-Finnish agreements that the Soviet government was confident would result in concessions to its demands for domination, but if rejected could trigger a Soviet attack on Norway and Sweden. Canada was another state that strongly advocated an effective treaty and was concerned that, as a result of discussions in the Senate, the treaty might be watered down so that it would not be much more than a Kellogg-Briand pact. On the other hand, Belgium was apprehensive about the provocative effect that any North Atlantic security treaty might have on the Soviet Union. While the Belgians were anxious to obtain immediate help from the United States, they floated ideas about the armed neutrality of Western Europe as perhaps being preferable to a formal Atlantic treaty relationship.[42]

It is not unreasonable to assume that the above concerns of selected prospective alliance member-states not only did reflect their urgent need for bolstering their security, but also that the public goods theory discussed earlier in this chapter may also explain their actions and those of other states. Obviously, the security of all the member-states would be enhanced by the alliance regardless of the size of the contributions they were to make in the future. In any case, agreement on the substance of the treaty was reached in April 1948 with an acceptable balance of obligations and rights of the parties.

With respect to the prospective members' obligations, the most controversial provision was the exact nature of the commitment to respond to armed attack on a treaty member-state. The United States did not want to and could not be obliged to use its armed forces automatically to aid a victim of an attack because the U.S. Constitution stipulates that only Congress can declare war. After many negotiating sessions and consultations with the foreign ministries of the prospective members and the Senate Foreign Relations Committee, the crucial Article 5 of the North Atlantic Treaty was to read as follows:

> The Parties agree that an armed attack against one or more of them in Europe or North America shall be considered an attack against them all, and consequently they agree that, if such an armed attack occurs, each of them, in exercise of the right of individual or collective self-defence recognized by Article 51 of the Charter of the United Nations, will assist the Party or Parties so attacked by taking forthwith, individually and in concert with the other Parties, such action as it deems necessary, including the use of armed force, to restore and maintain the security of the North Atlantic area.
>
> Any such armed attack and all measures taken as a result thereof shall immediately be reported to the Security Council. Such measures shall be terminated when the Security Council has taken the measures necessary to restore and maintain international peace and security.[43]

In spite of the qualifying words it was believed that Congress could be counted upon to back up the president with a declaration of war, particularly if the armed attack was not just an incident but a full-fledged initiation of extensive hostilities.

For the southern boundary of the territorial coverage of the treaty, the

Tropic of the Cancer was adopted (Article 6). This avoided involving any part of Africa or of the Latin American states as areas where an armed attack would constitute a casus belli. However, consultation on threats of or actual attack anywhere in the world was not restricted by the geographic parameters specified in the treaty. Indeed, consultations on possible threats is a major obligation of the member governments (Article 4). Although some European governments had insisted on a treaty duration of 50 years, the final agreement reached was limited to 20 years. It was doubtful that the Senate would have accepted a longer duration.

It should be noted that the treaty has an economic dimension. Article 2 emphasizes the elimination of conflict between the international economic policies of the member-states and encouragement of economic collaboration between "any or all of them." However, these provisions have been used only rarely; for example, when the NATO member-states pledged contributions to an assistance program for Turkey, which faced serious economic difficulties in the late 1970s.

In terms of rights, the member governments were given the right to be consulted, which is the other side of the coin of being obligated to consult each other in case of threats to their individual or collective security. It is noteworthy that the treaty negotiators did not spell out institutional and organizational details for the implementation of the agreement beyond stipulating the establishment of a council and committee, giving these organs the mandate to set up subsidiary bodies, including a defense committee. No mention was made of voting procedures, but the basic rule developed in the North Atlantic Council was that no government could be forced to take action against its will, but conversely, no government could prevent other governments from taking such collective action as they agree to take.[44] Figure 2.4 illustrates NATO's civil and military structure.

Finally, unanimous agreement is necessary to invite any state to accede to the North Atlantic Treaty. But only those states in a position to further the principles of the treaty and to contribute to the security of the North Atlantic area may be invited (Article 10). This shows that the member-states retained a maximum of flexibility for future decision making except for the obligations specified in Article 5 and for consultation.

The Origins of the European Communities (EC)

The basic motivation for the creation of the three European Communities in the early 1950s were primarily economic, but political and certain technological considerations also played a major role. The capabilities and resources of the six charter members (France, the Federal Republic of Germany, Italy, and the Benelux states) following World War II were clearly at a low ebb, strengthening their propensities to organize internationally to overcome

FIGURE 2.4

NATO Civil and Military Structures

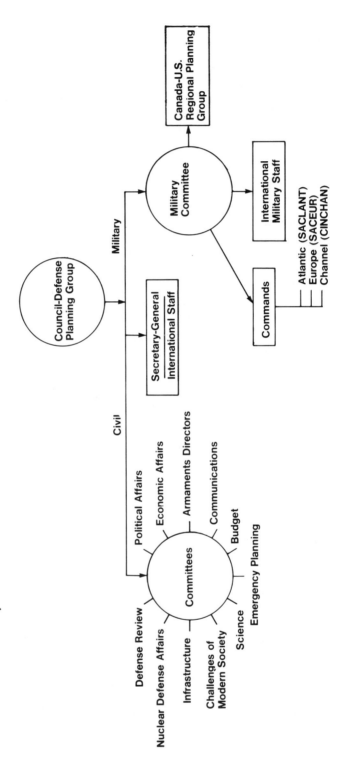

Source: The NATO Handbook (Brussels: NATO Information Service, March 1978), p.36.

national economic vulnerabilities and to pursue selected political goals successfully. Moreover, the political climate of opinion prevailing prior to the announcement of the plan for economic integration in 1950 was favorable.

In December 1946 the European Union of Federalists was founded. It established extensive national movements in Austria, Belgium, France, West Germany, Greece, Italy, and Switzerland. In Britain, a United Europe Movement was formed a year later. For the alleviation of traditional German-French antagonism, Winston Churchill asserted in May 1947 that this problem could not be solved "except within the framework and against the background of a United Europe." In May 1949 the various efforts toward European unity supported by many prestigious political leaders culminated in setting up the Council of Europe. Its Consultative Assembly held its first meeting in Strasbourg three months later and Paul-Henri Spaak of Belgium, the first president of the Assembly, said, "I came to Strasbourg convinced of the necessity of a United States of Europe. I am leaving it with the certitude that union is possible."[45]

When, in May 1950, French Foreign Minister Robert Schuman announced his famous plan for the creation of the European Coal and Steel Community (ECSC), he proposed not only an experiment in economic cooperation and integration; he also conceived this community to be the beginning of the political unification of Western Europe. He stated that the pooling of coal and steel would "mean the immediate establishment of common bases of industrial production, which is the first step toward European Federation and will change the destiny of regions that have long been devoted to the production of war armaments of which they themselves have been the constant victims."[46]

While this euphoric statement was shared by many governmental leaders in the prospective ECSC member-states, it is important to look in greater detail at the economic and political motivation of the two main powers involved in this integration experiment, West Germany and France. In West Germany, the direct economic benefits that might flow from a common market in the coal and steel sectors were not seen as being as persuasive as the indirect advantages of the proposed ECSC scheme. First, with the establishment of ECSC institutions, controls upon the West German economy were lifted, especially those of the International Authority of the Ruhr that under the direction of the French had limited the resurgence of that vital industrial region.[47] Second, the ECSC solution removed the Saar, which France had claimed as war reparations, from French administrative control and placed it in the hands of the ECSC authorities, where West Germany would have a degree of input concerning administration, and also could entertain some hope for eventual repatriation. Lastly, the ECSC provided domestic benefits clearly in the national interest, since it marked an end to export controls on West Germany's redeveloping its steel industry, and an end to tariff barriers against the export of West German coal—two major sources of revenue.

In terms of West German foreign policy objectives, the creation of the ECSC was also useful. Generally, it acknowledged West Germany's presence as a minimally sovereign state within Europe, equipped with the power to negotiate and conclude treaties. Additionally, the ECSC gave West Germany the opportunity to participate within regional cooperative institutions, as an equal to France and a superior to other Western European states. Thus, two important major goals of West German foreign policy were met.

For France, the direct economic benefits of the ECSC were also less important than certain political considerations. French foreign-policy planners were cognizant of the fact that West Germany could not be kept under Tripartite U.S.-U.K.-French Allied control for any extended period of time. This seemed especially true in the heavy industry sector where the Korean crisis had placed emphasis on the renewed production of European steel.

In fact, security planning dominated the French decision to propose the so-called Schuman Plan. The genesis of the plan came from the foreign policy planning of Jean Monnet, Etienne Hirsch, Pierre Uri, and Paul Reuter. In April 1950 a memorandum had been submitted to Prime Minister Georges Bidault that outlined the ECSC as a means of controlling West German industrial revitalization and of eliminating the possibility of renewed Franco-German hostilities on a long-range basis.[48] As Derek Bok noted, the ECSC presented France with the solution to a serious security dilemma:

> . . . without an expanding industry, and with the growing demand for steel production occasioned by the Korean War, France could not expect the controls upon German production to be continued indefinitely. At the same time, however, the French were fearful of an unbridled development of the Ruhr into a powerful arsenal which might once more become linked with the aggressive policies of a German government. Under these circumstances, the Schuman Plan was conceived by France as a compromise whereby she would give up a part of her sovereign power to secure a degree of international control over German coal and steel.[49]

The motivations of the other prospective ECSC members, Italy and the Benelux states, in support of the ECSC were less complex. They perceived that the prospects for domestic economic rehabilitation were enhanced and that political advantages were to be gained on the national as well as on the international level.

Great Britain was also invited to become a charter member of the ECSC, but turned down the invitation primarily on the grounds that it would not be beneficial either to its economic or political interests. At that time, economically, and perhaps also politically, Britain's relations with the Commonwealth states were regarded as holding the highest priority and, in addition, it was apprehensive about the supranational powers that were to be conferred upon the institutions of the ECSC.[50]

In the negotiations for the institutional framework, agreement was reached by the prospective ECSC member-states to set up a comprehensive structure for the management and performance of the tasks assigned to the organization. The most important organ was the High Authority, conceived to be the major executive and administrative agency and to be endowed with supranational powers to issue binding decisions (Article 14, ECSC Treaty) affecting coal and steel enterprises and individuals in the member-states. Other major organs were the Council, consisting of ministers of the member-states representing both the interests of these states and those of the ECSC (Articles 26–30); an Assembly composed of delegates appointed by the parliaments of the member-states and possessing only very limited powers (Articles 20–25); and a very powerful Court of Justice with extensive jurisdictional competencies (Articles 31–45). The voting procedures in the High Authority and the Council were based generally on majority rule, but in a number of cases the treaty required unanimity of the Council. The High Authority was given limited taxing powers, but its decisions to impose financial obligations were enforceable only through the use of the legal procedures of the member-states. National enterprises and member governments were given the right to appeal decisions or recommendations of the High Authority before the Court of Justice.

In terms of the degree to which member-states have transferred governmental powers to the institutions of an IGO, the ECSC undoubtedly ranks highest among all IGOs created so far. Indeed, it may well have set a high water mark since prospects for new supranational IGOs are bleak. Hence, the independence and freedom of action for the governments of the Six in the coal and steel sectors were reduced substantially by the provisions of the ECSC Treaty (also known as The Treaty of Paris) that was signed in 1951. But subsequent developments in the implementation of the treaty have gradually strengthened again the hands of the national governments and subtly weakened some of the pertinent supranational clauses. This also means that the obligations undertaken by the member-states with the ratification of this treaty have been watered down. On the other hand, their rights embodied in the treaty, such as the requirement of unanimity with respect to important decisions to be taken by the Council or their right to appeal decisions of the ECSC institutions, have so far remained unchanged, indeed, they were bolstered when in 1967 a modified decision-making approach in the Council enhanced the power of the member-states. We will return to this issue later.

Following the failure of the attempt to create a European Defense Community (EDC), when the French Assembly in 1954 refused to ratify the EDC Treaty signed two years earlier by the Six, thereby also smashing any hopes for the more ambitious scheme for a European Political Community, the attention of European unification enthusiasts turned again to economic integration. The idea was to expand the consumer market of coal and steel that had been put in place by the ECSC. This organization, which during the first few years seemed to be an instant success, began to run into some difficulties by the mid-1950s. The overall demand for coal had declined while oil and natural gas had become the preferred sources of energy. In some areas of the Community, especially in Belgium, the cost of domestic coal mining had risen so fast that the price of coal had lost its competitive edge, in particular vis-á-vis imported coal. Finally, the treaty's prohibition of cartels was flouted in West Germany and, to a lesser degree, in France.

On the other hand, the future creation of a common market for all goods produced in the six member-states promised to yield economic benefits that could not be gained by the national economies of the Six operating as separate units. Larger enterprises would be able to take advantage of the economies of scale that a market of 200 million consumers was going to offer. Political unification was viewed reflecting realistically the continuing progress toward economic integration, and thus became a powerful incentive for the negotiation of a European Economic Community (EEC) Treaty.

Talks on that treaty were opened in Messina, Italy in 1956. Agreement was reached with impressive speed; the Treaty of Rome was signed in March 1957 and came into force January 1, 1958. Despite the rapid pace of the negotiations, there were disparities of views among the six governments, and efforts especially by Jean Monnet, the dynamic and highly motivated first president of the ECSC High Authority, were necessary to overcome various obstacles. Concessions and counter concessions had to be made, and crucial compromises had to be offered and accepted. The EEC Treaty itself contained the guideposts to follow for the implementation of the common market, which was achieved ahead of the 12-year schedule of the transition period; it also suggested the necessary steps—such as the harmonization of national policies—to reach the goals of economic and monetary union. Voting rules in the Council of Ministers were to be changed in 1966 on important matters from unanimity to qualified majority rule, although this stipulation was largely ignored and modified by de facto consensus of the member governments. Finally, the treaty directed that there be eventual direct election of the Parliamentary Assembly and this was finally implemented in 1979. In summary, then, the path to political integration was opened by the treaty, and this prospect was a strong encouragement for the supporters of European unification.[51]

On the other hand, the treaty contained a small retreat from supranationalism inasmuch as the issue of binding rules on the people living in the member-states was more closely tied to joint action of the nine-man (later increased to 13) Commission (the independent executive of the EEC) with the Council of Ministers than was the case under the ECSC Treaty, which, in this respect, gave the High Authority greater freedom for independent action.

The third Community, the European Atomic Energy Community or EURATOM, was signed at the same time as the EEC Treaty and went into effect also in January 1958. EURATOM appeared to offer at the time of its establishment a significant instrument for political integration. Pooling the development of atomic energy resources seemed to be a logical step after the ECSC treaty had created a common market in coal and steel. Moreover, although in the coal industry many long-standing vested interests had grown up in the private and public sectors, most European enthusiasts believed that in the field of atomic energy fewer national interests existed that had to be accommodated. Hence, it was hoped that nuclear development for peaceful purposes could be placed successfully on a regional rather than national basis, if the appropriate resources for coordinated research could be made available. A joint agency for the supply of fissionable materials was to be established, and regional production targets for reactor projects were set. It was hoped that technological progress in the high-technology nuclear field could be made more rapidly and with less cost by pooling national resources and capabilities than proceeding separately solely through the national frameworks. These hopes were not fulfilled, however, primarily because the member governments and national industrial groups wanted to be in control of the development of this key source of energy. Consequently, national competitive pressures and other problems hampered the growth of EURATOM shortly after its establishment, and its contribution to regional integration has been minimal. Figure 2.5 illustrates the institutions of the European Communities in 1962.

Many Europeans felt in the 1950s that without Great Britain's membership in the Communities there was no realistic prospect of creating a truly unified Western Europe. The U.S. government generally shared this view and made efforts during the establishment of both the ECSC and the later two Communities to bring Great Britain into the fold as a charter member. But these efforts failed because Britain continued to place its priority on relations with the Commonwealth countries for economic and political power reasons and was opposed to any impairment of its sovereignty. Nevertheless, it became interested in some kind of low-level economic integration. Hence, in the late 1950s, the British government sponsored the European Free Trade Association (EFTA) that came into being in 1960 and included among its members the three Scandinavian states (Norway, Denmark, and Sweden), Austria, Switzerland, and Portugal.[52]

To the surprise of many on both sides of the Atlantic, the British

FIGURE 2.5

The Institutions of the European Communities, 1962

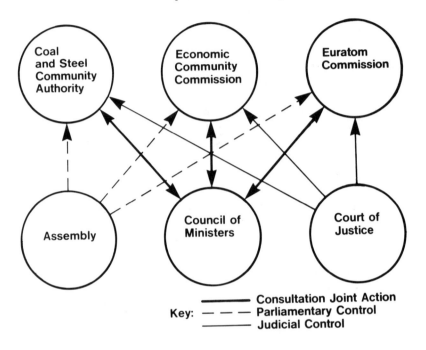

Key: ——— Consultation Joint Action
——— Parliamentary Control
——— Judicial Control

Source: J. Warren Nystrom and Peter Malof, *The Common Market: European Community in Action* (Princeton, N.J.: D. Van Nostrand Co., Inc., 1962), p.77.

government announced on July 31, 1961 that it now wanted to become a member of the Community. The reasons for this change of heart were both political and economic. Britain felt that it would be increasingly affected by whatever happened on the continent and that it had to take its place in the movement toward greater unity in Europe and perhaps ultimately in the free world. Britain was concerned about its serious balance-of-payments deficits caused in part by a sharp drop of exports to the Commonwealth. Moreover, EFTA turned out to be only a moderate success as a trading group. After long and difficult negotiations in 1961 and 1962, the prospects seemed good that an agreement could be reached for Britain to join the EEC. It was at that time, specifically on January 14, 1963, that General Charles de Gaulle cast his famous veto on the entry of Britain. General de Gaulle's professed reasons were his grave doubts about Britain's readiness for membership because its main orientation was insular and directed toward the other shore of the Atlantic, as well as to the Commonwealth. But perhaps the most significant consideration for the de Gaulle veto were strategic and political. The membership of Great Britain was likely to threaten France's leadership in the EEC and, in his view, Britain could constitute a trojan horse for the U.S. government—on the one hand impeding Western Europe's emergence as a unified power under French leadership, and on the other leading ultimately to an Atlantic Community under U.S. hegemony.[53] As a consequence, it took Great Britain another ten years before it could join the EC and at that time (January 1, 1973) Ireland and Denmark also became members.[54]

The institutional frameworks hammered out in the negotiations for the EEC and EURATOM were similar to that of the ECSC except that the main executive and administrative organs in both constituent treaties were called the Commission. A Council of Ministers performed basically the same functions as did the ECSC Council, but was given more power. It had the final word on all proposals submitted by the Commission, however, the intent of the two treaties was to draw a fine balance between the two organs so that it would require the active participation of both bodies to make decisions. However, as the evolution of the EC decision-making procedures has demonstrated, a shift of power toward the Council began in the middle 1960s and has continued slowly until today.

Several factors were responsible for the shift of power from the Commission to the Council. Nationalism began to be revived not only in France but in all the other Communities' member-states, rekindled principally, but not exclusively, by the actions and philosophies of Charles de Gaulle. Another factor was a slowly rising opposition to the progress of political integration on the part of basically nationalist-oriented bureaucracies in the member-states. Finally, French fears that a change of voting procedures in the Council from unanimity to a qualified majority for certain cases, scheduled to take effect in 1966 according to the EEC Treaty (Article III), would be harmful to France's vital interests, resulted in an ambiguous and inconclusive compromise among the Six that weakened much of the pro-integrationist bias of the treaty.

In the institutional framework of the EEC and EURATOM, two organs of the ECSC, the Assembly and the Court, were also used and exercised similar functions, but the Assembly's name later became the European Parliament. In 1967 the two Commissions (EEC and EURATOM) and the High Authority were merged into a unified Commission. The result was that four major organs: the Commission, the Council of Ministers, the European Parliament, and the Court were now operating the three Communities, but each one was continuing to function under its own constituent treaty. Figure 2.6 illustrates the restructured institutions of the European Communities.

It appears that the economic calculations and aspirations that the EC

FIGURE 2.6

The Institutions of the European Community, 1967

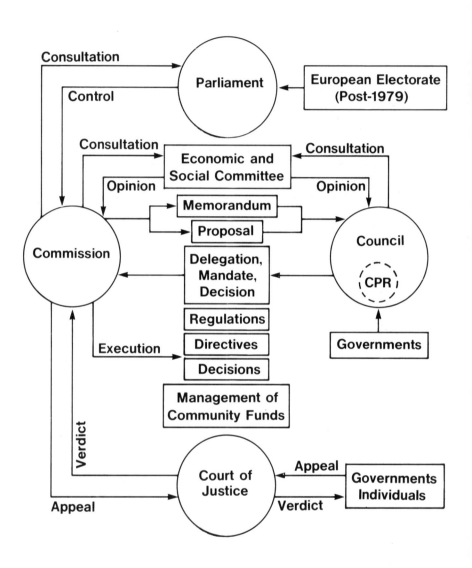

Source: European Communities Commission, *The Courrier: European Community-Africa-Caribbean-Pacific*, No. 48 (March-April 1978), p.36.

member-states motivated to set up the common market were confirmed and largely fulfilled by 1967. Within nine years from the beginning of the EEC, intra-Community trade had reached $24.5 billion, an increase of 326 percent over 1958. The standard of living in the EEC member-states continued to rise dramatically, and their general economic posture had attained impressive dimensions. At the same time, part of the independence and freedom of action sacrificed when the three treaties were signed has been regained over the years by the national governments of the member-states. Clearly, Community decision making carries more of a national imprint than was intended by the treaties; the obligations of the member-states have been softened and their rights bolstered. This will be discussed in greater detail in Chapter 5.

The Creation of the Council for Mutual Economic Assistance COMECON/ CMEA

The Council for Mutual Economic Assistance, best known in many Western states by its abbreviation of the English title COMECON,[55] but recently more frequently referred to as CMEA, was founded in January 1949 by the Soviet Union, Bulgaria, Czechoslovakia, Hungary, Poland, and Romania. Albania joined shortly thereafter, and the German Democratic Republic (GDR)—East Germany—was accepted in 1950. The major motivation for the Soviet Union to seek the establishment of COMECON was to counter the effects of the 1947 Marshall Plan through which the United States had offered financial aid not only to Western Europe, but also to the states of the Soviet bloc to overcome the ravages of World War II. However, the Soviet Union rejected this aid and compelled Czechoslovakia and Poland, which accepted the U.S. aid program, to reverse their actions and to follow the Soviet example. This initiative also provided an East European response to the Organization for European Economic Cooperation (OEEC) that was established to coordinate the distribution of Marshall Plan funds in Western Europe, to liberalize trade within the region, and to help in improving the international payment system among West European states. COMECON appeared to be an appropriate counter organization, although because of the fundamental difference in the West and East European economic systems, its functions differed from those of the OEEC. COMECON's major tasks were the exchange of economic experience among the members, coordinating foreign trade, extending technical aid to one another, and rendering mutual assistance with respect to raw materials, foodstuffs, machinery, and other items.[56]

For the Soviet Union, the underlying reasons for the creation of 1030MECON were both political and economic. It provided an instrument of Soviet control over the East and Central European economies, aided in assuring that the Soviet model would be faithfully followed in every sphere of their political, economic, and social life, and made it possible to coordinate intra- and extra-regional trade to the advantage of the Soviet Union by insisting on a favorable international division of labor among the COMECON member-states. For the non-Soviet member-states, economic motivations impelled them to participate in this regional cooperation experiment. Of course, the disparity in military and political power between the Soviet Union and the other members of the organization was such that the latter hardly could reject participation at the time COMECON was formed.

Although the capabilities and resources of the Soviet Union were clearly far superior to those of the other COMECON charter members, and therefore the Soviet propensity for international organization might have been relatively low, apparently the Soviet Union perceived potential benefits from COMECON. It was fortunate for the other COMECON members that the policy statement made after the constituent conference in 1949, a statement that served as a substitute for a constitution for 11 years, included the principle of sovereignty.[57] This protected, at least in a legal sense, the freedom of action and independence of the East European member-states, although they remained, of course, subject to Soviet political pressures. When in 1962 Nikita Khrushchev, following a Polish initiative, proposed a unified planning organ that would be empowered to compose common plans and to decide organizational matters, the proposal was rejected by Romania. Fearing that this proposal would transform COMECON into a supranational body, the Romanian government claimed that this would result in turning sovereignty "into a notion without a content" and would restrict "the fundamental, essential and inalienable attributes of sovereignty of the socialist state."[58]

In contrast to most IGOs, the institutional framework of COMECON developed very slowly over about 15 years. Up to 1956, the only body that met and discussed policy and possible actions was the Council and it did not hold any sessions between November 1950 and March 1954. The Council is composed of the chief executives of the member-states. Although the creation of a Secretariat was discussed at the constituent conference in January 1949, it was not until 1956 that a Secretariat with its seat in Moscow became a reality. The task of the COMECON Secretariat is to prepare for the sessions of the Council. When, in 1962, an executive committee was established whose members were deputy prime ministers of the member-states, the Secretariat had the additional mission to prepare for the bimonthly meetings of the committee. Finally, there are a number of standing commissions whose number now exceeds 20. Their fields of activity are linked to various economic sectors and industries such as coal or electronics. They are mainly concerned with the coordination of production plans. The establishment of priorities for outputs of certain key products, the formulation of foreign-trade agreements, and the selection of new investment projects.[59]

In accordance with the principle of sovereignty prevailing in COM-

ECON and also reflecting the rejection in 1962 of any conveying of supra-national powers to the organization's institutions, each member-state possesses one vote, and all decisions must be approved unanimously. However, in principle, a state that declares itself noninterested cannot veto an action agreed to by the other members (for example, on specialization of production in some sector). It can only refuse to participate.[60]

With this strong insistence on the right of maximum freedom of action on the part of the member-states, COMECON has not made the progress in economic integration as enjoyed by the EEC. Of course, in view of the difference in economic systems between Eastern and Western Europe, comparable development in integration may be impossible anyway. Nor has it been feasible to achieve the division of international socialist labor among the member-states that the Soviet Union had hoped to attain and for which, according to Khrushchev in 1962, the Soviet Union was prepared to reduce its output of some categories of manufactures if it proved more expedient to produce them in another COMECON state.[61] Nationalism and economic egocentric tendencies in most East European member-states have severely curtailed the potential for such a division of labor.[62] However, there has been increased border-crossing economic cooperation in such fields as energy supply (for example the Druzhba oil pipeline and an integrated electric power grid system), rail transportation (a railroad freight-car pool) and even links in industrial production as demonstrated by the collaboration of Czech and Polish tractor plants.[63] An International Bank for Economic Cooperation clears payments for COMECON's members.

In summary, then, some economic benefits from the COMECON arrangements, though varying in extent and nature, have accrued to all member-states, and it is noteworthy that 55 percent of all exports of the members move within COMECON. Hence, their overall capabilities and resources have been strengthened in return for a relatively low level of obligations to the organization and the retention of a high degree of national prerogatives. For the Soviet Union, however, political control over its East European satellite states through COMECON has not been bolstered materially. All of these states had by the 1970s turned to the West for financial aid for their further industrial development, both through the EC and bilaterally. Furthermore, while the Soviet Union may have gained certain economic benefits, its interdependence costs may turn out to be appreciable if the Polish internal struggle of the 1980s should prove contagious in the region and affect the general operations and activities of COMECON.

The Central American Common Market (CACM)

Efforts to unite the Central American states have a long history. After gaining independence from Spain in 1821, Guatemala, El Salvador, Nicaragua, Honduras, and Costa Rica formed a single political unit, the Federation of Central America in 1824 whose constitution was patterned after that of the United States.[64] This republic lasted until 1838, when it became apparent that it was impossible for the federal government to achieve full consolidation and therefore the Federation was dissolved.[65] Since then, several attempts were made to link the five states again into a political unit; in the 1890s it appeared that a loose confederation, called the Greater Republic of Central America, might succeed, but divergent politics in the individual states proved too strong and the attempt at creating a confederation ended in failure.[66]

Since all five Central American states have small populations (only Guatemala has more than five million inhabitants) and since they form a compact geographic unit, a strong case could be made for the advantages of economic cooperation among them, and this became a strong motivation for appropriate international organization. Strengthening this motivation was the economic doctrine developed by the United Nations Economic Commission for Latin American (ECLA) that put forth powerful and very persuasive reasons for international regional economic integration. The core of the ECLA recommendations was that the level of economic development could be raised only through the formation of a unified market, diversification of the Central American economies, greater industrialization, and changes in the makeup of foreign trade.[67] Adding further to the propensity of the five states to organize internationally were the history of attempts at political unification during the nineteenth century and their low level of economic capabilities and resources.

To translate the ECLA blueprint and to satisfy Central American aspirations for closer collaboration, the General Treaty of Central American Economic Integration, creating the Central American Common Market (CACM), was signed by Guatemala, El Salvador, Honduras, and Nicaragua in December 1960, and Costa Rica acceded to the treaty in July 1962. It obliged the states to eliminate tariffs on intraregional trade and to establish a common external tariff. It provided for the establishment of the Central American Bank for Economic Integration and set up a special regime for industrialization to aid the integration process. Industries that qualified for this regime would enjoy privileged status within the five states, including free trade, special consideration with respect to the reduction of import duties on imported raw materials, and preferences on needed imports.[68]

The institutional structure agreed upon in the General Treaty is limited. The highest organ is the Central American Economic Council, composed of the respective economic ministers; the task of the Council is to integrate the Central American economies and coordinate the economic policies of the member-states. Consensus appears to be necessary for all Council decisions. The application and administration of the treaty is entrusted to an executive council that consists of governmental representatives from each member government. Although it theoretically can adopt resolutions by majority vote, when ruling on a matter it must first determine by unanimous vote whether the matter is to be decided by unanimity or by simple majority (Article XXI). A Secretariat, with headquarters in Guatemala City, is headed by a secretary-general who is appointed by the Economic Council for a term of three years.

While it is apparent that the institutional voting procedures do not infringe on the autonomy of the member-states, the regime for integrating industries imposes obligations that affect their freedom of action. New industries are to be distributed to all member-states on as equal a basis as possible and once a particular industry is allocated to a specific state, a similar second plant cannot be built in the same or another member-state until all five member-states have been assigned their particular industrial facilities. Hence, the Central American scheme insists on direct and coordinated intervention in the distribution of industries in the region. This has provoked considerable criticism as being a restriction on the free operation of market forces. Moreover, once a plant in a particular integration industry is set up, its products enjoy the benefits of free trade within the region. Member governments are enjoined from imposing any kind of trade barriers on the border-crossing movements of these products.[69]

The hopes of many Central Americans that the CACM would turn out to be a successful experiment in economic integration seemed to become realized in the 1960s. By mid-1966 almost all of the tariffs on items in intra-CACM trade had been eliminated and by 1969 a common external tariff protected 97.5 percent of the tariff items that were imported into the region. Intraregional exports jumped from 8 percent of the member-states' exports in 1960 to 27 percent in 1970. Equally important, the structure of intraregional trade changed during that period with shipments of manufactured products increasing their share and foodstuffs and live animals decreasing percentagewise. On the other hand, the regime for integration industries yielded few results. Only Guatemala and Nicaragua experienced the establishment of such industries.[70] The likely reason was an unfavorable perception of prospective benefits by both entrepreneurs and governments, and for the latter a concern also about rising interdependence costs.

Toward the end of the 1960s and the early 1970s a number of problems arose that had their roots in governmental and elite perceptions in some of the member-states that benefits from the CACM were shared unequally, and that the consequent disadvantages outweighed the advantages. Some governments attributed their balance-of-payment difficulties to the progress of trade liberalization. Others felt that the integration industries scheme did not work properly.

Finally, as the result of the so-called soccer war in 1969 between El Salvador and Honduras, trade between the two states ceased and some of the CACM institutions stopped functioning. The level of intraregional exports as a proportion of total exports declined.[71] Moreover, internal conflicts in Nicaragua, El Salvador, and Guatemala had debilitating effects on the CACM. Thus it appears that the capabilities and resources of the five Central American member-states, which were strengthened initially during the 1960s, on balance may well have been weakened. National concerns with the unequal distribution of benefits among the members of the CACM, compounded by internal struggles for political power, caused cooperation through an IGO to appear as an exercise in futility, at least in the short run. Although Honduras and El Salvador concluded a peace treaty in 1980 and regional economic ministers meeting in Managua in April of that year reaffirmed their basic support for the CACM, it is too early to predict a revival of this IGO, especially in view of the continuing unrest in most of the member-states.

The Organization for African Unity (OAU)

The motivational background for the creation of the Organization for African Unity (OAU) flows from two different concepts: 1) a movement for the formation and consolidation of independent states within existing boundaries; and 2) a Pan-African movement hoping to join together all such states or groupings of them as were prepared to join forces for general or particular purposes. Whatever orientation, there was agreement among African leaders that unity and solidarity would not only assure a common front to safeguard African interests, but also would give African states a more effective voice in international politics, counter foreign influences in the solution of African problems, curb the danger of fragmentation among African states, and enhance their economic and social development.[72]

The problem of South Africa was also a major concern. Thus, the basic motivations for the establishment of the OAU were primarily political and this is confirmed in Article II of the OAU Charter, agreed upon by the Summit Conference of Independent African States in Addis Ababa in 1963. This article stresses the promotion of the unity and solidarity of the African states and the defense of their sovereignty, territorial integrity, and independence. With the capabilities and resources of the newly-independent African states very fragile, a high propensity for international organization to overcome their political weaknesses was almost a necessity.

In order to achieve the OAU objectives, the member-states, which now number more than 40, committed themselves in the OAU Charter to a number of obligations, but also they retained certain rights. There was, however, prior controversy about the extent of the commitment. For example, President Kwame Nkrumah of Ghana sought to set up a central political organization with powers to formulate a common policy in foreign affairs, defense, and economic matters. But the majority of the Addis Ababa conference participants rejected this attempt at supranationalism, and opted instead for the strict maintenance of the principle of sovereignty.[73] Indeed, the principles enumerated in Article III of the OAU charter include the sovereign equality of member-states, the noninterference in the internal affairs of these states, and respect for their sovereignty and integrity. On the other hand, the member governments pledged to settle all disputes among themselves by peaceful means (Article XIX) and affirmed a policy of nonalignment with regard to all blocs.

The supreme organ of the OAU is the Assembly of Heads of State and Government that meets at least once a year and can be convened in extraordinary session by a two-thirds majority of the member-states. Each member has one vote. It can only make nonbinding recommendations, which for their adoption require a two-thirds majority vote.[74]

The executive machinery of the OAU consists of a Council of Ministers and a Secretariat. The Council, whose power has increased over the years, is composed of the foreign ministers of the member governments or other ministers when appropriate. It adopts resolutions by simple majority.[75] It prepares for the meetings of the Assembly, implements the latter's decisions, and coordinates inter-African cooperation (Articles XII–XV). The head of the Secretariat is called administrative secretary-general, an indication that the member-states were anxious to limit the powers of the office and to prevent any kind of future aggrandizement of authority (Articles XVI–XVIII). Finally, a Commission of Mediation, Conciliation, and Arbitration was established, which is regarded as a principal organ. Consisting of 21 members elected by the Assembly for five year terms, it considers disputes between member-states with a view to finding an equitable settlement. However, despite a number of disputes between the members, the services of the commission have been rarely invoked. Instead, ad hoc commissions and committees have been set up to address the underlying problems of the disputes and to find acceptable solutions.[76] In 1977 the commission was replaced with a ten-member disputes committee that is charged with attempting to settle intra-African disputes.

The OAU has a mixed record in bringing about the settlement of the various—and all too frequent—disputes that have arisen among African states, in spite of the use of ad hoc bodies and mandates by either the Council of Ministers or by the Assembly to pressure the contending states to accept proposed solutions. For example, while in the Algerian-Moroccan border dispute of 1963 the fighting and hostilities ceased and tensions were lessened, no permanent settlement was ever formalized. In other instances, for example the guerrilla fighting along the borders of Somalia with Kenya and Ethiopia, mediating efforts were temporarily successful.[77]

Current issues occupying the OAU are the Polisario involvement in the Western Sahara, the continued South African presence in Namibia (formerly Southwest Africa), and the demand of Mauritius for the return of British-held Diego Garcia Island, located in the Indian Ocean. The Libyan intervention in Chad in 1980 prompted the OAU to establish a committee to investigate the crisis in this part of Africa.

For the promotion of national independence and racial equality, the OAU set up the Coordinating Committee in 1963 whose task was to harmonize the assistance given by African states to all national liberation movements and to administer a special fund that was established for this purpose. The Committee provided monetary aid and political assistance to movements fighting against colonialism in what used to be Rhodesia (Zimbabwe), Namibia, the territories formerly administered by Portugal, as well as against South Africa's policy of apartheid. It also furnished military training and advice, and distributed military equipment. While the efforts of the Committee in support of most liberation movements have been moderately effective, the struggle against South Africa could and can only be carried out through the comprehensive utilization of facilities offered by the United Nations. The Committee has sought to employ these means as much as possible, but ultimate results, of course, depend on the success of the various initiatives undertaken by the various relevant U.N. bodies.[78]

In sum and on balance, it appears that international organization by the African states in the form of the OAU has modestly strengthened their political capabilities and resources, although in the final analysis progress in economic development may be much more important for the individual states than political actions by the OAU. Nevertheless, the OAU has provided some benefits, if at times only psychological, to all of the member-states, and the interdependence costs have been minimal. A first OAU economic summit at Lagos, Nigeria, in April 1980 during which the conferees agreed on setting up an African Common Market by the year 2000, could result in additional substantive benefits if this plan could be realized effectively.

The International Civil Aviation Organization (ICAO)

Advances in technology and the necessity of border-crossing collaboration in order to enjoy the optimum benefits of the new technology are powerful motivations for international organization. An obvious example is the airplane, with its tremendous increase in range, speed, and carrying capacity. In a world of sovereign states international collaboration is an imperative that was recognized as early as 1917 when the International Commission for Air Navigation was established by the so-called Paris Convention, followed in 1929 by the creation of the Pan-American Convention for Air Navigation. An International Civil Aviation Conference, convened in the fall of 1944 and attended by representatives of 52 states, adopted an agreement for the establishment of the International Civil Aviation Organization (ICAO). This agreement reflected a compromise between the radical proposals of Australia and New Zealand that called for complete international ownership of world airspace and U.S. aspirations for maximum freedom of the air and unfettered competition. The agreement was ratified in 1947 by the necessary 26 states and, shortly thereafter, the ICAO became a specialized agency of the United Nations.[79]

The tasks of ICAO were to develop the principles and techniques of international air navigation and to foster the planning and development of international air transport. These tasks included as particular objectives: 1) the safe and orderly growth of international civil aviation throughout the world; 2) encouragement of the development of appropriate airways, airports, and air navigation facilities; 3) the assurance of safe, regular, efficient, and economical air transport; 4) ensuring respect for the rights of the member-states and their fair opportunities to operate international airlines; and 5) the promotion of flight safety in international air navigation. Clearly, these tasks require international organization; in the performance of these tasks the ICAO is aided by an INGO, the International Air Transport Association (IATA) that can be and is influenced by ICAO.[80]

In this connection, it should be pointed out that the world air-traffic market is far bigger than the sum of the bilateral air-traffic markets. Each state forms part of this world market. A state is not only origin and destination, but also a junction of international air service and international traffic.[81]

The ICAO structural framework consists of an Assembly in which every member-state is represented and that (as of 1977) is composed of 33 members elected for three-year terms. The Council is in permanent session and deals with the day-to-day activities of the organization. The Council also elects the 15 members of the Air Navigation Commission, who are chosen on the basis of their technical expertise in avionics. Another subsidiary organ is the Air Transport Committee; its members must be representatives of the Council.[82]

The ICAO Secretariat, another central body, is headed by the president of the Council, while the individual holding the title of secretary-general serves as deputy of the Council president in charge of administrative matters. As Robert McLaren points out, this means that the member governments are very much in control over the ICAO operations.[83]

The benefits of the ICAO for the member-states have been substantial. Many changes in air navigation infrastructures are processed every month (about 1,700) by the Secretariat personnel, and many other duties are performed to keep international air transport flowing. At the same time, each member-state retains its basic autonomy over running its fleets of airplanes wherever it best suits its purposes or those of the national carriers. The fact that governments often refer to their national carriers as a national instrument, thus identifying themselves with the management of the carriers, illustrates the protectionist (or national) approach of states to international civil aviation regulation.[84] A system has been created by the ICAO that regulates the admission of foreign carriers by a state to its national market in return for admission of its own carriers to other national markets.

An important ICAO activity has been its effort to develop effective deterrents to hijacking and air piracy. Under ICAO auspices, a number of conventions were drafted and signed at Tokyo in 1963, at The Hague in 1970, and in Montreal in 1971. These conventions have had a modest impact in reducing hijacking, but of course no matter how well a law or convention may be designed, it cannot stop all crimes if the motivation (and perceived advantages) to the perpetrators remains strong.

SUMMARY AND CONCLUSIONS

Perhaps the greatest challenge to all IGOs is the maintenance and stability of their task performance. Both domestic and external forces can sap the strength of the IGO institutions even after a certain level of performance has been achieved. The conflicting forces caused by the states' desire to buttress their national autonomy and enhance their national capabilities vis-à-vis the central management of capabilities and resources by the IGO institutions appear to be a common theme of all our cases. It can be seen in the problems of the U.N. Security Council, in the disparate views in and toward NATO, in the bickering in the EC and in COMECON, and in some of the disputes within the ICAO. A plateau in IGO task performance and/or regional integration had been attained in all of these cases, but any forward movement, especially if it hinted at supranationalism, as in the EC and CACM, resulted in a decided deterioration. The reasons for this phenomenon are discussed more fully in subsequent chapters. All we can conclude so far is that IGOs will, in the foreseeable future, remain vehicles through which nation-states conduct their affairs, but they are not likely to become decision-imposing entities on their member-states. The paradox is that the political, economic, scientific, and technological aspects of the world we live in are, at the same time, creating more and more interdependence, which in turn generates new or expanded expectations on and demands for IGOs.

Even though states may have a propensity for international organization, the force of nationalism and the desire of governments to attain short-term, immediate benefits rather than longer-term, more universal goals, have impeded any thrust toward either global or regional political unification. Nevertheless, the theoretical bases for the propensity of states to organize internationally depending on the extent of or constraints on their national capabilities and resources, and the concept of the collective good, provide useful comparative insights into the creation of IGOs. Indeed, the relevant variables explaining the genesis of IGOs can be extended beyond their creation, and can help us to understand the evolution, stability, and even the possible dismantling of IGOs.

An additional factor, not always explicit in the propensity model, is the impact of external forces on the genesis of IGOs. Such forces indirectly affect the capabilities and resources of nation-states, and therefore must inevitably be taken into account by prospective member governments in their calculations as to the benefits for them of creating or joining an IGO. The effort at the unification of Western Europe after World War II was encouraged by an external force, the United States, whose policy and influence, as the cases indicate, were reflected in the way the EC and NATO were devised. Also, the failures of the OAU can be attributed in part to the fact that states external to the region have intervened in various conflicts and (as in the case of the Ogadan conflict between Somalia and Ethiopia) sharp reversals of alliances can take place as a result. Such external impact can result in a decline in IGO task performance, which in turn will weaken its solidarity. The political turmoil in Central America, caused in part by conflicting objectives of the United States, the Soviet Union, and Cuba (all outside powers), has, for example, been responsible to a large degree for the decline of CACM in recent years.

NOTES

1. An exception is John Gerard Ruggie, "Collective Goods and Future International Collaboration," *American Political Science Review* 66 (September 1972): 874–93.

2. Ibid., pp. 877–82.

3. Ibid.

4. For a discussion of interdependence as viewed from the Third World, see Guy F. Erb and Valeriana Kallab, eds., *Beyond Dependency: The Developing World Speaks Out* (Washington, D.C.: Overseas Development Council, 1975).

5. Ibid., p. 882. This proposition is slightly paraphrased.

6. Ibid.

7. Ibid.

8. See M. Olson and R. Zeckhauser, "An Economic Theory of Alliances," *Review of Economics and Statistics* 48 (August 1966): 266–79; Todd Sandler and Jon Cauley, "On the Economic Theory of Alliances," *Journal of Conflict Resolution* 19 (1975): 330–48; Joe Oppenheimer, "Some Reflections on Clubs and Alliances," *Journal of Conflict Resolution* 24 (September, 1980): 349–57.

9. Various ways of looking at member-states' cost-benefit assessment of NATO are found in Karl H. Cerny and Henry W. Briefs, eds., *NATO in Quest of Cohesion* (New York: Praeger, 1965) and in Robert L. Rothstein, *Alliances and Small Powers* (New York: Columbia University Press, 1968).

10. For other examples see Sandler and Cauley, op. cit., pp. 334–35.

11. See, for example, Heinz M. Hauser, *A Financing System for Science and Technology for Development*, Science and Technology Working Paper, Series No. 13 (New York: United Nations Institute for Training and Research, 1982) and Eleanor B. Steinberg and Joseph A. Yager, *New Means of Financing International Needs* (Washington, D.C.: The Brookings Institution, 1978).

12. For an examination of Security Council practices, see Sydney D. Bailey, *Voting in the Security Council* (Bloomington, Ind.: Indiana University Press, 1969).

13. See Article 148 of the EEC Treaty. A thorough discussion of the legal powers of the EC, its members, and their exercise, can be found in A. W. Green, *Political Integration by Jurisprudence* (Leyden: A. W. Sijthoff, 1969).

14. For a thorough analysis of the earlier phase of Britain's relationship to the EC, see Miriam Camps, *Britain and the European Community, 1955–1963* (Princeton, N.J.: Princeton University Press, 1964).

15. For a thoughtful exposé of the dilemmas surrounding ensuring nation-state security, see Charles Yost, *The Insecurity of Nations: International Relations in the Twentieth Century* (New York: Praeger, 1968).

16. Quoted in Leland M. Goodrich, *The United Nations* (New York: Thomas Y. Crowell, 1959), p. 21. See also Theodore A. Wilson, *The First Summit: Roosevelt and Churchill at Placentia Bay*, 1941 (Boston: Houghton-Mifflin, 1969).

17. Goodrich, op. cit., p. 22. A definitive work on the history of the negotiations leading to the creation of the United Nations is Ruth B. Russell, *A History of the United Nations Charter: The Role of the United States, 1940–1945* (Washington, D.C.: The Brookings Institution, 1958).

18. Goodrich, op. cit., p. 23.

19. See Stephen S. Goodspeed, *The Nature and Function of International Organization*, 2nd ed. (New York: Oxford University Press, 1967), pp. 81–82.

20. Goodrich, op. cit., p. 22.

21. For background, see David A. Kay, *The New Nations in the United Nations, 1960–1967* (New York: Columbia University Press, 1970).

22. See, for background, Robert S. Jordan, ed., *International Administration: Its Evolution and Contemporary Applications* (New York: Oxford University Press, 1971).

23. Goodspeed, op. cit., p. 83 and pp. 528–65. See also Article 1 of the U.N. Charter.

24. Goodspeed, op. cit., p. 30.

25. Article 27, par. 3. France and the People's Republic of China are also permanent members in addition to the United States, Britain, and the Soviet Union. The number of nonpermanent members was increased to ten from six in 1976. For a further discussion of the powers of the Security Council, see Davidson Nicol, ed., *The United Nations Security Council: Towards Greater Effectiveness* (New York: United Nations Institute for Training and Research, 1982).

26. See Goodspeed, op. cit., p. 83.

27. For details of the conference and selected issues see ibid., pp. 85–102, and Russell, op. cit.

28. *Congressional Record* 91, Part 6 (July 23, 1945): 7957.

29. Inis Claude, *Swords into Plowshares*, 3rd ed. rev. (New York: Random House, 1964) p. 64.

30. For a detailed study of this period of postwar history, see Ernst H. Van der Beugel, *From Marshall Aid to Atlantic Partnership* (New York: Elsevier, 1966).

31. Eric Stein and Peter Hay, *Law and Institutions in the Atlantic Area* (Indianapolis: Bobbs-Merrill, 1967), p. 1032. For a survey of the institutions of NATO as well as the conclusion of the North Atlantic Treaty, see Robert S. Jordan, *The NATO International Staff Secretariat, 1952–1957: A Study in International Administration* (New York: Oxford University Press, 1967).

32. Stein and Hay, op. cit.

33. See Theodore Achilles, "U.S. Role in Negotiations that Led to Atlantic Alliance" *NATO Review* 27, (August 1979): pp. 11–14.

34. Quoted in Alexander Rendel "The Alliance's Anxious Birth," *NATO Review* 27 (June 1979): pp. 15–20.

35. Ibid., p. 17.

36. For a full discussion of these problems see ibid., pp. 17–20. See also Robert Strausz-Hupé, et. al., *Building the Atlantic World* (New York: Harper and Row, 1963).

37. Endicott Reid, "The Miraculous Birth of the North Atlantic Alliance," *NATO Review* 28 (December 1980): pp. 12–18.

38. Achilles, op. cit., pp. 12–13.

39. Paragraph 3 of Senate Resolution 239, June 11, 1948, 94 Congressional Record 7791, 7846.

40. Achilles, op. cit., p. 14. See also Edwin H. Fedder, *NATO: The Dynamics of Alliance in the Postwar World* (New York: Dodd, Mead, 1973).

41. Achilles, op. cit.

42. For details see Reid, op. cit., pp. 14–17.

43. Quoted in Theodore C. Achilles, "U.S. Role in Negotiations that Led to Atlantic Alliance," Part 2, *NATO Review* 27 (October 1979): pp. 16–19.

44. *New York Times*, May 15, 1947. For a survey of how the treaty provisions were applied in the first 20 years, see Robert S. Jordan, *Political Leadership in NATO: A Study in Multinational Diplomacy* (Boulder, Colorado: Westview Press, 1979).

45. Quoted in Richard Mayne, *The Community of Europe* (New York: Norton, 1963), p. 81. For background on why there was a propensity to form a regional IGO, see Lord Gladwyn, *The European Idea* (London: Weidenfeld and Nicolson, 1966).

46. Quoted in F. Roy Willis. *France, Germany, and the New Europe, 1945–1967* (London: Oxford University Press, 1968), p. 80. For a comparative summary of attempts at regional political unification, see Amitai Etzioni, *Political Unification: A Comparative Study of Leaders and Forces* (New York: Holt, Rinehart and Winston, 1965).

47. For details see Willis, op. cit., p. 105.

48. Richard Mayne, *The Recovery of Europe* (New York: Harper and Row, 1970), pp. 177–78.

49. Derek Bok, *The First Three Years of the Schuman Plan* (Princeton, N.J.: International Finance Section, Dept. of Economics and Sociology, 1955), p. 3.

50. For background on the nature of the Commonwealth during this period, see W. B. Hamilton, et. al., *A Decade of the Commonwealth, 1955–1964* (Durham, N.C.: Duke University Press, 1966).

51. A survey of the early history of the European Communities from the perspective of European union can be found in Susanne J. Bodenheimer, *Political Union: A Microcosm of European Politics, 1960–1966* (Leyden: A. W. Sijthoff, 1967).

52. For a description of the relationship of EFTA to other Western European IGOs, see J. Warren Nystrom and Peter Malof, *The Common Market: European Community in Action* (Princeton, N.J.: D. Van Nostrand, 1962). See also Thomas Franck and Edward Weisband, eds., *A Free Trade Association* (New York: New York University Press, 1968).

53. For details see Werner Feld, *The European Common Market and the World* (Englewood Cliffs, N.J.: Prentice-Hall, 1967), pp. 71–76. For a review of the special position of France, see Simon Serfaty, *France, de Gaulle, and Europe: The Policy of the Fourth and Fifth Republics Toward the Continent* (Baltimore: The Johns Hopkins Press, 1968).

54. For a good overview of the status of Britain at this time, see David Calleo, *Britain's Future* (New York: Horizon Press, 1968).

55. *Council for Mutual Economic Assistance.* The Soviet Union prefers "CMEA."

56. See Michael Kaser, *COMECON* (London: Oxford University Press, 1965), pp. 10–21; and Andrzej Korbonski, *COMECON* (New York: Carnegie Endowment for International Peace, 1964), no. 549, p. 2.

57. Kaser, op. cit., p. 11.

58. Quoted by Kaser, op. cit., p. 15. For additional details, see ibid., pp. 91–100 and Zdenek Suda, *La division internationale socialiste du travail* (Leydon: A. W. Sijthoff, 1967), pp. 42–45.

59. For details see Korbonski, op. cit., pp. 15–24.

60. Ibid., pp. 13–14.

61. Werner Feld, "The Utility of the EEC Experience for Eastern Europe," *Journal of Common Market Studies* 8 (March 1970): pp. 236–61 on p. 254.

62. Ibid., p. 258.

63. Ibid., p. 248 and Kaser, op. cit., pp. 133–34.

64. For background see Thomas L. Karnes, *The Failure of Union* (Chapel Hill, N.C.: The University of North Carolina Press, 1961), pp. 30–68.

65. Ibid., pp. 84–86.

66. Ibid., pp. 164–74.

67. James D. Cochrane, *The Politics of Regional Integration: The Central American Case* (New Orleans: Tulane Studies in Political Science, 1969), pp. 37–46.

68. For details see ibid., pp. 68–84.

69. For a more detailed analysis of this problem and experiences in other regions see Sidney Dell, *A Latin American Common Market* (London: Oxford University Press, 1966), pp. 53–57.

70. Harold K. Jacobson and Dusan Sidjanski. "Regional Pattern of Economic Cooperation" in *Comparative Regional Systems*, eds. Werner J. Feld and Gavin Boyd (New York: Pergamon Press, 1980), pp. 56–94 on p. 82.

71. For a comprehensive analysis of the CACM problem see Royce Q. Shaw, *Central America: Regional Integration and National Development* (Boulder, Col.: Westview Press, 1978), pp. 84–214.

72. Rupert Emerson, "Pan Africanism" in *Africa and World Order*, eds. N.J. Padelford and R. Emerson (New York: Praeger, 1963), p. 7.

73. Berhanykun Andemicael, *The OAU and the UN* (New York: Africana, 1976), p. 11.

74. Ibid., p. 31 and Articles VIII to XI of the charter.

75. Ibid., pp. 32–33.

76. Ibid., pp. 36–39.

77. For a detailed analysis of the major disputes see ibid., pp. 45–100.

78. For a very thorough analysis of the OAU-UN cooperation on this problem see ibid., 101–55.

79. Goodspeed, op. cit., p. 447.

80. Robert L. McLaren, *Civil Servants and Public Policy* (Waterloo, Ont. Canada: Wilfrid Laurier University Press, 1980), pp. 52–53.

81. H. A. Wassenbergh, *Aspects of Air Law and Civil Air Policy in the Seventies* (The Hague: Martinus Nijhoff, 1970), p. 32.

82. McLaren, op. cit., p. 53.

83. Ibid., p. 54. For additional details see Young W. Kihl, *Conflict Issues and International Civil Aviation Decisions* (Denver, Col.: The University of Denver, 1971), pp. 2–9.

84. Wassenbergh, op. cit., p. 10. For a discussion of other ICAO activities see ibid., pp. 51–152.

Chapter 3

Institutional and Bureaucratic Developments

We pointed out in Chapter 2 that the establishment of an IGO requires the determination as to what kind of a structure the prospective IGO is to have. The nature and shape of this institutional framework obviously must relate to the task performance and functions an IGO is expected to carry out but, as we have also seen in Chapter 2, political desiderata may impose constraints on purely rational considerations to set up an effective management model. These desiderata not only have an impact on the organizational details of the IGO institutions, but also on the power conferred upon them by the member-states.

THE RANGE OF INSTITUTIONAL PATTERNS

IGO Administration

All contemporary IGOs have a secretariat as the basic administrative organ, although the name for this organ may vary. For example, in some IGOs the name "bureau" is used—a case in point is the Universal Postal Union (UPU); in the European Communities it is the commission that is in charge of administration.

The executive head of an IGO may be called the secretary-general, as in the case of the United Nations, or president, the title of the head of the EC Commission. Director-general is another title for a chief administrator and this is used for the chief of the secretariat of the General Agreement on Tariffs and Trade (GATT), and throughout the United Nations.[1] It is important to note that these chief administrative officers often also have important executive functions that either flow from provisions in the constituent treaties (Article 99 of the U.N. Charter) or from the development of continuing practices such as those that have occurred in the case of GATT's director-general.

Plenary Organs

A large majority of IGOs have plenary organs on which all member-states are represented. Historically, these organs were known as conferences, going back to the Congress of Vienna, and this designation continues to be used today as exemplified by the General Conference of the ILO and UNESCO. Other names for plenary organs are congress (the Universal Postal Union and World Meteorological Organization use this term), assembly (the United Nations and the Council of Europe), and parliament (the European Communities).

The frequency of plenary organ meetings varies with the kind of function for which the IGO was created. Some plenary organs meet only once every five years—Universal Postal Union (UPU) and International Telecommunication Union (ITU)—while the European Parliament meets now four to five times each year and the U.N. General Assembly at least once a year, but this session lasts from September through mid-December. There also has been the tendency for the General Assembly to have resumed sessions sometime in the following year.

Plenary organs normally engage in deliberations on broad policy questions and make appropriate recommendations to member-states and IGO administrators. However, in some cases they become involved in IGO management or make proposals on more detailed issues. For example, the ITU Plenipotentiary Conference establishes the budget for the organization for the next five years,[2] the U.N. General Assembly, whether convened in general or special session, often makes detailed recommendations on economic matters such as the resolutions embracing the so-called New International Economic Order (NIEO) and the Consultative Assembly of the Council of Europe makes specific proposals on draft conventions of various kinds. In many cases, the plenary organs review and act on the work of standing committees whose membership is open to all members.

Organs of Limited Composition

The executive functions of management in an IGO are often performed by a council or an executive board or committee with limited membership. The members are elected usually by the plenary organ(s) of the IGO, and it is not unusual for stiff competition to arise between different member-states that want to be represented on these councils or boards, especially if they wield considerable power. The Security Council of the United Nations provides a prime example for such competition; in order to accommodate as many member-states as possible for the ten two-year terms of the non-permanent members of the council, the term has been split into two single-year terms.[3]

The size of the limited composition organs varies. The U.N. Economic and Social Council (ECOSOC) consists of 54 members, the ILO Governing Body has 40 representatives, ICAO 27, UNESCO 24, and the Inter-Governmental Maritime Organization (IMO) is composed of 16 members. It is interesting to note that some constituent treaties contain guidelines for the selection of council members. It is expected that the members should come from states with important interests in the subject matter for which IGO was created. For example, Article 50(b) of the ICAO treaty provides:

> In electing the members of the Council, the Assembly shall give adequate representation to (1) the States of chief importance in air transport; (2) the States not otherwise included which make the largest contribution to the provision of facilities for international civil air navigation; and (3) the States not otherwise included whose designation will insure that all the major geographical areas of the world are represented on the Council.

The IMO Convention in Article 17 states:

> (a) Six shall be Governments of the nations with the largest interest in providing international shipping services;
> (b) Six shall be Governments of other nations with the largest interest in international seaborne trade;
> (c) Two shall be elected by the Assembly from among the Governments of nations having a substantial interest in providing international shipping services, and
> (d) Two shall be elected by the Assembly from among the Governments of nations having a substantial interest in international seaborne trade.

Finally, it is important to point out that in regional organizations, councils as executive organs are composed of representatives of all member-states. This is the case in the EC Council of Ministers, in NATO, in the Standing Committee of the Association of South East Asian Nations (to be discussed in detail below), and others. The reason is the small number of member-states normally found in regional organizations; it does not affect the power and influence of these organs, which depend on other factors also to be examined in Chapter 5.

In most cases the organs of limited composition meet monthly or more frequently since they are engaged in the day-to-day operations of their IGO. Usually, they are authorized to set up subordinate committees or working groups on various issue areas to help them in managing the IGO's task performance. In regional IGOs these committees and other groups may not always have representation from all the states that compose the membership of the higher council. An example is NATO's Nuclear Planning Group, a seven-state suborgan ultimately responsible to the NATO Council.

Adjudicatory Organs

Only a few IGOs have adjudicatory organs. The United Nations has both the International Court of Justice in The Hague and the Secretariat's Administrative Tribunal. In terms of decisions rendered and complied with, the latter might have a better record caused mainly by its considerable involvement in intra-U.N. matters. In the European Communities the Court of Justice is a very viable adjudicatory organ that has rendered more than 1000 judgments and opinions since its establishment in 1953. The European Court of Human Rights is associated with the Council of Europe; the number of cases decided by this judicial body has remained small although its decisions have had a significant impact on administrations throughout Europe. The institutional framework of the East African Common Market had included a Court of Appeal, but with the demise of that organization the court has become inoperative, if, indeed, it ever was used. It is interesting to note that the Convention on the Law-of-the-Sea envisages the creation of an International Tribunal connected with the regime of the Enterprise that would be charged with the deep-seabed mining of the oceans. This suggests that as the number of IGOs and the scope of their activities expands further, we might witness the creation of additional adjudicative organs.

If we look at the many IGOs existing in the world today, we can observe a great variety of institutional frameworks. On the one hand, there are the very extensive and intricate frameworks of the United Nations and the European Communities, whose institutions are housed in skyscrapers and many other buildings in different cities and states. On the other hand, we can observe much smaller IGO structures, much less complicated, in political organizations such as the OAU and ASEAN, and even more so in smaller technical IGOs such as ICAO.

What are some of the basic factors that determine the extent and intricacy of an IGO's institutional framework? We believe that perhaps the most important factor is the scope and complexity of the tasks to be performed by the IGO. In some cases these tasks are in several issue areas, as is the case with the United Nations whose concerns range from dispute settlement and conflict resolution to economic and social development. In others, they require the issuance of detailed regulations for the management of various economic sectors—the best example is the EC and its detailed operation of the Common Agricultural Policy (CAP).

Another influential factor seems to be the kind of politics involved in the operation of particular IGOs—low politics or high politics. The former refers primarily to economic matters and technical problems, while the latter deals with strategic issues and political matters significantly affecting the national welfare. Although the distinction between low and high politics at times becomes blurred, we hypothesize that in low-politics areas, the more far-reaching and specific the tasks to be performed by an IGO the more extensive and comprehensive is the institutional framework; whereas, if the tasks to be carried out are relatively narrow, only a moderate framework is used. In high politics, we posit that if multiple tasks are to be performed, the framework will be extensive with attempts made to portion out functions in accordance with different perceived needs; on the other hand, if the tasks for the IGO are limited, the framework will be relatively simple although the issues involved may touch on the survival of the member-states. The matrix in Figure 3.1 provides a schematic picture; it should be noted, however, that in actuality, IGO institutional frameworks do not always fit tidily into any schema. The United Nations is generally a high-politics IGO with multiple tasks (peace keeping and concern for the global economy), but it also performs low-politics tasks, primarily through the specialized and affiliated agencies. NATO's high-politics task is limited, while the EC's is basically a multiple low-politics IGO with some high-politics aspirations. The Universal Postal Union is a typical low-politics IGO with narrow tasks.

TASK PERFORMANCE

As discussed in Chapter 1, the fundamental mission of IGO institutions is the management of cooperation in various fields in order to carry out the tasks for which the IGO was created. This involves the search for compromises in conflictual situations whose origins may have been military, political, and/or economic. It also involves the coordination of the member-states' national policies and activities in economic and security issue areas as far as it is needed to assure the success of the IGO's assigned functions, under the powers transferred to the institutions.[4]

Depending on the issue area with which the IGO is concerned, the institutional framework must provide the appropriate means for its task performance. This includes the necessary physical facilities for deliberation, consultation, and negotiations within and among institutions and between member-state governments and institutions.

The instrumentalities for task performance vary from IGO to IGO. However, all IGOs collect information on their issue areas and disseminate it to relevant institutional parties and to the member-states (usually through the governments but sometimes also directly to the people). The higher the quality of the information disseminated, the more it can contribute to the success of deliberations, consultations, and possible negotiations within the

FIGURE 3.1

Institutional Frameworks

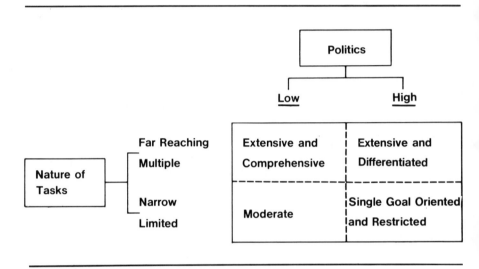

institutional framework. The Bank for International Settlements (BIS) is a good example of an IGO that generates a high quality of information with resulting success in task performance.

Another important instrumentality authorized for many IGOs is the formulation of pertinent policies. In some IGOs such as the United Nations and the EC, several institutions participate in policy making. The implementation of these policies is, in many if not most cases, carried out by member-state agencies; member governments opposed to the policies are therefore likely to forego implementation. However, in the EC limited implementation is performed by the Commission in the agricultural and antitrust sectors, and both the International Monetary Fund (IMF) and the

International Bank for Reconstruction and Development (better known as the World Bank) also implement their own policies by granting or refusing loans for different projects, although in the latter case, local bank officials may help in the implementation. Another example is the monitoring function of the International Atomic Energy Agency (IAEA), whose inspectors make checks of nuclear power facilities in member-states to prevent the use of fissionable materials for the production of nuclear weapons.

Policy making and implementation by IGOs involves a series of decisions within the institutional framework. A taxonomy of IGO decisions and other factors of decision making in IGO institutions will be examined in detail in Chapter 4.[5]

Regardless whether IGOs themselves carry out the implementation of their policies or whether this task is handled by the member governments, IGOs must be concerned with the supervision of the implementation process. In crisis situations, the power to investigate and to report to the major political organ reflects this function; for other IGO tasks, monitoring events and preparing reports for discussion and dissemination serve the function of supervision of policy implementation. This is therefore a very significant dimension of task performance, but at times it may be difficult to achieve as it may impinge on what member governments consider their national prerogatives or even is seen as interference in their domestic affairs. Indeed, the scope and success of IGO policy making and the successful supervision of the implementation process depends on the perceptions of the member governments as to how far IGO policies promote or hinder the attainment of national priority goals and important objectives of nongovernmental actors in the individual member-states. These questions will be discussed in detail in Chapter 5.

Less stringent institutional instrumentalities for task performance, yet not unimportant and often effective, are nonbinding recommendations and resolutions. Obviously, they do not have to be heeded by any government objecting to them, but the repeated passage of recommendations, especially in a politically visible body such as the U.N. General Assembly, is bound to affect world opinion and thereby could influence the decision-making processes of member governments in opposition.

Finally, in some cases IGO institutions are authorized to render judgments regarding obscure or ambiguous, factual or legal situations. For example, the U.N. Security Council may have to issue a judgment as to whether an act by a state is a violation of international peace, or the EC Commission must make a determination as to whether the behavior of a company in the Common Market constitutes an infringement of the EEC or ECSC antitrust provisions. The authority to make such findings is a significant instrument in the United Nations' or EC's performance of its various tasks.

MANAGEMENT EFFICIENCY

Management efficiency in the task performance of an IGO is high if its institutions have a good record in attaining desired outcomes. This, in turn, requires superior knowledge of cause-effect relationships and of political, social, and economic environmental elements in the issue areas in which a particular IGO is involved. The more limited this knowledge, the greater are the difficulties for goal achievements.[6] Task performance is also likely to be improved, or at least not likely to be impaired, if the relevant institutions can adjust themselves to constraints and contingencies not controlled by the IGO itself.

An important element in achieving good task performance is the leadership quality of the executive head of IGO institutions. According to Robert W. Cox, the executive head plays a big role in converting an IGO conceived as a framework for multilateral diplomacy into one that is an autonomous actor in the international system.[7] However, there are also significant constraints on the executive's leadership ability to bring about full management efficiency. These include bureaucratic immobilisme, increasing client control benefiting from intrabureaucratic balances of influences, and the patterns of conflict and national power alignments that make it difficult to mobilize uncommitted supporters for particular IGOs.

Of course the greatest thing an executive head can do for improving task performance efficiency is to alter the policies of the member-states so that they conform more with the decisions and interests of the IGO. In order to do this he must have: "(1) access to domestic groups having influence; (2) adequate intelligence concerning their goals and perceptions; and (3) ability to manipulate international action so that these groups can perceive an identity of interest" with the IGO.[8] Such a strategy is likely to work best in a pluralistic national political system and most states do not fall into this category. But even in pluralistic politics this is a difficult undertaking, except perhaps in small states. The president of the EC Commission has not been successful in persuading the larger EC member-states of this identity of interests, nor has the U.N. secretary-general been able to do this as far as the United States and other major powers are concerned. The coincidence of IGO member-state interests fluctuates according to the larger world political environment in which both rest.

Another factor affecting the efficiency of IGO task performance is the organizational structure of institutions. The EC Commission, which has grown tremendously between 1958 and 1976, has been declining in efficiency. Table 3.1 demonstrates this growth across the commission units.

Édouard Poullet and Gerard Deprez, who have made a careful study of the Commission's administrative efficiency, stress that "the multiplication and differentiations of principal administrative units [especially directorates-

TABLE 3.1: Development of Horizontal Differentiation, 1958–76

Year	Number of Directorates-General	Number of Directorates	Number of Divisions or Specialized Services	Number of Principal (Non D.G.) Administrative Units	Number of Divisions or Specialized Services [a]
1958	9	32	100	1	3
1965	9	36	124	2(+3)[b]	4(+25)[b]
1967	10	36	124	2(+3)[b]	4(+25)[b]
1968	20	66	238	7	30
1970	20	66	238	8	32
1972	18	64	246	10	38
1973	19	72	265	10	44
1974	19	73	284	10	46
1975	19	71	284	10	50
1976	19	71	288	12	50

[a] This column shows the development in the number of Divisions and Specialized Services pertaining to the Principal Administrative Units listed in the preceding column.

[b] The figures in parentheses correspond to the administrative units common to the three executives (EC Commission, Euratom, High Authority of the Coal and Steel Community), that is, the Statistical Office, the Legal Service, and the Press and Information Service.

Source: Christoph Sasse et al. Decision Making in the European Community (New York: Praeger Publishers, 1977) p. 149.

general and directorates] have contributed to the compartmentalization of policies and made the means for the coordination needed more numerous and expensive."[9] They conclude that the organizational pattern that has gradually developed has been imposed upon it by events and external pressure. They believe, however, that it represents in effect nothing other than the perpetuation of a simple hierarchical model which was well suited to a small organization, but is poorly suited to a large organization operating within a very complex system, which is what the EC now represents.[10] The consequence of the resulting organizational pattern of the Commission has been the breakdown of the organization internally into separate subsystems, each acting for its own account, defending its own interests, having recourse to its own policies, and coexisting rather than interacting with the others.[11] Efforts at restructuring the United Nations have also met with only limited success.

This raises the question of rationalization; that is, the process of attempting to remove duplication of activities between and among units, which is a perennial problem not only in IGO institutions, but of public administration in general. We will return to the relationship between task-performance efficiency of IGO institutions and organizational patterns in the cases that follow.

INSTITUTIONAL EXPANSION, PROLIFERATION, AND INNOVATION

The expansion of the EC Commission's organization reflects both the enlargement of the membership of the communities in 1973, as well as an increasing workload as the result of new tasks that needed to be performed by the EC's international civil service.[12] Examples are the ever-increasing functions that had to be performed to meet the needs of the Common Agricultural Policy (CAP) or the establishment of the Regional Development Fund in the early 1970s that will be examined in detail in Chapter 5. Does this development of the Commission's organizational structure suggest a confirmation of Mitrany's proposition that "form follows function"?[13] Or are other forces at work that generate not only the expansion of institutions, but also their proliferation?

Clearly, the neofunctionalist argument of spillover is attractive. If an IGO institution does not have the capability to carry out satisfactorily its assigned tasks, thus jeopardizing the goals pursued by those states that established the IGO, institutions are automatically expanded or new institutions are created to perform the tasks in order to attain the original goals.[14] But it may not be the functionalist logic that is the incentive for institutional expansion, but simply the desire for growth, which is a normal organizational goal.[15] In this respect the leadership role of the executive head may be crucial.[16]

Institutional clientele and bureaucracy are apt to be strong supporters of institutional growth and the former may provide the needed political interference on the national level to assist institutional expansion. Indeed, this clientele may also assist in bringing about a proliferation of institutions. For the bureaucracy of an IGO, institutional expansion or proliferation may offer greater specialization of expertise that in turn is likely to result in promotions and salary increases.

The efficiency of the management of task performance in IGO institutions may also be improved by innovations in the processes used to achieve the various tasks. In this respect the motto, "form follows function" might also apply. But whether this motto provides many answers is doubtful because innovation analysis is highly complex. Innovation may flow from various sources: intellectual vision, disillusionment with existing institutions and procedures, and substantive needs. Civil servants may undergo learning processes in their institutional positions that might trigger innovation. Also, crisis conditions (institutional survival) may stimulate innovative proposals and so will expectations of major rewards.[17] How far innovation stems from the operation of functionalist logic is difficult to judge, for functionalists have assumed that everybody (governments or peoples) will value the fruits of international cooperation in specific functional areas and that most participants will find the process in itself rewarding. However, basing innovation on expectations of concrete rewards seems to be more in line with realistic thought.[18]

To summarize the discussion so far, it has been our intention to identify criteria for comparing IGO institutions. A number of variables are useful for this purpose. They are the kind of IGO organs or institutions set up, that is, secretariats, organs with full or limited representation of member-states, and adjudicating organs; the type of instrumentalities available for task performance; the management efficiency for task performance; the impact of institutional structure on task-performance effectiveness; and possible reasons for institutional expansion, proliferation, and innovation. Some of the factors and forces that might promote these developments may also give us insights as to why institutions decline, since some of these forces (especially the competing institutional clienteles), may have reasons to want to do away with certain IGOs. Much of this depends of course on the civil servants who work in these international institutions. What are the basic criteria for evaluating the performance of the civil servants that compose the bureaucracies of IGOs? This subject will be examined in the next section.

CHARACTERISTICS OF AN INTERNATIONAL CIVIL SERVICE

The traditional concept of a truly international civil service is that it must serve the interests of the organization as a whole.[19] This concept can be said to consist of four basic principles. The first, and probably the most crucial, principle is that of loyalty: the employees of an IGO must shed their national loyalties to some extent and consider only the interests of the IGO that employs them in carrying out their professional responsibilities. A corollary to this first principle is that international civil servants, while in international employment, should not receive instructions of any kind from their own governments or attempt to represent the interests of their national governments in any manner.

The second principle is that of impartiality. International civil servants are to be administrators, not politicians. It is their function to implement conscientiously decisions that were reached elsewhere, and to avoid involvement in the controversy that often surrounds IGO decision making if at all possible. International civil servants should be apolitical in the sense that they will willingly implement whatever policy decisions are reached by the governing political bodies or organs (that is, those composed of representatives of the member-states). This principle is more easily practiced by nationals from the industrial democracies, where the capacity of the state to control a person's right to free speech and expression is circumscribed.

A third principle is that of independence. Independence, in the sense of international secretariats being independent of political pressure from any national government or group of member-states, is implied by the first principle discussed above. But the principle of independence of the international civil service has a very important organizational dimension as well. It has been suggested that for any international secretariat to maintain its independence, it must be composed of career civil servants who enjoy a considerable degree of job security. Hence, career or indefinite contracts should be given to international civil servants so that they can feel confident that if they promote the best interests of the organization, they will be free from retribution or from removal from office for political reasons. The expectation is that a predominantly career civil service would thus facilitate the creation of an international identity, or esprit de corps. In contrast, individuals seconded (on leave of absence from their national governments) to an IGO on a fixed-term contract would find it difficult not to retain their national political self-consciousness, and thus, (so the argument goes) would not develop the same type of nonnational attitudes and behavior patterns as individuals who knew that they were immune from the worry that their official actions could influence their subsequent national career fortunes.

The fourth and final principle relates to recruitment practices. Those persons who still adhere to the traditional concept of an international civil service, maintain that individuals should be recruited primarily on the basis of merit, "primarily" because it is recognized that a certain amount of geographical representation (or distribution) is also a prerequisite. The rationale for geographic representation is that IGOs basically reflect a common effort of the member-states, and nationals of all states should participate as civil servants in this effort. Consequently, because of decolonization and the rapid increase in new states, a form of international affirmative action has taken hold in the United Nations and many other IGOs, whereby the newer member-states, have claimed that geographical distribution should be equal to or even take priority over, merit and objective criteria of personal competence. States that have been the major financial contributors in such affected IGOs and that obviously have something to lose in terms of the numbers (and rank) of their nationals in the various secretariats, have protested this preoccupation with geographical representation. However, at least until 1981, no effective barrier to this trend has been erected. We will return to this issue in our illustrative cases.

THE PLACE OF BUREAUCRACIES IN IGOs

Bureaucracies are commonly considered to be a phenomenon of the rise of the modern industrial state. This does not mean that there were not cadres of officials who were concerned primarily with transacting the public's business before the industrial revolution. Obviously, they existed. All societies have had definable cadres of servants who have been accountable to the governing authority for their official actions. What makes modern states different is both the scale of their activities, and the pervasiveness of the bureaucracy into all aspects of daily living. As one observer put it:

> (Both) liberals and . . . conservatives often strongly objected to the bureaucracy and depicted it as a colossus which would engulf the various areas of life and cancel the traditional liberties of the people and which would engender a mechanized and oppressive civilization, choking the individual and regimenting his every activity.[20]

The nineteenth century expectation that the role of public administration at the national level was to help solve society's ills, gave way, by the second quarter of the twentieth century, to the belief that bureaucracy should be controlled. Ironically, this change in attitude occurred during the same period when greater confidence was being expressed about the desirability of creating more bureaucracies at the international level. For example, Jean Monnet, the Frenchman who became known as the foremost advocate of European unification, was successful by the end of the 1940s in convincing the major European industrial democracies that the creation of the bureaucracies of the European Communities would be for the mutual benefit of all participating member-states.[21] The growth of the civil service in such regional functional IGOs was paralleled by the rapid increase of the international bureaucracies of the United Nations and its specialized and affiliated agencies. Unfortunately, complaints of politicization and preoccupation with geographic distribution, to which we alluded earlier with respect to the United Nations and other IGOs, have also been heard concerning the bureaucracies of the EC; consequently, rather than increasing in prestige and in attracting the confidence of the member-states as their functions have expanded, they have diminished in prestige.[22] Thus, by the 1980s the bureaucracies of regional IGOs, derived as they are from the same tradition as the United Nations and its various affiliated agencies' bureaucracies, have been subjected to similar criticisms and suffer increasingly from low esteem.

Is this decline justified? If the conception of the proper role of international bureaucracies is to reflect the bureaucratic behavior of national bureaucracies, then, as regards Europe, both the Western European industrial democracies and the so-called Eastern European Socialist (or People's) democracies may well approve the decline. But when the governments of the newer member-states of the United Nations—and the Third World generally as represented by the Group of 77—are taken into account, then a sense of alarm can be detected. They are keenly aware that their national bureaucracies—most often the legacies of colonial rule—are either so fragile, or so inexperienced, that simply to leave them to their own administrative/bureaucratic devices would be to assign these states to a condition of permanent inferiority in the international political scheme. Quite naturally, the governments of these states are unwilling to see this happen, and so, from the 1960s onward, with accelerating pressure, the developing states of the Third World have been pressing for the creation of more international bureaucracies that are committed to promoting actively their interests and serving their pressing national needs.

Organizational Ideology

In every IGO, as indeed in every organization, some kind of organizational ideology develops that impinges on the effectiveness of the IGO's task performance. A basic concern of employees in any organization is the latter's continuity and, hopefully, its expansion. If an organization expands its functions, the prospects are good for promotion, greater personal prestige, higher salaries and other rewards, and these of course are major personal objectives of those working for the organization. But the organizational growth of most IGOs is not assured and in fact, as has been pointed out, the member-states may have little interest in an IGO's further growth. Both the Soviet Union and the United States, for example, have opposed the growth of the U.N. bureaucracy.

Since the civil servants of an IGO are also nationals drawn from the member-states, this situation exposes officials to conflicting loyalties and pressures. The result could well be a decline in the quality of task performance that could compound already existing dissatisfaction with the manner in which the normal functions of the IGO are carried out. This can create serious dilemmas for the executive leadership that would like to see maintained a firm commitment of its staff to a strong organizational ideology in order to ensure a high-quality performance of the assigned tasks. On the other hand, trying to accomodate the national policy goals of the member-states may result in a negative reaction of the bureaucracy and poor performance of the IGO's functions and tasks.

In our cases we will explore how much the basic principles of the international civil service have been maintained in such universal IGOs as the United Nations, and also in functional and regional IGOs. We will also look at some of the complaints voiced against international institutions and analyze the image they project to the outside world. How high is their professional competence? What kind of socialization processes take place among officials? How does working for an IGO change an official's attitude toward and support of the organization? What are the relations of international civil servants with the national bureaucracies? How does the organizational structure of international institutions affect the efficiency of the civil service?

The cases selected for discussion and comparative analysis in terms of the criteria developed above are divided into two categories. In the first category we focus on the institutions, and the IGOs to be examined will be five regional IGOs and two universal IGO's all of which differ in structure and purposes. They are: the Organization of American States (OAS), the Latin American Free Trade Association (LAFTA), the Economic Community of West African States (ECOWAS), the Association of Southeast Asian Nations (ASEAN), the General Agreement on Tariffs and Trade (GATT), and the U.N. Conference on Trade and Development (UNCTAD). The second category concentrates on international civil services. Since only the United Nations and the European Communities dispose of substantial numbers of civil servants, they can serve as models for problems and issues characteristic of all international bureaucracies regardless of the IGO's size.

ILLUSTRATIVE CASES

The Organization of American States (OAS)

In order to gain a full appreciation as to how the institutional framework of the OAS is related to its assigned tasks, a few remarks regarding the history and issues of the IGO are needed. At the first International Conference of American States in 1890, the International Union of American States was formed that became primarily a series of international conferences designed to promote commerce and the peaceful settlement of disputes. It was assisted by a Commercial Bureau whose original purpose was to ensure the prompt collection and distribution of commercial information. In 1910, the name of this organization was changed to the Union of American Republics and the Bureau was given the name of Pan-American Union.[23]

During the 1930s a collective security system gradually developed among the American states that was aided by the United States adopting in 1933 President Franklin D. Roosevelt's Good Neighbor policy and by the acceptance of the principle of consultation in 1936 between these states. In 1947 the Rio Treaty, properly termed the Inter-American Treaty of Reciprocal Assistance, gave definite form to a regional security system based on the principle that an attack against any one of the inter-American states constituted aggression against all. This principle was incorporated the following year, in 1948, into the Pact of Bogota that established the Organization of American States (OAS). Despite the broad name of this IGO, it should be noted that up to this writing Canada has not yet joined, although the former English-speaking colonies of the Caribbean have. Canada's reasons for not joining were the financial cost and hopes for a forthcoming charter change.

The aims of the OAS can be broken down into three categories. First, common action is to be taken for the peace and security of the continent and disputes among member-states are to be settled by pacific means (Article 4). Second, common political, juridical, and economic problems are to be solved through the facilities of the OAS, and third, cooperative action is to be taken to promote economic, social, and cultural development. These aims make the OAS a very comprehensive IGO.

To assure proper task performance, the institutional framework of the OAS is quite extensive. The supreme organ, in which each member-state has one vote, is the OAS General Assembly. Prior to 1970 this plenary organ was called the OAS Inter-American Conference. While the Conference normally met only once every five years, the Assembly convenes annually. It decides general action and policy, determines the structure and functions of the OAS' organs, and has the authority to consider any matter relating to friendly relations among the member-states (Article 33). Obviously, its terms of reference are very wide.

Another plenary body of the OAS is the permanent OAS Council, which meets very frequently and has executive functions. It operates at the ambassadorial level (through permanent representatives) and is the continuation of the former Governing Board. The Council's main tasks are to supervise the Pan-American Union that served as the international secretariat of the OAS, to coordinate the activities of specialized conferences and organizations, to promote collaboration with the United Nations and other

IGOs, and to adopt the budget. In addition, it formulates the statutes of its subsidiary organs that are themselves plenary bodies: the Inter-American Economic and Social Council, the Inter-American Juridical Committee, and the Inter-American Council for Education, Science, and Culture. Finally, the OAS Council has the authority to create its own committees; examples are the OAS General Committee, the OAS Committee on Finances, and the OAS Permanent Committee on Inter-American Conferences.

In order to carry out the OAS peace-keeping function, the OAS Meeting of Consultation of Ministers of Foreign Affairs plays a prominent role as a consulting organ. Its task is to consider problems of an urgent nature (Article 39) and to serve as the organ of consultation under the Rio Treaty. This body is also a plenary unit on which all member-states are represented. It can be convened by a majority of the OAS Council at the request of any member government.

However, a meeting is obligatory, and must be convened without delay in the event of an armed attack against a member-state or against the region as defined in the Rio Treaty; that is, the Western Hemisphere. If the Meeting of Consultation of Ministers of Foreign Affairs is not obligatory, the Council may constitute itself as the provisional organ of consultation. This gives the Council considerable political power, and in practice it has often been able to settle disputes without summoning a meeting of foreign ministers.[24] The instruments used by the Council are similar to those of the U.N. Security Council, including the appointment of investigating committees and receiving formal findings as to the responsibility of the parties involved.

The Pan-American Union was formerly the central and permanent bureaucratic organ of the OAS. This function is now carried out by the General Secretariat that has a budget of more than $75 million. It is located in Washington, D.C. and is headed by a secretary-general who is elected by the Council and who may participate in the work of any of the OAS organs. But the secretary-general does not have the right to vote. The Secretariat consists of 1,200 international civil servants who, in order to safeguard their independence, are under obligation not to seek or to receive outside instructions from the member-states that, in turn, are enjoined not to tempt them. Many of the civil servants are highly-skilled specialists in the various fields of OAS endeavor.

Aiding in the task performance of the OAS are the aforementioned OAS Inter-American Economic and Social Council and the OAS Inter-American Council for Education, Science, and Culture, which supervise extensive programs, draft treaties, and initiate conferences under OAS Assembly guidance. Specialized organizations working with the OAS deal with problems of agriculture, child welfare, health, women's affairs, and Indian issues.

To help with development problems, the OAS urged the establishment of the Inter-American Development Bank (IDB) that began operating in 1960.

Cumulative loans of the IDB now exceed $10 billion. It is interesting to note that 12 European states, Israel, and Japan have been admitted to membership and that the IDB has been successful in securing financing in private capital markets. [25]

Another collateral organization supporting OAS aims is the Inter-American Commission on Human Rights (IACHR). It was established in 1959 to promote the observance of standards for human rights by OAS members. It is composed of seven individuals nominated by member governments and selected by the OAS Permanent Council. Following the example of safeguarding human rights in Europe—the European Convention for the Protection of Human Rights and Fundamental Freedoms—a court has been set up in Costa Rica to apply and interpret the American Convention on Human Rights of 1960. [26]

If we add the IDB and IACHR as well as the OAS Specialized Conferences, which according to Article 93 can be convened by the OAS Assembly and have indeed been organized on such topics as copyrights, cartography, highways and others, to the Meeting of Consultation, and the Permanent Council, it is obvious that the formal and complementary institutional frameworks of the OAS, both permanent and temporary, are very extensive. [27] But how did they perform their tasks and what were the instrumentalities used?

In terms of the defense against states threatening from outside the hemisphere, Cuban indirect aggression in the form of subversion and military training as well as logistical support of guerrilla forces in more recent years had to be countered. This was done by the adoption of a number of resolutions during the 1950s urging safeguards against subversion, mostly in response to U.S. initiatives. Then, in 1962, Cuba was suspended from participation in the OAS and communism as such was declared incompatible with the principles of the OAS. Following the removal of certain Soviet weapons in the Cuban missile crisis, the OAS enacted anti-Cuban collective economic and diplomatic measures. In 1979, the Sandinista regime of Nicaragua, suspected of collaboration with Cuba, was censured after Nicaraguan planes had violated Costa Rican air space. However, OAS members could not agree regarding the role the OAS should play in the civil war there, nor was there any agreement about such a role in the struggle between government forces and left-wing guerrillas in El Salvador.

With respect to challenges to the OAS peace-keeping task posed by inter-American disputes, the institutions, especially the Council and the Meeting of Foreign Ministers, were successful in most cases. They include conflicts between Costa Rica and Nicaragua (1948–49, 1955–56, 1959), Honduras and Nicaragua (1957), Venezuela and the Dominican Republic (1960–61), Venezuela and Cuba (1963–64, 1967), the Dominican Republic and Haiti (1950, 1963–65), Panama and the United States (1964), and El Salvador and

Honduras (1969–70). The OAS also served as an instrument of support for the United States during the overthrow of Guatemala's president in 1954 and the intervention in the Dominican Republic in 1965. However, in the latter case, which aroused much controversy in Latin America and the United States, it was only with difficulty that the necessary two-thirds vote for an OAS force (mostly 1,200 Brazilian soliders) could be mustered in the Meeting of Foreign Ministers to replace the U.S. military contingents that had been sent earlier to Santo Domingo.[28]

In the field of economic and social development, the OAS, acting on an initiative by U.S. President John Kennedy, was involved in the formulation of a major policy complex, the Alliance for Progress. The terms of this program were outlined in the Charter of Punta del Este in 1961 and aimed at economic and administrative reforms throughout Latin America that would result in increases in per capita income, more equitable distribution of income, expanded investment from outside sources, more rapid industrialization, increased agricultural productivity and land reform, and the improvement of educational and medical facilities. The funds needed over a ten-year period for this program were estimated at $100 billion, with 80 percent to be generated internally in Latin America and 20 percent to come mainly from public and private sources in the United States.

Implementation of the Alliance fell far short of expectations. While a few states did enjoy substantial income growth, in most cases this growth fell far below the 2.5 percent targeted increase, and the land-reform goals were largely unfulfilled. The basic reasons for the implementation failure remain in dispute. Wood states:

> The fundamental decisions on the allocation and administration of grants and loans were made by the financial institutions including AID in the United States, and there was no Latin American body comparable to the Organization for European Economic Cooperation (OEEC) that received moneys and disbursed them in its discretion during the period of the Marshall Plan. That plan's success was not matched by the Alliance for Progress, and debate continues as to assessment of the latter's achievements. It is, however, intriguing to speculate whether, if allocation decisions had been surrendered to a Latin American OEEC, perhaps within the OAS, Latin American integration, and the Organization itself might have been strengthened.[29]

Although the Alliance for Progress scheme did not have the anticipated results, other, less politically sensitive OAS activities have helped economic, social, and scientific developments in Latin America. They include the provision of advisory services and training programs through national technical cooperation undertakings and technical studies and reviews of progress toward specific development goals.[30] The OAS also entered the field of technology transfer through the Regional Scientific and Technological Development Program (PRDCYT) that has been moderately successful through furnishing services, skills, information, and a network of contacts.[31] The IDB loans have been mentioned earlier for the pursuit of major broad development goals.

To complement OAS efforts with respect to raising the level of economic development, most Latin American OAS member-states participated in the creation in 1975 of the Latin American Economic System (SELA). The concept of SELA was initially advanced by President Luis Echeverria of Mexico and backed by President Carlos Andres Perez of Venezuela. SELA is a regional IGO in its own right, composed of a plenary Latin American Council, a number of so-called action committees, and a Secretariat. Its objectives are: to promote Latin American multinational enterprises, to foster the protection of basic commodities while, at the same time, to seek to ensure markets for regional exports, and scientific and technological cooperation. SELA is the successor to the Latin American Economic Coordination Committee, set up in 1964, that had as its mission to coordinate Latin American foreign economic policies, especially toward the more industrially advanced states.

Although many observers felt that SELA could make a significant contribution to regional integration in Latin America, those hopes so far have not been fulfilled. However, SELA has produced an agreement to create a regional monitoring system, and an accord was signed with the U.N. Industrial Development Organization (UNIDO) and the U.N. Development Program (UNDP) for industrial development projects in the energy and capital goods fields.

Indeed, to move forward on development, Latin American states have increasingly turned to another forum, the U.N. Conference on Trade and Development (UNCTAD), where some of the nationals of Latin American governments, especially Peru and Mexico, have assumed positions of leadership.

It is difficult to evaluate the management efficiency of the OAS unless the complete record of the IGO could be examined in detail. The civil service seems to be experienced and dedicated and the length of the tenure of the secretary-general—ten years—is a positive factor. With the exception of lack of success in one major development program, the Alliance for Progress, the record of the OAS in attaining desired outcomes in less ambitious fields is relatively good, although the full expectations of the parties involved may not always be fulfilled. As Yale Ferguson aptly remarked: "Rivalries among the major Latin American powers, differing ideologies, and smoldering territorial disputes will continue to undermine the processes of institution building at the inter-American, regional, and subnational levels."[32] There are clear political constraints and the foreign-policy behavior of the United States, including Latin American perceptions of this behavior, is an important factor. This point will be explored further in Chapter 5 with respect to Western Europe.

What are, nevertheless the reasons for regional institutional proliferation and for the creation of subsidiary and complementary bodies such as the various committees, commissions, and conferences? It is our view that the strong desire to satisfy perceived needs in various sectors of development is the major incentive for this proliferation. Hence, David Mitrany's maxim that form or structure follows function may well be the best explanation for this proliferation and expansion rather than simply organizational desire for growth. It is evident that the OAS is primarily a low-politics organization with far-reaching specific tasks and its institutional framework must therefore be extensive to assure task performance.

The Latin American Free Trade Association (LAFTA)

Inspired by studies of the U.N. Economic Commission for Latin America (ECLA) and emulating the initial successes of the three European Communities that were established in 1952 and 1958, the Latin American Free Trade Association became operational in 1961. The constituent document, the Treaty of Montevideo, was signed in February 1960 by Argentina, Brazil, Chile, Mexico, Paraguay, Peru, and Uruguay. Colombia and Ecuador joined in 1961 and Venezuela is now also a member.

The hopes were high that LAFTA would become a viable experiment in regional economic integration. However, the dismantling of tariff barriers, a very complicated and cumbersome process under the constituent treaty, allowed nationalist and protective tendencies of the member governments to block real progress in creating a true free-trading area. Moreover, the same tendencies made it very difficult to implement an ingenious scheme for region-wide integrated industrialization through so-called complementary agreements (Articles 14–17). The agreements were designed to establish a program of sectional integration through the liberalization of trade in the complementary products of a particular industrial sector.[33] The result has been that in spite of a promising start in the early 1960s, LAFTA has made little progress toward integration.

What, if any, has been the role of the institutions in this unfavorable development? The institutional framework of LAFTA is small, consisting mainly of the Conference of Contracting Parties, and the Permanent Executive Committee.

The Conference, a plenary body, normally meets once a year. It is responsible for engaging in periodic tariff-cutting negotiations as required by the treaty, but very little has been accomplished since the middle 1960s. It also elects the secretary of the Permanent Executive Committee for a three-year term and approves its budget. The Executive Committee, also a plenary organ, runs LAFTA's operations and supervises the implementation of the provisions of the Montevideo Treaty. It also convenes the conferences, prepares work programs and budget estimates, and initiates studies of various kinds. It represents LAFTA in dealing with third states and other IGOs. A Secretariat provides administrative support to the Committee, and the executive secretary participates in Committee deliberations but does not have a vote. The bureaucracy of LAFTA consists of 200 international civil servants, most of whom are dedicated technical experts who provide the staff for the various advisory and consultative committees. The 1976 budget was slightly above $2 million.[34] The headquarters is in Montevideo, Uruguay, but LAFTA's very modest administration building cannot compare with the magnificent splendor and grandeur of the EC headquarters in Brussels.

As already intimated, LAFTA's level of task performance has been low. The original plan was to achieve a complete free-trade area by 1973, but by 1967 it was clear that this goal was unachievable. It was then decided to aim for a common market by 1980, which would also incorporate Central America. This deadline passed without a successful outcome and the prospects are indeed bleak that an all Latin American common market will every be realized. In 1978, intrafree trade-zone exports of member-states reached only 13 percent of total exports. Only 21 complementary agreements to promote industrial integration had been signed by 1976 and they were concluded by subsidiaries of American multinational corporations located in different Latin American states and most of the agreements involved the "Big Three" (Argentina, Brazil, and Mexico).[35]

Clearly, the management efficiency of the LAFTA Executive Committee and LAFTA Secretariat is low and lacks the dynamic nature of the EC institutions. This is really not surprising because the Committee has not been given the same power of decision and action that had been conferred on the EC Council of Ministers. Nor were the central institutions of LAFTA in a position to acquire power above those conferred by the Treaty.[36]

The real reasons for the poor task performance of the LAFTA lie elsewhere. One reason is the strong nationalistic and protective character of most Latin American governments. The second reason is succinctly spelled out by Yale Ferguson:

> A sore issue over the years has been one that has usually plagued integration experiments, the matter of an unequal sharing of benefits. Most benefits have plainly accrued to the three leading exporters of manufactured goods—Argentina, Brazil, and Mexico—and primarily to foreign multinationals operating in these and other countries.[37]

In spite of LAFTA's inability to become a viable, economically integrated regional IGO, representatives of the member-states met in Acapulco in June 1980 to draft a treaty for a new regional IGO, called the Latin American Integration Association (LAIA). The treaty, signed in August of that year by the foreign ministers, aims at the establishment, in a gradual and progressive manner, of a Latin American common market. To avoid the mistakes of LAFTA, it emphasizes the differential treatment of member-states, depending on their level of economic development.[38] Existing tariff concessions, largely negotiated under the auspices of LAFTA, are to be renegotiated and in some instances suspended. New tariff negotiations are expected to include both reciprocal and preferential accords, but no deadlines have been set.

The structure of this new IGO consists of an annually-convened Conference of Contracting Parties (composed of the same members of LAFTA), a Council of Foreign Ministers (LAIA's principal political organ), and a Secretariat. Whether this new venture is nothing more than old wine poured into a new bottle, remains to be seen; we are quite skeptical.

The Economic Community of West African States (ECOWAS)

In spite of the lack of success recorded by LAFTA, and similar disappointing experiences with other regional Third World IGOs seeking to enhance Latin American or African economic development—the Central American Common Market and the East African Community are only two of many examples—the United Nations Economic Commissions for Latin America and for Africa (ECLA and ECA), as well as UNCTAD, have continued to encourage regional and subregional economic cooperative experiments. More recent attempts have tried to avoid the pitfalls of naiveté and overambition as exemplified by the CACM and LAFTA, and apply the lessons learned from previous failures. In Africa, the Economic Community of West African States (ECOWAS) is the latest manifestation of these attempts. It was established in 1975 by the Treaty of Lagos and, for the first time, brought together into one organization the former West African French, British, and Portuguese colonies. Its members consist of the following states: Benin, Cape Verde Islands, Gambia, Ghana, Guinea-Bissau, Ivory Coast, Liberia, Mali, Mauritania, Niger, Nigeria, Senegal, Sierra Leone, Togo, and Upper Volta. (The Gambia and Senegal are now joined as Senegambia).

The aims of ECOWAS are not only the establishment of a customs union over a 15-year period, but also the creation of a common commercial policy and the harmonization of the economic and industrial policies of the member-states. The ultimate goal is the elimination of the disparities in levels of development of these states. Nobody can deny that these goals are not very ambitious, especially considering a pronouncement by ECA stating that the West African region "is the most varied in Africa as to the size of the countries, degree of economic development, language, and economic internal and external links."[39]

The institutional framework for goal achievement is extensive. The primary plenary organ, which sets basic policy, is the Supreme Authority of Heads of State with a rotating chairmanship. The executive organ is a Council of Ministers consisting of two representatives from each member-state. The Council, headquartered in Lagos, Nigeria, is supported by an executive Secretariat whose head is appointed for a four-year period. Four specialized Commissions deal with trade, customs, immigration, and monetary matters. To settle disputes arising under the treaty, a Community Tribunal was established. Finally, an important organ is a Fund for Cooperation, Compensation and Development (FCCD) that is supported by contributions from the member-states and the revenues of Community enterprises. Located in Lome, Togo, one of the fund's tasks is to compensate member-states that suffer losses from the establishment of Community enterprises in a particular member-state and from the liberalization of trade.

It is too early to fully evaluate the quality of task performance of the ECOWAS institutions. At their fifth summit conference in May 1980, the Heads of State agreed to implement the elimination of tariff barriers and other restrictions. May 28, 1981 was set as the deadline for lifting customs duties and other barriers on local raw materials, while an eight-year timetable was drawn up for similar action on industrial products. It was also agreed that the removal of nontariff barriers (NTBs) should have a high priority, with the aim being their total dismantlement by 1985. At the same meeting, it was also stated that planning would continue for a common defense organization to safeguard Community institutions, an activity that appears to be most unusual for a regional economic IGO. Finally, it was decided to set up a special fund for telecommunications.[40]

Although the organizational framework appears to be adequate to carry out ECOWAS' assigned tasks, a number of factors cast doubt that the ECOWAS executive and administrative leaders will be able to manage successfully the economic and political cooperation necessary to attain the ECOWAS goals or to resolve emerging conflicts based on the national cost/benefit calculations of the member-states. While the technocrats in the international bureaucracy have played important roles in the evolution of ECOWAS, they have not been able to emerge as main decision makers, due to the fact that national politicians have retained their place at center stage and, therefore, have been reluctant to assign important roles to the ECOWAS civil service.[41] Moreover, because of the pervasive poverty of the region, matters that would be relatively uncontroversial in the context of the EC can become politically very sensitive in West Africa and therefore require for their solution the involvement of top political leaders of the member-states.

These conditions stem in part from the greater inequality in the economic size and power of the member-states. Table 3.2 illustrates this inequality and shows the predominance of Nigeria. This generates fear in some member-states of being controlled by an all-powerful neighbor, although so far the Nigerians seem to have acted most responsibly and have not engaged in any pressure tactics.[42] Indeed, Nigeria initially strongly supported the spirit of ECOWAS. This spirit was compromised in 1983 when Nigeria expelled on very short notice two million non-Nigerian West Africans working in Nigeria, thus violating the principle of freedom of movement among ECOWAS states.

For most of the governments of the member-states, the highest priority remains nation building and the consolidation of political authority, which often requires quick national solutions to such economic problems as excessive unemployment. Many of the ECOWAS governments cannot afford to see neighboring states flourish as the result of an economic integration scheme, while their own populations appear to have become disadvantaged by the same scheme.

Other problems compound the political sensitivities produced by perceptions of inferiority vis-à-vis a possibly dominating partner. Most ECOWAS states export primary products of either the agricultural or mineral

TABLE 3.2: GNP of ECOWAS Member-States

	GNP at Market Prices, 1974 (U.S. $ Millions)	Percent of Total
Benin	370	1.00
Cape Verde	140	.40
Gambia, The	90	.26
Ghana	4130	11.98
Guinea	630	1.82
Guinea-Bissau	210	.60
Ivory Coast	2930	8.50
Liberia	580	1.68
Mali	450	1.30
Mauritania	380	1.10
Niger	540	1.56
Nigeria	20810	60.38
Senegal	1590	4.61
Sierra Leone	540	1.56
Togo	550	1.59
Upper Volta	520	1.50
Total ECOWAS	34460	100.00

Source: GNP statistics from World Bank Atlas (Washington, D.C.: World Bank, 1976). Percentages computed.

variety. Their economies are therefore competitive rather than complementary which means that even when the customs union is implemented the expansion of trade will be modest. Moreover, much of the trade of the ECOWAS states is oriented toward extraregional partners. For example, 63 percent of Benin's imports came from the EC, while only 6.2 percent originated in other ECOWAS countries.[43] But even if trade could expand, it may be hampered by something characteristic of many Third World states, namely, a lack of intraregional transportation facilities.

Finally, a very serious problem for most ECOWAS member-states is their strong dependence on import duties as a form of revenue. For example, in 1971 Benin relied on import duties for 55 percent of its revenues, and the figure in 1973 for Upper Volta was 45 percent.[44] States with such heavy reliance on duties for their national revenue are naturally reluctant to give up this important source, although the ECOWAS Treaty provides for a mechanism to compensate member-states, at least partly, for such a loss, and of course, the collection of duties from imports originating in third states is not affected.

The question arises as to whether, in the face of these difficulties, ECOWAS' institutional framework should not be expanded to overcome the problems enumerated, and to achieve the necessary changes in the economic systems of the member-states in order to assure viable progress toward the objectives of ECOWAS. While some benefits may indeed flow from expanded institutions and from a larger bureaucracy, effective systemic change can only be produced if the West African economies could be wrested from their colonial moorings. Only then could task performance in line with the ECOWAS Treaty become truly effective, and the various instruments, such as the FCCD compensation payments arrangement used to full advantage. This would constitute a material boost for Third World enthusiasm for using regional IGOs to promote their economic development, and to achieve South-South solidarity. Moreover, if the success of ECOWAS could be achieved, it would be a real breakthrough considering the disappointing performance of regional economic IGOs in the Third World that occurred during the late 1960s and 1970s.

The Association of Southeast Asian Nations (ASEAN)

The main task of the LAFTA and ECOWAS institutions was or is to move forward regional economic integration, in the form either of a free-trade area or of a customs union. While so far, LAFTA clearly has failed to bring about the desired outcome, ECOWAS, having been created more recently, is still seeking to achieve a customs union or perhaps a common market. In contrast, ASEAN has developed into a regional IGO on the basis of political rather than economic motivations, and so initially it did not aim at regional economic

integration. Hence, ASEAN did not start out with a well-developed institutional framework; whatever modest institutions it has now evolved gradually as needed by the functions assigned to it.

ASEAN, when founded in 1967, had as its primary goal to assure
regional peace and stability. Its member-states—Thailand, Malaysia, Indonesia, the Philippines, and Singapore—called for "collective political defense"
to protect individual as well as group interests.[45] In dealing with third states,
they aimed at taking common positions in order to strengthen their bargaining
power. In the economic sphere, their objectives were to accelerate economic
growth, social progress, and cultural development through "close and beneficial cooperation," but no plans existed at the time of ASEAN formation
to set up a free-trade zone or customs union.[46] Nor was there any intention
by the member-states to confer national governmental powers on a central
body and indeed ASEAN operated without a secretariat until 1976.

The challenge of Vietnam put pressure on the ASEAN member-states
to function as a cohesive group on a continuing basis. Economic pressures
from Japan reinforced the necessity for cohesion. As a consequence, a summit
meeting of ASEAN member governments was held in February 1976 that
resulted in a Treaty of Amity and Cooperation in Southeast Asia, and in
some new institutions. A Secretariat was set up in Jakarta, Indonesia, and
a secretary-general was appointed. This post rotates every two years among
nationals of the member-states.

Prior to 1976, regular annual meetings were only attended by the foreign
ministers of the member-states. Now an ASEAN Economic Ministers Meeting has also become institutionalized as a formal structure for handling economic matters. Finally, a legal mechanism for the peaceful settlement of
disputes among ASEAN members was created by the Treaty of Amity and
Cooperation. A High Council is now available that is an ad hoc body of
mediators who, however, do not possess any enforcement powers. But ASEAN
member-states are legally bound to seek the help of the High Council before
turning to outside states in case of a dispute.[47]

Within the Annual Meeting of Foreign Ministers, there is a Standing
Committee that meets regularly between ministerial sessions and carries out
executive functions. The Standing Committee, which works closely with the
Secretariat, has a large number of permanent and ad hoc committees dealing
with various functional matters. A similar, though smaller, structure of committees also exists vis-à-vis the economic ministers. National ASEAN Secretariats have been formed that are subordinate to the international Secretariat.
This is a rather unusual institutional feature, perhaps either serving as a
channel to the national government for the ASEAN international Secretariat,
or as an oversight device by the latter to control the central organ.

At this writing, it is still too early to assess the task performance of the
ASEAN institutions, which are clearly quite limited in scope and extent.

However, the 1976 summit meeting also adopted the so-called ASEAN Concord that is a blueprint for economic cooperation. The ASEAN Concord includes preferential trade arrangements in basic commodities, joint investment in industrial projects, and trade promotion measures. There is also hope that by the turn of the century, a free-trade area will be a reality. These goals and appropriate implementing measures present major challenges to the ASEAN institutions, all the more since the economies of the five member-states are structurally more competitive than complementary. Nevertheless, the ASEAN Secretariat and the other institutions are functioning and the Secretariat has begun to make a positive impact on the task of economic cooperation leading gradually to economic integration.

The General Agreement on Tariffs and Trade (GATT)

We now proceed to an examination of an IGO that in theory is universal, although not all nation-states are members. From an initial membership in 1947 of 23, mostly the industrial democracies, GATT has grown to well over 100 members, including five East European states and about 75 developing states.[48] The Soviet Union, in 1983, applied for observer status, which reflects a sharp change in attitude toward GATT.

Occasionally the question has been raised as to whether GATT can be considered an IGO, because it consists mainly of a multilateral agreement embodying reciprocal rights and obligations designed to achieve certain objectives, followed up and sometimes amended by subsequent multilateral and bilateral agreements. Nonetheless, basic IGO principles and criteria seem to be useful for an evaluation of GATT's institutional framework and task performance. Initially, this framework consisted of a Secretariat headed by a director-general and a meeting of the Contracting Parties to the agreement. Usually, these meetings, lasting from two to three weeks take place at least once each year.

GATT's supervisory functions over tariffs, nontariff barriers (NTBs), and the conduct of trade made it necessary as early as 1951 to set up an Intersessional Committee to deal with exceptional restrictive measures on international trade. The Committee was authorized to conduct voting between the sessions of the Contracting Parties by mail or telegram and this made it possible for the parties to take joint action when they were not in session.[49]

In order to make GATT's work continuous and more effective, a Council of Representatives was established in 1960 that replaced the Intersessional Committee and was endowed with more extensive powers. The Council is an organ of limited composition; it consists of 49 representatives from those member governments willing to assume special responsibilities such as carrying out advisory work and recommending draft resolutions for mail or telegraphic approval by all the Contracting Parties.

Other bodies engaged in the performance of important tasks are the committee on trade in industrial products, the committee on trade and development, and the committee on agriculture. These committees, in turn, have various subsidiary working parties and groups to study GATT-related problems caused by changes in tariffs and NTBs or by contraventions of the rules established for the conduct of international trade and to offer suggestions for solutions.

The GATT Secretariat is relatively small (about 200 civil servants) and consists of about 50 percent professionals and 50 percent general service staff members.[50] The staff appears to be very capable and dedicated, inasmuch as it has been able to cope successfully with the increasing complexities of international trade, 80 percent of which moves under the auspices of GATT. Thus, GATT's efficiency in its task performance must be evaluated as being high, especially when we consider that all implementation of changes in the trade rules is ultimately in the hands of the member governments.

Since its inception in 1947, seven major trade negotiations under GATT auspices have taken place that have successfully reduced tariffs, and in some cases have eliminated duties completely. Efforts to dismantle so-called nontariff barriers (NTBs), such as quantitative restrictions of imports, preferences by governments for the purchase of products, and many other ingenious devices of a protectionist nature, have been much less successful. But the elimination of NTBs remains a high-priority GATT target. In response to the demands of the developing states for more appropriate treatment of their exports, the GATT members have added a number of new clauses to the GATT General Agreement (Part IV), to promote the participation of developing states in international trade, and to promote the sustained growth of their export earnings. For this purpose, GATT also established, in cooperation with UNCTAD, an International Trade Center in Geneva.

While thus, over the years, some of the barriers to trade have been lowered or eliminated by GATT and its institutions, other barriers are likely to tax severely GATT's ability to remain on top of the continual fluctuations in the global pattern of trade and economic competition. The trade tensions that have arisen in the early 1980s among Japan, the United States, and the EC states is a major case in point.

The U.N. Conference on Trade and Development (UNCTAD)

Another IGO also concerned, at least partially, with international trade, though primarily from the perspective of the developing countries, is the U.N. Conference on Trade and Development (UNCTAD), established as a permanent organ of the U.N. General Assembly by resolution 1995 on

December 30, 1964. Since that time UNCTAD has developed an impressive institutional framework, whose budget exceeded $33 million in 1978–79.[51] Joseph Nye has called UNCTAD the "poor nations' pressure group."[52]

The top layer of the institutional framework is the Triennial Conference, a plenary body open to all U.N. member and nonmember-states (for example, the Holy See and Switzerland are UNCTAD members). The Conferences formulate basic policies and guidelines in the fields of primary commodities, trade in manufactured and semimanufactured goods, development financing, transfer of technology to developing states, aid to the least developed and geographically disadvantaged states, economic cooperation among developing states regionally and otherwise, and problems of shipping and insurance. The last Conference, the fifth since the initial meeting in Geneva in 1964, was held in 1982.

The Conferences are huge affairs, lasting up to eight weeks and bringing together over 1,000 delegates from the member-states. In addition to a full representation of developing Third World states (Group A: Afro-Asian states and Yugoslavia as well as Group C: Latin America), developed states with market economies (Group B) and communist-bloc states (Group D) are also in attendance and participate in the deliberations.

A number of organs of limited composition operate below the Conference. The Trade and Development Board (TAB) is the permanent organ of the Conference; it meets at least once annually and more often if necessary. Composed of 55 member-states elected by the Conference, the TAB assures continuity of activities between the Conferences. It initiates studies and reports, maintains links with intergovernmental bodies whose work is relevant to UNCTAD, and keeps close liaison with the five regional economic commissions of the United Nations and with other relevant regional organizations.

Subsidiary to the Board are several committees and other subordinate working groups, all of limited composition. The most important committees are the committee on commodities (120 members), the committee on manufactures (89 members), the committee on invisibles and financing related to trade (94 members), and the committee on shipping (90 members). All members are elected by the Board, to which the committees report. Permanent committees exist also on the transfer of technology, tariff preferences, and economic cooperation among developing states.

UNCTAD is serviced by a full-time Secretariat functioning within the U.N. Secretariat and headed by the secretary-general of the Conference, who in turn is appointed by the secretary-general of the United Nations and confirmed by the U.N. General Assembly. The location of the UNCTAD Secretariat is Geneva, which gives this organization a considerable degree of independence. During the early 1970s the staff of UNCTAD consisted of about 500 civil servants, of which about 40 percent were professionals.[53]

Aiding in UNCTAD's task performance is the International Trade Center that is operated and managed in cooperation with GATT. This center provides various services, especially for the developing states.

The basic purposes of UNCTAD are the promotion of international trade in order to accelerate the economic growth of the developing states; in this respect, it has served as an advocacy IGO for the developing states' strong desire, through the NIEO proposals, to alter the pattern of international economic relations more in their favor. UNCTAD also formulates policies with respect to trade and development in general, to negotiate multilateral legal instruments—such as international commodity agreements (ICAs)— in the field of trade, and to harmonize the development policies of governments and regional groupings.

The task performance efficiency of UNCTAD has generally been high as far as lobbying for the Third World is concerned; but in terms of accomplishing its purposes, UNCTAD's record has been uneven. The most effective means have been the preparation of studies and the collection of information, the formulation of programs, the organization of conferences to promote UNCTAD's goals, the formation of working groups to deliberate on various and often controversial issues and then to articulate proposals, and the engineering of the adoption of supporting resolutions by ECOSOC and the U.N. General Assembly.[54] Coalitions have been formed with sympathetic national and international political organizations, such as with the states of the Non-Aligned Movement. The Movement itself has organized highly-publicized meetings in support of Third World causes endorsed by UNCTAD, and these have attracted Soviet-bloc endorsement.[55] UNCTAD also has focused attention on the U.N. Second and Third Development Decades. Part of the credit for these accomplishments must go to UNCTAD's articulate Secretaries-General, Raul Prebisch and then Gamani Corea, as well as the committed and enthusiastic international civil service.

Nonetheless, a full implementation of UNCTAD's goals favoring the developing states seems to be years, if not decades, away although some progress has been made in the preferences granted by developed states to the imports of manufactured and semimanufactured goods from the Third World, to the creation of funds countering commodity price fluctuations (for example, STABEX, which was created by the Lomé convention to give greater access of developing states to the EC), and special financial aid to the poorest of the poor developing states. Meanwhile, the spread between development levels of the latter states and Third World newly industrialized states (NICs) is widening, bringing with it gradual shifts of interests and objectives pursued by the states, which fall into the NIC category. While Third World solidarity—as expressed within the United Nations through the Group of 77—remains fairly high, cracks are likely to appear in the future as the interests of the NICs approach those of the Western industrialized states.

The U.N. Civil Service

The United Nations is the largest employer of an international civil service. Excluding the IBRD, IMF, and the regional banks, but including the specialized agencies it had 44,000 employees in 1979. If we exclude the specialized agencies, the U.N. organization had a total of 22,600 posts, of which only 10,513 were in the U.N. Secretariat under the regular budget and 12,087 posts were financed from extra-budgetary sources.[56] When we ask how much the basic principles of the international civil service have been maintained in the United Nations, we discover that because of many staff members recruited for short-term service, for technical cooperation projects or mission service, and for special language requirements, only 2,700 posts in fact were officially subject to the application of all the principles of truly international civil service, including the principle of geographic representation. Of the 2,700 posts, 40 percent went to the developing states and 60 percent to the developed states, including 49 percent to the Western industrial states.

But, as pointed out in the introduction to this chapter, subtle opposition to the principles of impartiality and complete independence of the U.N. bureaucracy lead to a greater degree of politicization of the civil servants by the insistence of the Third World that more of their nationals be recruited to maintain opportunities for the newer member-states' nationals. Of course, this should not be surprising in an organization that is not only highly political, but has a staff that is both multinational and multicultural.

Another factor contributing to the trend toward politicization is increased organizational concern with economic and social activities within the context of development, which in itself has become a highly sensitive political issue. As a consequence, greater emphasis has been placed on the recruitment of technical staff over the recruitment of generalists, and on the use of short-term staff and outside experts, all of which tends to undermine the concept of a traditional international civil service.

Politicization is also reflected in lobbying efforts by U.N. civil servants seeking to persuade delegations of particular member-states to take certain actions. The chairman of the Fifth Committee, dealing with U.N. administrative and budgetary matters, strongly criticized such activities and stated:

> No member of the Secretariat should be allowed in a conference room, unless officially authorized to be there by virtue of his functions. . . . That matter should be brought to the personal attention of the Secretary-General. It was particularly annoying and unacceptable to see self-styled emissaries of international civil servants preaching what they considered to be right while problems involving the material interests of the staff were being discussed.[57]

Politicization has also been fed by economic pressures caused by poor global economic conditions that have led to staff reductions and freezes in recruitment, and when recruitment does continue, often only fixed-term contracts are given. This has affected civil service morale and has brought about an increasingly strident tone in talks between the representatives of the U.N. civil servants, the staff union or The Federation of International Civil Servants Association (FICSA) and the U.N. assistant secretary-general for personnel services. Complaints have also been voiced by the unions about poor working conditions. To put pressure on the U.N. administration, staff strikes have been called in Geneva and New York, which in fact are becoming more frequent although they are strongly condemned by almost all member governments and by the secretary-general.[58]

It is interesting to note that the U.N. civil service's disenchantment is caused partly by the erosion of the application of the aforementioned principles, and the activism by the staff union is justified in part by their desire to conserve something close to the traditional concept of that civil service. The president of the staff committee, acting for the staff union, has stated what he considers are the conditions required to rescue the international civil service from demoralization:

1. A new dynamic and more progressive leadership based on . . . personal qualities of integrity, courage, and competence; . . .
2. A positive, open personnel policy based on merit which seeks out the best qualified of all countries without regard to political connections and which ensures a rational system of career development free from political interference;
3. A revitalized sense of accountability to the world public which provides the financial support for our work;
4. A unified international service which puts an end to dubious 'class' distinctions and recognizes that members, no matter where or in what capacity they serve are entitled to equal standards of dignity and treatment;
5. A renewed commitment to and respect for staff participation in decisions affecting the conditions of service and management of the various organizations as a means to maintain the active interest and involvement of the staff in the purpose of international service.[59]

This statement in itself may not reflect widespread staff consensus, but it is important in that it is illustrative of the effort by staff members to articulate broad principles as well as specific claims.

Kurt Waldheim, the former secretary-general, is also on record on the subject of the U.N. bureaucracy. He stated:

The concept of international civil service is at the heart of the problem of building an effective system of world order. The international civil service should be the objective executor of the decisions of intergovernmental bodies. It should be the point at which expertise, common sense, objective judgment and moderating influence converge. It should provide the common ground where governments can begin to harmonize their conflicting viewpoints.

I am increasingly concerned at the mounting pressure from all sides to secure jobs, especially at senior levels in the Secretariat. The top level of posts, under-secretaries-general and assistant secretaries-general, are certainly to be regarded to some extent as political appointments in which member states have a legitimate interest. At lower levels, however, the intergovernmental competition for posts is tending to become a severe impediment to the balanced and effective development of the Secretariat. I appeal to all member states to exercise great restraint in this matter in the interests of building an effective, balanced and representative international Secretariat, which will in the long run best serve the interests of all the members. The task of building an efficient and active international civil service will otherwise be seriously hampered. No civil service can hope long to survive if it fails to compensate adequately, through reasonable career prospects, those of its staff who have served it for long periods, conscientiously and with dedication. . . .[60]

Whether all member-states will heed the appeal of the secretary-general, is doubtful. Meanwhile, the International Civil Service Commission, composed of individuals who, acting in their private capacities, are to be competent and experienced in personnel management (no two of whom can be nationals of the same state) is making a serious effort to deal with questions of recruitment, career development, and the career concept. But whether this effort can be translated into useful results in the foreseeable future is far from certain because the Commission has become part of the politics that permeate the issues and principles of a genuine international civil service.[61]

There are, of course, proposals for upgrading the whole complex of the U.N. civil service through the formulation of career development programs that have originated from outside the U.N. institutional framework. One of these proposals, aiming at a program that differentiates between the capabilities and needs of the highly specialized technical organizations such as FAO, UNESCO, IFAA, and WHO, and more diversified organizations (the U.N. Secretariat, ILO, UNDP, and others), has been developed by Norman A. Graham and Robert S. Jordan.[62] But whether their detailed suggestions for recruitment, appointment policy, career management, training, and promotion/mobility opportunities might find acceptance during the turbulent phase through which the U.N. civil service is passing in the early 1980s, is unlikely. It seems that as long as member governments tend to look at recruitment and promotion first from their own national viewpoints rather than from the organization's overall perspective, the bureaucracy (whether management or labor) will tend to push its particular interests first. Furthermore, since there is no unified system of governance of the United Nations as a whole, there would appear to be little prospect of the emergence in the foreseeable future of a unified career concept or system.

The question may be asked whether a socialization process operating among U.N. civil servants might produce attitudes more supportive of U.N. principles and goals, thereby in turn strengthening their commitment to the ideal of an effective international civil service as outlined in Article 101, paragraph 3, of the U.N. Charter.[63] While a number of studies have been undertaken to test the learning process that national participants (mostly delegates in various U.N. bodies and specialized agencies) might be undergoing and to determine what cognitive, affective, and evaluative changes in their attitudes may have occurred,[64] similar research on U.N. civil servants appear to be lacking. The results of these studies have been far from uniform and they suggest multidimensional effects of the experiences on the attitudes of the participants. A positive socialization process and its intensity are likely to depend on the nationality of the participant, which would include the extent that domestic bureaucratic principles interfere with those of the United Nations, his or her general support of the United Nations, commitment to foreign aid and development in general, and his or her view on the principle that sovereignty is transferable.[65] Although some of the U.N. civil servants may be drawn from the national bureaucracies of the member-states and others may be on short-term contracts, it seems to be inappropriate to draw inferences from the results of the above-mentioned studies regarding the socialization process that may be at work on U.N. officials. Because of their career commitment to the United Nations or its specialized and affiliated agencies that, by itself, produces specific interests, beliefs, and goals, these individuals constitute an entirely different category from the more temporary participants in the work of various U.N. bodies and activities. In the absence of sufficient empirical evidence, any proposition or statement about the effects of a possible socialization process involving U.N. civil servants would be mere speculation, although some kind of socialization is likely to take place.[66]

Another factor that might influence not only the morale of U.N. civil servants, but also their commitment and interest in assuring that the principles of Article 101, par. 3, are fully maintained, could be the esteem in which they are held by their national colleagues and working partners and the quality of their relations with national officials. The higher the national officials value the competence and skills of the U.N. bureaucracy, and the more harmonious the interbureaucratic relationships, the greater may be the incentive of the latter to justify fully this evaluation and this, in turn, could engender a stronger desire to meet the requirements of a dedicated international civil service. Again, no relevant attitude surveys on these aspects of the U.N. bureaucracy appear to have been made and therefore, no definite propositions can be advanced.

In the absence, then, of clearly recognizable, uniformly strong motivations on the part of the U.N. bureaucracy to seek an improved career concept—which is also opposed by a growing number of the member-states—

we must look to the member governments as the ultimte source of support for such a concept. This brings up the issue of sufficient funding for the civil service. But since there is little agreement among the governments as to the most equitable way to finance the organization, there can be little prospect that the secretary-general can implement to the satisfaction of everyone the requirement to balance off equitable geographic representation with the highest standards of efficiency, competence, and integrity. For example, some of the developing states claim that their contributions come from the heart of their budgetary resources, whereas the largest contributors pay their contributions out of excess resources and therefore, logically, should pay much more percentagewise. Certainly the largest contributors—and especially the United States Congress—would not be pleased with this reasoning. At the same time, many member governments are often still very critical of efforts at eliminating or terminating what other states might regard as unnecessary or ineffective programs.

There has been in recent years a movement led by the Third World to restructure the United Nations and its affiliated bodies and agencies to respond more fully to their needs.[67] As regards the Secretariat of the United Nations itself, the most important single development was the creation in 1977 of the post of Director-General for Development and International Economic Cooperation. This post has been termed as ranking second only to the secretary-general in importance, and was meant to facilitate the process of making the U.N. system more responsive to the needs and goals of the Third World member-states.[68]

The Secretary-General: "A Man for all Seasons"

The chief international civil servant is, of course, the secretary-general. Even though the major (or principal) United Nations organs responsible for the peaceful settlement of disputes are the U.N. Security Council and the U.N. General Assembly, the secretary-general has often played a key role as a mediator in many disputes between the member-states.

The relationship of the secretary-general to the Security Council is central to multilateral decision making concerning threats to the peace. In more recent times, the office of president of the Security Council has taken on some of the functions entrusted to the secretary-general. Even though Article 98 of the U.N. Charter had provided that the secretary-general should perform such functions as asked of him by the other principal organs, the Security Council has occasionally entrusted the president of the Security Council with such tasks. This does not necessarily mean that the Council lacks confidence in the secretary-general; it could depend as much on the nature of the task at hand and its urgency. There have been instances, for example, where the Council has sent its own observers to report on the conditions of what might become a threat to the peace, rather than to rely only on the sources supplied through the secretary-general. Member-states always have their own national sources as well that the secretary-general has had at times to rely on.

The secretary-general has ample opportunity to function as a mediator, or adviser, and so on. He is expected, in fact, to perform this function, keeping the major political organs—and relevant member-states—informed along the way. His problem is not that there are too few opportunities for this kind of activity, but rather that he is called upon only too often to perform this task under the most unpromising circumstances. As Dr. Kurt Waldheim put it:

> A day seldom passes without approaches to the Secretary-General from one of the Member Governments for assistance in solving problems which have defied solution by other means. Even if the Secretary-General, as often happens, cannot succeed where others have failed, the fact that Governments can, in certain situations of crisis, place their worries before him and discuss them in full confidence can in itself be helpful to Governments.[69]

By 1956, Secretary-General Dag Hammarskjöld had taken the power of the office to its highest point when the General Assembly overwhelmingly approved his plan for a U.N. Emergency Force (UNEF) to resolve the Suez crisis. His handling of the crisis in such a fashion was important because it marked the first use of what Hammarskjöld came to term "preventive diplomacy"—that is, using the United Nations to intervene in order to forestall or preclude intervention by the major world powers, and in particular the two superpowers. Perhaps more important in practical political terms, the secretary-general had delegated to himself discretionary power to organize and administer an international military force. He became a commander-in-chief of his own army—a role which Sir Eric Drummond, the first secretary-general of the League of Nations would never have hoped for, or for that matter, wanted.[70]

But Hammarskjöld's success in promoting, through Suez, the notion that the United Nations must be capable of acting independently of the major world powers came to haunt him when he tried to do this in the Congo crisis. Even if the veto in the Security Council could be neutralized by a majority vote of the General Assembly through the so-called "Uniting for Peace" Resolution, in power terms the victory could be less in the long run than it would appear in the short run.

As to the Congo crisis, which erupted in June 1960, after Belgium precipitously granted independence, according to Hammarskjöld the United Nations Congo Force (ONUC) was to be organized along the same lines as

UNEF. The secretary-general was to have exclusive command of the force, and the troops composing it would not be drawn from either of the superpowers, or from the other major Western powers. Furthermore, almost contradictorily, the force was to remain neutral in internal Congolese political rivalries, but would have free movement throughout the country. This was truly intervention in the old-fashioned sense. At its height, the U.N. force came to number 20,000.

One of the reasons for the strong opposition of the Soviet Union to this peace-keeping operation was that, in its view, there was no clearly-established procedure in United Nations practice to halt such an operation once authorized, except by explicit resolution. The Congo crisis had become, through Uniting for Peace, the province of the General Assembly, and the Soviet Union was apparently unable to put through a resolution to have ONUC withdrawn. In the General Assembly, although an operation can be launched by a two-thirds majority of those member-states present and voting (or can be blocked by one-third plus one), an operation, once underway, can be halted only by an express decision of a two-thirds majority.

One of the criticisms of Hammarskjöld's conduct of the Congo crisis was that he had not integrated the new Afro-Asian states into the institutional structure of the United Nations. While this may or may not be valid, it did pose an irony in that Hammarskjöld viewed himself as enlightened when it came to decolonization and its political, social and economic ramifications. In fact, his concept of preventive diplomacy arose out of his concern that the de jure independence claimed for the new member-states should be de facto as well.

The growth of the responsibilities placed upon both the secretary-general and the Secretariat since Dag Hammarskjöld's death has been remarkable. A virtual doubling of the membership has shifted not only the political balance of the organization, it has altered fundamentally the nature of the political dialogue. Even though to many observers, the NIEO appeared at the outset of the 1970s to have burst with dramatic suddenness onto the international agenda, it was in fact ignited by a slow fuse that had been burning since the Hammarskjöld era.

Hammarskjöld's singular contributions, however, were his thoughtful innovations and efforts to building and keeping peace. He believed that ways of diplomacy can be improved through multilateral institutions and through a flexible use of these institutions. The manner in which he conducted the instrumentality of the United Nations was like a player with a large keyboard that included, among others, semiarbitrating groups, conciliation groups, high-level emissaries, and all the potentialities of multilateral diplomacy. In the solution of immediate conflicts and the preservation of peace through situations that remain precarious, multilateral diplomacy has historically had a watchdog function that he utilized. His contribution to international politics, therefore, has stood the test of time well in that his successors have continued to pursue his precedent of innovating ways of dealing with intractable diplomatic problems.

The European Communities' Civil Service

The civil service of the European Communities—the ECSC, EEC, and EURATOM—suffer from many of the same problems as the U.N. bureaucracy. Since 1958, when the EEC and EURATOM were established, the Eurocracy, as the Communities' civil service is often called, has grown steadily. Indeed, the size of the Commission staff alone rose from 1,108 in 1958 to nearly 8,000 in 1976 (see Table 3.3) and has expanded further since then to over 11,600 (January 1, 1980). But the staff of the Commission is only part of the total Eurocracy; other civil servants serve in the Council of Ministers (over 1,500), the European Parliament (about 1,300), the Court of Justice (about 300), and some smaller institutions such as the Economic and Social Council. The total of this impressive international bureaucracy, therefore, today may well exceed 15,000. But this represents only about 0.005 percent of the 1979 population of the nine member-states. Not surprisingly, this is a much smaller percentage than the bureaucracies of the EC member-states; after all, the Eurocracy deals only with a very limited range of functions and not with all the aspects and levels of administration of the national civil services.

The civil service of the Communities is divided into four basic categories: A, B, C, and D. The officials in category A constitute the administrative elite and they, in turn, are divided into seven groups (A1-A7). The highest positions of leadership are assigned to the A-1 group. They are the directors-general and their deputies. Directors are normally A-2s, and a chef de division usually holds the rank of A-3. Below them are various classes of senior administrators.

While, as we have seen, ideally an international civil service should be recruited from individuals untainted by service in the national administrations of IGO member-states in order to insure complete independence and full commitment to the goals of the organization, the need for immediate administrative competence and political problems have produced a different situation from the start of the three Communities. In order to assure the developmental maximization of the Communities during their fledgling years, they resorted to secondment from the national bureaucracies of their member-states to provide much of the initial staffing in the A category of the Eurocracy. It was felt that seconded national administrators already know their way through the corridors of national power and politics and therefore they could ease very markedly the burden of the neophyte organization. A seconded official, by definition, is expected to return to his national service,

TABLE 3.3: Development in Size of the EC Commission (1958–76)

Year	Absolute figures	Growth Index (1958 = 100)	Annual Growth (percent)
1958	1,108[a]	100	–
1959	1,480	133	+ 33.0
1960	1,686	152	+ 14.0
1961	1,848	167	+ 9.4
1962	2,156	195	+ 16.7
1963	2,346	212	+ 8.8
1964	2,643	239	+ 12.7
1965	2,738	247	+ 3.6
1966	2,738	247	0.0
1967(1)	2,924[b]	264	+ 6.8
(2)	5,149	465	+ 76.1
1968	4,953	447	– 3.8
1969	5,003	451	+ 1.0
1970	5,300	478	+ 6.0
1971	5,575	503	+ 5.1
1972	5,962	538	+ 6.9
1973	6,907	623	+ 15.9
1974	7,375	665	+ 6.7
1975	7,776	701	+ 5.4
1976	7,983	720	+ 2.7

Note: Total of permanent and temporary appointments authorized by the Council of Ministers. These are the end-of-year figures for authorized appointments and include contingent supplementary appointments authorized in the course of the year concerned.

[a] For the year 1958, we took the total number of persons recruited or appointed by the Commission as of February 28, 1959. There is therefore a slight distortion in relation to the end-of-year 1958.

[b] For 1967 (1), these are posts authorized by the Council for the Commission prior to the merger of executives. For 1967 (2), this is the cumulative total of authorized permanent and temporary appointments for the three Commissions or executives at the time of the coming into force of the Merger Treaty.

Source: Christoph Sasse et al., Decision Making in the European Community (New York: Praeger Publishers, 1977), p. 144.

but some have made a career out of the Communities' civil service. While others, after an initial attempt to pursue such a career, have changed their minds and returned to their capitals.[71]

It is difficult to determine exactly how many national officials were tempted by the integration adventure to move to Luxembourg (ECSC) or to Brussels, and it is even more difficult to find out how many have returned to their national services after their allotted time expired. But clearly a large number of Eurocrats came initially from the national civil services. In his pilot study on the EEC, Leon N. Lindberg noted that of the commission bureaucracy in 1961:

> . . . approximately 50 percent . . . has been drawn from the administrative services of the Member States. This figure however, rises to 75 percent for the major administrative posts (Category A), and if we take only the major policy-making posts (Categories A-1 and A-2), 57 of which are authorized in the 1961 budget, we find that all are drawn from the national administrations.[72]

More recent data (1973–74) confirm the pattern that the higher the officials are placed within the A category, the greater the likelihood that they had been employed by their national governments. Of the A-3 officials, 46 percent had prior experience in public service, while only 28.6 percent of the A-4 through 7 civil servants indicated to have had such service.[73]

As with all major international civil services, the European Communities have attempted to reconcile, in their recruitment and selection, the principles of maintaining the highest professional competence with equitable geographic distribution. Up to the accession of Greece in January 1981, each of the four largest member-states (Great Britain, France, West Germany, and Italy) were allocated an 18 percent quota while the remaining 28 percent were given to the five other members, 9 percent to Belgium and The Netherlands, 5 percent each to Denmark and Ireland, and 2 percent to Luxembourg. A slight modification took place with the expansion of the EC membership to ten.

The implications of the quota system are far reaching. In staff changes nationality is likely to become overemphasized with insufficient attention paid to administrative competence and quality. Every member government seeks to retain the balance it has in the different directorates-general—the basic organizational units of the Commission. Promotions are difficult because, for the positions of director-general, his deputy, and division chiefs, the member governments may insist on appointing their preferred choices. Hence, less-qualified persons may be appointed or promoted and as a consequence overall morale may suffer severely. The promotion situation is compounded by the need for bargaining between the superior of an official who is being considered for advancement and the unions representing all EC civil servants. The unions are often reluctant to make competence and merit the decisive criteria for promotion; instead, they prefer promotions to be based on age and seniority.[74] At the same time, it may become very difficult to remove an official even if he is clearly incompetent, because it could unbalance the geographic quota system unless the superior can find a qualified substitute of the same nationality and unless the unions do not oppose the dismissal.

When the Communities were first established in the 1950s, the greatest appeal for many of the job applicants was not high pay, but the opportunity to participate in an exciting experiment, namely to create the United States of Europe. Today, the spirit of Europe as a motivation for service in the Community has receded, if not entirely vanished. Meanwhile, the financial emoluments for the Eurocrats have become extremely attractive and this attractiveness has been further strengthened by various tax advantages that although not as favorable in 1981 as they were in the early 1960s, still are the envy of the national bureaucracies.

Indeed, the salaries of the Eurocrats are very high by any standard. In the middle and junior grades they are paid two to three times as much as they would receive if they were employed by their national governments. For example, an EC chauffeur has a take-home pay equal to the salary of minister in the Belgian government. On higher levels Eurocrats earn roughly twice the salary of comparable civil servants in the EC member-states, often up to and over $100,000. In addition, EC civil servants benefit from special privileges. They can buy subsidized liquor in the Commission's own super-market and they receive discounts on gasoline purchases. They can also send their children to free, special European schools.[75]

The high salaries of the Eurocracy and the various privileges granted them have not set well with the national civil services of the member-states whose salaries, as we have seen, are substantially lower. At the same time, elite survey research has indicated that national civil servants in the member-states do not have the highest esteem of the working habits and qualifications of their colleagues in the Communities.[76] However, these perceptions of the national officials interviewed may have been colored by concerns that the EC institutions might expand their powers at the expense of national pre-rogatives and by understandable envy of the Eurocrats' much higher salaries and other benefits. Indeed, this envy, which exists in all member-states, has induced the Council of Ministers to seek a gradual harmonization between the salaries of Community and member-government bureaucracies.[77]

For the Eurocrats, the Council decision conjured up vistas of net losses in their incomes and the possibility of the nationalization of the Communities' civil service. Hence, a rash of protest strikes by the Eurocracy broke out in the winter and spring of 1981, bringing most EC activities on several occasions to a complete standstill.[78] A compromise between the Council and the Commission, which had opposed the Council's suggestions, settled the dispute.

Our examination of selected aspects of the U.N. and EC bureaucracies suggest a number of similar developments in the structural and political spheres that tend to weaken their prestige, influence, and image. The ideological support for a united Europe has declined and so has much support for the United Nations, at least in the United States and perhaps in some other states as well. This has affected the morale and spirit of their respective bureaucracies.

There was much hope in the 1950s and 1960s that member-state officials who went to work for the Communities would adopt more intensive European values and that through this socialization process these values would spread among the national bureaucracies. While this process seemed to work successfully at the beginning, counter-organizational socialization forces by the national bureaucracies and adverse attitudes of national civil servants toward the possible transfer of power to the EC institutions seem to have carried the day. Although a continually increasing number of these officials (well above 12,000) are called to serve in Commission study and working groups every year, during the second half of the 1970s and early 1980s the EC institutions have been losing political ground vis-à-vis the national governments.

There is little doubt that we are witnessing in Western Europe a trend toward the renationalization of policy and perhaps EC institutional authority, despite some rhetoric to the contrary by some of the leaders of the member governments. The onslaught on EC salaries may be part of this trend, ultimately aiming to abolish the Eurocrats' status as a truly international civil service. The Eurocracy has become vulnerable to this attack and the Commission's personnel management of the top levels in the directorates-general may have been a contributory cause. This, in turn, was prompted by the national governments, that prefer a pliable commission to a strong one and that show little interest in abandoning the principle of national allocation of senior posts. In many ways, this is the root of the problems discussed here. In the long run, it does not bode well for either the Eurocracy or the Communities' institutions unless the political climate in the member-states were to change through a new infusion of European enthusiasm. This is not likely to happen.

SUMMARY AND CONCLUSIONS

It is quite clear from the foregoing discussion that even though the numbers of IGOs—and their consequent bureaucracies—have increased, their prestige and overall effectiveness have been diminishing. It is apparent that the level of task performance has generally been high at the inception of these IGOs—to which the idealism of the initial United Nations and European Communities' civil servants bears testimony. But, as the various bureaucracies gained more responsibilities, and became more formalized administratively, the governments of the member-states began to resist either the growth of the budgets or the distribution of the benefits and this has resulted in increasing acrimony within the governing bodies.

Along with this almost inevitable evolution in the life of bureaucracies of all kinds, can be added the tension that is growing between the so-called rich and poor states, as the latter attempt to induce changes in the international economic system that would favor their interests. UNCTAD has perhaps the most involved bureaucracy, followed by LAFTA and ECOWAS. GATT has been more concerned with the problems of trade among industrial states rather than between industrial and developing states. The attempt to broaden GATT's role in development has met with fierce resistance from the world's major trading partners, who are slipping into postures of competition and of employing restrictive trade practices among themselves.

Regionally, the expectation that a community of interests could be achieved if smaller numbers of more cohesive states were involved, has proven somewhat illusory. Ancient grievances that continually have exacerbated relations among the partners, have crippled LAFTA and has kept ECOWAS at a very low level of economic activity. ASEAN, on the other hand, for reasons of pursuing mutual interest through coordination of foreign policy, has adapted itself from being primarily a political IGO concerned about the security of its members, to an IGO interested increasingly in economic cooperation.

The notion that sustained interaction among international civil servants, preferably committed to the career concept, would lead to a greater institutional socialization that in turn would break down nationalistic sentiments among the member-states, has not been fulfilled. Resistance by the member-states to the career concept in all the IGOs—some for budgetary and program management reasons and some to expand their nationals' career opportunities—has led to unrest among the various civil service unions. Anxiety that their privileges would be eroded has contributed to the generally low morale of all the international civil services, and this has left them vulnerable to political influence peddling by their own or other member governments. Thus, the executive heads have found it more difficult to preserve the institutional autonomy of their IGOs, and to exercise their administrative authority.

The general weakening of the dispute settlement functions of the U.N. secretary-general has not given this office the prestige that is required to slow down or to reduce the trends described above. In fact, in recent years the secretary-general has appeared willing to compromise the integrity of the civil service in order not to antagonize the member governments to the extent that his overall political effectiveness is curtailed even more. Nonetheless, the quality of the executive leadership of the U.N. and all IGOs is an essential feature of the ability of the organization to adapt to the political, economic, and social environments in which they must exist and that is essential if IGOs are to fulfill their very important, indeed vital, functions.

NOTES

1. For a summary discussion of the origins of the office of secretary-general, see Robert S. Jordan, "The Influence of the British Secretariat Tradition on the Formation of the League of Nations," in *International Administration: Its Evolution and Contemporary Applications*, ed., Robert S. Jordan (New York: Oxford University Press, 1971). See also Robert S. Jordan, ed., *Dag Hammarskjöld Reconsidered: The U.N. Secretary-General as a Force in World Politics* (Durham, N.C.: Carolina Academic Press, 1983).

2. D. W. Bowett, *The Law of International Institutions* (New York: Praeger, 1963), p. 108.

3. For an elaboration on the powers and functions of the Security Council, see Davidson Nicol, ed., *The United Nations Security Council: Towards Greater Effectiveness* (New York: United Nations Institute for Training and Research, 1982).

4. See in this connection James M. McCormick, "Intergovernmental Organizations and Cooperation Among Nations," *International Studies Quarterly* 24 (March 1980), pp. 75–95.

5. See also Johan Kaufmann, *United Nations Decision-Making* (Rockville, Md.: Sijthoff and Noordhoff, 1980).

6. See James D. Thompson, *Organizations in Action* (New York: McGraw-Hill, 1967), pp. 14–24, 159–60.

7. Robert W. Cox, "The Executive Head: An Essay on Leadership in International Organization," *International Organization* 23 (Spring 1969), pp. 205–30.

8. Ibid., p. 230.

9. Christoph Sasse, Edouard Poullet, David Coombes, Gerard Deprez, *Decision Making in the European Community* (New York: Praeger, 1977), p. 176.

10. Ibid., p. 178.

11. Ibid., p. 157. See also Hans J. Michelmann, *Organizational Effectiveness in a Multinational Bureaucracy* (Westmead, England: Saxon House, Teakfield Limited, 1978).

12. See, for example, Lawrence Scheinman, "Economic Regionalism and International Administration: The European Communities' Experience," in Jordan, op. cit.

13. David Mitrany, "The Prospect of Integration: Federal or Functional?" in *Functionalism*, eds. A. J. R. Groom and Paul Taylor, (New York: Crane, Russak, 1975), pp. 53–78, 71–72.

14. See Philippe Schmitter, "Three Neo-Functional Hypotheses about International Integration," *International Organization* 23 (Winter 1969), pp. 162–64.

15. See Norman F. Dufty, "Organization Growth and Goal Structure: The Case of the IGO," *International Organization* 26 (Summer 1972), pp. 479–98.

16. See Cox, op. cit., pp. 213–26.

17. See some of the comments made by Henry Nau, "From Integration to Interdependence: Gains, Losses, and Continuing Gaps," *International Organization* 33 (Winter 1979), pp. 119–47. See also R. G. Havelock, *Planning for Innovation Through Dissemination and Utilization of Knowledge* (Ann Arbor, Mich.: Institute for Social Research, University of Michigan, 1973) and James Q. Wilson, "Innovation in Organization: Notes Toward a Theory" in James D. Thompson, ed., *Approaches to Organizational Design* (Pittsburgh: University of Pittsburgh Press, 1963), pp. 194–218.

18. See the revealing study by Robert E. Riggs "The Bank, The IMF, and the WHO," *Journal of Conflict Resolution* 24 (June 1980), pp. 329–57, and his "The FAO and the USDA: Implications for Functionalistic Learning," *Western Political Quarterly* 33 (Sept. 1980), pp. 314–29.

19. Portions of this section are derived from chapter 1 of Norman A. Graham and Robert S. Jordan, eds., *The International Civil Service: Changing Role and Concepts*, (New York: Pergamon Press, 1980). See also Sydney D. Bailey, *The Secretariat of the United Nations* (New York: Carnegie Endowment for International Peace, 1962).

20. S. N. Eisenstadt, *Essays on Comparative Institutions* (New York: Wiley, 1965), p. 180; see also Paul Reuter, *International Institutions* (London: Allen and Unwin, 1958).

21. See C. Grove Haines, ed., *European Integration* (Baltimore: The Johns Hopkins Press, 1957).

22. See Werner J. Feld, "The European Community's Civil Service: Bureaucracy in Crisis," unpublished paper delivered at the annual convention of the Southern Political Science Association, Memphis, Tennessee (November 5–7, 1981)

23. Bowett, op. cit., p. 183 and *Yearbook of International Organizations*, 17th ed. (Brussels, Belgium: Union of International Organizations, 1978), hereafter referred to as *Yearbook.*

24. Bowett, op. cit., p. 188.

25. Bryce Wood, "The Organization of American States" in *The Yearbook of World Affairs* (Boulder, Col.: Westview Press, 1979), pp. 148–66 on p. 155.

26. A good advocacy position can be found in the 28th Report of the Commission to Study the Organization of Peace, *Regional Promotion and Protection of Human Rights.* (New York: CSOP, 1979).

27. Bowett, op. cit., p. 189.

28. For more details see Wood, op. cit., p. 156 and G. Connell-Smith, *The Inter-American System* (London: Oxford University Press, 1966) p. 337.

29. Wood, op. cit., p. 155.

30. Detailed data are found in ibid., pp. 161–62.

31. For details see Ernst B. Haas, "Technological Self-Reliance for Latin America: The OAS Contribution", *International Organization* 34 (Autumn 1980), pp. 541–70.

32. Yale H. Ferguson, "Latin America," in *Comparative Regional Systems*, eds. Werner J. Feld and Gavin Boyd (New York: Pergamon Press, 1980), p. 342.

33. For details see Sidney Dell, *A Latin American Common Market?* (London: Oxford University Press, 1966), pp. 125–34.

34. *Yearbook*, A 2879g.

35. Ferguson, op. cit., p. 332. Multinationals were attracted by the favorable investment climates in those states, especially Argentina and Brazil, and the large internal markets these states offered.

36. For details see Dell, op. cit., pp. 197–205.

37. Ferguson, op. cit.

38. *Business America* (April 6, 1981), p. 15.

39. Quoted in John F. Renninger, *Multinational Cooperation for Development in West Africa* (New York: Pergamon Press, 1979), p. 45.

40. See *Political Handbook of the World* (1981), p. 594.

41. Renninger, op. cit., p. 53.

42. See also Oatunde J. B. Ojo, "Nigeria and the Formation of ECOWAS," *International Organization* 34 (Autumn 1980), pp. 571–604.

43. Renninger, op. cit., p. 50.

44. United Nations, *African Statistical Yearbook, 1975*, Part 2, West Africa.

45. Charles E. Morrison and Astri Suhrke, *Strategies of Survival: The Foreign Policy Dilemmas of Smaller Asian States* (New York: St. Martin's Press, 1978), p. 265.

46. Quoted by Termsak Chalermpalanuapap, "A Novel Approach to Regional Integration," paper presented at the 1982 Louisiana Political Science Association Meeting, New Orleans (March 12–13, 1982), p. 7.

47. Ibid., p. 17.

48. Czechoslovakia, Poland, Hungary, Romania, and Yugoslavia.

49. Cox and Jacobson, op. cit., p. 30.

50. Ibid., p. 303.

51. *Yearbook*, # B 3381g. See also Jack A. Finlayson and Mark W. Zacher, "The GATT and the Regulation of Trade Barriers: Regime Dynamics and Functions," *International Organization* 35 (Autumn 1981), pp. 561–602.

52. Joseph S. Nye, "UNCTAD: Poor Nations' Pressure Group" in Cox and Jacobson, op. cit. pp. 334–70.

53. Ibid., pp. 335–38.

54. For example, in 1981 UNCTAD asked member governments for information about vessels owned by their nationals that sail under flags-of-convenience in order to formulate rules that would phase out this practice. The Western shipping states were almost uniformly opposed to UNCTAD's involvement in this activity, but nevertheless an intergovernmental preparatory group was set up to draw up basic principles for this purpose. *Journal of Commerce* (July 17 and October 16, 1981).

55. For a detailed discussion of this process, see Odette Jankowitsch and Karl P. Sauvant, "The Initiating Role of the Non-Aligned Countries" in *Changing Priorities on the International Agenda*, ed., Karl P. Sauvant (New York: Pergamon Press, 1980), pp. 41–77.

56. Robert S. Jordan, "What has Happened to our International Civil Service? The Case of the United Nations," *Public Administration Review* (March/April 1981), pp. 236–45.

57. U.N. General Assembly, Doc. A/C.5/34/SR88, January 4, 1980.

58. Jordan, op. cit., p. 239.

59. Quoted in ibid.

60. U.N. Document A/33/I, Section II, September 12, 1978.

61. Jordan, op. cit., pp. 241–42.

62. *The International Civil Service: Changing Role and Concepts* (New York: Pergamon Press, 1980), pp. 148–67.

63. "The paramount consideration in the employment of the staff and in the determination of the conditions of service shall be the necessity of securing the highest standards of efficiency, competence, and integrity. Due regard shall be paid to the importance of recruiting the staff on as wide a geographic basis as possible."

64. See Riggs, "The FAO and USDA," op. cit. and the detailed literature listed there as well as Riggs, "The Bank, The IMF, and WHO," op. cit.

65. Riggs, "The FAO and USDA," pp. 317–18.

66. David A. Kay, "Secondment in the United Nations Secretariat: An Alternative View," *International Organization* 20 (Winter 1966), pp. 63–75 focuses on the European experience to draw a few inferences for the Secretariat, but has no data with respect to that organ.

67. For a useful background document, see *Restructuring the United Nations System for Economic and Social Cooperation for Development* (New York: Commission to Study the Organization of Peace, 1980) and *A New United Nations Structure for Global Economic Cooperation* (New York: United Nations Document, Sales no. E.75.11.A.7). See also Harold K. Jacobson and Dusan Sidjanski, eds., *The Emerging International Economic Order-Dynamic Processes, Constraints, and Opportunities* (Beverly Hills: Sage Publication, 1982).

68. The Director-General's duties were described as " . . . ensuring the provision of effective leadership to the various components of the United Nations system in the field of development and international economic cooperation and exercising over-all coordination within the system in order to ensure a multidisciplinary approach to the problems of development on a system-wide basis." U.N. General Assembly, *Report* of the Ad Hoc Committee on the Restructuring of the Economic and Social Sectors of the United Nations System, A/32/34, pp. 25–26.

69. Kurt Waldheim, *Building the Future Order*, ed. Robert L. Schiffer (New York: The Free Press, 1980), Intro., p. xxii.

70. For a survey of the evolution of all aspects of international administration, see Robert

S. Jordan, ed., *International Administration: Its Evolution and Contemporary Applications* (New York: Oxford University Press, 1971). For a discussion of Dag Hammarskjöld, see ed. Robert S. Jordan, *Dag Hammarskjöld Reconsidered*, op cit.

71. For details see Lawrence Scheinman and Werner Feld, "The European Economic Community and National Civil Servants of the Member States," *International Organization* 26 (Winter 1972), pp. 121–35.

72. Leon N. Lindberg, *The Political Dynamics of European Economic Integration* (Stanford, Calif.: Stanford University Press, 1963), p. 55.

73. For a much more detailed discussion of this problem see Hans J. Michelmann, *Organizational Effectiveness in a Multinational Bureaucracy* (Westmead, England: Saxon House, Teakfeld Limited, 1978), pp. 23–38.

74. *The Times* (London), April 22, 1980, pp. 14–15.

75. *The Guardian* (Manchester), January 24, 1981, p. 19.

76. See Werner J. Feld and John K. Wildgen, *Domestic Political Realities and European Unification* (Boulder, Col.: Westview Press, 1976), p. 126.

77. *The Economist* (February 14, 1981), p. 48.

78. *Europe* (March-April 1981), p. 45.

Chapter 4

Decision-Making Processes and Policy-Making Scope

The creation of IGO institutions and the employment of civil servants in these institutions have as their major purpose to accomplish the tasks for which the IGOs were created. The attainment of this goal requires national and multinational decision making that form the basis of IGO policies and implementing actions. For a comparative analysis and evaluation of IGO decision- and policy-making processes we will examine in the following pages the voting systems used in IGOs; the scope and level of decisions authorized in the constituent treaties including a taxonomy of decisions; changes in the locus of decision making and their implications; special strategies used in IGO decision making such as bloc voting or package deals; and the implementation and evaluation of decisions.

In most cases the IGO decision-making process consists of many activities and actions prior to the actual making of a particular decision and is followed by other activities and measures to implement the decision. Hence, David Easton's input-output model[1] can serve as a useful background for understanding the political environment that is likely to surround IGO decision making. Easton suggests that, just as in national decision making, it is reasonable to expect a variety of efforts by interested parties to influence the shape of the decisions that are eventually made in IGO institutions. These efforts may consist of logrolling, corridor deals, and the many other activities normally associated with inputs into national political decisions. We will return to this subject in more detail in our illustrative cases and voting analyses.

VOTING SYSTEMS

Majority Rule

There is a clear historical trend away from the rule of unanimity to majority rule in decisions made within IGOs. In the course of drafting the Covenant of the League of Nations, Lord Robert Cecil declared that "all international decisions must, by the nature of things, be unanimous."[2] Therefore, it is not surprising that in the Covenant the unanimity rule was generally preserved, although some explicit exceptions were made in which majority voting sufficed. These exceptions included procedural questions, the admission of new members, and other instances in Assembly voting and even in a few situations in Council decisions.[3] In the United Nations, majority vote has become the rule in most bodies except the Security Council. In the General Assembly the basic rule is that a simple majority is sufficient unless the decision to be made deals with an important question (Article 18).

Majority rule also prevails in the specialized agencies of the United Nations. In fact, because of the technical nature of their task performance, so-called public unions, some of which were the predecessors of these agencies—for example the Universal Postal Union formed in 1894—employed majority rule much earlier than the IGOs.[4] On the other hand, unanimity (or, rather, the absence of a negative vote) remains the basic rule in the Committee of Ministers in the Council of Europe, the Council of the OECD, the Council of the Arab League, COMECON, the Political Consultative Committee of the Warsaw Treaty Organization (WTO) and the NATO Council. In the Council of Ministers of the EC unanimity is basically retained when prospective decisions affect the vital interests of member-states.

At times there are differences in the voting system depending on whether procedural or substantive issues are involved. In the latter case, the majority requirements are often a two-thirds vote rather than a simple majority. There are also instances when continuing practices may change voting systems and this change develops into customary law. Examples will be provided later in this chapter.

VARIATIONS IN THE EQUALITY OF VOTING POWER

If one were to follow strictly the principle of cosovereign equality, each member-state of an IGO should have the same voting power. However, in the real world of unequal power distribution and considering the concern of especially the large states to retain as much of their political freedom of action as possible, some means had to be found to deviate from this principle. One way has been to allow a state extra representation through assigning sovereign status to territorial units within a state. This was the reason for admitting Byelorussia and the Ukraine to full status as member-states in the United Nations. It is reasonable to assume that these two states usually vote the same way as does the Soviet Union.

Another means of breaking the principle of one state-one vote is weighting the votes of IGO members. This has been defined as a system that assigns to members of IGOs votes proportioned on the basis of predetermined relevant criteria.[5] Such criteria may be the financial contributions of member-states to the IGO as is done in the World Bank, the International Monetary Fund (IMF), and the International Development Association (IDA), or the size and economic power of the member-states as exemplified in the voting arrangements of the Council of Ministers of the EC. Under this arrangement, the four largest members (France, West Germany, Italy, and the United Kingdom) have ten votes each; Belgium, Greece, and The Netherlands, have five each; Denmark and Ireland three each; and Luxembourg two.[6]

Other systems of weighting have been proposed. For example, the suggestion has been made to base the voting system in the U.N. General Assembly on population figures.[7] While an interesting suggestion, it was politically unacceptable. Finally, the one state-one vote principle is circumvented when some member-states are given a veto power over decisions. The obvious case is the U.N. Security Council where the five permanent members (the United States, Soviet Union, China, Great Britain, and France) can veto any substantive decision of the council.

In summarizing our discussion of voting systems, it appears that the more technical or perhaps low politics the issue areas in which an IGO is concerned, the greater the chances that simple majorities are employed for the approval of decisions. Conversely, the more high politics are involved in particular decison making within IGOs, the greater is the tendency to insist on unanimity in voting. In this way, it is not likely that perceived vital interests of member-states may be adversely affected. Where the issues are very general, such as those that compose the NIEO, reliance on consensus decision making has helped to paper over real and specific differences that have hampered effective implementation.

THE SCOPE AND LEVEL OF DECISIONS

The term decision in our discussion covers all types of action taken by vote, whether framed as resolution, recommendation, directive, or other description. Most decisions are not automatically binding on the member-states of an IGO; indeed the majority may be nonbinding and often programmatic, especially as far as those in the U.N. family are concerned.

Decisions may be rendered at different levels of an IGO's activities. Usually, decisions at lower levels, for example in committees, will become building blocks for the decisions at the top levels. The international political significance of decisions of IGOs depends in large part on the level where it has been made although in some cases—such as the large body of antiapartheid resolutions passed in U.N. organs—the higher political level has not resulted in a significant change in national policies. On the other hand, a resolution by the U.N. Economic and Social Council (ECOSOC) on some development issue will gain considerably in importance if endorsed by an appropriate resolution in the U.N. General Assembly. Also, a decision of the European Parliament will have saliency only if the EC Council of Ministers adopts it and gives it political and legal support.

The circle of decision makers in IGOs does not only consist of IGO civil servants. While these individuals, especially those in high or top executive positions, play the main roles in decisions made in the secretariats or the organs they serve, in the plenary bodies and councils of the organization it is the representatives of the member governments who, as the appointed delegates of their governments, has the prime responsibility in the decision-making process. In some cases, these individuals, who may either be national civil servants or legislators or ad hoc appointees, may also participate in preliminary decisions, either in IGO committees, their diplomatic missions at the seat of the IGO, or in committees composed of mission staffs such as the Committee of Permanent Representatives serving the EC or the Council of Permanent Representatives of NATO. In some instances, a government may use representatives of interest groups or commercial enterprises as participants at various levels in the IGO decision-making process. This method is often employed by the United States and offers splendid opportunities to interest groups and enterprises to influence directly the IGO decision-making process. The ILO is the most obvious case in point.

In many IGO decisions, the economic and political stakes are high and therefore the utilization of appropriate strategies may be crucial. This may require launching particular initiatives by some participants in the decision-making process, expressing support for these initiatives by others, or seeking to kill them by still another group of actors. Others again may serve as power brokers or consensus builders depending on the particular interests pursued by governments and private groups.[8]

A Taxonomy of Decisions

Robert Cox and Harold Jacobson have developed a taxonomy of seven categories of decisions that we have found useful for the comparative analysis of IGOs.

1. *Programmatic decisions* refer to the strategic allocation of the IGO's resources among different types and fields of activity. Such decisions are frequently made in the framework of the budget and are inherently related to the effective task performances of the organization.

2. *Rule-creating decisions* produce the rules within the substantive scope of the IGO and also relate to task performance. They include binding norms on governments and individuals if such decisions are authorized in the constituent treaties, as is the

case with the ECSC and EEC. They may also include directives to governments where authorized. In addition, they may take the form of agreements, as, for example, GATT's activity in the conclusion of tariff accords and codes on nontariff barriers, or labor conventions by the ILO.

3. *Operational decisions* refer to the utilization of resources for task performance and the IGO's provision of services in accordance with established programs and policies. Operational decisions are often made between national civil servants of the member-states and international bureaus, and may suffer from pressures by various clienteles who seek to promote their own objectives.

4. *Rule-supervisory decisions* deal with the application of approved rules and supervision over the proper implementation of approved programs. One example is the implementation of the safeguard provisions of the International Atomic Energy Agency (IAEA). Supervision may be carried out by national and international civil servants acting singly or jointly, or by private specialists. Where realistic enforcement is possible, supervision can be crucial for proper task performance.

5. *Representational decisions* are concerned with membership issues in the IGO and representation in international bodies. Who is to be admitted to membership and who should be expelled if the possibility of expulsion is stipulated in the constituent treaty? Other issues include the validity of credentials and the determination of representation on executive organs and committees.

6. *Boundary decisions* refer to an IGO's relations with other universal and regional IGOs regarding their respective scope and competence, cooperation among the different units, and various kinds of interaction.

7. *Symbolic decisions* are primarily tests of "the acceptability of goals and ideologies intensely espoused by one group of actors or the legitimacy of long-accepted norms of dominant elites."[9] These decisions have no practical consequences in the form of actions that flow directly from them, but they may provide a sensitive measure of changes in the internal distribution of influence.

Some or all of these categories of decisions may appear in our cases and they will give us a clearer insight into the operations of IGOs.

CHANGES IN THE LOCUS OF DECISION MAKING

We have intimated in our preceding discussion in this section that national governments (and some nongovernmental actors) participate in IGO decision making in various ways. This raises the question as to where the primary locus of the decision-making process is in particular issue areas. It also raises the question of the extent of integration on IGO displays that, as pointed out in Chapter 1, can range from a very loose and limited organization with very restricted decision-making authority, to an IGO that is tightly organized, possesses an extensive institutional framework and is endowed with supranational powers. As defined in Chapter 1, these powers permit IGO institutions to make decisions that are directly binding on the member-states without specific action by the governments and/or legislatures.

If IGOs have such powers, it implies that slices of sovereignty have been transferred from the member governments to the IGO. Functionalist theory claims that this transfer occurred as the result of functional border-crossing cooperation satisfying the needs of the people in the collaborating states. The neofunctionalists might contend that this process is the consequence of sector and institutional spillovers and of appropriate strategies employed by IGO technocrats.[10] Still others argue that the degree of integration progress depends on the foreign policy goals of the member-states intertwined with the need to meet domestic political demands by various constituencies.[11]

Regardless of the theory favored, Leon N. Lindberg and Stuart A. Scheingold have developed a useful scale of the locus of decison making in their study of the EC that can have application to other IGOs.[12] They explore movement from a situation in which individual national governments make all fundamental policy choices by means of a purely internal process of decision making or make them in nonnational settings like NATO, to a terminal situation where all these choices are subject to joint decision within an IGO. To show various points on the integrative continuum, they prepared an illustrative table that we have reproduced. Table 4.1 suggests different loci of decision making on this continuum or, in other words, different levels on which decisions are made. We should note that a higher level of decision making does not automatically broaden the scope of decisions authorized for an IGO, although upward movement of this scope may occur in individual cases and conceivably continuing practice may bring about such a result. This has happened in the EC as demonstrated by Lindberg and Scheingold.[13]

As we will see in our cases, the trend of movement in the locus of decisions in an IGO may also go in the opposite direction and result in a gradual renationalization of the IGO decision-making process. Such a trend has been observed more in regional IGOs in the Third World than in universal IGOs. However, it has also happened in U.N. units. For example,

TABLE 4.1: A Scale of the Locus of Decision Making

Low Integration
1. All policy decisions by national processes
2. Only the beginnings of Community decision processes
3. Policy decisions in both but national activity predominates
4. Policy decisions in both but Community activity predominates
5. All policy decisions by joint Community processes
High Integration

Source: Leon N. Lindberg and Stuart A. Scheingold, *Europe's Would-Be Polity* (Englewood Cliffs, N.J.: Prentice Hall, 1970), p. 69.

we find that the U.N. agency established after the 1972 Stockholm Conference on the Human Environment to create a global program—the U.N. Environment Program (UNEP)—has been losing the support of its participating member-states. Preoccupation with failing economies, shortages and global inflation has taken precedence over supporting environmental concerns.[14] The projects of the U.N. Development Program (UNDP) are now almost entirely subject to host government control, which was not the case a decade ago.

SPECIAL STRATEGIES IN DECISION MAKING

Special strategies in IGO decision making are employed by the IGO leadership, international civil servants, and member governments and are designed to attain important goals in which these actors are particularly interested. These strategies may include the utilization of conferences first to prepare and then to vote on relevant issues, the use of special sessions in various deliberative IGO bodies, the repeated introduction and passage of the same pertinent resolution first in subsidiary bodies and later in such top-level plenary bodies as the U.N. General Assembly, proposals by IGO executives for package deals in stalemated negotiations, and the formation of voting blocs by states with common or converging interests.

Conference and Related Strategies

Since the emergence of the Third World as a major bargaining force in the international political process, there has been a tendency to view conference diplomacy as a primary strategy to achieve the goals of the Group of 77. Thus, challenges to the global status quo have been expressed multilaterally through IGOs, as well as through other forms of coalitions. Single-issue, or ad hoc, conferences have received a great deal of attention in this regard. They have been utilized, mostly but not always under the sponsorship of the United Nations, to give expression to the desires of the Third World for a change in international economic relationships. These conferences have been charged to consider such particular issues as food, population, energy, the role of women, and science and technology for development. Their value has been summarized thus:

> If one views global, ad hoc conferences as vehicles for the interaction of public and private, national and international bureaucracies, an appropriate question to ask is, "What would have happened without the conference?" Our answer lies in investigating the two important functions of these conferences: 1. to give publicity to an issue-area and to change

the dominant attitudes surrounding the definition of the issue-area; 2. to initiate actions designed to alleviate the problem by an agreement on how to strengthen the existing institutions or an agreement on new and more appropriate institutional machinery.[15]

A second strategy in conference decision making is the use of special sessions of the U.N. General Assembly to take up important issues outside its normal program of work or traditional U.N. Charter responsibilities. The special sessions on disarmament, held in 1978 and 1982, could be considered in this category, as also can the sixth (1974) and seventh (1975) special sessions dealing with New International Economic Order (NIEO) issues, and even possibly the U.N. General Assembly's Committee of the Whole, which was charged in 1980 with reconciling the issues that comprise the so-called North-South dialogue, but which had to report in 1980 to another special session its inability to do so.[16]

Probably the apex of the use of the General Assembly as a special-issue negotiating forum was the eleventh special session, held in August 1981, presumably to launch global negotiations that theretofore had not succeeded in other forums. The reason for the failure of this session, therefore, can be traced to the general inability of intergovernmental conferences—whether ad hoc, specialized agency sponsored, or General Assembly special sessions—to resolve issues of immense complexity and that address the vital interests of major participating states. As one study put it:

> As is well known, the breakdown at the 11th Special Session was attributed to disagreement over procedural issues. But questions of centralization, decentralization, linkage, integrity and competence of specialized agencies and other procedural issues are all tied to matters of substance. Procedure is in some sense a smokescreen for more fundamental kinds of questions. At the 11th Special Session procedural questions masked quite fundamental substantive disagreements on two agenda areas: (1) energy and (2) money and finance. For there to be agreement on procedures some kind of trade-off had to be achieved as to substantive outcomes in these two issue areas.[17]

A third strategy in promoting particular goals through appropriate decisions is the practice in the United Nations of making use of subsidiary bodies, or of the specialized agencies, to serve as the convenor of a conference and to provide the secretariat. This was done, for example, for the World Employment Conference of 1976 for which the ILO was the convenor, and for the World Conference on Agrarian Reform and Rural Development of 1979 for which the FAO was the convenor.

Resolutions introduced and approved by basically sympathetic delegates to these conferences and subsidiary bodies are then moved to higher bodies for further approval and ultimately are presented to the U.N. General Assembly for consideration. Given the substantial Third World majority in the Assembly, it is not surprising that these resolutions are adopted in that body, receiving thereby the highest legitimacy within the U.N. framework.

A final step in the use of General Assembly resolutions is the movement toward global negotiations in the Assembly. The hopes (so far unrealized) of the developing states that compose the Group of 77 has been that through such negotiations their economic and political objectives will find acceptance by the industrialized states, perhaps with the help of a sympathetic global public opinion.

While we have focused here on the United Nations, the three strategies conceivably can also be employed in regional IGOs if they have a hierarchical structure as has the U.N. family of IGOs. However, success depends also on the distribution of decision-making powers to subsidiary organs and on the fervor with which conflicting interests are pursued. Hence, a regional IGO such as the OAS might be suitable for the employment of these strategies, but this can only be determined in the context of an illustrative case.

"Package Deals"

When negotiations on an important issue are stalled in an IGO and votes on that issue either cannot be scheduled or are likely to be inconclusive, package deals can be and have been used successfully by the executive heads of an IGO, or by the conference chairman or president, to break the stalemate and achieve an acceptable outcome of the negotiations. A reason for such success is the comprehensive knowledge possessed by the IGO executive regarding all elements of the issue, which enables him and his colleagues to prepare a solution with an acceptable distribution of gains and concessions for all parties. Such package deals have become a stock-in-trade of the EC Commission over the years, and has been employed successfully on several occasions by the director-general of GATT.[18] But these IGOs may be only the best examples; package deals may be found in other IGOs as well.

Somewhat similar to proposals of a package deal is the utilization of a chairman's text to galvanize consensus and movement on outstanding issues, mostly in working groups set up by U.N. bodies and specialized agencies. The chairman of such a group will formulate a proposed text for an international convention such as an accord on the code of conduct for the transfer of technology. This tool, which may contain agreed and nonagreed portions of articles and clauses of the prospective convention, can serve as a stimulus for further negotiations by the parties involved and has been effective in reaching final consensus on contested parts of the convention. An example of this device to aid the decision-making process will be presented in Chapter

7. An example of an attempt that has failed is the use of a package deal approach to the Law-of-the-Sea.[19]

VOTING BLOCS

Although the term "voting bloc" is frequently used in the literature when voting in the U.N. General Assembly or in other plenary bodies is discussed, the term "caucusing group" might be more appropriate because continuous solid bloc voting is rare except perhaps with respect to the Soviet Union and the East European states. A bloc may be defined as a group of states that meet regularly in caucus, has some degree of formal organization, and is concerned with substantive issues and related procedural matters that may come to a vote in plenary IGO organs.[20] These groupings include the developing states (the Group of 77), which may be broken down further into Afro-Asian, Latin American, and other Third World regional units. Another group is the EC states, sometimes voting with other Western states such as the United States, Canada, and Japan and, of course, another bloc is composed of the Soviet Union and the so-called People's Democracies (but not the People's Republic of China).

Group cohesion in voting depends on the issues and caucus leadership. Anticolonialism and the NIEO have been powerful stimulants to coalesce Third World states. Caucus leadership is closely related to persuasive skill, careful presentation of issues and possible outcomes, and the charisma of the caucus leader.

It is interesting to note that the United States and the Soviet Union voted more often against the majority in the U.N. General Assembly than most U.N. members. Our voting analyses later in this chapter will offer detailed insights into the intricacies of bloc voting and possible motivation for states joining different caucuses and on what issues.[21]

While it is important in both theoretical and practical terms to understand the political and economic implications of voting patterns in IGO plenary organs as well as to comprehend the reasons for these patterns, it would be even more valuable if one could predict future voting outcomes in IGO institutions. Jack E. Vincent has attempted to correlate national attributes of member-states with their voting record in the General Assembly. His findings are that a state's degree of economic development is one of the most important predictors of future voting behavior. With respect to attitudes toward the work and task performance of the United Nations, this might signify that highly developed states may be inclined to show negative tendencie because their capabilities and resources are already high and contributions of IGOs to these capabilities might be relatively insignificant. On the other hand, economically underdeveloped states are more apt to want to expand the work of IGOs because it offers prospects of substantial improvements of their capabilities. Other important attributes according to Vincent are democracy as the political system used in particular states and relations with the United States.[22] We will return to this issue later in this chapter.

OUTPUT IMPLEMENTATIONS

An important question to be explored in more detail relates to the tools that an IGO can use to implement decisions and the degree of effectiveness of the implementation method. Several methods are available to IGOs; the constituent treaties specify which method can be employed in particular circumstances and not all methods are permitted for all IGOs. In many cases, member-state agencies or bureaucracies (both public and private) must be used by IGOs to implement decisions and policies.

Member-states concerned that the balance between national and IGO policy making should favor their governments may not consider that the effectiveness of implementation is the most desirable objective, since it may undermine national prerogatives. The history of disarmament and arms control negotiations bears eloquent witness to this observation. Even in low-politics issue areas, states may have only a limited interest in seeing the functionalist logic work too successfully unless the tasks to be performed by the IGO institutions are completely beyond the reach of their capabilities or are perceived as relatively unimportant.

The least circumscribed method for IGO output implementation is the dissemination of information. The effectiveness of this method depends on the issue area. The more technical the subject or issue areas and the less political they are, the better chances for its effectiveness, and for its acceptability to IGO member-states. Information on health matters or agricultural production by the World Health Organization or the Food and Agriculture Organization (FAO) are cases in point. The use of U.N. agencies to disseminate such political information as apartheid and South Africa, or the plight of the Palestinians and Israel, has aroused resistance and opposition.

A recommendation, which is normally nonbinding, is a method through which an IGO can move things forward, especially if the same recommendation is passed again and again. In particular, if a recommendation is approved by an important body such as the U.N. General Assembly, it can have a decisive effect on world public opinion. Opponents will be pushed in a corner when the same recommendation is passed with increasing majorities and it will take a strongly-held view of a member-state for that state to remain in the opposition year after year. The votes recommending the expulsion of South Africa from the U.N. General Assembly, if not from U.N. membership, and the recent recommended sanctions against Israel to punish that state for the annexation of the Golan Heights are indicative of the problem. Voting on the expulsion of the Republic of China (Taiwan) and admission of the People's Republic of China (Peking), as shown in Figure 4.1, illustrates this point.

Directives authorizing IGOs to issue an enforceable order are not frequent. The U.N. Charter's Chapter VII grants the Security Council such authority, but of course five U.N. member-states have veto rights in the Council. Moreover, actual enforcement action of an order has never been undertaken. Furthermore, the use of Article 19 of the Charter to compel financing of peace-keeping operations authorized by the Security Council has not been successful.[23] In the EC system, however, directives as imple-

FIGURE 4.1

Voting in the General Assembly on the Representation of China

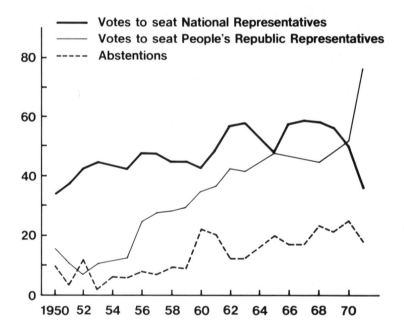

Source: A. LeRoy Bennett, *International Organizations*, 2nd ed. (Englewood Cliffs, N.J.: Prentice-Hall, Inc., 1980), p. 87.

menting tools for policy decision are used more often and in most cases member governments comply.

While directives, wherever authorized, are addressed to the member governments, a very few IGOs are empowered to implement policies with regulations (ordinances) that are directly binding on member-states without positive implementing legislation or decrees by the national parliaments or executive administrations. The prominent examples of this type of output implementation are the ECSC and EEC. In this kind of a legal situation, the member governments and the nongovernmental actors must keep a very watchful eye on the entire IGO decision-making process in order to assure that their major interests are protected and their various national policy goals enhanced as much as possible. Indeed, in some cases member governments may be anxious to frustrate completely the IGO implementation process if they are dissatisfied with a decision.

IMPLEMENTATION EVALUATION

The evaluation of the implementation of IGO decisions is largely an unexplored field, although in the domestic policy area a fairly extensive literature has built up during the last few years.[24] At the heart of the evaluation of decision or policy implementation is the notion of causality. A decision that requires implementation is expected to have a particular causal effect. If the intended effect is achieved, implementation has been successful; if the effect is not achieved and perhaps the outcome of the attempted implementation is quite different from what the decision makers had intended to accomplish, something may have gone awry with the implementation process or the goals chosen for implementation were unrealistic or inappropriate. What are some of the pertinent variables on which evaluation research should focus in order to determine on a comparative, cross-national basis the reasons for failures of IGO decision making and policy implementation processes?

The dependent variable in such an evaluation is implementation effectiveness. A decision or policy is effectively implemented according to the degree to which the decision or policy goals are realized within the specified time period and within the budget allocated for this purpose.

The independent variables can be divided into three clusters.[25] The first cluster is concerned with aspects of the IGO subsystems consisting of its member-states. The particular variables are the nature of the political structure of these states, their political culture, and their economic characteristics. We must remember that implementation of IGO decisions and policies in most cases requires the assistance of member-state agencies. Hence, these variables are very relevant for an evaluation of implementation processes. With respect to culture, public opinion may be crucial: what are the attitudes of various target groups in the IGO member-states regarding particular IGO goals and programs? Among the economic characteristics the rate of inflation and unemployment in different member-states are likely to affect the effectiveness of the implementation processes.

The second cluster of variables focuses on bureaucratic particularities. How strong is an IGO institution's commitment to a goal or program and how high is the implementing state agency's priority to realize pertinent IGO decisions and policies? How well has the particular IGO policy whose implementation is being evaluated, been funded compared with those of other IGO and national policies and programs? What are the levels of bureaucratic expertise and relevant experiences of the IGO civil service involved in implementation? How extensive is the authority of IGO bureaucrats to oversee implementation and how centralized or decentralized is this authority, especially if state agencies are the prime implementors?

The third cluster of variables deals with operational problems. Since many IGO decisions and programs affect different groups in the member-states, questions arise about the degree of support given by these groups and their willingness to participate in individual IGO-sponsored programs. Collaboration of local administrative subdivisions and political party organizations may be a salient element for effectiveness of program and policy implementation, while nonsupportive target groups and antagonistic political forces strengthen the potential for delays and cost overruns in the implementing process. Some of these issues will become more apparent in our illustrative cases.[26]

ILLUSTRATIVE CASES

The United Nations:
Voting Practices and Decision Strategies

The Veto

One of the perennial complaints about the U.N. Security Council has been the veto. However, it is important to note that the veto has been somewhat softened by practices that have evolved over the years into customary law.

Article 27, paragraph 3, of the U.N. Charter that establishes the veto of the five permanent members of the Security Council, states that for a favorable vote on substantive matters before the Council "the concurring votes of the permanent members" must be included. It does not stipulate all the members. Hence, very early in the history of the Security Council, the usage developed that abstention of permanent members from the vote on a substantive matter should not constitute a veto.[27] This usage has given the permanent Council members greater latitude in the expression of their views and the implementation of their foreign policies. At the same time, it has significantly reduced the negative impact of the veto on the working of the Council.

The Security Council adopted a similar practice with respect to the physical absence of a permanent member. Absence, therefore, does not have the effect of a veto. The best-known case for this interpretation of Article 27 was the Korean crisis of June 1950 although earlier precedents existed.[28] The Soviet Union representatives had absented themselves from Security Council proceedings from January to August 1950 in protest against occupation of the Chinese seat by a representative of the Republic of China, the nationalist government on what was then called Formosa. The absence of the Soviet representative during the deliberations on the North Korean aggression on South Korea made it possible to pass important resolutions, including the recommendations of enforcement measures for the first time in the history of the United Nations.[29] These resolutions embodied both operational and rule-supervisory decisions. The Soviet Union denied the legality of these resolutions, but it has in fact not consistently opposed the thesis that "the absence of a permanent member should be construed as acquiescent abstention rather than veto in *absentia*."[30]

Another resolution passed by the General Assembly in November 1950, and called the Uniting for Peace Resolution, also undermined the power of the veto in the Security Council. As explained in Chapter 3, it authorized the General Assembly to confer upon the secretary-general the authority to take a number of measures when the Security Council is unable to act as the result of a veto being cast. The measures range from the establishment of peace observation commissions to the recruitment and dispatch of military contingents as peace-keeping forces. This resolution, then, can be characterized as an operational decision that allocated various resources to the secretary-general beyond the formal powers specified for him in the U.N. Charter.

It is interesting to note that the United States and the Western permanent members of the Security Council have changed their view about the evil of the veto. Being outvoted in the General Assembly by the Third World (that is, the Group of 77) - Soviet bloc coalition during much of the 1960s and 1970s, these states now see a virtue in the veto that offers them opportunities to effectively counter these majorities, at least in those peace-related cases that are brought before the Security Council. The contemporary usefulness of these innovations are illustrated by the fact that Britain used the veto in its 1982 Falkland Islands dispute with Argentina, and the Uniting for Peace Resolution was used in 1981 to overcome a Soviet veto of what it considered a hostile resolution in the Security Council concerning the Soviet military presence in Afghanistan.

Conference Strategies

In the introduction to this chapter we pointed out that the use of ad hoc global conferences as a means to obtain favorable decisions is perceived especially by the Third World as a valuable strategy for the attainment of goals that cannot be realized through well-meaning, nonbinding resolutions passed by the U.N. General Assembly or other U.N. bodies. In other words, conferences on particular important issues may reflect more concretely the interests and power of the Third World vis-à-vis the advanced industrial states than would be possible in other forums and thereby could achieve important results.

Johan Kaufmann, in discussing U.N. decision making has stressed the role of global conferences in the past two decades that mostly under U.N. auspices, are increasingly being used to deal with certain world-wide issues that do not lend themselves to handling by a single agency.[31] The consequence of this development is that the international political community is much more aware of the importance and of the complexity of economic issues. Even though the world is still very much fragmented politically into competing/cooperating states, economically the world has grown increasingly interdependent. This interdependence requires multilateral methods to be employed in avoiding or in resolving disputes. Closely related to this multilateralism is the use of groups of states to participate in such negotiations. These groups can perform the following conference functions: to exchange information on all or part of the agenda of a conference, either in advance or during the conference; to develop common general positions on important agenda items, without definite voting commitment; to develop common positions on certain agenda items or initiatives with agreement on how to vote; to agree on candidates to be put forward by the group or on a common vote for candidates outside the group; to agree on a common spokesman, and on the contents of the statement to be delivered; to undertake joint action for or against a proposal.[32]

During the past ten years, the two-week long, single-agenda-item global conferences, sponsored by the United Nations and dealing with critical economic and social problems of a developmental nature, have become so much a part of the U.N. that they must be seen collectively as a separate, powerful strand in the growing web of dialogue dealing with North-South issues. In fact, in the opinion of some qualified governmental observers, these conferences should be recognized by development experts as representing a new and innovative technique for achieving policy change at the national level.[33]

Not only have these global conferences sponsored a host of new institutions, new funds, and new mechanisms for action at both the national and international levels, but also they have been responsible for generating two new developmental ideas; one, putting much greater emphasis on the provision of basic human needs to the poorer states, while the other calls for greater self-reliance on the part of the Third World states by advocating technical cooperation among them. These ideas are having a major impact on the thinking of development planners in many parts of the world.

The first in this series of conferences was the 1972 global meeting on the environment at Stockholm. Three years in the planning, it grew out of the West's concern about runaway industrial growth and focused particularly on the impact of this growth on man's total environment, including air and water pollution. It did not attract high-level attention from the developing states until shortly before the conference opened, when concern began to spread that environmental cleanup costs in the industrial West would be passed on to the Third World via higher prices, and thereby could slow their development process. There was also a concern that any obligation to observe environmental standards would slow the industrialization of developing states (the right to pollute argument).

A plan of action was adopted at Stockholm laying out recommendations for national, regional, and international action. It also called for the creation of a new agency within the United Nations (UNEP—the U.N. Environment Program), a secretariat to staff the agency, a special voluntary fund for technical assistance projects, an intergovernmental council to supervise the new agency, and a new body in the U.N. Secretariat to coordinate the work of the existing U.N. agencies who were already working on various aspects of the environmental problem. Stockholm has turned out to be one of the most successful conferences in this series. Aside from developing such innovative programs as an international treaty that has as its goal a pollution-free Mediterranean and that has been signed by every state bordering the sea except Albania, UNEP has stimulated the creation of intergovernmental mechanisms for the coordination of national environmental programs in more than 100 states around the world.

The second single-agenda-item conference concerned population and took place at Bucharest in August of 1974. It, too, was three years in the making. The draft plan of action was carefully put together by a small intergovernmental preparatory committee made up of national population and demographic experts who, it turned out, were out of touch with their political mentors. The conference declaration and plan of action were finally adopted by consensus but only after over 100 votes on specific language changes had been taken at the committee level. In the reshaping of the plan of action, the politicians on the delegations of the developing states placed the population issue in the context of the New International Economic Order (NIEO), which had been proclaimed a few months earlier at the sixth special session of the U.N. General Assembly. They forced a broadening of the population experts' narrow focus on family planning objectives and emphasized instead the general developmental aspects of the population problem.

This world conference demonstrated the significance of timing and the linkage of specific global concerns outside the trade and aid field with the North-South dialogue.

In spite of these problems, Bucharest should be viewed as a success since many persons did not think it was possible even to convene a world meeting on the subject of population. No new institutions or funds were established, but the existing U.N. Fund for Population Activities (UNFPA) was strengthened and a great deal of high-level political attention was focused on this major developmental issue.

The third conference in this series was on food and took place in Rome in November 1974. It was organized in a remarkably short time. In early September 1973, the heads of state of the nonaligned states, responding to a proposal made by their host, President Houari Boumedienne of Algeria, urged the holding of a joint FAO-UNCTAD conference to discuss "the serious food crises confronting vast areas and populations of the world." The United States picked up this idea at the U.N. General Assembly a few weeks later and called for a U.N. World Food Conference.[34]

In December 1973, the U.N. General Assembly agreed to host the conference in Rome the following November. Considering the shortness of time involved in planning for such a complicated gathering, this was a remarkably successful conference. It was one of the few times the nonaligned states and the United States were in full agreement on the urgent need for substantial action on a given subject, and so the usual U.N. political issues and even the NIEO did not hamper the conference outcome. The conference plan of action was adopted by consensus and was seen by almost everyone as a positive step forward in the North-South dialogue. It focused national and global attention on the food problem and stimulated governments to take positive action toward solving those problems. Two new U.N. agencies were established by the conference, over the objection of the Food and Agriculture Organization (FAO) that is the primary U.N. body to deal with food matters. The World Food Council (WFC) was designed to establish global food policies, and the International Fund for Agricultural Development (IFAD) was designed to serve as a financial source for agricultural projects in the Third World.

These three conferences were followed by global meetings dealing with women and development (Mexico City, 1975), basic human needs (Geneva, 1976), human settlements (Vancouver, 1976), water (Mar del Plata, 1977), deserts (Nairobi, 1977), technical cooperation among developing countries [TCDC] (Buenos Aires, 1978), rural development (Rome, 1979), science and technology for development (Vienna, 1979), women (Copenhagen, 1980), new and renewable energy (Nairobi, 1981), problems of the least developed countries (Paris, 1981), and the World Assembly on Aging (Vienna, 1982).

These global conferences have a number of things in common: 1) their convening was blessed by a unanimous resolution of the U.N. General Assembly, primarily a programmatic decision though with symbolic overtones; 2) the documentation for conference consideration was prepared by existing or newly-created units within the U.N. family of agencies; 3) the conferences were of two weeks' duration; 4) they had parallel meetings of interested nongovernmental organizations going on in the same city; 5) they often generated a new U.N. entity or U.N. fund designed to focus more attention on the subject as part of the post-conference follow-up; 6) the conference plan of action was usually adopted by consensus; 7) the recommendations were approved by the subsequent U.N. General Assembly; and 8) they were all designed to change attitudes, to stimulate political will, and to raise the level of national and global interest in the subject.

Clearly, some of these conferences were more effective and had a greater impact on the world scene than others, but they all succeeded in focusing governmental attention on often neglected or emerging problems. Frequently there were intrusions of political issues that clearly had no place in such conferences, but by and large those were dealt with and were widely perceived as diversions from the purposes for which the conferences had been called. When a global conference is carefully planned and orchestrated, it is well worth the effort because it can highlight the complexity of problems surrounding a particular development issue.

The four strands described in this overview on conference strategy each make up an important aspect of the North-South dialogue, and each has its strengths and weaknesses. The developing states will continue to work for a world economic system that will be more to its advantage and for commitments from individual donor governments that will advance the South's goal of a more favorable distribution of the world's resources and income. The industrialized states for their part must continue the dialogue, in its own enlightened self-interest.[35]

Conferences as strategies for favorable decisions to be taken ultimately in plenary bodies, seem to be more characteristic of the U.N. family of IGOs. As suggested, they have become especially prominent in economic issues within the North-South dialogue. These strategies have little utility in other IGOs whose membership is much smaller and rarely as polarized as is the case in the United Nations. Hence other strategies for favorable decisions must be employed, including package deals and intergovernmental and interbureaucratic lobbying and trade-offs.

U.N. Bloc Voting: An Analysis

There are a number of studies in the literature that have dealt with the definition and identification of voting blocs or caucusing groups within IGOs—the U.N. General Assembly has received most of the attention—as well as some empirical studies on the measurement of such blocs' degree of cohesive behavior/level of voting agreement. More recently, some studies have offered some predictor variables of voting behavior within the United Nations. A good review of the earlier work has been presented by Arend Lijphart.[36]

As Lijphart writes, one of the major weaknesses of the early analyses of bloc politics in the General Assembly was "the lack of a satisfactory identification of blocs" because most provided a list of blocs or groups "without attempting to give any rigorous definition of these terms, and often without attempting to distinguish between different types of blocs." In addition, these studies were quite deficient in their avoidance of precise empirical measurement. Notwithstanding these weaknesses, however, there were strands of common agreement across the various descriptions: the Afro-Asian, Arab, Latin American, Soviet, West European-North American states, the Commonwealth, and NATO were all identified as blocs or groups.

But as mentioned above, most of these analyses did not provide very precise definitions nor did they distinguish between the different groups in the General Assembly. These defects were addressed by Thomas Hovet, Jr. whose *Bloc Politics in the United Nations*[37] was mentioned earlier in this chapter. Hovet identified different types of blocs and groups and he employed explicit terms when defining each type: caucusing blocs, caucusing groups, geographical distribution groups, regional organizational groups, common interest groups, and temporary groups. Hovet identified nine caucusing groups: the Afro-Asian, Arab, African, Benelux, Commonwealth, Latin-American, Scandinavian, Soviet, and Western European caucusing groups. Some members of the U.N. (U.S., China, Israel, South Africa) were not located in any caucusing group and, conversely, some members were placed in more than one group.

Lijphart himself has examined bloc voting in the General Assembly (44 roll calls on colonial issues from 1956–58). The method employed was Lijphart's adaptation of the Rice-Beyle Index of Voting Agreement.[38] The underlying principle of this method, as Lijphart writes, is that instead of first "postulating the existence of certain blocs and then measuring their cohesiveness, it performs both tasks—identification of blocs and measurement of their cohesion—simultaneously on the basis of the voting records." The Rice-Beyle method compares the vote of every single member to the vote of every other member and a bloc is defined as a group of members "between all possible pairs of whom the voting agreement is equal to or greater than an assigned minimum figure."

Lijphart's application of the Rice-Beyle method to the 44 roll calls on colonial issues discovered several voting blocs located at differing levels on the 0–100 voting agreement index. The bloc composed of the Soviet Union, its two Union Republics, and its East European satellites (but not Poland) was at the 100 level; at the 95.5 level were Iraq, Saudi Arabia, Jordan, and

Libya, all members of the Arab caucusing group; Ceylon (Sri Lanka), India, and Nepal were at 90; Australia, Canada, New Zealand, and the United Kingdom were also at 90; there were two large voting blocs at the 75 level: a 29-member Asian-African-Soviet bloc and an 18-member Western bloc. Chapter 5 contains a discussion of the Rice-Beyle method as applied to the analysis of voting in both the European Parliament and of the EC within the United Nations.

Later analyses of voting behavior and bloc cohesiveness have employed quite sophisticated methodological approaches. Two such examples—one by Hayward R. Alker, Jr. and the other by Bruce M. Russett[39]—applied the techniques of factor analysis to the voting in the U.N. General Assembly. Factor analysis is a rather common technique and does not require at this point any lengthy description. The most common technique is R-analysis, where every variable is correlated to every other variable using the product-moment correlation coefficient (Pearson's rho). R-analysis is then a data-reduction technique—those variables that show high correlations among themselves and very low correlation with other variables are seen as pointing to a single underlying dimension or factor. The factors themselves are un-correlated with each other. Q-analysis treats the states as variables and the roll calls themselves become observations. If the matrix is factor-analyzed, the correlations identify states with similar voting patterns and the factors point to voting groups or blocs.

Alker employed the R-analysis to the XVI Session of the United Nations (1961–62). Seventy votes were examined—they included all distinct, nonu-nanimous, nonprocedural, plenary roll calls as well as 26 of the most im-portant committee votes. Alker's findings can be summarized as follows: six major factors were identified and eight main groupings emerged. The main blocs or groups were seen to be the Old Europeans, Latin caucus, Soviet bloc, Arab caucus, Casablanca group, Brazzaville group (mostly former French colonies), Africans, and Asians (Yugoslavia, Israel, and Nationalist China were not listed within any group). The factors of conflict identified by Alker were East versus West, North versus South, self-determination, cold war, Moslem questions, and U.N. supranationalism. Russett applied the Q-anal-ysis to the XVIII Session and examined all plenary and committee roll calls except those seen as virtually unanimous (more than 90 percent on any one side). A total of 66 votes were analyzed by Russett. Russett's analysis found six factors but with Q-analysis, the factors are the country groupings or blocs. These six were the Western community, Brazzaville Africans, Afro-Asians, communist bloc, conservative Arabs, and Iberia.

While most of the studies cited above dealt with the identification of blocs/groups, the measurement of such groups' degree of cohesion, and the dimensions of conflict within the United Nations, a series of articles by Jack E. Vincent[40] correlated national attributes of member-states with their voting record in order to predict future voting outcomes. The techniques employed by Vincent included survey data, correlation techniques, factor analysis, and canonical correlation. In one study, Vincent identified the roll-calls' content areas as votes East, votes South, votes East in cold war, self-determination, supranationalism, pro-Arab, and against U.N. intervention; the voting groups were identified as Western community, Brazzaville Africans, Afro-Asians, communist bloc, conservative Arabs, and Iberia.

Table 4.2 presents a summary of Vincent's findings. Vincent writes that although the studies listed in Table 4.2 include a number of variables other than just the economic variable, "it can be seen that, compared to other predictors, economic development measures have emerged again and again as primarily important. Further, concerning the United Nations system, high development tends to predict negativism . . . whether one is dealing with attitudes toward specific organs, procedures, or voting behavior."[41] Vincent's findings tend to corroborate the general view that IGO member-states with greater capabilities tend to have more negative attitudes toward the IGO (at least within the U.N. system). This is a very pessimistic finding in light of the fact that the more economically developed countries are—and will continue to be—the main source of financial support of the United Nations.

The European Communities: The Role of the Council of Ministers

Examples of weighted voting as well as of continuing practices developing into something akin to customary law can be found in the EC. We have already mentioned in the introduction of this chapter the voting system in the Council of Ministers where the votes of the large states have a weight of ten, while Luxembourg's vote has only a weight of two, with the remainder of the member-states having weights in between these two values. However, this voting arrangement is only part of a complicated decision-making process outlined in the constituent treaties, a process that has become much more complex through practices that have developed during the last 20 years.

According to the ingenious arrangement devised by the treaty framers, it is the Commission that is to act as the driving force of the decision-making apparatus. It is the initiator of proposals upon which the Council is called to act. As the Common Market moved through the three stages of a transitional period from 1958 to 1970, the Council was authorized increasingly to make its decisions with a qualified majority.[42] However, it cannot amend a Commission proposal except by unanimous vote. In the majority of cases the Council is not able to make a decision unless a Commission proposal has been offered, and it does not have a legal tool to force the Commission to submit a specific proposal. On the other hand, the Commission can modify,

TABLE 4.2:   Summary of Findings on Predictor Variables

Year	Subject	Findings
1. 1961–62	U.N. caucusing groups	Average per capita GNP of the members of caucusing groups predicts attitudes held by delegate members in groups. High development predicts negative attitudes.
2. 1965–66	U.N. delegate attitudes toward organs	Economic development predicts negative attitudes.
3. 1967–68	Relationship of voting and attitudes	Western voting states have negative attitudes. Afro-Asian, African, and communist voting states have positive attitudes.
4. 1967–68	U.N. caucusing groups	Economic development predicts nonsupranational structures and negative attitudes.
5. 1968	U.N. delegate attitudes toward organs	Economic development receives largest weight in canonical correlation between attitudes and predictors, predicting negative attitudes.
6. 1969	Regional groups	Economic development discriminates four regional groups better than any other predictor, followed by democracy and U.S. relations.
7. 1970	General Assembly voting	Economic development best predictor of negative voting, followed by democracy and U.S. relations.
8. 1971	U.N. delegate attitudes toward the IR system	Economic development predicts negative attitudes while democracy and U.S. relations predict positive attitudes.

Source: Jack E. Vincent, "An Application of Attribute Theory to General Assembly Voting and Some Implications," *International Organization* 26 (Summer 1972), Table 7, "Summary of Studies," p. 576.

substitute, or withdraw its proposal at any point up to the last moment prior to the Council's decision unless the timetables of the treaties preclude such withdrawal. Thus the treaties have drawn a careful balance of power between the two organs, which forces them to cooperate in governing the affairs of the Community. However, in practice, as we will see, there is considerable imbalance, weighing heavily in favor of the Council.

A third organ, the Committee of Permanent Representatives (CPR or COREPER, following the French title) has the duty of preparing the sessions and decisions of the Council (which usually meets only a few days each month) and of carrying out any tasks assigned to it by the Council. In addition, the staff of the CPR is frequently consulted informally by the Commission before it submits a formal proposal to the Council. In order to accomplish these missions, the CPR, composed of the ambassadors from the ten member-states and their staffs, totaling more than 400 civil servants, has established a number of working groups, subcommittees, and special ad hoc committees patterned after the administrative structure of the Commission.[43]

Clearly, the CPR, as handmaiden of the Council, has gained over the years in importance and influence and has materially contributed to the shift in the balance of power from the Commission to the Council. Prior to submitting a proposal to the Council, the Commission engages in preliminary and informal consultations with the staff members of the CPR in order to gain more knowledge about the views of the member governments. Information is also sought through meetings with national officials who possess expert knowledge on the matter under consideration and through formal meetings or informal contacts with national and European-level interest group associations.

The power of the Commission and indeed the entire integration process of the EC sustained further damage when in 1965 the implementation of the EEC Treaty's provisions for decision making by qualified majority in the Council regarding a number of policy issues was refused by France. Using as a pretext certain problems in the financing of the Common Agricultural Policy (CAP), the French government started in July 1965 to boycott all EC proceedings, an action that became known as the policy of the empty chair. The basic rationale for this policy was de Gaulle's opposition to strengthening in any way the political powers of the Community's central institutions. When in January 1966 the Luxembourg Conference of the EC Foreign Ministers settled the crisis provoked by the French boycott it was on the basis of allowing any member-state a veto on matters it considers of vital national importance.[44] As a consequence, although in recent years member governments occasionally have abstained rather than blocked an agreement, unanimity in decision making was the fundamental rule for the Council of Ministers. However, in May 1982, when Great Britain invoked its vital interest in the Council in order to block the annual price increases under the Common

Agricultural Policy, the nine other member-states rejected the British veto and adopted the increase in farm prices with a qualified majority vote.[45] Whether this means that the Luxembourg arrangement is dead and the EEC Treaty provisions regarding qualified voting have been resuscitated, is unclear at this writing. Our view is that the vital national interest will again be invoked on future issues by the more powerful member-states such as France if it suits their overall purposes and if a less powerful political constituency is involved than the very influential and politically astute farmers of Western Europe. Hence, it remains essential that the Commission's proposals on most types of decisions have to be formulated in such a way that they are acceptable to most, if not all, member-states in order to have a reasonable chance for approval. This means that these proposals must search for the lowest-common-denominator level and this reduces the role of the Commission and lowers its ability to represent truly the overall interests of the Community.

In spite of its weakened position, the Commission can still make at times a major contribution to the final decision of the Council. Because of its usually superior technical knowledge of all aspects of the situation with which the Council is faced, it can propose a package deal that may not fully satisfy all participants and all the interests of the member-states, but may represent an acceptable compromise. Especially after marathon sessions of bargaining often lasting around the clock, a compromise submitted by the Commission may look very attractive and an ultimate decision by the Council is achieved.

In terms of decision-making locus, this is a clear case where the formal procedures of the EEC Treaty specifying balanced collaboration between the Commission and the Council with an eventual tilt in power to the former have not been maintained in practice. Rather, the decision-making locus has shifted to some degree to the control by the member governments, although nominal decision making continues to be carried out within the EC institutions. Programmatic and symbolic decisions usually escape the severe scrutiny by member governments that is given to proposals for other types of decisions.

The International Monetary Fund (IMF)

Another example of weighted voting in an IGO, although quite different from the EC, is found in the International Monetary Fund (IMF). To understand this system requires a brief discussion of the IMF's history, structure, and functions.

The IMF is one of two key IGOs that emerged from the Bretton Woods Conference in New Hampshire in July 1944; the other IGO was the International Bank for Reconstruction and Development, better known as the World Bank. The basic purposes for the creation of the IMF were to safeguard international financial and monetary stability and to provide financial backing for the revival and expansion of international trade.

Although initially the product mostly of Anglo-American discussions, the Articles of Agreement of the Fund, its basic constituent treaty, was ratified by 28 states before the end of 1945 and formal IMF operations began March 1, 1947. At present more than 140 states are members of the Fund, but most communist countries, including the Soviet Union, have refused to join.

The two bodies in the Fund formally responsible for making decisions are the Board of Governors and the Executive Board. The Board of Governors is composed of one representative from each member-state (usually the minister of finance or economics) and meets once a year. It constitutes the deliberative organ of the IMF. However, while each member-state is represented on this organ, the governors wield unequal votes, based on a system of quotas. The size of the quotas of individual member-states depends on their contributions to the Fund, which in turn determines its borrowing rights and its voting power. The largest contributor currently is the United States, which has 19.83 percent of the voting power; the smallest contributors have considerably less than 1 percent each. Over the years the quotas have undergone changes and through one of these changes the EC's quota now exceeds 15 percent. A sharp increase in the U.S. contribution, along with others, of nearly 50 percent was authorized in 1983 by the IMF's policy-making interim committee, to help avoid bankruptcies in the Third World.

This change was important because the Articles of Agreement require not only qualified majorities of weighted votes on important issues, but also a miniumum number of member-states for the approval of proposed resolutions in particular cases. For example, any general revisions of quotas in the Fund must be approved by a four-fifths majority of the total voting power. Any changes in the Articles of Agreement has to have the concurrence of three-fifths of the members having four-fifths of the votes. Such a change was made to increase the minimum total votes from four-fifths to 85 percent in 1968[46] and as a consequence, the United States and the EC were placed in the position of being able to veto important decisions. It should be noted that on less important issues a simple majority of the voting rights of the member-states is sufficient.[47] Between the annual sessions of the governors, votes can be taken by mail or other means.

The Board of Governors has delegated many of its powers to the Executive Board but has retained its authority over the admission of new members, quota changes, and the election of executive-board members. The latter body is, in effect, in permanent session in Washington. It consists of a total of 22 directors, five of whom are appointed and the others elected. The appointed directors are nominated by and represent the five states with the largest quotas of the Fund, that is, the United States, the United Kingdom,

West Germany, France, and Japan. The elected directors are nominated by and act for groups of member-states. The chairman of the Executive Board is the Fund's managing director and is also the head of 1,400 staff members.

In 1974 a 22-member interim committee on the International Monetary System was established to advise the Board of Governors regarding the management and adaptation of this system. This body also makes recommendations to the Board on how to deal with sudden disturbances that threaten the system. The committee has now been transformed into the IMF Council that concerns itself with global liquidity and monetary adjustment problems.

The IMF's central function is to assist members in meeting short-term, balance-of-payments difficulties by permitting them to draw temporarily upon the Fund's reserves. An instrument in carrying this function has been the creation of new international reserves in 1968 through the establishment of special drawing rights (SDRs) over and above the drawing rights already available to Fund members. Since then the quotas have been increased substantially; 33 percent in 1976 and 1978, and a further 50 percent in 1980.[48]

A second major IMF responsibility has been to supervise the operation of the international exchange-rate system in order to maintain stability among the world currencies and prevent competitive devaluations. A second amendment to the Articles of Agreement, which entered into force in 1978, legalized the system of floating exchange arrangements and ended the existing system of par values based on gold.

Finally, a most essential function of the IMF is assistance to developing states. For this task it conducts a program of technical assistance—largely in the field of banking and fiscal problems—through its own staff and outside experts and through a training program organized by the IMF Institute in Washington. Stand-by credits are granted to developing states, but only if certain conditions are met such as the reduction of imports, the devaluation of currencies, and tightening domestic money supplies. A number of states have protested the imposition of what is called the IMF's standard package for the provision of loans and have called for a reform of its procedures.[49] However, it is doubtful whether the IMF will accede to these demands, and if at all, changes will come very slowly considering the current distribution of weighted votes. This also shows the tremendous importance of weighted votes for the Western industrialized states that are the strongest financial contributors to the IMF. On the other hand, the developing states also benefit from this arrangement because without the protection of the influence that the Western states enjoy through the voting system, the resources of the IMF in all likelihood would be much smaller, which is one important reason why all recent U.S. presidents, regardless of party, have resisted congressional efforts to limit U.S. contributions to international financial agencies.

The Andean Common Market:
Defeat of a Fragile Decision-Making Approach

After it had become clear in the second half of the 1960s that LAFTA was not living up to the expectations of most of the member-states, the dissatisfaction was especially pronounced among the Andean states (Colombia, Chile, Ecuador, Peru, Bolivia, and Venezuela). One aspect of this dissatisfaction was the growing sense among the Andean states that they were simply trading dependence upon extra-regional states for dependence upon the Big Three states of LAFTA—Brazil, Mexico, and Argentina. For example, during the 1960s, Brazil, Mexico, and Argentina enjoyed increasing proportions of intraregional trade, especially among manufactured products, and much of this was simply diverted trade from the smaller states of LAFTA that otherwise would have gone outside the region.

Interlocked with this growing sense of diverted dependence, was the sense that the costs and benefits of LAFTA integration were not being shared equally among all members.[50] With no controls on foreign investment or distribution of industrialization, the Big Three, already partially developed economies, were able to attract more capital investment and benefited more than the other members for the majority of industrial agreements.

In order to seek more rapid developmental gains and at the same time to counter Brazil's push for regional political leadership, the Andean states began to look for a new framework. The resulting Cartagena Treaty of 1969 establishing the Andean Common Market (ANCOM) represented a compromise among the Andean states regarding national development policies. Among the less-developed states, Bolivia, Ecuador, and Peru, the basis for development was perceived to be joint industrial planning. The prime movers of the Andean Pact, Chile and Colombia, however, focused upon the developmental stimulus of trade liberalization and pushed for swifter movement toward free trade in the region than within LAFTA. Working from a shared conception of regionalism as a developmental tool, the Cartagena signatories opted to include both positions in order to get ANCOM off the ground.

Organizationally, there are two main institutions within the Andean Group, the Commission and the Junta. The Commission consists of representatives from the member-states (one each) and it is charged with the key decision making for the group and the implementation of proposals. However, the power of the Commission is hampered by three provisos. First, the Commission, unlike the EC Commission, meets only three times a year and not continuously. Second, decision making is hampered by the voting rules. Although most decisions, including the annual budget, are approved by a two-thirds majority, some matters are subject to veto by any state. They include treaty amendments, the approval of regional development plans, and the acceleration of trade liberalization. Moreover, Bolivia and Ecuador can veto the free circulation of certain commodities of special interest to them, although they were supposed to move immediately to full trade.[51] Lastly, since the Commission has no independent grant of authority, decisions are not automatically binding upon the member-states but must be ratified and made a part of the legal code of each member.

The second institution, and the one that is most involved with both planning and executing policy within ANCOM, is the three-man Junta of technocrats, appointed by the Commission. It is the Junta, acting in the role of a secretariat, that formulates and proposes policies for the Commission. Moreover, the Junta carries out the decisions of the Commission and acts as a pressure group within the pact to stimulate regional cooperation.

Functionally, the Cartagena Treaty presented an almost perfect expression of the economic thought promoted by the U.N. Economic Commission for Latin America (ECLA). Regional development was based upon a three-pronged approach: trade liberalization, sectoral development programs, and control of private foreign investment. Unlike the negotiation approach taken by LAFTA, trade liberalization plans were written into the Cartagena Treaty. Regarding external trade, the Cartagena agreement called for the Andean states to reach agreement on a common minimum external tariff structure and it required a complete common external tariff structure to be gradually implemented by member states from 1977 to 1980. Regarding internal trade, the members were committed to automatic gradual reductions of most tariffs, with Bolivia and Ecuador granted possibilities for delays in implementation.

The second prong of the attack on dependence was the Sectoral Programs of Industrial Development (SPIDs). In order to take advantage of the potential size of the market, the Cartagena Treaty called for the rationalization of industrial planning on a region-wide basis.

The third prong of the attack on dependence was the decision concerning treatment of foreign capital, known as Decision 24, adopted by the Commission in December 1970 and clearly an example of a rule-creating decision. This was a policy designed to limit the impact of foreign private investment in national economies as well as to control existing foreign capital investments. The first broad element of Decision 24 was the classification of industries based upon the mixture of capital investment: a company with less than 51 percent investment by native capital was considered to be a foreign firm; a company with between 51 percent and 80 percent local capital and under local management control was considered mixed; and, firms with 80 percent or more local capital participation was considered to be a local firm.

The second and perhaps the most controversial aspect was the divestment requirement imposed on foreign capital. Foreign owned corporations were given 15 years in Chile, Colombia, and Peru, and 20 years in Bolivia and Ecuador to transfer capital holdings to local investors.[52]

The third aspect of Decision 24 was the limitations placed on new investments within the region. Outside of limited opportunities in industry, there was little opportunity for new investment in other sectors of the economy.

During the early years of its existence, ANCOM seemed to be a very successful IGO. By December 1971, Decision 24 had been accepted by all the member-states. Venezuela, which had participated in the ANCOM negotiations, finally joined the Pact in 1973. Lastly, agreement was reached on the first two SPIDs for the region, metal working and metallurgy (except automobiles) in August 1972[53] and in petrochemicals in September 1975.[54] However, the Chilean withdrawal almost immediately weakened the faith placed in ANCOM by the remaining members. The Protocol of Lima, issued after a summit meeting in November 1976, made changes throughout the ANCOM action program and as such can be characterized as another rule-creating decision. The target for full tariff-free regional trade was extended from 1985 until 1989 and the negotiation of the common external tariff was extended.

The Protocol also made sweeping changes that gutted many of the key provisions of Decision 24. Tourism and agro-industry in Bolivia and Ecuador (which with Chile had been the chief agitators for reform) were exempted from the divestiture provision. Levels of profit remittance were raised from 14 percent to 20 percent with the implication that each member could set it higher if they preferred.

Following the Protocol of Lima, integration within ANCOM continued to decline. The industrial development program for the automobile industry, which had been signed in June 1977, after three years of negotiations, was scuttled by Peru in only two months. Furthermore, the new deadlines for trade liberalization set in Lima in 1976 were extended even further at summit meetings in Arequipa in 1978, Cartagena in 1979, and Sochogota, Colombia, in 1981.

One important lesson can be learned from the decline of ANCOM from the heady days of the early 1970s. A fragile decision-making approach within the central institutions will only work properly if there is enthusiastic support for the integration experiment that a regional IGO has been commissioned to carry out. Once the original consensus of the member-states begins to crumble, the central decision-making process is likely to be fatally wounded. Part of the breakup of the consensus was due to changes in the regimes of the member-states. Indeed, only two member-states have experienced stable civilian governments since the Cartagena Treaty was signed. They are Colombia and Venezuela and they have been the strongest and most consistent advocates of salvaging the organization. On the other hand, the changes in the regimes in the remaining member-states with the consequent restructuring of national interests, have more than anything played havoc with the development of ANCOM as a viable regional integration scheme. In late

1976 Chile gave formal notice of withdrawal. The early successes of ANCOM came as a result of shared perceptions regarding dependence and development. With changeover in regimes came a break in this consensus, and changed interests of the member-states have led them away from the organizational structure and along different paths to development.

The Warsaw Treaty Organization (WTO)

In May 1955 the Soviet Union and its East European allies established the Warsaw Treaty Organization (WTO), also known as the Warsaw Pact, as a direct response to NATO and West Germany's membership in that organization. The basic legal provisions and institutions of WTO clearly mirror those of NATO. In the event of an attack on any of the WTO members, assistance to the victim of aggression is mandatory; however, the use of armed force as a means of aiding the attacked member-state or states is not obligatory.

Like NATO, the WTO has a dual structure of civilian and military institutions. The highest civilian organ is the Political Consultative Committee that coordinates all activities apart from purely military matters. It is composed of the first secretaries of the communist parties, heads of governments, and foreign and defense ministers of member-states. In 1977 the WTO established a permanent Committee of Foreign Ministers that is subordinate to the Consultative Committee and is concerned mainly with political consultation. Administrative support comes from a Secretariat under a Soviet director-general. All decisions in these bodies is by consensus.

The military structure of WTO is headed by the Committee of Defense Ministers. A joint command organization is required by the WTO treaty and the top echelon consists of a commander-in-chief and a military council. Meeting under the chairmanship of the commander, the council includes the chief-of-staff and permanent representatives from each of the allied armed forces. The positions of commander-in-chief and chief-of-staff have been invariably Soviet officers; not surprisingly, the headquarters of WTO is in Moscow.

The maverick of WTO has been Romania. It refused to participate with other WTO forces in the occupation of Czechoslovakia in 1968; it insisted during the reorganization of 1969 on the relaxation of the tight control over WTO exercised by the Soviet government and obtained some concessions; and it advocates the concurrent dissolution of WTO and NATO.[55]

Decision Making in NATO: France's Withdrawal from NATO's Military Structure[56]

The highest organ of NATO is the Council, which meets twice a year on the ministerial level, but is in permanent session on the ambassadorial level.

In the latter case, the heads of the member-states' permanent diplomatic missions to NATO represent their governments. A number of committees support and prepare the work of the Council. They include the committees dealing with defense planning, political affairs, economic affairs, and the budget. In some cases, the Council itself may sit as the Defense Planning Committee (DPC).

Decisions in the Council require unanimity. Consensus is of course easy when noncontroversial issues come before the Council, but the situation can become very difficult when the Council has to face complex problems that might lead to a breakup of the alliance. This was the case when France expressed the desire to sever its ties with NATO's military organization. This organization is headed by the Military Staff that prepares plans and supervises policy implementation. Three major commands covering the North Atlantic Treaty area form the framework through which, in the event of hostilities, the military operations would be carried out. Figure 2.4 (in Chapter 2) provides an illustration of NATO's civil and military structure.

At his first press conference after his reelection to a second term as president of France, General Charles de Gaulle reiterated his intention to break with the obsolete forms of NATO. Two weeks later he sent handwritten messages to U.S. President Lyndon Johnson, U.K. Prime Minister Harold Wilson, West German Chancellor Ludwig Erhard, and Italian President Giuseppe Saragat in which he detailed reasons for severing all French ties with NATO's military organization. He added, however, that unless in the coming three years events were to change the basic facts underlying East-West relations, France would in 1969 and beyond, be determined to fight on the side of her allies in the event one of them should be the object of an unprovoked aggression. De Gaulle also referred to the infringement on French sovereignty by the presence of NATO's military organization. In reply, Johnson stated the American belief that something more than a firm commitment was needed to achieve effective deterrence and maintain peace in the North Atlantic area. Johnson, therefore, endorsed the alliance's collective efforts to assure its members' security and expressed bewilderment over de Gaulle's claim of NATO's infringement on French sovereignty. The next day the French Foreign Ministry delivered memoranda to the other 14 governments of the Atlantic alliance informing them of France's simultaneous decision to withdraw from the integrated commands and to have the headquarters of these commands removed from French territory. It is worth noting that these communications were sent to the respective states' ambassadors to France and not to their permanent representatives to the NATO Council. The memoranda to Canada, the United States, and West Germany included a text referring to individual bilateral arrangements or agreements concluded to implement NATO military plans.

The United States, in an aide-mémoire, acknowledged the French message and requested details and clarification. In a second aide-mémoire of March 29, 1966, the French government set the dates for the implementation of its decisions and offered to discuss, either bilaterally or multilaterally, the many problems they entailed. The termination of the assignment of French military personnel to allied commands was to be effective on July 1, 1966. Excepted were the French participants in the courses at the NATO Defense College, who would remain until the end of the current session, July 23, 1966. The allied commands in France were to complete their transfer by April 1, 1967, and the United States and Canada were asked to complete the evacuation of their various installations by the same date.

The reaction at NATO's Paris headquarters at the Porte Dauphine to the French withdrawal was one of dismay; it was barely conceivable that de Gaulle would put such an abrupt end to so many agreements. There existed also a bit of confusion as to the appropriateness of a response by the North Atlantic Council. The Council, which had come to rely on NATO Secretary-General Manlio Brosio's preparation and coordination of its operations, suddenly found itself adrift: the secretary-general was convinced that he and the Staff/Secretariat should not become involved in an affair between alliance members. Brosio perceived himself as the secretary-general of the whole organization, and as such it would not be appropriate for him to defend any one faction no matter how dominant. Brosio felt that if he were to exercise the function of the chairman of any of its bodies, every member-state had a right to be present: none could be excluded.

André de Staercke, still Belgian permanent representative and doyen of the NATO diplomatic corps, immediately stepped forward to fill the diplomatic gap left by Brosio's retreat to the sidelines. De Staercke offered to convene the 14 NATO representatives and sit as chairman. The U.S. representative approved, as he was quite happy to have someone else take the initiative and bear the criticism, if any should arise. Thus, the fourteen, or *les quatorze* as they were known in Paris, meeting sometimes in de Staercke's apartment, went to work on a statement of their common commitment to NATO. In ten days of continuous consultations, starting with a British draft, they hammered out a simple declaration of their belief in the essentiality of NATO and its military organization to the security of their countries, and of their determination to continue in the joint enterprise. This declaration, a programmatic and symbolic decision, was officially agreed to by the 14 governments and was released simultaneously in each of their capitals. It was not, however, a NATO document.

On March 16, Brosio accepted a strictly limited mandate from the full 15-member NATO Council, which instructed him to conduct a study of the implications of the French withdrawal for the alliance. His staff quickly identified no fewer than 50 problems brought about by the withdrawal. Because of the size of the task, the bulk of the work regarding the French action was handled directly among the 14 delegations. In 1966 the United States had a network of more than 25 bases and over 750,000 tons of equipment on French territory. This was the result of five bilateral accords, which France denounced, as it did those with Canada, in its aide-mémoire of March 10. Necessarily then, the United States alone faced a multitude of problems in complying with the French request, which included substantial financial claims against the French government for the expenses incurred in moving! Here especially, U.S. domestic political factors influenced the bilateral negotiations and caused them to drag on.

De Staercke energetically chaired meetings of the fourteen when they collectively considered the issues posed by the French withdrawal. Their discussions included such topics as the determination of liability for the termination of contracts with French firms and nationals, the cost of moving supplies and equipment, and reparations to NATO for the jointly financed permanent facilities—infrastructure, buildings and other nonmovable improvements. The fourteen continued their work until the early 1970s, when the crisis atmosphere finally subsided. Brosio, by his own choice, was excluded from a good part of the intense activity of *les quatorze*. Reports on their proceedings would be relayed informally to the secretary-general, however.

The central questions faced by the alliance concerned the possible removal of NATO's civilian headquarters and the transfer and reorganization of its military structure. The decisions affecting the military organization, examples of the operational type, were relatively easy to make. The first casualty was the U.S.-U.K.-France standing group, which was a Washington link of the military committee that had not proved very effective. It was summarily abolished. The military committee itself was moved to the alliance's European headquarters, and the fourteen also agreed to give the military committee the planning functions previously assigned to the standing group and attached to it an international military staff for that purpose. The foreign ministers ratified these decisions at a meeting the day before the regularly scheduled ministerial session of the Council in Brussels in June. The implications of the French withdrawal constituted the main subject of the Ministerial Council, although relations with the East, West German security, disarmament, and Cyprus were also reviewed.

The more difficult problems facing the fourteen involved the removal and the relocation of the new headquaters of the European Command (SHAPE). De Gaulle's letter and the French memoranda gave the impression that the status of NATO in Paris would be unaffected. Yet when the fourteen assembled, it was one of the first questions to come under study. Smaller member states like Greece, Portugal, and, most of all, Denmark wanted to encourage France to remain active in the alliance, partly to counterbalance the ever-growing strength of the other major continental power, the Federal

Republic of Germany. To varying degrees, therefore, they favored staying in Paris. Consultations were carried on among the other members to see whether or not a consensus could be obtained. The British definitely wanted to leave France, and there was some speculation that NATO would move back to its original headquarters in London. The Belgians were hesitant to endanger their traditional amity with France, and the West Germans were reluctant to cool the Franco-German rapprochement. The position of the U.S. government was that as long as NATO could not be certain that France would support the allies in the event of hostilities, it would be unwise to run the risk of having its communication lines cut off in a crisis.

Brosio felt that it was important to restrict the French break to NATO's military arm in order to salvage the NATO Ministerial Council's usefulness in political consultation. Then later, when de Gaulle would be gone, defense cooperation could perhaps be reinstituted. It was understood all along that de Gaulle did not intend to sever completely France's relationship with the alliance. Brosio emphasized this fact, pointing to the confirming evidence of French public opinion in bolstering a conciliatory attitude among the four-teen. The tense nature of the situation reinforced his instinct and inclination for patient, quiet, behind-the-scenes diplomacy. Therefore Brosio tried to suppress any tendency to dramatize the crisis.

The French withdrawal not only produced changes in NATO's military structure but also led to adaptations in the political sphere. In response to the French action, the commitment of the United States to the alliance remained firm. U.S. troops would be maintained in Europe and the U.S. nuclear deterrent would continue to guarantee Western Europe's security. At the same time, the attitude of the United States toward de Gaulle's invitation to leave France had been restrained: the Americans would leave quietly, efficiently, and ahead of time, though without formally accepting French deadlines. Instructions were issued that de Gaulle was to be treated with the utmost respect; no attacks on him by U.S. officials would be tol-erated. The French also showed a desire to make accommodations with their allies in NATO.

At the ministerial meeting of 1966, both member-states welcomed a proposal by Belgian Foreign Minister Pierre Harmel to chart the future course of the alliance in light of the changing international political environment. Officially, as reported in the communique, the ministers agreed "to undertake a broad analysis of international developments since the signing of the North Atlantic Treaty in 1949," in order "to determine the influence of such de-velopments on the Alliance and to identify the tasks which lie before it in order to strengthen the Alliance as a factor for durable peace." The United States and the other allies hoped that this exercise, later dubbed the Harmel Report, would serve as a means whereby France might be drawn back into the mainstream of the alliance. The French likewise desired an agreement on a set of political principles as a basis on which future common action by NATO might be prepared.

De Gaulle's trip to the Soviet Union in 1966 had revealed a new dimension in French foreign policy, and the failure of the French to contribute adequately during the drafting sessions led to uncertainty as to the future direction of French policy. During the consultation between the Americans and the French over wording and punctuation, the secretary-general and other representatives found themselves removed from the process. But eventually, everyone found the document acceptable, and the Report on the Future Tasks of the Alliance (or Harmel Report) was unanimously approved at the ministerial meeting of December 1967, the first to be held in the new headquarters near Brussels.

The major aim of the report—to engage France in redefining the alliance's political assumptions—had been accomplished. The report endorsed greater consultation among NATO's members, and emphasized the continuing relevance of the alliance's twin political and military functions and stressed NATO's ability to adapt to changing conditions. Finally, the report defined two specific tasks for the alliance, one military and the other political. In the military realm, it noted the vital need to defend the exposed areas of the alliance, particularly the Mediterranean, where events like the Six-Day (Arab-Israeli) War of June 1967 had led to an expansion of Soviet activity. Politically, the report assigned top priority to the formulation of proposals for reducing tension between East and West. The keynotes of the report—defense and detente—have remained the main themes of the alliance well into the 1980s. The adoption of the Harmel Report also marked the disappearance of the possibility of a total French withdrawal from the organization, and afterwards Brosio was once more confident that NATO could proceed with its principal mission without debilitating internal dissension. This lasted until the Reagan Administration's negative policy toward East-West trade, and especially toward the West's helping the Soviet Union finance a major natural gas pipeline to Western Europe.

The International Labor Organization (ILO): Unusual Decision Making

The International Labor Organization (ILO) is set apart from other IGOs because, although its members are nation-states, their representatives in the major organs of the ILO are not only government officials, but also individuals representing the views of employers and workers.

The ILO is one of the oldest IGOs; it was established in April 1919 as an autonomous organization associated with the League of Nations. In 1946 it became associated with the United Nations as a specialized agency.

Major goals of the ILO include full employment, raising the standard of living, the assurance of proper earnings and working conditions, the provision of adequate training facilities, effective recognition of the right of collective bargaining, and appropriate social security measures.[57]

The General Conference is the top-level plenary organ of the ILO. Each member-state is represented by two government delegates, one employers' delegate and one workers' delegate. In the choice of employers' and workers' delegates, the member governments are obligated to consult "with the industrial organizations, if such organizations exist, as the case may be, in their respective countries."[58] Each delegate has one individual vote. Most of the decisions of the Conference deal with setting standards for the improvement of working conditions and require a two-thirds vote for adoption. The decisions are in the form of draft conventions and recommendations. They fall into the category of rule-creating decisions, but they are not binding on the member-states, but are expected to be ratified by the approximately 130 member governments for incorporation into their national law. While France and Belgium, for example, have ratified more than 70 of these international instruments, the United States, a member of the ILO since 1934, has ratified only seven.

Below the Conference is an organ of limited membership, the Governing Body, whose composition also follows the tripartite pattern. It consists of 24 government officials, 12 employers' and 12 workers' representatives. Ten of the government representatives are required to be from the states of "chief industrial importance" and the employers' and workers' representatives are to be "elected respectively by the employers' delegates and workers' delegates to the Conference.[59] The functions of the Governing Body include the selection of the director-general of the International Labor Office (the Secretariat of the ILO) and the supervision of this organ and the many subsidiary committees and commissions of the ILO. The staff of the labor office is large and numbers above 3,000.

On November 5, 1975, then Secretary of State Henry Kissinger notified the ILO of the United States' intention to withdraw its membership, setting out "four matters of fundamental concern" that were the main—but not the only—reasons for leaving the Organization: 1) the erosion of tripartite representation, 2) selective concern for human rights, 3) disregard of due process, and 4) the increasing politicization of the Organization.[60]

At least four other concerns were apparently in the minds of government, labor, and management representatives (the tripartite character of the ILO): 5) declining ILO interest in the development of technical standards through conventions and recommendations; 6) excessive use of flexibility devices that permit developing countries and others to avoid the full obligations of conventions; 7) lack of connection between ILO technical cooperation programs and the supervision and enforcement of labor standards; and 8) misdirection or inappropriateness of International Labor Office research and publications.

Despite a two-year effort by both the United States and the ILO to change the things the United States did not like, the United States decided on November 5, 1977, to allow its withdrawal to take effect. Thus on that date it ceased to be a member of the ILO.

This step was significant because actual withdrawal from the United Nations or one of its specialized agencies or activities weakens the notion of universality and/or equality of membership that is one of the cornerstones of the present political configuration of world politics. It also signified, in a more fundamental sense, that one of the major supporters of international organizations—the United States—was becoming disenchanted with the benefits that such support presumably was to bring! Without the political and financial sustenance of the United States, many international organizations would be hard pressed to continue the range and variety of their programs.

Following the withdrawal, President Jimmy Carter established a cabinet-level committee to monitor developments and to advise him on ILO matters. Reflecting the ILO's tripartite structure, the AFL-CIO, the U.S. Council of the International Chamber of Commerce, and U.S. government representatives all were given an equal voice on the committee.

An underlying condition that set the stage for this development was the fact that the initial dominance in the ILO of industrial states with market economies, had given way to a more varied membership, with important parts being played by the centrally planned economies of Eastern Europe, many newly independent states, and the Third World in general.[61] In fact, Secretary Kissinger had asserted that the United States could not accept a growing tendency for workers' and employers' groups to fall under the domination of governments.

Specifically, in 1970 the new ILO Director-General Wilfred Jenks of the United Kingdom, as one of his first official acts, appointed a Soviet Assistant Director-General. The hostile reaction of the AFL-CIO, which has a very strong anticommunist tradition, led the U.S. Congress to suspend temporarily the payment of the U.S. contribution to the Organization. To make matters worse, in 1975, the ILO granted observer status to the Palestine Liberation Organization (PLO), and this created widespread resentment in the United States.

Nonetheless, there was great uneasiness among some informed sectors of the American public that by withdrawing from the ILO, the United States would be sacrificing the necessary political leverage needed to bring about the reforms or other changes that it desired. In other words, working from within would be better than simply walking away. Furthermore, examples could be found where the system of tripartite voting had indeed benefitted U.S. interests, even though one of the United States' major complaints was that the ILO reports and complaints procedures were biased against the Western industrial states, with especially the socialist states of the Soviet bloc being given less intensive scrutiny, even to the point of averting the ILO's eyes to blatant violations of workers' rights. The report of the private, nonpartisan Commission to Study the Organization of Peace put this question of politicization in the following way:

> Since ILO voting rights extend beyond governments, empowering non-government delegates to vote on issues normally reserved to governments, the ILO should be even more careful than the other Specialized Agencies to avoid involvment [sic] in issues of international politics unrelated to ILO's substantive work. Assuming that a particular political issue is extraneous or tangential to the central core of ILO's mandate, there is even less reason for workers' or employers' delegates to become involved than there is for governments to seek to raise such issues in an ILO forum. When such issues are raised, however, in some circumstances workers' and employers' delegates may be able to exercise greater freedom of action than governments. In such a case, tripartism, fortified by the new secret ballot rule, can help to insulate the ILO from excessively political use.[62]

As an example, in the 1978 General Conference, a Syrian resolution condemning Israel received the support of a bare majority of the governments represented at the Conference (63 out of 125 states), but failed of adoption because a number of employers' and workers' delegates failed to vote with their governments in favor of the resolution. From the U.S. viewpoint, the Syrian resolution would not have been proper for General Conference adoption, but, as it happened, its defeat would not have occurred were it not for the independent vote exercised by workers' and employers' delegates.[63] The resolution had sought to extend a 1974 resolution that had condemned Israel without any investigation of the facts. Consequently, a new mechanism to eliminate resolutions representing such violations of due process was negotiated by Western and Third World governments, thus making the fact-finding aspect of the ILO's functions more balanced.

Another reform was to strengthen the tripartite decision-making system itself. For example, as mentioned above, a new General-Conference, secret-ballot procedure was instituted over the strong resistance of the Soviet Union. By instituting a secret ballot, the employers' and workers' respresentatives are encouraged to vote their consciences without fear of governmental recrimination.

In the area of human rights, the ILO began applying its human-rights machinery to Eastern Europe. In November 1978, the ILO Governing Body censured Czechoslovakia for illegally firing dissidents from their jobs, an action exemplifying rule-supervisory decisions. By 1980 it was examining worker complaints against the Soviet Union and Poland for violating trade union rights. By following the ILO procedures for handling complaints of workers against their governments, what would otherwise have been a do-mestic quarrel between a government and its employers' or workers' organ-izations becomes internationalized, thus bringing to bear the weight of international public opinion. Without a doubt, the strong support of the Western trade unions in support of the Polish Solidarity trade union gave the indigenous movement much more international significance.[64]

Further evidence that the ILO meetings had become less politicized (that is, less anti-Western), came during the speech of the Egyptian Labor Minister in the 1979 conference, when those Arab representatives that walked out were joined only by the communist delegates; other Third World represen-tatives refused to engage in an anti-Egyptian demonstration. The ILO also sent two missions to investigate the working conditions of the Palestinians in the Israeli-occupied territories, and in view of the United States the reports were well-balanced and accepted by both Arabs and Israelis at the 1978 and 1979 General Conferences, with the result that no political resolutions were offered on this subject.[65]

Thus, the stage was set for the United States' return, which came in February 1980, when the cabinet-level committee recommended such action to President Carter. The rationale that proved persuasive was that although withdrawal may have promoted reforms, continuing to remain outside the ILO would not have yielded additional benefits to the United States. Those ILO members who worked to achieve the gains that were made would have felt disillusioned if the United States had failed to return. Also, the United States' lead in human rights issues would have been sorely missed, even though the Western group of members had become more cohesive and ef-fective.

Specific reasons for rejoining were:

1. The opportunity to participate in and to influence the formation of interna-tional labor standards, which directly affect labor codes in developing countries;

2. The opportunity to participate in and to influence voluntary agreements such as codes of conduct for multinational enterprises, the ILO version of which is regarded by United States labor and business as the most constructive yet developed;

3. A framework in which the United States labor movement and business com-munity can be in contact with their counterpart organizations throughout the world;

4. Influence over ILO execution of United Nations Development Program (UNDP) projects, totaling about $40 million in 1980;

5. Participation in the United Nations system's most effective mechanism for promoting the human rights of workers; and

6. Participation in the ILO's studies of development, which pioneered the basic human needs approach to development and directly influenced World Bank and AID programs.

This experience of withdrawal rested on such a unique organizational structure and political circumstances, that it is difficult to draw the conclusion that the interests of the United States are better served by taking this unusual step. Attempts by the United States to withhold funds from international organizations in order to exert political pressure are becoming more common, with such resolutions increasingly showing up on the agenda of both houses of the U.S. Congress. Usually the administration opposes such resolutions because to allow the Congress to make such determinations leaves open too many opportunities for a consistent U.S. policy toward the international organization at issue to become a casualty of domestic politics—especially in an election year. Nonetheless, such congressional pressure on the administration has served to help the government in its negotiations with other governments in trying to bring about reforms in those international organizations in which the United States is a member.

From the decision- and policy-making perspective the withdrawal of the United States set in motion an informal review of decision and policy outcomes—the appointment of the Soviet Assistant Director-General, the granting of observer status to the PLO, and the catalog of Kissinger complaints enumerated earlier—which produced policy changes that induced not only the United States to return to ILO membership, but may have improved the task performance of the organization in general. This case then is an example of the benefit of evaluating the formulation of policies and the effects they may have on member-states and on the execution of the manifold functions of the ILO.

Disenchantment of Member-States with IGO Performance: The East African Community (EAC)

In contrast to the ANCOM case depicting a gradually weakening decision-making process, this case deals with the complete disintegration of a regional IGO whose performance was viewed by some of its members as increasingly unacceptable and in fact harmful to national interests. This is the case of the East African Community (EAC). The three member states—Kenya, Uganda, and Tanzania—inherited an extensive integrative framework when they gained independence from Great Britain in the early 1960s. After an initial flurry of activity directed at moving from shared services to political amalgamation immediately after independence, the East African experience became a long slow process of movement toward total disintegration, culminating, 15 years after independence in complete disarray with two member-states, Uganda and Tanzania, engaged in full-scale war and the shared borders of all three states virtually closed.

The history of integration in East Africa dates back to the turn of the twentieth century.[66] Although the colonies of Kenya and Uganda were run rather autonomously through the colonial office, joint services were established early on. In 1902, rail service between Kenya and Uganda was placed under a common authority. A joint currency for the two colonies was established in 1905, and a postal union in 1911. Finally, in 1917, a customs union was formed between Kenya and Uganda. In the 1920s and 1930s, Tanganyika was gradually merged into the common services network. It joined the customs union in 1923, and in 1933 Tanganyika, the forerunner of Tanzania, became part of the postal union.[67]

Following World War II, the British government decided to give the various common services a central governing organization. This decision resulted in the establishment in January 1948 of the East African High Commission, consisting of the governors of the three colonies as the executive authority for all the common services. Additionally, a central legislature was planned that would consist of representatives from the three colonies, as well as a regional customs and excise department to administer the customs union and a regional railways and harbors administration. Importantly, for the first time, the common services were placed under a single legal umbrella. With independence approaching, the London Conference of June 1961 attended by representatives of the three colonies and Great Britain, changed both the name and the structure of the colonial arrangements and the East African Common Services Organization (EACSO) was formed. The High Commission was replaced by the High Authority, which included, initially, the colonial governors of the three states, who were replaced by the heads of state as each of the three members became independent. A 45-member central legislative assembly, to decide on the budget and other legal aspects of EACSO authority, was also established,[68] and met initially in May 1962.[69]

The reorganization of the Common Services into EACSO reflects more than mere disgruntlement over the mangement by the British Colonial Office and the desire of soon-to-become independent states to manage their own affairs. The creation of EACSO reflects as well the movement for the creation of a political federation within the region. As early as 1959, Julius K. Nyerere of Tanganyika endorsed the East African High Commission as a basis for the political federation of the region following independence. In March 1961, the political parties in Kenya expressed approval of the idea of federation of the three colonies and in August 1961 established a special committee in the legislative council to begin studying the problems of federation.[70]

In 1963 the idea of an East African Federation gained momentum and in June 1963 the heads of state of the three East African states involved agreed in Nairobi to establish such a federation by the end of that year. However, no consensus was possible on the details of this new federation. Although Kenya and Tanganyika agreed on the necessity of a federal foreign policy and federal citizenship rather than national foreign policies and national citizenships in the federation, Uganda adamantly opposed both these propositions and "was not prepared to lose its identity as a sovereign member of the international community and was particularly anxious to retain its separate representation in the United Nations."[71] Other intractable problems were the location of the capital and the division of powers, both between the two houses of parliament that were envisioned and between the federation and the constituent states.[72]

With federation having become a dead issue, interest turned toward the creation of an IGO to handle economic integration. To move ahead with this concept, there was a need to address the concrete issue of economic imbalance within the region. This was done during a meeting in Kampala, Uganda in May 1964. Since colonial days, Kenya had been the leading economic power within the region, enjoying greater industrialization than the other two states and a near constant trade surplus with its partners. The agreement reached at Kampala specified that new industries would henceforth be allocated among the three states at a ratio of five for Tanzania, two for Uganda, and one for Kenya[73] in an effort to redress the imbalanced development. Additionally, the agreement called for measures to adjust trade imbalances among the three.[74] Agreement on the economic restructuring of the region, however, proved to be as ephemeral as federation. Kenya withdrew its support for allocation when local investors announced plans to build an automobile plant similar to one that had been allocated to Tanzania. In the end, Kenya never ratified the Kampala Agreement and it was never implemented in the region.[75]

Faced with increasing disintegration, the heads of state again met in Mombassa in September 1965. After Kenya made a veiled threat to pull out of EACSO, the other member-states went along with the Kenyan suggestion to revamp the current common services arrangement, and a nine-man commission was appointed to study the economic and political problems of the region.[76] The report was finally delivered to the three heads of state and laid the basis for the East African Community (EAC) that was inaugurated in December 1967.[77]

Under the EAC the services generating their own operating funds such as the railways and harbors administration, the post and telecommunications administration, and East African Airways were converted into corporations owned by the Community. Furthermore, the headquarters of the EAC was decentralized. Headquarters for the airline and the rail corporation remained in Nairobi. The harbors corporation was moved to Dar-es-Salaam and the post and telecommunications corporation to Kampala. The headquarters of the Community itself, including the customs union and the Common Market, was established in Arusha, Tanzania.

The new EAC also made provisions for more balanced regional development through two new provisions, the East African Development Bank and the transfer tax system. Rather than attempting to allocate new industries, the Bank was to be a means of providing incentives for new investment in Tanzania and Uganda.

The transfer tax system was created to correct the trade imbalances among the three states. From immediately after independence until the eventual collapse of the Community, Kenya maintained a massive trade surplus with the other two member-states. The transfer tax system allowed deficit states (Tanzania and Uganda) to impose taxes on goods imported from surplus states that they either already produced or were expecting to produce within three months. The taxes were seen as a temporary measure to protect infant industries and were to be phased out within 15 years from the inception of the EAC.[78]

Soon after the EAC and its complex organizational and decision-making framework had been put into effect, disintegrative strains began to reemerge in East Africa. In July 1970 the East African University was dismembered and separate universities were established in each of the member-states.[79] Very severe strains were placed upon the Community after the coup in Uganda in January 1971, when Idi Amin ousted Prime Minister Milton Obote. Following the coup, President Nyerere announced that Tanzania would not recognize the new regime.[80]

In 1971 Uganda closed its border with Tanzania and, in response, Tanzania refused entry to Ugandans who were employed by the EAC offices in Arusha and Dar-es-Salaam.[81] Things went from bad to worse during the 1970s. In 1977 Tanzania permanently closed its border with Kenya.[82] The curtain fell on the EAC in June 1977, when Kenya announced its formal withdrawal from the EAC and recalled its personnel from Arusha. Uganda and Tanzania attempted to keep the Community alive, but in August, they announced that they, too, were withdrawing personnel.[83] In January 1978 the three ex-partners appointed Victor Umbricht, a U.N. official, to act as the arbitrator in the division of assets of the defunct Community.[84]

As a writer in the *New York Times* observed early in 1968, after the creation of the EAC, "With their headstart, it was assumed that Kenya, Tanzania, and Uganda would lead Africa in the process of unification."[85] The failure to achieve a federation in the period following independence is a crucial element in understanding the disintegrative story of East Africa because it set into motion forces that would lead to the eventual collapse of East African regionalism in the late 1970s.

A major problem that the three states were never able to come to grips with was the question of correcting the asymmetric interdependence that existed among the three. Uganda and Tanzania, the two deficit states, viewed Kenya as exploiting the common services and the Community for its own benefit and practicing subimperialism in the region. Kenya, on the other hand, felt that as the most propserous of the three states, it was forced to carry a disproportionate burden in the Community.[86]

Furthermore, efforts to correct the asymmmetry within the Community were counter productive. Import quotas put up by Tanzania and Uganda actually served to divert trade away from the region in the mid-1960s, rather than correct structural imbalances in regional imports and exports.[87] The transfer tax system, which was put into place under the Treaty for Cooperation did not promote rational industrial planning in the region. "Rather," as John Ravenhill remarks, "the tax merely encouraged deficit countries to duplicate those industrial plants that were already established in Kenya."[88] As shown in Figure 4.2, the transfer tax system had little or no effect on the balance of trade in the region. In fact, the Kenyan surplus in intraregional trade increased substantially. Tanzania was able to maintain the level of its

FIGURE 4.2

Intraregional Trade Surplus/Deficit, 1964–76

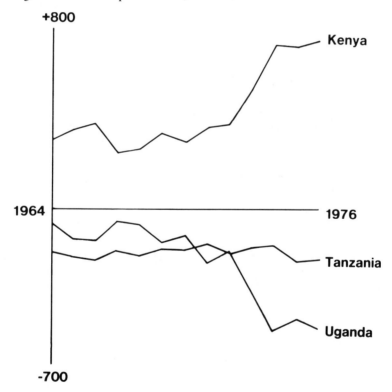

Source: Derived from John Ravenhill, "The Theory and Practice of Regional Integration in East Africa," in Christian P. Potholm and Richard A. Fredland, eds., *Integration and Disintegration in East Africa* (Lanham, MD: University Press of America, 1980), pp. 58-9.

modest deficit, but Uganda's deficit became worse over time, partly because of the slow economic collapse of the Amin government.

Finally, the major program to correct imbalances, the decentralization of Community headquarters, moving the majority of offices from Nairobi to Kampala and Dar-es-Salaam, had little positive effect upon the imbalances in the region. In the long run, this deconsolidation, like other measures, was counterproductive. It contributed to the ease with which the common services were renationalized in the 1970s.

The case of East Africa demonstrates that under certain conditions-nation-states decide to disengage from a network of regional cooperation embodied in an IGO and terminate its existence. Apart from perceptions of unequal cost and benefits, different economic and foreign policy perspectives play important roles. Soon after independence, the three East African states began to approach common problems, especially the transcendant problem of economic asymmetry, from divergent outlooks. Where Kenyan linkages were drawn to the more developed states of Western Europe, the Commonwealth, and the United States, and the development of an economy linked with the industrial West, Tanzanian linkages followed ideological trails to the more radical states of Southern Africa, such as Zambia and Mozambique and to the PRC and members of the Soviet bloc. Uganda's problems arose from serious domestic controversies and conflicts that aggravated the economic difficulties arising from the economic asymmetries existing in the region. All these divergencies resulted in regional conflict rather than regional cooperation in East Africa. As Raymond Copson remarked, "regional cooperation in East Africa became the victim of conflict rather than a force to limit conflict."[89]

It is interesting to note that in the East African economic integration experiment intensive efforts were made from 1963 to 1965 to evaluate the impact of the policies developed by the East African leaders. The best example is the Kampala meeting in 1969 which attempted to find viable solutions to the problem of unequal cost and benefits for the three member-states. However, the tax transfer system that was devised in Kampala to remedy the evolving disparities did not achieve its intended goal and a few years later political forces motivated by narrow nationalism, suspicion, and envy destroyed the regional IGO.

NOTES

1. David Easton, *A Framework for Political Analysis* (Englewood Cliffs, N.J.: Prentice-Hall, 1965). Other input-output models of decision making placing special emphasis on cybernetics are also useful.

2. Quoted in D. W. Bowett, *The Law of International Institutions* (New York: Praeger, 1963), p. 326.

3. Articles 1, 5, 15, 16 of the Covenant.

4. Bowett, op. cit., p. 327.

5. Ibid.

6. Articles 148 (2) EEC Treaty, 118 (2) EURATOM Treaty, and 28 (4) ECSC Treaty as amended.

7. Grenville Clark and Louis B. Sohn, *World Peace Through World Law*, 2nd revised ed. (Cambridge, Mass.: Harvard University Press, 1960), pp. 20–23, 25–31.

8. See Robert W. Cox and Harold K. Jacobson, *The Anatomy of Influence* (New Haven, Conn.: Yale University Press, 1973), p. 12.

9. For more details, see ibid., pp. 9–11.

10. See Philippe C. Schmitter, "Three Neo-Functional Hypotheses About International Integration," *International Organization* 23 (1969).

11. Charles A. Duffy and Werner J. Feld, "Wither Regional Integration Theory?" in Werner J. Feld and Gavin Boyd, *Comparative Regional Systems* (New York: Pergamon Press, 1980), pp. 497–522.

12. Leon N. Lindberg and Stuart A. Scheingold, *Europe's Would-Be Polity* (Englewood Cliffs, N.J.: Prentice-Hall, 1970), pp. 68–70.

13. Ibid., p. 71, Table 3.1.

14. John Worrall, "UN Watch on Environment Gets Lonelier," *The Christian Science Monitor*, January 12, 1982, p. 5.

15. Thomas G. Weiss and Robert S. Jordan, *The World Food Conference and Global Problem Solving* (New York: Praeger, 1976), p. 4.

16. For a review of the somewhat tortured progress of the negotiations between North and South, see Robert S. Jordan, "Why an NIEO: The View From the Third World," in *The Emerging International Economic Order: Dynamic Processes, Constraints and Opportunities*, eds. Harold K. Jacobson and Dusan Sidjanski (Beverly Hills, Calif.: Sage, 1982). See also George A. Codding, "Influence in International Conferences," *International Organization* 35 (Autumn 1981).

17. John P. Renninger with James Zech, *The 11th Special Session and the Future of Global Negotiations*, Policy and Efficacy Studies No. 5 (New York: United Nations Institute for Training and Research, 1981), p. 3.

18. Regarding the action by GATT's Director-General Mr. Wyndham White at the end of the Kennedy Round negotiations, see Feld, *The European Community in World Affairs*, op. cit., p. 184.

19. For a discussion of a package deal, attempt at a single negotiating text, and consensus, see Mohamed El Baradei and Chloe Garvin, *Crowded Agendas, Crowded Rooms: Institutional Arrangements at UNCLOS III: Some Lessons in Global Negotiations*, Policy and Efficacy Studies No. 3 (New York: United Nations Institute for Training and Research, 1981).

20. For somewhat similar definitions see Thomas Hovet, Jr., *Bloc Voting in the United Nations* (Cambridge, Mass.: Harvard University Press, 1960), p. 31 and Jack C. Plano and Robert E. Riggs, *Forging World Order* (New York: Macmillan, 1967), p. 148. See also Weiss and Jordan, op. cit., p. 27ff. for a discussion of bloc voting definitions in U.N. conferences; for a discussion of caucusing within conferences, see ibid., p. 110ff.

21. For a discussion of the role of groups, see Johan Kaufmann, *United Nations Decision Making* (Rockville, Md.: Sijthoff and Noordhoff, 1980), p. 87ff.

22. Jack E. Vincent, "Predicting Voting Patterns in the General Assembly," *American Political Science Review* 65 (June 1971), pp. 471–95; "National Attributes as Predictors of Delegate Attitudes at the United Nations", *American Political Science Review* 62 (September 1968), pp. 916–32; "An Application of Attribute Theory to General Assembly Voting Patterns, and Some

Implications," *International Organization* 26 (Summer 1972), pp. 551–82. We discuss the general tendencies of a state toward international organization in Chapter 1 of this text.

23. See Joel Larus, ed., *From Collective Security to Preventive Diplomacy* (New York: Wiley, 1965), p. 490ff. for a discussion of the state of affairs toward financing U.N. peacekeeping as a result of the Congo crisis.

24. See for example David Nachmias, *Public Policy Evaluation* (New York: St. Martin's Press, 1979).

25. This discussion leans on the conceptualizations developed by James D. Slack, "The Cross-National Analysis of Implementation Effectiveness," paper presented at the 1979 Annual Meeting of the Southern Political Science Association, Gatlinburg, Tenn., November 1–3, 1973.

26. Kaufmann, op. cit., discusses many of these questions.

27. See Inis L. Claude, Jr., *Swords Into Plowshares*, 4th ed. (New York: Random House, 1971), p. 143 and Stephen Goodspeed, *The Nature and Function of International Organization*, 2nd ed. (New York: Oxford University Press, 1967), pp. 148–49. For a general discussion, see Sydney D. Bailey, *Voting in the Security Council* (Bloomington, Ind.: Indiana University Press, 1969). On Security Council leadership and procedures, see Davidson Nicol, ed., *Paths to Peace: The U.N. Security Council and Its Presidency* (New York: Pergamon Press, 1981), especially the chapter by Sir Colin Crowe, "Some Observations on the Operation of the Security Council Including the Use of the Veto."

28. For details see Goodspeed, op. cit., p. 149.

29. Ibid.

30. Claude, op. cit., p. 143. See also Leon Gordenker, *The U.N. Secretary-General and the Maintenance of Peace* (New York: Columbia University Press, 1967), especially Part Four.

31. Johan Kaufmann, op. cit., p. 73.

32. Ibid., pp. 90–92.

33. The following pages are drawn from John W. McDonald, Jr., *The North-South Dialogue and the United Nations*, an Occasional Paper of the Institute for the Study of Diplomacy, Edmund A. Walsh School of Foreign Service, Georgetown University, pp. 17–22.

34. For a detailed discussion of the World Food Conference, see Weiss and Jordan, op. cit.

35. For a complete discussion of this dialogue, see Jacobson and Sidjanski, op. cit.

36. Arend Lijphart, "The Analysis of Bloc Voting in the General Assembly," *American Political Science Review* 57 (December 1963): 902–17. Among the works cited by Lijphart are: M. Margaret Ball, "Bloc Voting in the General Assembly," *International Organization* 5 (February 1951), 3–31; John A. Houston, *Latin America in the United Nations*, United Nations Studies, no. 8 (New York: Carnegie Endowment for International Peace, 1956); F. H. Soward, "The Changing Balance of Power in the United Nations," *The Political Quarterly* 28 (October-December 1957); Robert E. Riggs, *Politics in the United Nations: A Study of United States Influence in the General Assembly*, Illinois Studies in the Social Sciences 41 (Urbana: The University of Illinois Press, 1958); Geoffrey Goodwin, "The Expanding United Nations, I—Voting Patterns," *International Affairs* 36 (April 1960); and Roderick C. Ogley, "Voting and Politics in the General Assembly," *International Relations* 2 (April 1961).

37. Thomas Hovet, Jr., *Bloc Politics in the United Nations* (Cambridge, Mass.: Harvard University Press, 1960).

38. The Rice-Beyle Method is discussed in greater detail below in Chapter 5.

39. Hayward R. Alker, Jr., "Dimensions of Conflict in the General Assembly," *American Political Science Review* 58 (September 1964): 642–57; Bruce M. Rusett, "Discovering Voting Groups in the United Nations," *American Political Science Review* 60 (June 1966): 327–39.

40. The series of studies by Jack E. Vincent are: *The Caucusing Groups of the United Nations: An Examination of Their Attitudes Toward the Organization* (Stillwater: Oklahoma State University

Press, 1965); "National Attributes as Predictors of Delegate Attitudes at the United Nations," *American Political Science Review* 62 (September 1968): 916–31; "The Convergence of Voting and Attitude Patterns at the United Nations," *Journal of Politics* 31 (1969): 952–83; "An Analysis of Caucusing Group Activity at the United Nations," *Journal of Peace Research* 2 (1970): 133–50; "An Analysis of Attitude Patterns at the United Nations," *Quarterly Journal of the Florida Academy of Sciences* 32 (1969): 185–209; "Generating Some Empirically Based Indices for International Alliance and Regional Systems Operating in the Early 1960's," *International Studies Quarterly* 15 (1971): 465–525; "Predicting Voting Patterns in the General Assembly," *American Political Science Review* 65 (June 1971): 471–98; and "Testing Some Hypotheses About Delegate Attitudes in the United Nations and Some Implications for Theory Building," *Research Report No. 52*, Dimensionality of Nations Project, University of Hawaii (1971).

41. Jack E. Vincent, "An Application of Attribute Theory to General Assembly Voting Patterns and Some Implications," *International Organization* 26 (Summer 1972): p. 576.

42. When decisions require a qualified majority for their adoption, 45 votes (considering their weighted value) are necessary for adoption. Moreover, the concurring votes of at least six member-states are required for a favorable decision.

43. For an exhaustive study of the CPR see Dimitri Tsikouris, "Institution of the Permanent Representatives of the Member States of the European Community," unpublished MA thesis, University of New Orleans, 1981.

44. For details see John Lambert, "The Constitutional Crisis 1965–66," *Journal of Common Market Studies* 6 (May 1966), pp. 195–228.

45. *Agence Europe Bulletin*, May 20, 1982.

46. Articles of Agreement as amended, Articles XXIV and XXVII, in *The International Monetary Fund 1945–1965*, (Vol. III: Documents), pp. 504–5 and Susan Strange, "IMF: Monetary Managers," in Cox and Jacobson, op. cit., pp. 263–97, fn. 4.

47. Article XII, see 4 (d).

48. *The Political Handbook of the World 1981*, eds. Arthur S. Banks and William Overstreet (New York: McGraw-Hill, 1982) p. 655.

49. Ibid., p. 656.

50. Kevin C. Kearns, "The Andean Common Market: A New Thrust of Economic Integration in Latin America," *Journal of Inter-American Studies and World Affairs* 14 (May 1972), pp. 228–29.

51. See Edward S. Milensky, "From Integration to Developmental Nationalism: The Andean Group 1965–1971," *Inter-American Economic Affairs* 25 (Winter 1971), pp. 79, 85.

52. For details see Ralph A. Diez, "The Andean Common Market: Challenge to Foreign Investors," *Columbia Journal of World Business* 6 (July-August 1971), p. 23.

53. *New York Times*, August 26, 1972.

54. *New York Times*, September 6, 1975.

55. *The Political Handbook of the World 1981*, pp. 665–66. See also John Erickson, "The Internal Evolution of the Warsaw Pact and the European Balance," *Spettatore Internazionale* 14 (Jan.-March 1979), pp. 45–58.

56. This case is drawn from Robert S. Jordan, *Political Leadership in NATO: A Study in Multinational Diplomacy* (Boulder, Col.: Westview Press, 1979), pp. 194–205.

57. Article III of the Declaration Concerning Aims and Purposes of May 10, 1944.

58. Article 3, section 5, ILO Constitution.

59. Article 7, ibid.

60. The points made in these paragraphs are drawn from: *The United States and the International Labor Organization*, Twenty-Sixth Report of the Commission to Study the Organization of Peace, December, 1979, Introduction.

61. This information is drawn from the ILO entry in *The Political Handbook of the World*, 1981, Arthur S. Banks and William Overstreet, eds., (New York: McGraw-Hill, 1982).

62. Report, op. cit., p. 76.

63. Ibid.

64. ILO's formal complaints procedures can also be invoked by employers' and workers' organization in two ways. First, delegates to the ILO Conference are competent to lodge complaints charging a member-state with failure to give effect to a labor convention ratified by that member. Such complaints can be made by workers' and employers' delegates against their own governments. The complaint process can result in the convening of a Commission of Enquiry empowered to make findings of fact and law, and to the government involved. Second, under the ILO Freedom of Association procedure, workers' and employers' organizations are permitted to raise complaints concerning infringements of trade-union rights. Such complaints are referred to the Governing Body's Committee on Freedom of Association and may result in the convening of a Fact-finding and Conciliation Commission having powers similar to those of a Commission of Enquiry. Again, complaints of this nature may be raised by an employers' or workers' organization concerning actions of its own goverment. Ibid., pp. 75–76.

65. These comments, and the observations that follow, are drawn from an information statement, "US Re-entry into the ILO," published in February 1980 by the Bureau of Public Affairs, U.S. Department of State.

66. Carl G. Rosberg and Aaron Segal, "An East African Federation," *International Conciliation* 543 (May 1963), p. 5. For more detailed analyses of regional integration in East Africa prior to independence, see Robert I. Rotberg, "The Federation Movement in British East and Central Africa, 1889–1953," *Journal of Commonwealth Political Studies* 2 (May 1964), pp. 141–60 and Joseph S. Nye, Jr., *Pan-Africanism and East African Integration* (Cambridge, Mass.: Harvard University Press, 1965), pp. 86–94.

67. Tanganyika, formerly German territory, became a League of Nations mandate, administered by Great Britain, following World War I. Tanganyika and Zanzibar were merged in April 1964 into the United Republic of Tanganyika and Zanzibar. In October 1964 the name Tanzania was adopted.

68. Joseph S. Nye, Jr., "East African Economic Integration" *Journal of Modern African Studies* 1 (December 1963), p. 479.

69. *New York Times*, May 23, 1962, p. 3.

70. *New York Times*, August 14, 1961, p. 3.

71. J. H. Proctor, "The Effort to Federate East Africa: A Post-Mortem," *The Political Quarterly* 37 (January-March 1966), p. 54.

72. Ibid., pp. 52–53.

73. Apolo Robin Nsibambi, "Political Commitment and Economic Integration: East Africa's Experience," *The African Review* 2 (June 1972), p. 199.

74. John Ravenhill, "Regional Integration and Development in Africa: Lessons From the East African Community," *Journal of Commonwealth and Comparative Politics 17* (November 1979), p. 236.

75. Ibid., p. 237.

76. *New York Times*, September 17, 1965, Supp., p. 2.

77. *New York Times*, December 3, 1967, p. 8.

78. See Phillip Ndegwa, "Transfer Taxes are a Challenge—Not an Obstacle," *East Africa Trade and Industry* 13 (July 1967), pp. 25–28.

79. *New York Times*, September 15, 1970, p. 10.

80. *New York Times*, February 13, 1971, p. 8.

81. *New York Times*, July 9, 1971, p. 3.

82. *New York Times*, May 18, 1977, p. 6.

83. Richard Hodder-Williams, "Changing Perspectives in East Africa," *World Today* 34 (May 1978), p. 166.

84. *New York Times*, January 15, 1978, p. 23.

85. *New York Times*, January 26, 1968, p. 58.

86. Agrippah T. Mugomba, "Regional Organizations and African Underdevelopment; The Collapse of the East African Community," *Journal of Modern African Studies* 16 (June 1978), p. 263.

87. David Segal, "On Making Customs Unions Fair: An East African Example," *Yale Economic Essays* 10 (Fall 1970), p. 116.

88. Ravenhill, op. cit., p. 237.

89. Raymond W. Copson, "African International Politics: Underdevelopment and Conflict in the Seventies," *Orbis* 22 (Spring 1978), p. 231ff.

Chapter 5

IGO Interactions with Member-States and Other IGOs: Domestic Politics and the Pursuit of Foreign Policy Goals

When we discussed in Chapter 2 the genesis of IGOs, we stressed that these organizations are the creatures of the member-states, established for the basic purpose of achieving objectives and carrying out functions perceived by the prospective member governments to be in some way beyond the reach of their national resources. Hence, IGOs are instruments of policy for member governments whose aspirations and expectations ride on the appropriate task performance of the IGOs created or joined by them. Inevitably, member governments make cost-benefit calculations regarding the usefulness of their IGOs; they want to retain their influence in and perhaps exercise control over these IGOs and decidedly they do not want to slide into the position of Geothe's Sorcerer's Apprentice, who, after having magically transformed an old broom into an efficient water carrier, lost complete control over his creation and was unable to stop its persevering, untiring activities.

The desire to minimize loss of freedom in national policy making and to guide, if not control, the task performance of IGOs permeates the relations between member governments and international institutions. This is the case in universal organizations such as the United Nations, its specialized agencies and other multilateral units such as UNCTAD, as well as in regional organizations, for example, the EC and others. The desire for influence is especially pronounced in the international financial organizations.

The influence of individual member-states on the activities of IGOs varies and may change over time. For example, the influence of the United States in the various bodies of the United Nations has been declining over the years while that of some Third World states has increased. For the latter, the United Nations has become a major instrument for the implementation of their foreign policies; for the United States a contrary, unilateral trend has been observed. In the EC the influence of France on EC policy making has waned somewhat, while that of West Germany has risen.

For a systematic analysis of the relationship between member-states and IGOs, a number of specific questions need to be formulated that can serve as useful criteria for comparison.

IGOs AS INSTRUMENTS OF NATIONAL POLICIES

To what extent and for which domestic and foreign policy goals do national decision makers consider IGOs as useful instruments of policy implementation? The answers will, of course, depend very much on the interests pursued by national governments (security, economic, political, technological) that led to the participation in the IGO in the first place. It also depends on the competences and powers conferred on particular IGOs.

INFLUENCE ON IGO DECISIONS

What means are available to member governments to influence the input and output of the decision making processes in individual IGOs? A variety of possibilities come to mind. On the formal level, participatory and representational mechanisms are available to shape inputs and outputs. These may take the form of shaping particular IGO policies, recommendations, resolutions, or even legal, binding pronouncements. For example, in the EC the Council of Ministers, composed of the ministers of the member-states competent for a particular issue before the Council, has a major role in influencing inputs and in shaping the decisional output. In other words, the ministers actually participate in various phases of the decision-making process. In the same manner, members of the European Parliament (EP), the assembly in the institutional framework of the EC, participate in the decisions of this body. Votes in the EP conceivably can be used to promote the goals of the member-states. How much this actually is the case will be seen from our voting analysis in the EP case.

A representational mechanism is illustrated by the permanent missions of the member-states to the United Nations. The members of these diplomatic missions accredited to the United Nations represent the viewpoints of the member governments and, therefore, are in a position to promote the national policies of their governments. Staff members of these missions, however, also participate in the decision making itself by acting as delegates in various U.N. bodies.[1]

On the informal level, personal contacts and other kinds of interface between national and IGO bureaucracies can be used to influence the IGO decision-making process in the direction of objectives sought by one or more member governments. So-called corridor deals during sessions of the U.N. General Assembly and other organs as well as during the U.N. conferences come to mind. Even if carefully organized, these contacts may not always be successful; the perceptions held by national civil servants of their IGO counterparts are likely to play an important role and, to a lesser degree, so do the images of the national bureaucracies formed in the minds of the IGO civil servants. While IGO officials, especially for those in higher positions, may provide significant channels for the attainment of member-states' goals, it should be noted that informal contacts between IGO and national government officials also can be used to persuade member-states of the merits of IGO policy proposals.

Informal interactions also take place between national and international INGOs and IGO institutions and their bureaucrats that often have as their aim to influence IGO decision making in accordance with interest group goals and, at times, converging member-state national objectives. Interest groups pursue goals in a variety of issue areas, such as economic, humanitarian, religious, ethnic, and disarmament, and therefore, depending on the particular goals pursued, every type of IGO and especially its individual organs might be perceived as useful targets.[2]

COALITIONS

To what extent are transgovernmental, interbureaucratic, and transnational coalitions formed to enhance member-state goals? Coalitions may be formed: 1) by national governments exclusively, 2) by national bureaucracies either entirely from member-states or, in exceptional circumstances, with selected segments of IGO bureaucracies, and 3) between interest groups, working in some cases with national bureaucrats or even leaders of member governments. Interest groups may also seek to work with IGO officials if that may enhance the achievement of their objectives. The Group of 77 is a prime example of a governmental coalition, and the national bureaucracies of the members of this Group are more likely than not to cooperate to achieve their various goals. In contrast, the Non-Aligned Movement is not nearly as cohesive. In certain instances, IGO bureaucracies are drawn into this endeavor; in fact, the bureaucracies of such development-oriented agencies of the United Nations as UNCTAD or UNIDO are mandated to do so. The negotiations regarding the U.N. code of conduct for transnational corporations, which began under the auspices of the U.N. Economic and Social Council in 1974 and are still in process, illustrate different attempts at such coalition formation when interest groups in the advanced industrial states solicited the cooperation and support of the officials of the U.N. Center for Transnational

Corporations. This organization was set up by the secretary-general to provide administrative support for the negotiations. This is discussed further in Chapter 7.

In the search for coalition partners, member governments of an IGO may seek the support of third states. For example, during the early years of the European Coal and Steel Community and the European Economic Community, the support of the United States for regional integration was sought by the member-states of the two Communities; this support was given with enthusiasm and contributed to a large degree to the initial success of the EC.

IGOs as formal coalition structures may also be employed by member governments to influence the decision-making process in another IGO. The institutionalized practices for external policy coordination in the EC furnish an example. Whatever issue may come up in U.N. bodies, the member-states of the EC seek to coordinate their approach and voting behavior in these bodies to promote their particular objectives. How successful this coordination has been in the past can be seen from voting analyses presented later in this chapter.

Another aspect of coalition building is the fact that many states are members of many IGOs. The United States has memberships in over 50 major IGOs.[3] A number of other advanced industrial states also are members of many of these organizations. This makes it possible for them to expand channels and instruments for the promotion of their national policies. For example, the influence exerted by the U.S. government in the IMF, GATT, and the OECD makes it possible for the United States to attempt coordination of policies in those IGOs in such a way as to support U.S. national policies vis-à-vis selected socialist bloc or Third World states. Other member-states of these three IGOs can, of course, make similar policy-influencing efforts, and these attempts may be at variance with those of the United States.

INTER-IGO RELATIONS

An intriguing question is whether relations among IGOs may also be affected by the attempts of member governments to use and perhaps to manipulate the operations of one IGO in order to influence the activities and policies of another IGO for the purpose of enhancing national interests. In some cases, the form and scope of inter-IGO relations are stipulated in the constituent treaties. For example, the EEC Treaty contains a number of provisions prescribing this organizations's formal relations with the United Nations, the Council of Europe, and other IGOs (Articles 229–231). Although these relations under international law are between the IGOs as the result of their recognized legal personalities, it is quite conceivable that in political terms they may well be influenced and perhaps shaped in varying degrees by the interests pursued by some or all of the member-states of the interacting organizations.[4] That is likely to be more the case in relations among IGOs within a particular region such as among the EC and the Council of Europe, or the OAU and ECOWAS, as well as between the OAU and the U.N. Economic Commission for Africa and NATO and the OECD. In relations between units of the U.N. family, administration and bureaucratic considerations—for example budget concerns—may play a more significant role, but economic and political concerns may also induce the member-states to exert some influence on interunit relationships that they might perceive to be in the interest of the entire membership.[5]

IGO-IGO interactions have so far not been explored systematically. Perhaps our illlustrative cases later in this chapter may shed some light on this issue and may provide insights into the question of how competitive or cooperative IGOs are in their relations with each other.[6]

EXERCISE OF INFLUENCE AND ORGANIZATIONAL EFFECTIVENESS

While it is obviously important to identify and to analyze the various means and channels emanating from member-state sources that are used to shape the input into an IGO's decision-making process, it is equally important to determine how these efforts affect IGO organizational efficiency and performance. Undoubtedly, the leadership and subordinate personnel of every IGO can be presumed to be interested in effectively achieving the goals and carrying out the functions for which the IGO has been established. For this purpose it wants to exercise the legal powers conferred by the member governments in the constituent treaties to the fullest extent and with the utmost efficiency.

But the member governments may become apprehensive of the new "broom," to use again the phrase in Goethe's poem. This may lead to subtle (and not so subtle) interventions by member governments in the operations of IGOs and their decision-implementation processes that are apt to undermine the authority and the power of the IGO insitutions, and adversely affect the morale and esprit de corps of their civil servants. The declining power and esteem of the EC Commission during the 1970s is a case in point and has resulted in reduced organizational efficiency and performance in all three European Communities.[7] Our discussion of a number of illustrative cases later in this chapter will show similar developments in other regional and universal IGOs.

EXPULSION

Can an IGO, possessing legal personality under international law, expel a member-state? Obviously, such an action would be the ultimate affront to a member-state in its relationship with an IGO, the most extraordinary display of power of the "broom"—in Goethe's sense—against its master.

The League of Nations had the authority under the Covenant to declare that a state was no longer a member. It required the concurring vote of all member-states except, of course, that of the expellee. This authority was used in 1939 when the Soviet Union was expelled.

The United Nations also has a provision for expulsion (Article 6) but such action can be taken only by the General Assembly upon recommendation of the Security Council. In view of the veto, the permanent members of that Council cannot be expelled and they can hold their protective umbrella over other states that they do not want to see expelled. In any event, it seems that since World War II no IGO has used the power of expulsion provided for in its constituent treaty.[8] However, other methods of reprobation have been attempted. South Africa was prevented from participating in the work of the General Assembly in 1974, but the president of the Assembly clearly indicated that this did not imply expulsion from the United Nations. Other U.N.-related organizations, such as the ILO, endeavored to exclude South Africa from the meetings of their major organs.[9] However, in all such cases the legal situation was doubtful since the U.N. Charter has a specific provision on expulsion and unless the actions of the various bodies conform with these provisions, the rights of the member-states can be curtailed illegally and the exercise of their membership suspended without a basis in law.

ILLUSTRATIVE CASES

Multilevel Bargaining between
IGO Institutions and Member-states:
The EEC Regional Development Fund

The aim of member governments to influence IGO policies is not confined to universal IGOs such as UNESCO; national efforts to influence these policies are also exerted in regional IGOs. The development of regional development policies in the EC and the creation and operation of the European Regional Development Fund (ERDF) are prime examples of the bargaining on the European, national, and subnational levels to influence the nature and direction of EC policies in this issue area.

The establishment of the ERDF was approved by the EC Council of Ministers in March 1975 for the three-year experimental period. It followed two years of intensive and often bitter discussion among all parties involved, especially the member governments, and culminated earlier, unsuccessful attempts by the Commission to institute a common regional policy. However, the initial resources allocated to the Fund were very modest and many looked upon it as primarily a quid pro quo for cooperation in other areas of Community activity. As Helen Wallace points out, it was felt that the creation of the new Fund "would allow for budgetary transfers that would ease, even cancel out, unfavorable financial commitments incurred on other common policies."[10]

The negotiations over the establishment of the ERDF took place within the decision-making framework of the EC, but were dominated by serious controversies among member governments, in particular between Britain and West Germany. Moreover, different ministries in the national capitals got into the act, trying to promote their own institutional interests through suggestions as to how their governments should respond to repeated, though different Commission policy proposals. Finally, subnational units such as the West German states (Länder), Italian regional governments, and Scotland and Wales in Britain had particular interests in regional development that they were anxious to pursue as EC development policies were discussed and formulated.

The basic tenets of a community regional policy had been under consideration for several years, but the formulation of such a policy did not become a major issue until the Summit Conference in 1972. This Conference was particularly important because of the enlargement of the EC that was to come in force in 1973 and brought in two states, Ireland and Great Britain, both of which had serious regional problems. In addition, the negotiations about the Fund came at a time when questions were raised about the effective use of resources in the Community budget and which priorities should be assigned to EC expenditures.

Point 5 of the final communiqué of the Conference of Heads of State or of Government held in Paris from October 19 to 21, 1972 stated the following:

> The Heads of State or of Government agreed that a high priority should be given to the aim of correcting, in the Community, the structural and regional imbalances which might affect the realisation of Economic and Monetary Union.
>
> The Heads of State or of Government invite the Commission to prepare without delay a report analysing the regional problems which arise in the enlarged Community and to put forward appropriate proposals.
>
> From now on, they undertake to coordinate their (national) regional policies. Desirous of directing that effort towards finding a Community solution to regional problems, they invite the Community Institutions to create a Regional Development Fund . . . . Intervention by the Fund in coordination with national aids should permit, progressively with the realization of Economic and Monetary Union, the correction of the main

>regional imbalances in the enlarged Community, and particularly those
>resulting from the preponderance of agriculture and from industrial change
>and structure underemployment.[11]

In general, the regions with agricultural problems tend to be situated on the periphery of the EC, and over recent years they have known a sharp decline in the proportion of employment devoted to agriculture. Severe structural underemployment is characteristic and in some cases long-term unemployment is also high. These disadvantages are particularly significant in the cases of Ireland and the Italian Mezzogiorno. But whatever the variations in this respect, the features common to all these areas are relatively low income per capita and high dependence on agricultural employment.[12]

The areas suffering from industrial change have usually been those highly dependent for employment on aging industries such as steel. The Walloon region of Belgium is another example. Their difficulties with economic transformation are often underlined by a constantly slow growth rate and by high levels of unemployment stretching over many years. To a varying extent both the agricultural and the industrial problem areas are affected by outward migration: in some cases this is extremely high, both qualitatively and quantitatively, reaching an annual rate of 15 for every 1,000 inhabitants. Some areas—Wales, for instance—are further handicapped by the lack of means of communication, industrial infrastructure, and educational and training facilities. Moreover, the geographical situation of certain areas, such as Greenland, gives rise to exceptional economic and social problems.

In statistical terms, in two major areas in which 9 percent of the total EC population lives—namely, Ireland and southern Italy—the regional per capita income is less than 60 percent of the EC average. In two other zones—central and northeast Italy, and Scotland and northeast England—people have to be content with only 60 to 80 percent of the EC average level of prosperity. This statistical group also includes isolated areas of West Germany and parts of Benelux.

Although, until 1972, there was no comprehensive EC regional policy, in certain cases the expenditure of Community resources has had salutary regional effects. Operations of the European Investment Bank (EIB) are relevant in this context. Substantial loans from 1958 to 1972 were allocated to regional development schemes. Reconversion and readaptation financing, pursuant to Article 56 of the ECSC Treaty, contributed to the creation of 110,000 new jobs and made readaptation possible for nearly half a million workers of the coal and steel industries. The Social Fund, in providing resources for settlement and training of workers, had a regional impact, as had the guidance section of the European Agriculture Guidance and Guarantee Fund (EAGGF), where large amounts of money have so far been spent on modernizing and providing higher living standards in agriculture.

However, more was needed, and the Commission presented proposals for a regional policy based on the following guidelines:

1. Community regional policy cannot be a substitute for the national regional policies which Member States have been conducting for many years. It must complement them with the aim of reducing the main disparities across the Community . . . .

2. Since overconcentration of economic activity in some regions is a major social and economic problem which tends to become more and more acute, the Community, as well as giving aid to the poorer regions, should seek agreement between the Member States on common policies to reduce concentration in the congested regions . . . .

3. If Community regional policy is to be successful, it requires not only new incentives but coordination of the various common policies and financial instruments which exist at Community level with a view to their improved utilization for regional objectives . . . .

4. The principal vehicle for mobilizing Community resources as a complement to actions presently carried out in the member-states should be the Regional Development Fund. The assistance of the Fund should be devoted entirely to the medium and long term development of the less developed and declining regions within the Member States, with the aim of bringing about self-sustaining growth . . . .

5. The Fund will have to concentrate its expenditure very largely in those regions which are the most in need in relation to the Community as a whole. In other words there must be standards to ensure that the means available to the Fund are used in a manner quite independent of any criterion of *juste retour* . . . . The acceptance of this principle will be an important test of Community solidarity . . . .[13]

Yet in proposing to go beyond assistance to the hard core of neglected areas and take into consideration the accommodation of members' national interests and goals, the Commission gave the impression of "being a watering can . . . sprinkling a little in everyone's direction" so that no member government would oppose it.[14] It based its position on the expanding suburban sprawl, the housing problem in Europe, the difficulty of coping with commuter traffic, and the pollution of air and water for which financial aid should be make available from the Regional Development Fund. Therefore, affluent areas as well as poorer regions were to be beneficiaries.

The amount of the Fund was set at 1.3 billion UAs (units of account) (about $1.5 billion in current exchange rates) to be expended over three years. The West German government was to supply 30 percent of the total and the French 20 percent. Neither the British nor the Italians considered the size of the Regional Development Fund sufficient. The Germans, on the other hand, thought the amount too high and the distribution formula unacceptable. Their position was that only the poorer countries should benefit and that Great Britain, Denmark (for Greenland* and the Faroe Islands),

*A large island located between 60 degrees north and the North Pole, close to the North American continent, but administratively fully integrated into Denmark.

Ireland, and Italy should draw the same net figure; regions eligible for aid should be those with a gross national product at least 10 percent lower than the Community average. Under the German proposal France would not have benefited at all from the Fund, nor would The Netherlands, Belgium, or Luxembourg. The French opposed the idea of not being able to draw from the regional purse for their less developed areas, and later a compromise was drafted, leaning toward concentration on the most needy regions and accepted at the December 1974 summit meeting of heads of government in Paris.[15]

How effective has been the ERDF in improving the economics of the depressed regions and what are the likely EC development policies of the future? First, the gap between the richer and the poorer regions has widened instead of narrowing. The ratio between the richest regions and the poorest regions was 2.9:1 in 1970; at the end of the decade it had risen to 4:1.[16] This development occurred despite the fact that the annual size of the Fund quadrupled from 1975 to 1980. Obviously, the policy has not attained its intended purpose.

Second, questions have been raised whether the national quota system, which controls 95 percent of the ERDF expenditures may have been responsible for the Fund's poor record in helping the poorer regions. Of these expenditures, 74 percent went into infrastructure improvement and only 26 percent into industrial projects.[17] Assuming that the strict adhesion to the quota system was indeed harmful to the achievements of an effective regional development policy, the Commission recommended new policy outlines in July 1981. In a memorandum published at that time, the following points were stressed:

1. The Commission notes the urgent need for the EEC to reverse the trend of increasing regional differences, in evidence since the common market was first founded.

2. ERDF funds should be concentrated more on regions that lag far behind the EEC average (rather than base aid on national averages) so as to give ERDF aid greater impact.

3. The ERDF's top priority should be to create new jobs, taking due account of population trends and the fact that there will be less mobility between regions than in the past (this is not in itself a negative factor since the EEC must work to prevent over-concentration of economic activity in certain areas that are already well provided for, which merely puts outlying regions even further behind).

4. The Community should make the most of local development potential in the regions that need assistance: manpower, of course, as well as alternative sources of energy, and latent industrial potential, especially in small and medium-scale industries.

5. Coordination of the different EEC instruments should be improved and strengthened and a guarantee should be given that EEC aid is to match national efforts and not replace them.[18]

Although the Commission did not suggest the complete elimination of quotas, only states with extensive regional economic problems were to be allocated quotas and these quotas were to be increased. Table 5.1 provides data on the allocations from the 1981–82 period to 1983. It is important to note that in the future total quota allocations of the Fund were to be reduced to 80 percent from 95 percent, providing considerably larger amounts of money to nonquota projects.

The basic rationale for the Commission's enlargement of the nonquota portion of the ERDF seems to make sense. Problem regions at times straddle the territories of several countries and do not necessarily coincide with as-sisted areas as defined by member-states for their own national assistance to troubled areas. Moreover, multiannual programs can be developed that may have a much more significant impact on the poorest than annual projects that are often poorly integrated.

Whether this new approach will be fully acceptable to national EC governments and subnational governmental units remains to be seen. There are voices of support from the European Parliament, but rumbling of op-position from the chambers of commerce and industry groups. It is note-worthy that permanent observers by the German Länder as well as by Scotland and Wales are installed in Brussels and that these observers are likely to inject themselves in regional issues.[19] The regions will, of course, also seek to exert influence on the national governments in order to enhance their particular interests. The regions may also interact with each other in creating coalitions for the advancement of their goals.

The preceding pages demonstrate the significant influence that domestic

TABLE 5.1: Shift of ERDF Quota Amounts, 1981–82 to 1983

	1981-82 (percent)	1983 (percent)
Italy	35.5	43.7
Britain	23.8	29.8
France	13.6	2.5[a]
Greece	13.0	16.0
Ireland	5.9	7.3
Germany	4.7	0
The Netherlands	1.2	0
Denmark	1.1	0.3[b]
Belgium	1.1	0
Luxembourg	0.1	0

[a] French Overseas Departments
[b] Greenland
Source: The Economist, October 24, 1981, p. 38.

politics have in the issue area of regional development on the relation between the Community institutions and the member-states as well as on the direction and content of policy formulation and perhaps also implementation. Obviously, to evolve a truly rational, common policy is extremely difficult. Compromises to satisfy the interests of various groups, subnational units, and national governmental agencies are a continuing part of the policy-making process that is further compounded by a pervasive economic recession. The *retour juste* remains a persisting concern in the minds of national leaders. Nevertheless, progress has been made on the policy level and this progress, involving the ever-larger dispension of financial aid, is likely to strengthen the legitimacy of the EC institutions. In longer terms, even the economic conditions of the aid recipients may be improved and the gap between the rich and poor regions of Western Europe narrowed, if not closed.

As for the progress achieved, considerable credit must be given to the Commission whose patience and persistence coupled with a measure of flexibility achieved essentially its original goal for the ERDF. Thus we see evidence in this case that in spite of differing perceptions and objectives on the part of the member-states, central IGO institutions can evolve compromises for policies that are eventually accepted and that are in line with the fulfillment of important IGO objectives. At the same time member governments are satisfied with the IGO performance because they see in this particular case the enhancement of their own national interests.

UNESCO and the "New World Information Order"

We pointed out in the introduction to this chapter that IGO member-states want to use central institutions and specialized units as instruments to achieve their particular goals. This often requires the exercise of influence over the operations of institutions and units to direct their activities into desired directions. An interesting case regarding UNESCO illustrates this point.

UNESCO was created as a specialized agency of the United Nations to work—as its constitution puts it— for "the unrestricted pursuit of objective truth and the free exchange of ideas and knowledge . . ." and, to that end, "to increase the means of communication between peoples."

In 1976, in an effort to reveal the total dimensions of such a mandate, UNESCO established an International Commission for the Study of Communication Programs under the presidency of Mr. Sean MacBride of Ireland. The need for such a Commission arose because of an international debate that had arisen in the 1970s as to whether Third World protests against the dominant flow of news from the Western industrialized states were attacks on the free flow of information, and if so, what appropriately should be done about it to satisfy both parties.

Referring to the state, the Commission observed:

The framework within which communication takes place is ultimately determined by the political and social struggles which have shaped the prevailing social consensus in a given society. The way communications are organized in a democratic society is basically a political decision reflecting the values of the existing social system. At a pragmatic level, solutions to the political problems of communication depend on finding a balance between the legitimate interests of the State and the rights of access to information that may be extended to diverse sections of opinion. These solutions will necessarily vary according to the political structure, the degree of development, and the size and resources of each nation. But neither practical necessities nor the claims of ideology should be invoked to exclude freedom of expression from its proper place.[20]

The dilemma that has confronted UNESCO is that there is not world-wide agreement as to the proper place for, or even the rightful existence of, this freedom of expression.

In 1970, UNESCO had announced that it was switching its attention from providing technical assistance to Third World media to focus instead on the content of information. These two aspects of journalism became the object of the subsequent international debate ever since. This change of UNESCO reflected a growing awareness by Third World states of the implications of the fact that nearly 90 percent of the international news circulated worldwide is supplied by four main agencies—Associated Press (U.S.), Reuters (U.K.), Agence-France Presse (French), and United Press International (U.S.). But it was not only the dominance of the Western press that had come under attack; the model of a free press was also being rejected as alien and undesirable. This goes beyond the familiar arguments of national leaders that their societies are too vulnerable to permit an independent press to function freely. It led to pressure through UNESCO for control over the activities of the international press.[21]

In contrast, the West viewed some of the proposed reforms as efforts to legitimize government control over the news, and the Soviet bloc and Third World governments' habit of expelling Western journalists and banning publications that offend those in power. This they would accomplish by having UNESCO declare that news organizations have a duty to support government policies and promote good causes such as economic development and peace, while opposing bad ones, such as fascism, warmongering, and racism. In addition, UNESCO was asked to draw up an international code of journalistic ethics imposing these obligations on journalists, who would also receive special safe-conduct passes, or licenses, that could be withdrawn if they broke the code.

At the 1976 General Conference of UNESCO, held in Nairobi, the Soviet Union supported a resolution that states should have the power to control the content of news. The effect of this declaration was to move the debate away from legitimate Third World grievances to the question of freedom versus sovereignty. Then, at the UNESCO General Conference held in 1980 in Belgrade, Yugoslavia, a proposal was made to pledge assistance to professional organizations and other bodies interested in devising measures to protect journalists in their work. It also sought universal definitions of responsible reporting and ways to help strengthen the propaganda capability of various liberation movements, such as the Palestine Liberation Organization. Thereafter, a Commission for the Protection of Journalists was proposed that would issue identification cards to reporters on dangerous assignments, in war zones, or working abroad. It would also judge complaints about their professional conduct and have the power to withdraw their identity cards, making it difficult and perhaps impossible for them to work in many countries. UNESCO officials claimed that the main purpose of the Commission would be to reduce journalists' risks on dangerous assignments by "enabling them to identify themselves rapidly in all circumstances." The idea would be to persuade governments to incorporate the Commission's recommendation into their national legislation, thus giving a code of journalistic ethics the force of law.[22]

This proposal engendered a lively debate about the need for an international agency to arbitrate the rights, responsibilities, and protection of journalists. Some Western newspapers exhorted their governments to quit UNESCO or to withhold their financial contribution in protest. In Washington, for example, Representative Robin L. Beard, Jr. of Tennessee offered an amendment (which was opposed by the Administration) to a bill authorizing funds for the State Department that would mandate a yearly accounting of actions by UNESCO affecting international communications. If UNESCO should attempt to license or censor journalists, or to introduce a binding code of conduct, the United States would be required to stop all payment to the organization—about 25 percent of the budget. Other "sense of Congress" resolutions—which are not binding on the Administration—have been introduced to reduce U.S. contributions rather than to end them, and to call upon UNESCO to cease its efforts to control the activities of journalists or the flow of news.[23]

In a joint declaration of a conference held in France in May 1981, some leaders of print and broadcasting organizations from 20 mostly Western states asserted that press freedom was "a basic human right" and declared that they were resolved to resist "any encroachment" on it. Furthermore, they urged UNESCO "to abandon attempts to regulate news content and formulate rules for press conduct," claiming that these attempts violated UNESCO's own charter, the Universal Declaration of Human Rights and the Helsinki Declaration on Human Rights, and was inconsistent with the United Nations Charter. They pledged to expand the "free flow of information worldwide," and would support efforts by international bodies, governments, and private agencies to help developing countries build up a healthy and free press of their own. Specifically, they rejected "the view of press theoreticians and those national or international officials who claim that while people in some countries are ready for a free press, those in other countries are insufficiently developed to enjoy that freedom." This Declaration of Talloires served as a riposte to the controversial efforts of UNESCO's Director-General, Amadou Mahter M'Bow of Senegal, to create a "new world information order," with the support of the Soviet bloc of states in the United Nations aligned with the Third World states.[24]

Advocates of such an order continued to complain that the business of disseminating news and information around the world is dominated by the West, and that as a consequence news and information unfavorable to the Soviet bloc and the Third World gets more attention than favorable news and information. Their objective was to obtain a more balanced flow of news and information by reserving a bigger share of the airwaves for developing states so that their voices could be heard more easily, by giving them greater access to satellite communications, and by encouraging them to develop their new organizations.

At the initiative of the United States in 1980, the West, in response to the movement to limit journalistic freedom, and to meet these other complaints, supported in UNESCO the creation of an International Program for the Development of Communication. It was an effort to get UNESCO back on the track of providing technical assistance. The U.N. General Assembly at its thirty-sixth session in December 1981 adopted Resolution 36/149 that called upon all member-states to support the Program. (The resolution was passed without a vote.) This Program thus became an attempt by the West and the Third World to find concrete ways of increasing Third World participation in the international flow of news, without, at the same time, compromising on the principle of the freedom of the press.

But by January 1982 it became clear that the U.N. resolution notwithstanding, the United States was unwilling to provide more than nominal financing for the International Program for the Development of Communication, and instead proposed projects that would be supported by the U.S. private sector. Director-General Amadou M'Bow criticized this approach as being "more in keeping with the preoccupation of the donors than with the wishes of the recipients and creating an inegalitarian type of relationship between the two parties."[25] In contrast, the Program focused attention on the idea of the Pan-African News Agency and an Asia-Pacific News Network.

Without a doubt, this debate will not be resolved either easily or soon. The fundamental differences in the current pluralistic international political system simply make it extremely difficult to bridge such competing or contrasting political, cultural, and social values. In spite of the considerable influence exercised by the Third World over U.N. bodies and agencies including UNESCO, and in spite of a seeming compromise reached by all member-states, the ideological and philosophical differences have remained, evidenced by the lagging U.S. implementation of the International Program for the Development of Communication. Thus, frustrations and frictions on this issue are likely to continue weakening, although perhaps only to a small degree, the effectiveness of UNESCO task performance.

The Capacity of IGOs to Deal with the Food Issue

As mentioned in the beginning of this chapter, IGOs have often had difficulty in implementing their own policies. Indeed, it frequently takes beneficial interaction among U.N. institutions, specialized agencies, and member governments to carry out effectively the missions for which the international organization(s) have been created. An illustrative example is the capacity of IGOs to deal with the food issue, as revealed in the discussion that follows.

Even though the World Food Conference, held in 1974, was considered one of the most successful of the global conferences, its long-term effect outside the United Nations system may not have been as important as the changes on the system itself. This is because global institutions are marginal in their ability to influence directly national decisions on food issues. The seeds of a globally organized food regime have been cast on the stony soil of sovereignty. As two skeptical scholars put it:

> . . . the World Food Conference set about proliferating new food institutions, as constitutionally impotent as ever, but with the explanation that the older ones don't work. Needless to say, if some institutions could work, propensities to pathological behavior in the global food system might be controlled. But, then, the pathologies result, after all, precisely from the fact that the current regime is distinctly inhospitable to the notion of "working international organizations."[26]

Global dimensions of food issues intersect and interact with domestic dimensions: it strains credulity to think that governments are on the verge of ceding a significant measure of control over their economic life to any other institutions. Moreover, the current performance of international institutions probably has political utility for states as a mode of symbolic reassurance. Governments can direct attention to the inadequacies of global policy-making institutions to divert attention from their own policies and their consequences. A World Food Conference is a necessarily rare event, cast as a major confrontation between diverse views and competing priorities, an exercise in high politics over a subject otherwise thought of as low politics. But unless it results in concrete action, it looks more like a typical exercise in conceding and compromising on symbolic positions than a harbinger of changes in resource allocation or patterns of behavior.

Even if states had the political will to establish governing organs for a global food system, international institutions would remain marginal to the overwhelming bulk of the human and social transactions that can be said to make up a world food system. In the recent past, no more than 10 percent to 12 percent of world grain production has moved internationally, as compared with 50 percent of oil production.

Even if states were committed to eradicating hunger as a first priority, the commitment would be irrelevant in the absence of a comprehensive analysis and plan of action that treated food behavior as if it were a global system. Most of the efforts of the Food and Agriculture Organization (FAO) and other United Nations agencies have taken a global view of food issues. The Freedom from Hunger Campaign, the World Food Program, the Indicative Plan of UNCTAD, and the World Food Council were all efforts at a relatively comprehensive global approach. Along the same line, those who concentrate on international food markets and/or commodities agreements can lay claim to a global perspective. Since production of surplus food is concentrated in a few states and separated from the hungry by geographic and political barriers, there are significant advantages to looking from the top down, as it were.[27]

What made the World Food Conference significant was the fact that in 1972, the total global production of food fell for the first time since World War II, a startling reduction of some 33 million tons. Since output must expand at the rate of 25 million tons annually to keep abreast of increases in population, the lack of approximately 60 million tons was felt and resulted in short supplies and increased prices. Although the 1973 harvest represented a good recovery from 1972, the main problem was that the biggest increases (in the U.S.S.R. and the Far East) did nothing to replenish the depleted stocks of the main cereal exporters. The world's margin of security against starvation dropped from 96 days in early 1972 to only 26 days by mid-1973. The sense of crisis in food and agricultural matters was heightened by the deteriorating trade position of developing countries, galloping worldwide inflation, and a four-fold increase in the price of petroleum and fertilizers.[28]

Because of this critical situation, the Fourth Conference of the Heads of State of Non-Aligned Nations, which met in Algiers of September 5–9, 1973, urged that a joint, emergency conference of the FAO and UNCTAD should be convened at the ministerial level. In the opinion of these leaders of developing countries, the serious food shortages confronting vast areas and populations of the world necessitated a program of international cooperation. An important impetus for a high-level international discussion of food problems came on September 24, 1973. Then U.S. Secretary of State Henry A. Kissinger proposed that a world food conference under United

Nations auspices be convened as rapidly as possible to mobilize all the resources of the international community to maintain adequate food supplies.

It is interesting to note that FAO perceived Kissinger's proposal as vital from the perspective of convening an international meeting that had a chance of succeeding. An internal policy memorandum from the director of one FAO division, for instance, noted:

> The most important positive feature of this proposal is that it has come from the United States in a major policy statement and the United States would therefore remain interested in the success of the Conference. In the past 25 years almost all important proposals for international food reserves—in one form or another or for a longer term international food aid policy were thwarted because the United States has not been prepared to accept greater international control of its food and food aid policy. We cannot of course jump to the conclusion that this proposal constitutes a major shift in the United States policy but the fact remains that Henry Kissinger, with his unorthodox approach to international diplomacy, has made this proposal and it therefore offers at least some scope for some major initiatives.[29]

The U.S. government followed this initial suggestion on October 4 with a proposal that such an item be included on the agenda of the twenty-eighth session of the General Assembly, which in turn assigned it to the second committee. A similar item was then included on the agenda of the resumed 55th session of the Economic and Social Council (ECOSOC). ECOSOC, in turn, decided on October 18 to recommend that such a conference be held in 1974 and requested that the governing bodies of all agencies within the U.N. system discuss their own contributions to such a meeting as an item of top priority.

As the specialized agency whose mandate was food and agriculture, the reaction of FAO's biennial Conference in Rome in November 1973 was of vital importance. Recognizing that the United Nations itself and the Secretariat could best generate the political momentum to sustain the nature of such a conference, the FAO Conference welcomed such an effort under U.N. auspices, and recommended that the proposed conference should focus upon the resolution of food problems within the larger context of overall economic development. Echoing this point, in an address to ECOSOC, then Director-General of FAO A. H. Boerma pointed out that constraints on agriculture are constraints on development and went on to identify the most important constraints. Weather topped the list, followed closely by the failure of governments to "accord sufficient priority to agriculture and rural areas in general. More than any other sector, agriculture has suffered from a lack of sustained political will and commitment on the part of governments."[30] Land tenure systems and poverty were also high on Boerma's list; both are factors intimately related to the stability, if not the survival, of any Third World regimes.

On December 1, 1973, ECOSOC took special note of the remarks of the FAO body in Resolution 1831 (LV), and recommended to the General Assembly that a world food conference be convened under general U.N. auspices. General Assembly Resolution 3180 (XXVII) on December 17 proposed to accept the offer from the Italian government and convene the World Food Conference in November 1974 in Rome; recommended that the meeting be at the ministerial level; gave ECOSOC overall coordinating authority; authorized the secretary-general, in consultation with the director-general of FAO and the secretary-general of UNCTAD, to appoint a secretary-general for the Conference and to initiate a small Secretariat; and recommended that this Secretariat, in preparing for the Conference, should consider the recommendation of all governing bodies of U.N. agencies, in particular those of the seventeenth session of the FAO conference.

On February 1, 1974, in spite of U.S. reservations, Sayed Ahmed Marei of Egypt was named secretary-general of the World Food Conference, and shortly thereafter the first session of the Preparatory Committee, open to all governments and recognized observers, was held at United Nations headquarters in New York on February 11–15. ECOSOC, on May 15, 1974, took note of the Preparatory Committee in Resolution 1840 (LVI) and decided to convene the World Food Conference in Rome on November 5–16. Before the historic meeting occurred two more sessions of the Preparatory Committee were held, in Geneva from June 4–8 and in Rome from September 23 to October 4.

From a macroorganizational perspective, the seventeenth session of the FAO Conference held on November 10–29, 1973, was extremely important. It provided an interesting example of a bureaucratic structure reacting under outside pressure. The formal U.S. proposal—subsequently supported by well-known international figures such as Algerian President Houari Boumedienne and West German Chancellor Willy Brandt in the General Assembly—can be interpreted as a call for immediate action and an indirect criticism of past performances of international organizations concerned with food problems. Hence, this global awakening did not go unnoticed in Rome, the headquarters of FAO. Although many FAO officials saw the proposal for a conference as an excellent opportunity to use the politicians' preoccupation with the immediacy of the situation to get them to finally implement programs to combat long-standing problems, other officials reported that they, along with Director-General Boerma, were perturbed by the prospects that new activities on food might detract from FAO's image and mandate. The call for a food conference under U.N.—rather than FAO—auspices was indeed interpreted by some as a criticism of FAO's past performance. FAO supported Marei for secretary-general of the Conference because they thought he would be more amenable to FAO. As it turned out, this was not necessarily the case.[31]

Despite the criticism of FAO implied by the proposal of the United Nations to hold a food conference, the FAO's Secretariat and the FAO Conference quickly set about insuring a maximum feasible role for themselves in the preparations for a followup of such a global, ad hoc conference. While admitting that some of the programs necessary to alleviate the problems of food and agricultural development would be beyond the competence of FAO, the FAO Conference in November 1973 nonetheless wished to ensure that the special role of FAO should be given full recognition when such arrangements are made. While the necessity to arrange a ministerial-level, ad hoc conference that could solicit the participation of all states—particularly of the U.S.S.R. that is not a member of FAO—has been frankly admitted, the FAO's Conference and Secretariat anticipated that the recommendations of the World Food Conference were subsequently to be carried out through existing international machinery.

In fact, the Conference produced both the World Food Council, which the United States favored, and the International Fund for Agricultural Development (IFAD), along with a renewed mandate for FAO. Clearly the international system is in a period of profound transformation. One of the symptoms of that transformation is the perception that institutions and arrangements rooted in the world of the 1950s and 1960s no longer work. It is unlikely that an effective set of institutions dealing with food will emerge until the period of transition nears an end. But, in the interim, global institutions like the World Food Council and the FAO serve two vital functions.[32]

First, they provide an intelligence capability for decision makers. Gathering and analyzing statistics, developing some expertise in advising policy makers on successful strategies for dealing with local problems or wooing potential donors (a prime purpose of both the FAO staff and the consultative group on food production and investment composed of the World Bank, FAO, and the U.N. Development Program) is not a dramatic enterprise. But if policies are to be implemented at any level that in fact increases the amount of food on people's tables, it is a necessary one.

Second, if a new global consensus does arise, it will do so only through a quasidialectical process of confrontation, bargaining, and compromise, replete with symbolic appeals, posturing, and rhetoric. International institutions provide an established, focused, and continuing arena within which the politics of food can be played out. Not surprisingly, the arenas themselves become issues, as the pattern of events surrounding the 1974 Rome Conference illustrate. Institutional reform and restructuring makes sense when changes can be measured against a criterion of efficiency and the issues are competitive means to a given end. Disagreement about basic goals cannot be dealt with by debating alternative programs of work or reorganizing the management of agencies.

Intergovernmentalism and IGO Effectiveness:
The European Political Cooperation (EPC)

While it is frequently contended with justification that increased intergovernmental interaction among IGO member-states tends to undermine the effectiveness of the central institutions, there are areas where intergovernmentalism might strengthen particular functions of these institutions. This is the case with the so-called European Political Cooperation (EPC), a foreign policy coordinating mechanism established by the EC member-states that evolved during the 1970s.

The constituent treaties of the European Communities contain provisions for the formulation of selected external policies and for relations with other IGOs, but the full acceptance and use of these provisions has been slow and often troublesome. Undoubtedly the EEC Treaty has the most extensive provisions that include the creation of common commercial policies toward nonmember-states and the conclusion of association agreements with third states.[33] Although a number of these agreements have been signed since the early 1960s and progress has been made in the formulation of EEC commercial policies, many West Europeans expressed the desire to see their states speak with one voice in international affairs. As a consequence, efforts were made to search for other means to produce common foreign policies on the part of the member-states.

As a result of these efforts, an alternative structure outside the EC decision-making framework as specified in the three Community treaties was created to coordinate the foreign policies of the EC member-states. This structure, generally known as EPC, has only very loose, poorly-defined ties to the EC system. Its origins were in the so-called Fouchet Plans, which were elaborated in 1961 and 1962 by a committee of diplomats chaired by Christian Fouchet, then the French ambassador to Denmark. The basic idea of the Fouchet Plans—there were two somewhat different proposals made by the committee—was the creation of a council at the level of heads of state and government, which was to meet every four months and, acting by unanimity, was to coordinate foreign and defense policy. To assist the council and to prepare policy proposals, an intergovernmental European political commission, perhaps in the form of a permanent secretariat, was to be established. It was to be composed of senior officials in the national foreign services and to be located in Paris.[34]

Although a chance for success seemed to exist in the early stages of the negotiations on the essentially Gaullist draft treaty for policy coordination, no synthesis between the divergent positions of France and her EC partners could be evolved. In 1969 initiatives were again launched to find new paths for the construction of some kind of European union. One of these initiatives was the creation of a committee composed of high foreign-ministry officials of the Six under the chairmanship of Vicomte Etienne Davignon of the Belgian Foreign Ministry. The results of the deliberations of the Davignon Committee were published on July 20, 1970.[35] In accordance with this report, the foreign ministers of the Six began to schedule joint meetings every six months. In important cases, a conference of chiefs of state and government could also be called when crucial issues justified such a meeting.

To prepare the sessions of the foreign ministers, a special committee was created composed of the political directors of the Six foreign ministries, to which were added in 1973 their counterparts of the three new member-states, and in 1981 a Greek member. This committee was named the Political Committee and was to meet at least four times a year, but actually has met more often. Subordinate to this Committee are various working groups and groups of experts, which have the mission to investigate particular problems and recommend possible solutions. The place for the sessions of the Political Committee is rotated from one member-state to the other in accordance with whatever country chairs the EC Council of Ministers, whose presidency changes every six months. In line with the rotation of this presidency, the chairmanship of the Committee also changes every six months.

The major task of the periodic sessions of foreign ministers is the consideration of important questions of foreign policy. The member governments can suggest any issue for consideration that may pertain not only to general foreign policy problems but also to such matters as monetary affairs, energy, and security. Whenever the work of the Political Committee or of the foreign ministers impinges on the competence and activities of the EC, the Commission is requested to submit its own position on the matter under consideration and is invited to send a representative. It is interesting to note that during the discussion in the Political Committee regarding the preparatory conference on European security and cooperation in Helsinki, it was felt that this subject was likely to deal with problems affecting the activities and competences of the EC in the international trade field. Therefore, a Community representative was invited and the president of the Commission, then Franco Malfatti, participated in some of the sessions.

The foreign policy coordination activities of the Political Committee are supplemented by periodic sessions of staff members in the embassies of the Ten, located in different capitals. The commercial counselor of the embassy of the member-state that holds the presidency in the Council of Ministers of the EC at a particular time prepares a report on these meetings. These reports are addressed to the president of the Council and are also distributed to the permanent respresentatives in Brussels and a number of national governmental agencies. If no objections are raised by a member government within eight days, a copy of this report is furnished to the Commission. When Community affairs are discussed in the embassy meetings, officials of the EC Information Service participate if the Service has an office in a particular capital, such as Washington or Geneva. In such cases, the Community officials make a direct report to the president of the Commission.

Policy coordination meetings have also been held in the United Nations to assure the maximum cohesion in voting and policy positions of the member-states. The influence of the Commission staff in these meetings may well have been increased when the EC was granted official observer status by the United Nations.[36] An analysis of the cohesion of the EC member-states in voting in the U.N. General Assembly on various issues will be presented in the next section of this chapter.

The emergence of the Political Committee as an important factor in the formulation of common foreign policies is pitting three organizational and bureaucratic groups against each other. One group consists of the officials of the foreign ministries operating through the Political Committee and perhaps in the future through a permanent secretariat, which will be concerned with the coordination of a wide range of foreign policy issues and thereby may invade the competences of the Communities. Second, we have the EC decision-making process with its own group of civil servants striving to produce and implement external policies in accordance with the provision of the EC treaties. It is noteworthy that in this process, which originally was to be dominated by the international civil service of the EC, we find expanding control by a third group of national officials.

These officials operate through the offices of the permanent representatives, who, as we have seen in Chapter 4, have played an increasingly important role in the EC decision-making process but have not been able to exert the same kind of influence within the EPC process. Some of these national officials come from the foreign ministries of the member-states, and others are assigned by the ministries of economic, agriculture, and finance as technical experts. This may change in the future since some kind of liaison between the EPC structure and the CPR is now envisaged through ad hoc groups of senior civil servants of the foreign and other ministries on matters affecting EC affairs.[37]

We therefore see not only a subversion of the original concepts of Community decision making in the field of foreign policy by the national officials, but we can also discern competition and interpenetration between two distinct national bureaucratic groups struggling, perhaps subtly, to extend their own competencies and those of their institutions. Indeed, as Helen Wallace reports, the endeavor of different government departments in the member-states to stake out their own areas of responsibility for formulation policy has provoked tensions between foreign ministries and domestic departments, as foreign ministries have had to increase their awareness of domestic policy considerations and ministries concerned with domestic problems had to involve themselves more in international negotiations. At the same time, the permanent missions have come to enjoy a special status and to acquire a certain solidarity with each other[38] to play their traditional roles without being inundated by innovative proposals from the Commission experts.

Whatever the bureaucratic interplay and its effect on the morale of the Eurocracy, the range of activities by the staff of the Political Committee that might lead to common action is impressive. They include:

1. An average of some 100 communications transmitted every week over a common telex-system called COREU.

2. More than 100 sessions of common working groups composed of national diplomats to analyze important international problems.

3. Political Committee meetings held twice a month to exchange information about the work and operations of the various foreign ministries that are relevant to EPC. A crisis procedure is in the planning stage that will assure meetings of the Committee within 48 hours.

4. Representation of the Ten at international conferences and in IGOs carried out by one delegation.

5. Consultation among diplomatic missions of the EC countries that has been placed on an institutionalized basis in various third-country capitals to coordinate positions and actions.

6. Meetings of the heads of government four times in the European Council, where discussion of issues before the Political Committee is included.[39]

As a result of the EC's particular external policy competences and the EPC mechanism, third states have become aware that their own foreign-policy developments must take into serious consideration both processes and, in order to influence the foreign policies of the Ten the foreign ministries of third states should know as much as possible of what is happening in the EPC deliberations on various international issues. The United States has been especially sensitive to this set of problems and was particularly concerned with events and policies during the Yom Kippur War in October 1973 and the initiation of the Euro-Arab dialogue in 1974. To satisfy the concerns of the United States, a compromise agreement was concluded among the foreign ministers of the EC states. This made it possible for the United States to participate in EPC deliberations prior to a final decision by the EC foreign ministers if a member-state desires consultation with Washington on a particular issue and the remaining member-states agree to that procedure. If unanimity about the invitation of such consultation cannot be attained, then contacts and consultations with the United States can only be conducted on a bilateral basis.[40] This arrangement has worked well and seems to have satisfied all parties.

The success story of EPC is mixed. Although the Political Committee has been involved in a number of important international issues during the 1970s, clear-cut successful accomplishments have been rare. The most significant achievement of the EPC has been the coordination of policies leading to a common position during the preparatory phase of negotiations with respect to the Conference on Security and Cooperation in Europe (CSCE) from 1973 to 1979 and the followup evaluation meetings in Belgrade in 1977–78 and in Madrid during 1981–82. The EC Commission participated vigorously and effectively in the deliberations on economic issues and contributed materially to shaping the common stand ultimately taken by the Nine. Consultations between the United States and the EPC members of the CSCE issue were concluded with the framework of NATO: Washington accepted the leading role of the Nine in the preparation of the CSCE negotiations as far as nonmilitary matters were concerned; and, as a consequence, the Final Act of Helsinki carries the imprint of conclusions reached in the EPC deliberations.[41] Clearly this is an example of effective policy harmonization of both the member-states and the EC proper, although the specific competences of the latter were not directly involved.

Another major foreign-policy effort in which the EPC mechanism is used jointly with the EC external relations system is the Euro-Arab dialogue that was initiated in 1975 and continues in 1982. The delegation for the EC and its member-states is led by the government chairing the EPC and by the Commission president or his representative.[42] The delegation of the Arab League, the dialogue partner, is led by the state holding the rotating presidency of the League.

A number of conflicts of interest burden the dialogue partners; since so far the problems of oil prices and guaranteed supplies have been excluded from the dialogue, it is hard to see how other major economic questions can be tackled realistically. Nevertheless, the Arab states seek support to develop their own refineries and petrochemical industries in order to expand earnings from their oil resources. They also want to establish steel mills and fertilizer plants. However, the West Europeans find it difficult to encourage such ventures in view of already existing excess capacities. Finally, the Arab League states would like to conclude a comprehensive preferential trade agreement with the EC and to have economic assistance and tariff preferences not extended to Israel suspended. This has been consistently rejected by the EC institutions.[43]

In spite of these economic problems, the Euro-Arab dialogue has not been without benefits for the EC states. The framework of contacts and interpersonal relations built up through the dialogue has considerable political value in itself, on occasion including support of West European foreign-policy goals.

Other major issues in which EPC was involved include: the Greek-

Turkish dispute in 1974 over Cyprus, but no solution acceptable to the contesting states was found; the democratization of Portugal and Spain in which EPC worked very closely with the EC Commission; the civil war in Angola and the problem of Namibia for which no acceptable solutions were found; the invasion of Afghanistan in 1979, but none of the proposals of the Ten found approval by the Soviet Union that considered the EPC suggestions as unrealistic; and the Falklands crisis of 1982 in which EPC and the EC institutions worked closely together in the imposition of trade sanctions on Argentina.[44]

While it is obviously in the nature of the EC that its external policies should concentrate mostly on economic issues, it is equally evident that the EPC is mainly concerned with political and selected matters such as Cyprus, Afghanistan, and some aspects of CSCE. Hence, while EPC complements the external activities of the EC, it serves as a fully harmonizing agent for overall policy only insofar as it draws the Commission into deliberations on a particular issue. Nevertheless, some long-range benefits for the operations of the EC institutions may flow from the operations of the EPC mechanism. It is quite evident that at the present this mechanism and the EC external policy-making process operate side-by-side in a useful pragmatic manner. While so far no particular integrative effect by the EPC on the EC system can be observed and while, in fact, EPC may have strengthened intergovernmentalist trends in the relations between the member-states and the EC institutions, seen in longer terms, EPC may become a building stone for developing the necessary preconditions for integrative forward movement. Meanwhile, the aspirations of many West Europeans to see their region speak with one voice in international affairs have received a strong boost by the EPC operations during the last decade.

In terms of IGO task performance, EPC has strengthened the effectiveness of commercial policy formulation and implementation assigned to the Commission. From the member-states' point of view, the EC has become a more important instrument of national policy through the EPC coordination effort. EPC also tends to strengthen EC relations with other IGOs as well as to increase the influence of both the Commission and the member-states in the decision-making process of their IGOs. However, EPC, by its very nature, shows the increased utilization of the EC as a separate foreign-policy instrument and no attempt has been made by the member-states to move in this direction. This attitude of the member-states with respect to handling their foreign policy activities is not unique. As McCormick and Kihl have shown, the conduct of foreign affairs through IGOs by their member-states has not increased despite the rising number of these organizations since World War II. They have been used only selectively as instruments for gaining foreign policy objectives.[45]

The European Communities' Influence in U.N. Decision Making:
Levels of EC Cohesion

Member-states of IGOs frequently employ coalition strategies in order to influence the decision-making process, especially if the states concerned already belong to another relatively cohesive IGO. The institutionalized practices for external policy coordination by the EC member-states in the U.N. General Assembly is a good example of this coalition formation behavior. Whatever issue may come up in the United Nations, the EC member-states attempt to coordinate their approach in order to promote their particular national objectives. The voting analysis below can illustrate how successful this coordination has been.

Such a voting analysis is important for several reasons. Integration within an IGO such as the EC is not only increasing the transaction of goods, services, and people or the sharing of common attitudinal maps. The process of EC integration also includes the ability of the component states to coordinate their external behavior and to form a consensus on external questions. External here means the relationships vis-à-vis non-EC states; relationships between and among the EC member-states themselves are seen as domestic transactions. The EC may be integrated in domestic dimensions but there might be little spillover from, say, a common agricultural policy or the standardization of nomenclatures to a common stance in the U.N. General Assembly on decolonization or disarmament/arms control. In addition, such a voting analysis can examine the linkage, if any, between the establishment of a formal IGO such as the EC (and the subsequent entry of new states to the IGO) and the subsequent behavior patterns of the component member-states.

The Rice-Beyle method, which produces an Index of Voting Cohesion (IVC), is utilized to note the degree of voting cohesiveness/common external policy of the EC in the various broad areas of U.N. resolution content.[46] The Index of Voting Cohesion ranges from 0 (denoting low cohesion) to 100 (denoting high cohesion).

Table 5.2, "External Cohesion Level of the Original EC Members," presents the Index of Voting Cohesion (IVC) broken down into the *U.N. Yearbook*-defined content categories. One content category—the Hungarian crisis of 1956, with 15 recorded votes—is at the maximum cohesion level of 100, although there has not been a recorded roll-call vote in this category since Session 17 (1962–63). Three categories—the Korean question, human rights, and the Middle East—are at the 90+ level, but Korea has not been the subject of a roll-call vote in quite a few years. This 90+ IVC level is arbitrarily termed a high degree of external cohesion/common foreign policy, although the votes contained in these four categories represent only 23.5

TABLE 5.2:   External Cohesion Level of the Original EC Members
             (Sessions 3–34, 1948/49–1979/80)

Category	Rank	Votes	IVC
Hungary	1	15	100.00
Korea	2	19	98.95
Human rights	3	83	94.04
Palestine/Israeli- Arab dispute/Middle East	4	133	92.22
Trade/development/ aid/the environment/ NIEO	5	58	89.66
Disarmament/arms control	6	192	88.00
U.N. internal affairs- budget/committees/ administration/ membership	7	104	87.95
Self-determination/ decolonization/ trusteeships/ South Africa	8	399	85.53
International law	9	29	85.42
China	10	20	80.61
The Congo	11	9	74.03
		1061	88.18

Source: Data generated by the authors from an examination of the U.N. General Assembly's plenary roll-call votes as reported in the United Nations *Yearbooks*.

percent of the total recorded roll-call and two of the four categories are almost obsolete.

The original EC scores a medium level of cohesion/common foreign policy—the 80–90 range—on six of the voting categories with 802 votes (75.5 percent). A low level of external cohesion—the 70–80 range on the IVC—includes only what is now an obsolete voting area (the Congo crisis).

The aggregate IVC score for all 1,061 votes across all categories is 88.18, a medium-high level of external cohesion/common foreign policy within the U.N. General Assembly. This 88 + value can most certainly be interpreted as evidence that the original EC member-states do exhibit a relatively strong area of consensus within the United Nations although this 88 + level is the result of the summation of high and low areas of cohesion and is not the result of a cross-sectional 88 + cohesiveness. Conflict and disagreement do exist, however, especially within the self-determination/decolonization voting category and the original EC member-states do not present a unified stance on all issues.

Table 5.3 "Impact of EC Formation upon IVC Levels, Original EC Members," shows that of the 11 *U.N. Yearbook*-defined content categories, only two (Palestine/Israeli-Arab dispute/Middle East and human rights) registered an increase in the degree of voting cohesion/common foreign policy in the post-EC period compared to the pre-EC period. The remaining nine categories were unchanged, decreased, or were not applicable to the pre/post-EC distinction. The aggregate IVC level declined 2.73 percent (87.95 from 90.42) in the post-EC period. This decline (2.47 IVC points) is not very large but it is significant.

The hypothesis that the original six EC member-states should exhibit a higher level of external cohesion/common foreign policy within the U.N. General Assembly once they had formed the EC is just not validated by the data. On the contrary, holding constant the countless other variables, the formal creation of this particular IGO has brought with it decreased levels of external cohesion and thus higher fractionalization levels within the EC at the U.N. General Assembly than existed among the same states before the establishment of the EC. It appears that the EC is moving against a large segment of European public opinion concerning the latter's desire for a common European foreign policy and for a coordinated approach to external affairs.

It can be only conjecture at this point in time to offer explanations of why the original EC member-states' cohesion levels declined in the post-EC period, but a few intuitive comments may indicate some possible reasons. One tentative variable might concern the perceived immediate post-World War II threat of the communism/Soviet Union/cold war nexus and the pressing need to exhibit intra-European solidarity in the face of this perceived threat. As these factors became less and less salient, perhaps the EC member-states based their foreign policy decision-making process upon other independent but mutually antagonistic concerns.

A second possible explanation for the decline (however small) in the degree of a common EC foreign policy within another IGO (the United Nations) might lie within the EC itself. Perhaps the very success of the EC—success in terms of increased experience in cooperation and consensus formation, greater understanding, and ability to communicate—had led to a greater psychological independence of the EC member-states. Assured of a solid floor of group support and consensus (for example, the EC's support of the United Kingdom against Argentina over the Falkland Islands), the EC members may be thus able to pursue a more independent foreign policy in areas that do not directly impinge upon the Rome Treaties (for example,

TABLE 5.3: Impact of EC Formation Upon IVC Levels, Original EC Members (Sessions 3–34, 1948/49–1979/80)

Category	Pre-EC		Post-EC		Change	Percent Change
	Votes	IVC	Votes	IVC		
Palestine/Middle East	14	73.86	119	94.39	+20.53	+27.79
Human rights	9	84.23	74	95.24	+11.01	+13.07
Hungary	11	100.00	4	100.00	–	–
International law	10	85.82	19	85.23	– 0.59	– 0.68
Korea	8	100.00	11	98.17	– 1.83	– 1.83
U.N. internal affairs	11	92.40	93	87.44	– 4.96	– 5.67
Self-determination/decolonization	32	92.26	367	84.94	– 7.32	– 7.93
Trade/development	3	100.00	55	89.10	–10.90	–10.90
China	5	100.00	15	74.15	–25.85	–25.85
Disarmament/arms control	–	–	192	88.00	–	–
Congo	–	–	9	74.03	–	–
Total	103	90.42	958	87.95	– 2.47	– 2.73*

Source: Data generated by the authors from an examination of the U.N. General Assembly's plenary roll-call votes as reported in the United Nations Yearbooks.

*Percentage change of IVC levels from pre-EC to post-EC period.

France's atmospheric nuclear testing in summer 1973). But these are only exploratory remarks and additional research is necessary before they could be employed as explanatory variables.

Table 5.4, "External Cohesion Level of the New Three EC Members, Sessions 3–34," shows that, when the new three (excluding Greece) are compared to the original six, the two subgroups mirror each other in the first four categories, both on category position and IVC-level range. Of the 11 voting categories, the new three score 100 on one category, 90–99 on four, 80–89 on four, one (Self-Determination) is at the 73 + level, and the lowest IVC level is at 48 + (the obsolete China category). What is interesting in Table 5.4 is the relatively low (73.97) IVC score for the new three on the category Self-determination/decolonization/trusteeships/South Africa. This

TABLE 5.4: External Cohesion Level of the New Three EC Members (Sessions 3–34, 1948/49–1979/80)

Category	Rank	Votes	IVC
Hungary	1	15	100.00
Korea	2	19	98.23
Human rights	3	83	94.06
Palestine/Israeli- Arab dispute/ Middle East	4	133	92.38
U.N. internal affairs- budget/committees/ administration/ membership	5	104	91.08
Disarmament/arms control	6	192	89.58
The Congo	7	9	88.43
International law	8	29	85.49
Trade/development/ aid/NIEO/the environment	9	58	85.41
Self-determination/ decolonization/ trusteeships/ South Africa	10	399	73.97
China	11	20	48.25
Total		1061	83.68*

Source: Data generated by the authors from an examination of the U.N. General Assembly's plenary roll-call votes as reported in the United Nations *Yearbooks*.
*IVC level

voting category represents approximately 37 percent of the total coded resolutions and represents a majority of all the resolutions considered by the General Assembly. This 73.97 IVC score can be compared to the original six EC members' IVC level of 85.53 for the same category. The aggregate IVC score for the new three stands at 83.68, 4.50 IVC units below the original members' aggregate score of 88.18.

Table 5.5, "Impact of EC Entry Upon IVC Levels, New Three EC Members," shows that of the 11 broad categories (discounting the five categories that were not applicable after 1973), all registered an increase in the degree of voting cohesion/common foreign policy in the post-EC entry period compared to the pre-entry period. The aggregate level increased over 11 percent (8.80 IVC points) to 87.98 in the post-entry period. Although as discussed above, the original EC members may have declined in terms of IVC levels in the post-EC period (however small), the new three—as Table 5.5 shows, increased their coordination and degree of common foreign policy once they entered the European Communities. The fact of belonging to one IGO—the EC—has influenced the decision-making process and behavior of the component states in another IGO (the U.N. General Assembly).

The preceding voting analysis was concerned with 1) the level of external cohesion exhibited by the EC and 2) the impact of the formation of, and entry into, the EC has had upon these external policy coordination levels. A side calculation of the aggregate IVC level for the expanded EC (nine states, 36 A-B pairs) for all 1,061 coded resolutions results in an IVC of 86.56. It appears that this level will remain relatively constant over the next few years.

The institutionalized practices for external policy coordination by the EC member-states in the U.N. General Assembly has been shown to be a good example of coalition formation by members of one IGO in another IGO. On the whole, the EC member-states attempt to coordinate their approach in order to promote their particular national objectives. They realize that only through coordination will they be able to exert a measure of influence in U.N. bodies that are dominated by Third World states. Although our analysis has centered on the General Assembly, there is evidence that in other organs and committees of the United Nations the EC member-states have also employed coordination in their approaches to dealing with various problems. This was clearly the case in the ECOSOC negotiations on the code of conduct for transnational corporations, which is discussed in some detail in Chapter 7.

What we see, then, in this illustrative case is the use of an IGO, the EC, as an instrument for the pursuit of national policies by its member-states. The Communities are used as the core for coalition formation, with national and EC civil servants playing important roles through the EPC mechanism. However, it is important to note that the EC coordination efforts

TABLE 5.5: Impact of EC Entry Upon IVC Levels, New Three EC Members (Sessions 3–34, 1948/49–1979/80)

| Category | Pre-Entry | | Post-Entry | | | |
	Votes	IVC	Votes	IVC	Change	Percent Change
Self-determination/decolonization	226	70.23	173	78.86	+ 8.63	+ 12.28
Palestine/Middle East	43	88.50	90	94.24	+ 5.74	+ 6.48
Disarmament/arms control	59	85.93	133	91.21	+ 5.28	+ 6.14
U.N. internal affairs	48	89.06	56	92.82	+ 3.76	+ 4.22
Human rights	28	91.58	55	95.33	+ 3.75	+ 4.09
Trade/development	22	84.64	36	85.89	+ 1.25	+ 1.47
Hungary	15	100.00	–	–	–	–
Korea	19	98.23	–	–	–	–
The Congo	9	88.43	–	–	–	–
International law	29	85.49	–	–	–	–
China	20	48.25	–	–	–	–
Total	518	79.18	543	87.98	+ 8.80*	+ 11.11*

Source: Data generated by the authors from an examination of the U.N. General Assembly's plenary roll-call votes as reported in the United Nations *Yearbooks*.

*Percentage changes of IVC levels for pre-EC to post-EC period.

have not led to a special relationship between the EC and the United Nations, although interbureaucratic contacts between EC and U.N. civil servants may well have been intensified.

Interface between Regional and National Interests in the European Parliament

As mentioned above, there are several means available to member governments to influence the input and output of the decision-making process in a specific IGO. One such avenue is the formal participation of the members of the European Parliament within the EC.

This case has one limited objective: to identify the degree to which the members of the EP vote along partisan-ideological lines compared to national-interest lines. The fact that some beginnings have been made to formulate transnational party platforms across the EC and that the groupings have been established in the Parliament leads to the hypothesis that transnational party affiliation will be a stronger explanatory variable for the observed voting differences than will national identity (for example, a socialist will agree more with other socialists, regardless of country than with fellow nationals of different parties).

The findings will allow some comments regarding possible future conflict/consensus within the Parliament, depending upon the scope of bloc-like behavior and voting similarities. Strong transnational party groups may encourage EC interest groups to use their electoral weight to bargain for changes. A more balanced representation of interests at the European level might then be secured for, until now, the most influential interest groups have been producers and employers. Cohesive parties in Parliament—at least those on the left—may be more sympathetic to trade unions and consumer and environmental groups.

Finally, some comments can be offered on the scope of the erosion of long-held national mind-sets by Europeans and the emergence of truly transnational attitudes. It would be significant for the future of Europe if the representatives in Parliament actually behave (vote) as European socialists or Christian Democrats than as, say, West Germans, Danes, or Italians. This would intimate that nationalism is breaking down and, while not necessarily decreasing levels of conflict in the short run (ideological conflict would be simply substituted for nationalism), elite consensus and cooperation appear to be more readily attainable when based upon explicit and bargainable political goals rather than when based upon the subconsciousness of national identity.

The degree of voting similarity between and among this study's various subgroups (the nine national delegations and the six major transnational party groupings) is noted by utilizing the Index of Likeness Between Groups (IVL), devised by Stuart A. Rice.[47]

Table 5.6, "Index of Voting Likeness—Country and Party Comparisons," contains the data for the 12 largest specific country/party groups. It seems to confirm the hypothesis that partisan political ideology (defined as membership in one of the transnational party groups in the European Parliament) is a stronger explanatory variable for the observed voting differences than national interest (defined by country of representation) and is seen to be correct in nine of the 12 specific groups analyzed. The differences in IVL values between party identification and national identification for the nine confirmed cases range from a high of 48.31 (the West German PPE) to a low of 2.11 (the UK socialists). The three groups that do not agree with the hypothesis are the French communists (-5.89), the Italian communists (-6.75), and the French socialists (-16.53). These latter three groups show a higher level of voting agreement with the rest of their country representatives than with the rest of their transnational party group in the European Parliament.

Table 5.6 could be explained at length but this section will only discuss

TABLE 5.6: Index of Voting Likeness — Party and Country Comparisons

Group [a]	N [b]	IVL to Rest of Party [c]	IVL to Rest of Country [d]	Change
German PPE	42	95.74	47.43	+ 48.31
German SOC	35	70.26	42.63	+ 27.63
Netherlands PPE	10	93.05	65.60	+ 27.45
Italian PPE	29	91.70	64.86	+ 26.84
Belgian PPE	10	91.78	71.26	+ 20.52
French PD	16	88.09	80.55	+ 7.54
French LIB	16	87.63	82.88	+ 4.75
Italian SOC	13	78.99	76.83	+ 2.16
UK SOC	17	78.29	76.18	+ 2.11
French COM	19	63.70	69.59	− 5.89
Italian COM	23	64.71	71.46	− 6.75
French SOC	21	62.04	78.57	− 16.53

a. The UK conservatives are not included in this table. The UK conservatives represent 61 of the 64 members of the European democrat group in parliament. The remaining three EDs is simply too small a group to compare to the 61 UK EDs.

b. Only those groups with at least ten members are analyzed.

c. This IVL is calculated by comparing the specific group's voting to the same transnational party group less the specific group's members.

d. This IVL is calculated by comparing the specific group's voting to the same country group less the specific group's members.

Source: Data generated by the authors from an examination of the European Parliament's plenary roll-call votes as reported in the *Official Journal* of the European Communities.

a couple of the more interesting results. The most striking aspect of Table 5.6 is the degree to which the West Germans (at least 77 of 81) exhibit the least amount of nationalism. The 42 West German members of the PPE have an IVL value of 47.43 against the remaining West German members of the Parliament—a 48.31 IVL difference when compared to their IVL against the other PPE members in Parliament; the 35 West German members of the socialist group have a 42.63 IVL score against the remaining West German members—a 27.63 difference compared to other socialists. The West Germans appear to be approaching the votes in Parliament not as Germans but as members of transnational party groups—the partisan ideology of Christian democracy (PPE) and of socialism has, at least for the West Germans, surpassed the national interest mind-set. Perhaps guilt feelings about the excesses of German nationalism bringing on World War II may be an explanation of this pattern.

But as the West Germans are deemphasizing nationalism, the French and the Italians, especially the communists and the French socialists appear to value national identity more than transnational party ideology. This is doubly striking since our conventional wisdom has the parties of the left as more monolithic, coherent, and more internationally oriented. The French socialists' IVL to the rest of the French delegation is 16.53 points higher than to the rest of the socialist group in the European Parliament.

The degree to which the French and Italian communists agree more with other French-Italian representatives than with other European communists is also striking. The reason for this can be isolated but, as above, cannot as yet be explained adequately. The low IVLs for the rest of the party is directly attributable to the Italy-France pair (Italy and France have 42 of the 44 members of the Parliament's communist and allies group). The French communists show a low IVL with other communists because they have a low IVL with the Italian communists; just the obverse is true with the Italian communists. This may locate where the difference is but it only poses an additional question: Why do the French and Italian communists show the rather low level of voting agreement?

One possible preliminary reason could be the very real differences in the political outlook and behavior of these two parties, both in their respective domestic environments and their international positions. The French have been much more Moscow-oriented than the Italians and, conversely, the Italians are the leading voice for Eurocommunism. Additional research may provide a better explanation of their behavior, however.

The transnational political groups in the European Parliament do attempt to work out common positions on the major policy issues but the degree of internal cohesiveness, although higher for the political groups than for the country delegations, does not reach significant levels. It is all too obvious that members frequently vote counter to the majority view of their group. The very fact of direct elections may contribute to this comparative independence of the individual MEP. No longer responsible to the party hierarchy in the home parliament, the MEP has much more leeway when he is now accountable to an amorphous electorate and the links between MEPs and their constituents are often very tenous.

In any case, it may not be realistice to expect a high degree of cohesiveness or degree of bloc-like behavior from members of a political group who have been elected not as a member of a European political party but, rather, as a member of one of 55 separate national parties. The political groups are not (yet) transnational political parties. The groups are only broad coalitions/alliances composed of different national parties.

The transnational political groups in the European Parliament may develop into transnational parties in the future but, in order to do so, they will first have to present candidates for the EP across the 10 member-states under a single label and with a single, common platform. At present, there are three parties linked at the European level—the socialists, European Peoples Party (PPE), and the liberals. These federations attempted to coordinate the 1979 campaign and they attempt to maintain links between the EP groups and the national political parties. But these federations still cannot be called transnational political parties.

In terms of utilizing the European Parliament as part of the EC institutional framework for the promotion of national interests of the EC member-states, this illustrative case does not offer much supporting evidence. On the other hand, votes cast on the basis of similar views by the European party groupings have not effectively enhanced the integraton process. One reason is the very limited power of the Parliament under the EC treaties that so far has been only marginally increased despite its somewhat improved legitimacy as a result of the direct election process. The other reason is that communications between the MEP and his huge constituency are fragmentary. Although the EC Commission has allied itself closely with the Parliament, the main channel for the exertion of influence on EC decisions remains the Council of Ministers, representing mainly national interests. Thus, in spite of wide-ranging transnational coalition possibilities among MEPs, interest groups, and Eurocrats, the directly elected European Parliament is nothing more than a very weak link in the EC decision-making apparatus.

NOTES

1. See Johan Kaufmann, *United Nations Decision Making* (Rockville, Md.: Sijthoff and Noordhoff, 1980), esp. Chapter 6.
2. See Chapter 6 of this book for a discussion of the role that INGOs play in this process.

3. See Werner J. Feld and John K. Wildgen, *Domestic Political Realities and European Unification* (Boulder, Col.: Westview Press, 1976), pp. 119–44.

4. Article 51 of the U.N. Charter is cited by both the North Atlantic Treaty (NATO) and the Warsaw Treaty, but this is more pro forma than otherwise.

5. Charles W. Kegley and Eugene R. Wittkopf, *American Foreign Policy* (New York, St. Martin's Press, 1979), p. 34.

6. For some background, see Martin Hill, *The United Nations System: Coordinating Its Economic and Social Work* (Cambridge and New York: Cambridge University Press, 1968) and Mahdi Elmandjra, *The United Nations Systems: An Analysis* (London: Faber and Faber, 1973).

7. See Hans J. Michelmann, *Organizational Effectiveness in a Multinational Bureaucracy* (Westmead, England: Saxon House, 1978), passim. Former U.N. Secretary-General Kurt Waldheim makes this point in the Introduction to his book, *Building the Future Order* (New York: The Free Press, 1980).

8. See Felice Morgenstern, "Legality in International Organizations," *The British Yearbook of International Law* 48 (1976–77), pp. 241–57. See also Ruth B. Russell, *A History of the United Nations Charter* (Washington, D.C.: The Brookings Institution, 1958), pp. 847–54.

9. For details, see ibid., pp. 243–44. We should note that voluntary total or partial withdrawal from membership is not encouraged in most IGOs, although for political reasons attempts are made. See in Chapter 4 the case on France's withdrawal from NATO's military structure.

10. Helen Wallace, "The Establishment of the Regional Development Fund: Common Policy or Pork Barrel," in Helen Wallace, William Wallace and Carole Webb, *Policy-Making in the European Community* (New York: Wiley, 1977), pp. 137–63.

11. Quoted in "Report on the Regional Problems in the Enlarged Community," Supplement 8/73 to the "Bulletin of European Communities," published in Brussels.

12. See Dudley Seers et al., *Underdeveloped Europe: Studies in Core-Periphery Relationships*, The Institute of Development Studies (Atlantic Highlands, N.J.: Humanities Press, 1979).

13. Quoted in "Report on the Regional Problems in the Enlarged Community," op. cit.

14. *Die Zeit*, December 14, 1973.

15. *Agence Europe Bulletin*, January 25 and 26, 1974, November 1, 1974, and December 12, 1974. It is interesting that France managed to obtain at least a small portion of the Fund's disbursement (15 percent) and even West Germany received 6.4 percent

16. *Agence Europe Bulletin*, December 4, 1980.

17. *The Economist*, October 24, 1981, p. 38.

18. *Agence Europe Bulletin*, July 16, 1981.

19. See *Agence Europe Bulletin*, January 28 and March 25, 1982.

20. Sean MacBride, *Many Voices, One World*, Report by the International Commission for the Study of Communication Problems (New York: Unipub., 1980), p. 21.

21. These paragraphs are drawn from "The Global News Battle," *World Press Review*, October 1981, pp. 41–43.

22. See J. Clement Jones, *Mass Media Codes of Ethics and Councils: A Comparative International Study on Professional Standards* (Paris: UNESCO, 1980).

23. Barbas Crossette, "Bid to Curb Funds for UNESCO is Set," *New York Times*, September 16, 1981.

24. These quotations are drawn from Paul Lewis, "West's News Organizations Vow to Fight UNESCO on Press Curbs," *New York Times*, May 17, 1981.

25. Alan Riding, "UNESCO Parley on the Press Opens With U.S. Opposing Many Plans," *New York Times*, January 19, 1982.

26. D. Puchala and R. Hopkins, "Toward Innovation in the Global Food Regime," *International Organization*, Summer 1978, p. 624. These paragraphs are drawn from David N. Balaam and Michael J. Carey, *Food Politics: The Regional Conflict* (Monclair, N.J.: Allanheld, Osmun, 1981), pp. 198–200.

27. Ibid., p. 202. Also, H. Nau, "The Diplomacy of World Food: Goals, Capabilities, Issues and Arenas," *International Organization*, Summer 1978, p. 780.

28. These paragraphs are drawn from Thomas G. Weiss and Robert S. Jordan, *The World Food Conference and Global Problem Solving* (New York: Praeger, 1976), pp. 10–12.

29. Quoted in ibid., p. 11.

30. Quoted in Balaam and Carey, op. cit., p. 199. The entire reference to Director-General Boerma is from p. 199. The remainder of this discussion is from Weiss and Jordan, op. cit., p. 12. For an examination of the dilemma posed for the U.S., see Seth King, "Experts See No New Way to Treat an Old Problem," *New York Times*, August 15, 1982.

31. These paragraphs are drawn from Weiss and Jordan, op. cit., pp. 13–14. The fact that the Soviet Union is not a member of FAO was an important reason for going to the United Nations.

32. These paragraphs are drawn from Balaam and Carey, op. cit., pp. 203–04.

33. For details see Alessandro Silj, *Europe's Political Puzzle* (Cambridge, Mass.: Harvard University Center for International Affairs, December 1967, Occasional Paper no. 17).

34. For details see "Bericht der Aussenminister der Mitgliedstaaten der Europäischen Gemeinschaften and die Staatsbzw. Juli 1970, betr. mogkucge Fortschritte auf dem Gebiet der politischen Einigung," *Europa Archiv* 25 (1970), D520–D524.

35. *Agence Europe Bulletin*, September 18, 1975.

36. G. Bonvicini, "Der Dualismus zwischen EPZ und Gemeinschaft," in *Die Europäische Politische Zusammenarbeit*, ed. Reinhardt Rummel and Wolfgang Wessels (Bonn: Europa Union Verlag, 1978), pp. 89–90.

37. Helen Wallace, *National Governments and the European Communities* (London: Chatham House: PEP, 1973), p. 84.

38. For Greater detail see Wolfgang Wessels, "New Forms of Foreign Policy in Western Europe," in *Western Europe's Global Reach*, ed. Werner J. Feld (New York: Pergamon Press, 1980), pp. 12–29; and *Agence Europe Bulletin*, October 16, 1981.

39. For details see Beate Kohler, "Die Europäisch-Amerikanischen Beziehunger-Die EPZ als Vehikelder Emanzipation?" in *Die Europäisch Politische Zusammenarbeit*, ed. Reinhardt Rummel and Wolfgang Wessels (Bonn: Europa Union Verlag, 1978), pp. 167–88 on pp. 178–80.

40. For details see Goetz von Groll, "The Helsinki Consultations" and "The Geneva Final Act of the CSCE," *Aussenpolitik* 24 (1973), 123–29 and 26 (1975), 247–69, respectively.

41. EC Commission, *Ninth General Report* (1975), pp. 260–61.

42. *Agence Europe Bulletin*, October 27, 1977 and November 7/8, 1977.

43. *Agence Europe Bulletin*, July 13/14, 1981.

44. *Agence Europe Bulletin*, April 13/14, 1982.

45. James M. McCormick and Young W. Kihl, "Intergovernmental Organizations and Foreign Policy Behavior: Some Empirical Findings," *American Political Science Review* 73 (June 1979), pp. 494–504.

46. The Rice-Beyle Method produces an index of voting agreement between pairs of voters by pairing every voter within each group to every other voter in the same group on every vote. The Index of Voting Cohesion (IVC) is a result of the following expression:

$$\text{IVC} = \frac{f + \frac{1}{2}g}{t} \times 100 \text{ percent, where}$$

IVC = ranges between 0 (denoting maximum disagreement) and 100 (denoting maximum cohesion);

f = the number of votes in which each A-B pair of voters vote in an identical manner (A and B both vote pro, con, or abstain);

g = the number of votes in which each A-B pair of voters display partial cohesion (A votes pro or con, B abstains); and

t = the total number of votes in which each A-B pair participates.

Aggregated IVCs are calculated by summing the individual IVCs within each group and dividing by the number of A-B pairs: $\text{IVC} = \Sigma \text{IVCi}/n$. For aggregated IVCs where the number of votes are not identical, $\text{IVC} = \Sigma(\text{IVCi} \times [ti/\Sigma t])$. See Leon Hurwitz, "The EEC in the United Nations: The Voting Behavior of Eight Countries, 1958–1973," *Journal of Common Market Studies* 13 (March, 1975): 224–43 and "The EEC and Decolonization: The Voting Behaviour of the Nine in the UN General Assembly," *Political Studies* (Oxford) 24 (December, 1976): 435–47.

47. The Index of Voting Likeness (IVL) Between Groups is expressed as follows:

IVL = 100-/A-B/, where

A = percentage of subgroup A voting pro on resolution Z,

B = percentage of subgroup B voting pro on resolution Z,

/A-B/ = absolute value of A-B, and where IVL ranges between 0 (maximum disagreement) and 100 (maximum voting similarity).

Aggregated IVLs are calculated as $\text{IVL} = \Sigma \text{IVLiz}/i$. For aggregated IVLs where the number of votes are not identical, $\text{IVL} = \Sigma(\text{IVLiz}) \times 1/\Sigma z$. See Stuart A. Rice, *Quantitative Methods in Politics* (New York: Knopf, 1928) as discussed by Leroy N. Rieselbach, "Quantitative Techniques for Studying Voting Behavior in the UN General Assembly," *International Organization* 14 (Spring, 1960): 290–306.

Chapter 6

The Role of International Nongovernmental Organizations in IGO Decision Making

INTRODUCTION

In Chapter 1 we discussed the nature and growth of International NGOs. In this chapter we want to examine the goals pursued and supported by INGOs, to focus on the effectiveness of INGO goal attainment in the international arena, and to assess some of the means used by them for this purpose. Since INGOs, as discussed in Chapter 1, pursue a variety of interests, the decision as to whether or not to establish a particular INGO must take into consideration a careful calculation of benefits and costs regarding the potential for attaining the goals that are viewed as essential in advancing the organization's interests. It might appear that this attainment potential is small because INGOs lack the attributes of sovereignty and are inherently quite different from nation-states. However, the notion of benefits vis-á-vis especially interdependence costs is useful because INGOs, just as states, pursue various interests. If the attainment potential of a national NGO can be enhanced through contacts and action on the international level, including consultation status with selected IGO bodies, then the decision about organizing above the national level is likely to be positive.

The judgment as to whether or not to engage in international organization can be affected by the perceived usefulness of different strategies to achieve the INGO's international, national, or even subnational goals. These strategies can be broken down into three groups:

1. To call for and insist upon the formulation of appropriate policies by national governments and/or IGOs or, if possible, to institute such policies through INGOs themselves, with the explicit or tacit authorization of, or at least assurance of noninterference by, governments. This assurance may be presumed to be given when

governments do not object to transnational policies introduced without their advance knowledge.

2. To promote, modify, or oppose existing policies and policy goals of global and regional IGOs in accordance with INGO objectives.

3. To support, modify, or oppose existing policies and policy goals of national governments in accordance with INGO objectives.

The aims included in groups 2 and 3 are likely to be functions of the specific objectives encompassed by the first category, but this is not necessarily the case when it comes to general, often ideological, goals. It is also quite conceivable that a particular INGO will support specific IGO goals but oppose national goals of a particular government. Therefore, IGOs and national governments may perceive an individual INGO as either friendly or hostile, and these perceptions may differ from case to case.[1]

The general support goals pursued by INGOs for the achievement of their particular objectives can be gleaned from responses to a detailed questionnaire sent to 2,196 organizations in 1967 by the International Peace Research Institute in Oslo. More than 800 INGOs returned completed questionnaires. Based on the responses, Table 6.1 presents a rank ordering of six general support goals according to their relative frequency. These goals reflect the emphasis placed by INGOs on transactional flows and the potential of interdependence.

The creation of IGOs by itself is, of course, not sufficient to exert the necessary influence for successful goal attainment. This requires organizational effectiveness and adequate resources of individual INGOs to spread their gospel.

TABLE 6.1: General Support Goals of International NGOs

	Percent Response
To improve communication between members in the special field of the organization so that they can do a better job	87
To promote general cooperation and friendship between the members	79
To let members know each other so that they have contacts in other countries for travel, correspondence, and so forth.	56
To work for social and economic development in the world.	51
To improve general cooperation and friendship between all human beings	48
To work for peace between all nations and peoples in the world	45

Source: Kjell Skjelsbaëk, "A Survey of International Nongovernmental Organizations," International Associations (May 1974), pp. 267–70.

INGOs AND THE U.N. SYSTEM

For the United States, the constitutional right of a citizen to petition his government for redress of a grievance or to influence governmental action, is a domestic expression of the INGO tradition. It is thus no great leap conceptually, to embrace the notion that groups of citizens can petition their governments concerning their governments' participation in an IGO, and by extension, petition the IGO itself.

In fact, this was clearly set forth in Article 71 of the U.N. Charter that provided:

> The Economic and Social Council may make suitable arrangements for consultation with nongovernmental organizations which are concerned with matters within its competence. Such arrangements may be made with international organizations and, where appropriate, with national organizations after consultation with the member of the United Nations concerned.

These words, according to one author, are humble and couched in "rather condescending terminology"[2] and thus envisaged an insignificant, or at best a peripheral, role for INGOs in relation to the overall activities of the organization.[3] As of January 1980, approximtely 800 INGOs had consultative status, divided into three categories:

A. Category I: Organizations that are concerned with most of the activities of the Council and can demonstrate to the satisfaction of the Council that they have marked and sustained contributions to make to the achievement of the objectives of the United Nations (with respect to international, economic, social, cultural, educational, health, scientific, technological and related matters, and to questions of human rights), and are closely involved with the economic and social life of the peoples of the areas they represent and whose membership, which should be considerable, is broadly representative of major segments of population in a large number of countries.

B. Category II: Organizations that have a special competence in, and are concerned specifically with, only a few of the fields of activity covered by the Council, and that are known internationally within the fields for which they have or seek consultative status.

C. Roster: Other organizations that do not have general or special consultative status by which the Council, or the secretary-general of the United Nations in consultation with the Council or its Committee on Non-Governmental Organizations, considers can make occasional and useful contributions to the work of the Council, or its subsidiary bodies or other United Nations bodies within their competence.

Granting consultative status entitles the organization to propose agenda items for consideration by the council or its subsidiary bodies (Category I), attend meetings

(Categories I and II and Roster), submit written statements (Categories I and II and Roster) and be granted hearings (Categories I and II).[4]

These formal provisions have not, however, resulted in an expansion of the influence of INGOs in the work of ECOSOC. This is because ECOSOC itself has not played the role in the United Nations system that was envisaged for it. The rapid expansion of the membership resulted in a greater interest in using the General Assembly—where all member-states are equal in voting rights—rather than ECOSOC to deal with economic and social matters.

A further discouraging feature with respect to INGO influence has been the failure of the so-called restructuring effort of the United Nations system to restore ECOSOC to a position of genuine influence. The fault lies with the developing states, which have preferred to use the General Assembly as their primary forum for carrying on the North-South dialogue, thus bypassing ECOSOC.[5] The developing states have preferred in particular the General Assembly's second (economic and financial) and third (social, humanitarian, and cultural) committees over ECOSOC. This development began in the 1960s and accelerated in the 1970s. As one observer summarized it:

> ECOSOC was among the first of the Third World's targets. With the arrival of close to two score members from Africa the Council came under heavy attack. It was called completely unrepresentative of the total United Nations membership and a tool of the rich. One African delegate proclaimed in public session that his chief purpose in serving on the Economic and Social Council was to destroy it. In 1964–65, the effectiveness of the Council was severely impaired. A majority of the LDCs reinterpreted Chapters IX and X (of the Charter) as vesting all responsibilities for economic and social matters in the General Assembly. They denied that the Council had any real function or power, particularly to coordinate programs and activities.[6]

In 1979, at the thirty-fourth session of the General Assembly, an attempt was made to restore some vitality to ECOSOC. It was proposed that ECOSOC's membership should be expanded by amending the U.N. Charter, thus making it representative of the total membership. No action was taken on this recommendation. Consequently, influencing either ad hoc conferences—such as the Stockholm Conference on the Human Environment and others that were held in the 1970s—or continuing conferences—such as the General Assembly—became strong goals for both national and international NGOs. In fact, the level of interest of INGOs and their participation in IGO conference activities were generally and dramatically enhanced after the 1972 Stockholm Conference, in which participation went beyond those INGOs in the traditional consultative status to include a broader spectrum of NGO activity. Grass-roots organizations concerned with all aspects of environmental issues gained valuable experience operating as public interest groups at the conference.[7]

Some INGOs view themselves as single-issue oriented. They concentrate on a particular issue over many years and have drawn to them persons with a particular commitment to that issue. One of the reasons for this orientation is the efficiency achieved by an INGO that concentrates on a single issue rather than risking dissipating its scarce volunteer and other resources on a wider range of issues. It is not uncommon around the United Nations to encounter INGO representatives who are trying to make the point that their particular issue is pivotal to all others, but of course this may not necessarily be so. Most issues that are taken up through conferences are interrelated with other issues to the extent that mutually reinforcing coalitions of INGOs often prove more effective. Recognizing this, an International Coalition for Development Action (ICDA) was created in the late 1970s to enhance the effectiveness of INGOs in ad hoc conferences.

In any event, the relations of the United Nations and the specialized agencies with INGOs based usually on specific provisions of their constituent instruments, rules of procedure and resolutions, are diverse even though the general principles and objectives of consultative relationships are basically similar.[8]

On the basis of parallel legal provisions, the various specialized agencies have established consultative relations with those different sets of INGOs particularly relevant to their work. For easy reference, the respective legal bases of the consultative arrangements for INGOs within the U.N. system and the methods of classification of INGOs are given in Table 6.2.

In general, the main purposes for the consultative and cooperative arrangements within the U.N. system are: 1) to secure advice and technical cooperation from competent INGOs; 2) to enable organizations that represent important elements of public opinion in many states to express their views; and 3) to advance the objectives of the U.N. system through promotional activities and projects of INGOs. In broad terms, to acquire consultative status, INGOs should be: 1) particularly interested in matters within the competence of the U.N. body or agency concerned; 2) able and willing to make an effective contribution to the achievement of its objectives; and 3) internationally recognized and broadly representative of interested groups in a substantial number of states. However, the specific requirements for classifying INGOs and the corresponding privileges and obligations are far from uniform.

Like ECOSOC, several specialized agencies, particularly the ILO, FAO, and UNESCO, classify INGOs into three consultative categories; but the other agencies and activities maintain an undifferentiated list of INGOs in consultative status. Among the relevant economic and social bodies under

TABLE 6.2: INGOS and the United Nations System: Consultative Arrangements

U.N. Bodies and Agencies:

Basis for Arrangements	INGO Consultative Categories			Undifferentiated
	First	Second	Third	
	Category I	Category II	Roster	
ECOSOC Art. 71, U.N. Charter; ECOSOC res. 1296 (XLIV)	NGOs concerned with most of ECOSOC activities; making marked contribution towards its objectives; broadly representative.	NGOs concerned specially with some fields of ECOSOC activity; known internationally in such fields; or having as primary objective the promotion of U.N. purposes.	NGOs making occasional, useful contribution to ECOSOC work; or having consultative status with a specialized agency or a U.N. body.	
UNCTAD General Assembly res. 1995 (XIX). para. 11; Rule 79. UNCTAD rules of procedure; UNCTAD TD B res. 14 (II)				NGOs concerned with trade and development.
UNIDO General Assembly res. 2152 (XXI), para. 36; Rule 76, IDB rules of procedure.				NGOs concerned with industrial development.
UNEP General Assembly res. 2997 (XXVII), para.				NGOs having regular contacts with UNEP.

Body (legal basis)	Category I as in ECOSOC	Category II as in ECOSOC	Roster as in ECOSOC
UNEP IV.5; Rule 69, UNEP rules of procedure			
UNHCR Rules 9, 10, 11 of the rules of procedures of UNHCR Advisory Committee on Refugees			
UNICEF General Assembly res. 57 (I), para. 2, and res. 417 (V), paras. 3, 6.	NGOs in consultative status with ECOSOC (including Roster).		
UNDP ECOSOC res. 1739 (LIV); Directive UNDP/ADM/226	National (local) NGOs; technical assistance NGOs; international NGOs.		
IAEA Art. XVI, IAEA Statute; GC (II)/Res. 20	NGOs concerned with atomic energy and able to contribute to IAEA work; of recognized international standing.		
ILO Art. 12 (3), ILO Constitution	1 General Interest Consultative Status; concerned with wide range of ILO activities.	2 Special Interest Consultative Status; concerned with particular sector.	Special List: interested in some aspects of ILO work.

U.N. Bodies and Agencies:

Basis for Arrangements	INGO Consultative Categories			
	First	Second	Third	Undifferentiated
UNESCO Art. XI, UNESCO Constitution, Directives approved by eleventh session of General Conference, as amended at its fourteenth session.	Category A Consultative Associate. Broadly international; of proven competence in a major UNESCO field; with record of major contribution to UNESCO work; capable of advising on preparation and participating in execution of UNESCO programs; able to help coordinate NGO work in field.	Category B Information and Consultative. Record of effective assistance to UNESCO for at least 2 years; proven ability to assist in UNESCO programs.	Category C Mutual Information. Able and willing to make effective contribution to achievement of UNESCO objectives; broadly representative with international directing body.	
FAO Art. XIII (3), FAO Constitution; Rule XVII, general rules of FAO; Conference res. nos. 37/53, 74/51, 37/53, 39/57;	Consultative Status; Concerned with substantial portion of FAO's field; broadly international and suf-	Specialized Consultative Status. Concerned with particular portion of FAO's field; representative of its	Liaison Status. Concerned with a portion of FAO's field; able to give practical assistance; sufficiently	

"FAO Policy Concerning Relations with International Non-Governmental Organizations."	ficiently representative of its field of interest; of recognized standing.	specialized field.	representative of its field.	
WHO Art. 71, WHO Constitution; "Relations with Non-Governmental Organizations" (WHO, *Basic Documents*, 25th ed., 1975, pp. 67–70).				NGOs concerned with world health, normally international, widely representative and of recognized standing.
IMO Art. 48, IMO Convention; Rules Governing Relationships with Non-Governmental International Organizations, approved by IMO Assembly on April 13, 1961.				NGOs concerned with shipping and other maritime questions; able to make substantive contribution.
WMO Art. 26, WMO Convention, WMO Executive Committee res. 2 (EC-IV).				NGOs concerned with world meteorological matters
ITU Art. 27, ITU Convention.				NGOs concerned with telecommunications matters.

U.N. Bodies and Agencies:

	INGO Consultative Categories		
Basis for Arrangements	First	Second	Third	Undifferentiated
UPU Art. 15, para. 6 (c), UPU Convention				NGOs concerned with postal matters.
WIPO Art. 13, WIPO Convention.				NGOs concerned with intellectual property.
ICAO Art. 65, ICAO Convention				NGOs concerned with air travel.

Source:

the General Assembly, only the Advisory Commitee of the UNHCR applies the ECOSOC classification in its relations with INGOs: UNCTAD, UN-IDO, UNEP, UNICEF, and UNDP maintain so far single lists of INGOs. In all cases, a distinction is made between the INGOs on the official list and those not having consultative status with which each organization maintains informal working relations.

While the United Nations and its various specialized and other agencies embrace the largest number of INGOs in consultative status, other non-United Nations IGOs, such as the Council of Europe and the Organization of American States, also have adopted similar relationships with INGOs.

The classification takes two forms. The first form, based on the scope of INGO activities relative to the competence of a U.N. body or agency, has been adopted by ECOSOC, UNHCR, ILO, and FAO. It distinguishes INGOs possessing a wide-ranging interest from those with a specialized interest, and both from those with a more limited or occasional interest in the work of a U.N. body or agency. The second form, used by UNESCO, takes account of the capacity for and record of effective contribution to the achievement of the agency's objectives. In accordance with the extent and quality of its contribution, an INGO with a mutual information status (category C) may be promoted after two years to the information and consultative status (category B) and eventually to the consultative and associate status (category A), each involving greater privileges and obligations.

The third category of INGOs, which includes a special list prepared by the Secretariat, normally maintains with a U.N. agency relations limited to exchange of relevant information and documentation, attendance of certain meetings and, occasionally upon request, the preparation of specific studies or papers and the circulation of short statements within a subsidiary body. There is little difference among agencies in their relations with INGOs in this liaison category. However, in the second and first categories representing specialized and general consultative status, the diversity of agency practices is considerable. For the second category of INGOs, ECOSOC allows modest privileges in addition to those of the liaison category, including oral statements on a major subject not covered by a subsidiary body. For the first category, ECOSOC allows, in addition, the privilege to suggest, through ECOSOC's INGO Committee, items for its provisional agenda and the right to make an expository statement. In contrast, UNESCO's second and first categories may not only give advice and assistance regarding its studies and contribute by their activities to the execution of its programs but, significantly, they may receive from UNESCO financial aid in the form of either subventions or contracts for conducting their activities. In addition, the IN-GOs in the first category are closely associated with the various stages of planning and execution of relevant UNESCO activities and assist in the efforts to promote international coordination among related INGOs.

The striking features of other agencies' relations with INGOs pertain to the cooperative arrangements going beyond the consultative system. Because of its tripartite nature, ILO provides employees and labor representatives ample opportunity for official participation in decision making. In addition, it carries out development projects in cooperation with major INGOs having large-scale technical assistance programs for promoting the cooperative movement, the rights of women and young workers, occupational safety, and vocational training. FAO's Freedom from Hunger Campaign/Action for Development (FFH/AD), which operates through a network of INGOs and national committees, serves to stimulate a critical awareness of development issues and to promote the involvement of the people in their own development. Based upon local and national initiatives, the FFH/AD represents dynamic nongovernmental programs of education and action with the technical support of the FAO Secretariat.

A major task of fund raising is undertaken by voluntary agencies associated with the programs of UNICEF and the UNHCR. Those INGOs perform a major role in developing public understanding of the emergency needs and in helping to carry out field projects. The promotion of basic health services provided by church and other nongovernmental groups complement significantly the efforts of WHO and member governments.

In order to win greater opinion support for the objectives of the United Nations and to influence governments toward more active policies for the advancement of developing states, various U.N. bodies are involved in practical collaboration with INGOs. The conventional role of dissemination of information conducted by the INGOs associated with the U.N. Department of Public Information is now being supplemented by new approaches such as the formation by UNCTAD and CESI of an international coalition of INGOs for development aiming at national lobbying. With regard to the environment, INGOs maintain close working relations with UNEP through an Environment Liaison Board and carry out INGO programs for environmental action with financial assistance from UNEP.

According to a recent survey, the external technical assistance provided by INGOs to low-income states in 1973 was estimated to be over $1 billion. As a number of those INGOs are now moving toward longer-term technical assistance in addition to their huge relief assistance, the UNDP has set up procedures for mutual consultation and effective coordination of activites at the field level. The purpose is to benefit from the full potential of INGO contribution to development in harmony with the priorities and projects of intergovernmental agencies and national governments.[9]

INGO INFLUENCE ON DECISION MAKING[10]

The diverse nature of INGOs and the huge differences in their organizational attributes make it difficult to assess their overall influence on national governments, IGOs, and other nongovernmental actors. Clearly, many INGOs do not possess great financial resources and, therefore, their impact on the policy making of national governments and IGOs is likely to be the pinprick variety. Nevertheless, as the Soviet delegation observed during an ECOSOC review of the human rights organizations, governments at times perceive INGO activities as an infringement of national sovereignty.

In evaluating the effect of INGO activities on governmental policy making, it is perhaps useful to distinguish among them. The first distinction refers to the nature of the group's action. One category of INGOs bases its capabilities on technical expertise, as does the International Organization for Standardization. Others exert influence by leading and representing large segments of the public in various societies. In the latter category fall trade-union federations and religious organizations, which pursue objectives based on widespread interests.

Another useful distinction derives from the fields in which they are active. One group operates in areas of major concern to national governments, such as industry (including armaments), commerce, finance and technology; a second category is concerned with essentially noneconomic matters, such as sports, religious affairs, and so forth. Since the first group has more influence on the politics of individual states, its impact on national governmental decision makers is likely to be greater than that of the second group and the reactions of the governments more severe. It is also significant that the number of INGOs that belong to the first group, concerned with economic matters, has been growing more rapidly than the number in the second group, as shown in Table 6.3.

A third distinction refers to the states in which they carry out their transnational activities. As a general rule, economically developed, pluralistic states have many more INGOs operating in their midst than do developing states or socialist-bloc states. This is one reason why the developing states view INGOs with some suspicion—they are seen as pro-Western.

From this, one may conclude that, generally at least, the effects of INGOs on transnational policy making are more pronounced in the industrially advanced states with pluralistic political systems, and that interest groups concerned with economic, social, and humanitarian affairs are likely to have a greater impact than those in other fields. In general, it is fair to assume that the more the demands and objectives of INGOs support high-priority goals of governmental actors and national decision-making elites, the greater are the prospects of successfully influencing the policy-making process. This is illustrated by the shifting fortunes of the concern of INGOs for human rights according to the shifting priorities of U.S. presidents and the leaders of the other Western advanced industrial states.

There is another aspect of transnational INGO activity that deserves to be mentioned, particularly as it has minimal political implications for national governments. This aspect relates to INGO activity that may provide much-

TABLE 6.3: Growth of INGOS by Functional Groupings, 1909–72

Category	1909 A	1954 A	1954 B	1954 C	1960 A	1960 B	1960 C	1966 A	1966 B	1966 C	1966 D	1972 A	1972 B	1972 C
Education/ communication	35	124	12	5.6	159	12	4.7	219	11	6.2	87	277	11	4.3
Religion	21	79	7	6.1	87	6	1.7	93	4	1.0	60	112	4	3.3
Social/health	42	258	25	11.4	301	23	2.7	419	21	6.5	135	574	23	6.0
Scientific/ technical	29	115	11	6.6	143	11	4.0	220	11	8.8	75	317	12	7.3
Political	28	137	13	8.6	159	12	2.7	189	9	3.0	153	243	9	4.7
Economic	21	295	29	29.0	419	33	7.0	795	41	14.8	140	947	38	3.2
Total	176	1008	97*	10.5	1268	97*	4.2	1935	97*	8.7	650	2470	97*	4.5

A = number of existing INGOS
B = percentage of total INGOS
C = average yearly increase (percentage)
D = defunct or inactive INGOS
* Error due to rounding
Source: UIA 1972–73, passim.

needed assistance outside the normal realm of governmental concern without suggesting any kind of patronage. In such cases national policy makers may consider it useful to adopt a policy of noninterference and to let INGOs act as their informal agents in achieving worthwhile, though low-priority, goals. This has occurred on many occasions when visible activity at the government level might have been impossible in the context of existing relations. A hospital built on the edge of a desert in Africa through the efforts of an INGO can bring comfort and health to the surrounding villages without the government of the recipient state having to sacrifice any of its declared international positions. For this reason alone INGOs have been able to operate and achieve outstanding successes in such humanitarian activities as providing child care and medical aid, providing food to the hungry, and providing educational benefits in states that have thereby obtained these benefits without having to abandon their independence and freedom of action in the international community.

DEVELOPMENTS IN INGO CONFERENCE ACTIVITY

Although conferences—whether ad hoc or continuing—are providing greater opportunities for INGOs to influence international policy making, there is nonetheless a spirit of frustration among them with a succession of U.N. conferences whose results have appeared only to have revealed the limitations of multilateral decision making. As one observer commented in an article discussing the fact that 1982 was the tenth anniversary of the Stockholm Conference:

> There is no likelihood of a repeat performance of the Stockholm conference, which was financed by governments; and in any case the conference did not directly create public awareness *do novo*. Stockholm was able to focus existing interest and then to amplify it, thus encouraging and lending respectability to many other citizen action groups which were perhaps short of confidence, impetus and material until then. In the end the net result was more public interest—but it was created by indirect pumping. It will not be done twice.[11]

Right or wrong, there has emerged among many INGOs an increasingly critical view of the U.N. Secretariat's apparent inability to repeat the Stockholm success at other conferences, and a growing despondency about the role of certain states that appear to be working against the use of multilateral means to deal with global problems.

There is also an increasing concern felt by INGOs that they should not become trapped into the U.N. agenda. They resent the temptation to work on particular issues merely because these are the issues inscribed on an official conference agenda. An example of an INGO departure from an official agenda occurred at the eleventh Special Session of the General Assembly on Economic Issues (UNGASS), held in New York during August and September 1980, when INGOs focused on the role of transnational corporations in development because they felt that this issue was not adequately addressed on the official agenda.

Another interesting development is that INGOs are spending as much time lobbying media representatives at intergovernmental conferences as they are lobbying the official delegates, thereby acquiescing in the political cliché that what is said is not as important as how it is reported or portrayed to the public (whether governmental or otherwise). Many INGOs come to international conferences or to the U.N. General Assembly sessions with press accreditation for local newspapers or radio stations. They file reports and mix with the press corps. At UNCTAD V in Manila, for example, of a team of approximately 40 people working with the International Coalition for Development Action, two-thirds had press accreditation and were writing stories and sending radio reports back to their capitals.

Toward the end of the 1970s, INGOs seemed to be doing more than merely recasting and redefining the various agendas of these conference activities, they were concerned mostly with the economic and social issues commonly termed the New International Economic Order. INGOs are now pursuing independent paths or strategies that could possibly enhance the realization of some of these economic and social goals, in spite of official conference stalemates and deadlocks. The international negotiating environment had become increasingly intransigent by the early 1980s because 1) East-West polemics reminiscent of the cold war era were gaining more attention; 2) the advanced industrial states were overwhelmed by their own problems of inflation, recession, and unemployment; and 3) the unwillingness of these industrial states—especially the United States, West Germany, and Britain—to compromise diminished as the NIEO cluster of proposals and issues were viewed as less politically attractive domestically.

This is not to imply that INGOs will pursue their programs and activities irrespective of the governmental dialogue. Nevertheless, it does suggest that the INGOs are recognizing that links directly to the public opinion play a role in the formation of governmental policies. Thus, by relying on this direct access, and by carefully concentrating on issues that would be likely to provoke public response, INGOs hope to pressure their governments more effectively. Whether this approach will ameliorate the developing states' suspicion that INGOs are still predominantly pro-Western, remains to be seen.

Clearly, the role of INGOs is increasing in importance, but whether that role has resulted in significant shifts in governmental or IGO policy making is difficult to discern. In the view of many INGO representatives, unless there are dramatic changes in the way in which the U.N. system operates, INGOs will lose interest in attempting to influence policy making at the international level, and instead will focus even more at the national level. Aside from the fact that it is becoming prohibitively expensive to send INGO representatives all over the world to conferences, if national policy is determined before the conference, or if it is perceived by INGOs that decision making on a given policy issue occurs at the national level rather than through the dialogue of U.N. bodies or conferences, then an increase in INGO activities at the national level would be more effective.

As it has become more and more evident that many of the issues that separate the industrial states from the developing states are not going to be resolved either easily or soon through multilateral means (with the inclusion of the Law-of-the-Sea), INGOs are finding it more useful to concentrate their efforts in educating and sensitizing general public opinion and in lobbying at the national centers of power. Unless there is a change in this situation the 1980s will perhaps witness the increased formation of national NGO coalitions. At the beginning of the 1970s, INGOs became visible at intergovernmental conferences in order to help call attention to the issues, but they also were anxious to gather information and material for developing education at the national level. With the increasing concern globally about the threat of nuclear weapons, INGOs—especially in Western Europe and North America—have played a very active role in pressuring governments to be predisposed to negotiate on these complex issues.

Nonetheless, in this period of nationalistic preoccupations, it will be important for INGOs to retain their contacts at the international level. Aside from very large multinational corporations, governments still hold a monopoly on international decison making; in spite of the polemics and platitudes about the importance of public or popular participation in the international political decision-making process, as exemplified by the activities of international INGOs, the nation-state paradigm has continued to inhibit such participation, especially within the U.N. structure. But, as the illustrative cases that follow demonstrate, INGOs can have beneficial effects on international and national decision making and through this role INGOs may contribute to a better world community.

ILLUSTRATIVE CASES

Patterns of INGO Activities at the World Conference on Agrarian Reform and Rural Development

At the beginning of the 1970s, many INGOs were represented at IGO conferences by individuals or by very small groups. There had been some coordination among INGOs up to a point, but it was not until the Stockholm Conference, the World Population Conference in Bucharest, and the World Food Conference in Rome, the latter two held in 1974, that the role of the INGOs at single-issue global conferences was enhanced.

One reason for this was that the presence and activities of INGOs at these conferences helped to ensure that central issues were not ignored. INGOs, through publications or lobbying, can demythologize the official rhetoric, can urge a focus on facts, figures, and people. The World Conference on Agrarian Reform and Rural Development (WCARRD), held in Rome in 1979, provides a good illustration of this. INGO activity at WCARRD went a long way in recasting the issues of the Conference in light of INGO experience derived from rural development projects at the field level, and from independent research activities.

The representatives of governments at these conferences tend to downplay the inconsistencies and failures at home, instead taking every public opportunity to call international attention to their achievements. For example, in the case of WCARRD, they pointed "proudly to land reform legislation that decorates the statute books of dozens of countries around the world and argued that they are with the poor and the landless in spirit—even if a few local difficulties stood in the way of implementation."[12] In contrast, the final INGO statement to WCARRD reflected a significant departure from the official conference dialogue. While the WCARRD Secretariat and the delegations carefully worded their resolutions and the program of action to ensure that no serious or definite commitment would be imposed on them, the INGO statement highlighted the following perceptions and prescription:

> Official documents frequently refer to the rural poor as "target groups" and thus treat them as the *objects* of someone else's actions rather than the principal actors in their own development. NGOs, whose perception of these problems is drawn largely from first-hand relationships with rural people reject the attitudes which give rise to such terminology.
>
> National and international strategies up to now have not been merely inadequate: the fact is that in most cases they have been the *wrong* strategies. They have often had negative effects on the rural poor who were meant to be the main beneficiaries. We believe that the root causes of underdevelopment and rural poverty go much deeper and demand a radical rethinking of policies and a radical reorganization of the power structure that impoverishes these poor.
>
> A new model for rural development is needed and this model must involve a substantial transfer of power to the rural poor. This only emphasizes the need for structural reforms as a basis for real rural development.[13]

In the case of WCARRD, INGO-generated facts on the condition and progress of rural development often contradicted or contrasted with official statements. For example, the Rome Declaration Group—the NGO-sponsored counter conference—organized public discussion on the following topics: multinational corporations, food aid, the World Bank, repression of peasants, women and rural development, land reform, agricultural crises in the industrial states, and "more trade: progress or problem?"[14] Representing a consortium of 70 INGOs, the Group submitted, along with their formal statement to the Conference four position papers as appendixes:

1. *The Case for Alternative Development of the People, for the People, and by the People*, by the Asian INGO Coalition for Agricultural Reform and Rural Development;
2. *The Chance for a New Start*, by a number of European INGOs;
3. *Land for People*, by Oxfam; and
4. *The Rome Declaration on Agrarian Conflict: False Premises/False Promises*, by the Rome Declaration Group and other INGO signatories.

Of these, *Land for People*, which was considered very critical of the rural development policies of governments, was at first denied circulation through the official conference channels by FAO, an action for which no explanation was offered.

PAN, the INGO newspaper at WCARRD illustrates the variety of ways such newspapers serve the interests of the INGOs as well as of the conference dialogue. PAN was sponsored by Oxfam-UK and became the chief vehicle for the expression of opinion, research, criticisms, and comments of INGOs and governmental representatives. That the perceptions of the Conference priorities of the official delegations differed markedly from those of the INGOs was brought out in the very first issue of PAN in an article entitled, "Power of Elites Barrier to Real Change," in which the following comments were made:

> . . . governments hope to divert attention from themselves as causes of rural suffering by laying the blame elsewhere—on obstinate local rural elites, on the scarcity of funds, on unavoidable conflicts in priorities.
> . . . . the function of this conference is to portray good intentions when in fact the intentions are to protect vested interests; to portray progress when in fact there is great suffering; to portray as friends of the poor those actively involved in repressing them.

While the official negotiators carefully worded the Program of Action to be founded in principles, the INGOs through the Rome Declaration Group and articles in PAN, focused early on what they considered to be basic impediments to any definitive improvements in rural conditions. These included such items as unequal participation of developing states in the world economy and emphasis by many Third World governments on a national economy that gave first priority to export-led industrialization and that neglected rural development policies and basic needs. PAN had a print run of 5,500 and was read by all the delegations, thus becoming a source of shared information by all participants that the official information handouts and the govermental statements and speeches could not rival.

As to the use of an alternative conference to the official conference—a pattern of activity that has appeared in different forms at all of the ad hoc global conferences—note must be taken of the work of the International Peace Research Association (IPRA). IPRA's Food Policy Study, which consisted of persons mainly involved in social reforms of a radical nature in industrial and developing states, helped to form the Rome Declaration Group at WCARRD, which in turn organized the WCARRD counterconference. They released the statement, *False Premises: False Promises* on the day WCARRD opened. One person assessed the work of the Rome Declaration Group as follows:

> a) that it was significantly more radical than previous parallel or alternative conferences; b) that it succeeded in influencing some of the media coverage of the official conference; *Le Monde*, for instance, carried stories from their special envoy on the basis of the counter-evidence provided by the Rome Declaration Group; c) that it provided a genuine dialectic analysis of the conference agenda in north-south terms—a perspective which was largely absent from the official conference documentation which viewed the problem as a developing country one.[15]

The IPRA experiment with the Rome Declaration Group received a lot of attention from INGOs. Its format responded to the INGO frustration over the more traditional style of conference diplomacy, and allowed an opportunity for the publication or display of the considerable amount of INGO research done on many of the issues of the WCARRD.

In summary, INGO effectiveness appears to be dependent on two primary factors: their ability to interrelate their goals with those of other INGOs and with relevant international organizations, and their ability to penetrate the decision-making apparatus of national governments. Given their generally weak financial and staffing conditions, INGOs must depend on the goodwill of the general, concerned publics that they desire to inform and to speak on behalf of. There is no doubt, however, that the nature of the issues that face the international community, and the rapid growth of INGO activity in recent years, demonstrates that there is a legitimate role of INGOs even though the nation-state system is still dominated by governments rather than by publics.

International Scientific and Professional Associations and Their Role at the International Level[16]

There has been increasing interest in International Scientific and Professional Associations (ISPAs) and their role at the international level, because of their participation in the nongovernmental forums and counterconferences that have accompanied each of the recent major ad hoc global conferences organized by the United Nations. While much publicity was accorded to the unofficial forums that took place coincident with the United Nations conferences on the environment, population, food, status of women, human settlements, and trade and development, little is known about the role and contribution of ISPAs in the resolution of problems of international concern.

The *1974 Yearbook of International Organizations* lists 901 ISPAs in the following categories: social sciences; law, administration; professions, employers, economics, finance; technology; science; health, medicine. At the Stockholm Conference on the Human Environment, 73 had observer status. The numbers varied from conference to conference, with 36 having observer status at the Vancouver Conference on Human Settlements. These numbers refer solely to ISPAs and not to nongovernmental organizations (INGOs) in general.

ISPAs range from relatively loosely structured associations such as the Pugwash group (which has held 24 conferences and 25 symposia, or a total of 49 meetings, in 20 years) to complex associations such as the Committee on Space Research (COSPAR). COSPAR is a member of the International Council of Scientific Unions (ICSU) and together with the International Union of Radio Sciences and the International Astronomical Union forms the Inter-Union Committee on Frequency Allocation. COSPAR's membership consists of 35 nations and 11 international scientific unions. It has a president, two vice-presidents, a bureau, an executive council, a small secretariat, seven working groups, and several subgroups. Within this range of ISPAs fall the more traditional scientific unions that are grouped in a federation under a council. The purposes and methods of ISPAs vary accordingly.

ISPAs, particularly those that are members of ICSU, are forums for organizing and maintaining international contact among their membership, particularly with a view to the presentation and stimulation of research and the diffusion of findings; they are forums for the planning and organization of cooperative international research projects such as the International Geophysical Year (IGY); they are centers for the aggregation and articulation of interests in particular disciplines, and as such lobby at both the national and international levels; they are used by the international community as repositories of highly technical advice; and they seek comparability of data within particular fields. They are also forums in which compromise solutions to intractable international problems can be explored, and in which mutual understanding can be developed.

There are a number of ways in which individual members of ISPAs can have an effect on policy on questions of international concern. At the national level, as lobbyists, expert consultants, members of advisory committees, or staff of government agencies, they can influence the development of national policy on international questions. At the level of national representation in international organizations, as expert advisors to official delegations, as members of delegations, or as lobbyists they can have an influence on the articulation and implementation of national policy and in the adjustment of national policy in the process of transnational negotiation. At the international level, as technical advisors or consultants to international secretariats, as lobbyists, or as members of international secretariats, they can have an influence on the articulation and implementation of internationally agreed policies.

Although ISPAs are nongovernmental, as is evident from the foregoing, they are not necessarily entirely free from the influence government can exert on them, inasmuch as their members are scientists and professionals drawn from government as well as from academia, industry, and the business world including transnational enterprises. In general, this intermix of governmental with the nongovernmental is considered advantageous as it permits access to governments with a view to making known the ISPAs' ideas that are themselves the product of transnational interchange. From the point of view of governments, ISPAs bring together scientists and professionals of different nationalities in an atmosphere that can minimize political considerations.

The constructive role of ISPAs is thus seen as aggregating and articulating the ideas of scientists and professionals from different parts of the world, mobilizing their members on any issue that appears important to them, and informing and educating governments about such issues. The governing bodies of certain ISPAs can also function as coherent transnational delegations on issues of interest to them. In order for ISPAs to be effective there must be a unified viewpoint within the ISPA on a given subject, and the members must have access to the centers of government decision making.

Where issues are controversial, involvement entails high risks for the ISPA and success is a matter of skill. One of the determinants of success is quality of leadership. In this respect, it is interesting to note that in a setting and an era of increasing complexity, it has often been one man or relatively few men who have acted as the driving force—as a catalyst, or as a transmitter of ideas. Each of the individuals who are members of ISPAs also have a multiplicity of personal and organizational links.

Other important variables for success are levels of funding, changes in the internal or external environment of the ISPA, and culturally determined differences in role perception. The viability of ISPAs, or at least some of them, appears to be related to the actual and potential demand for their services.

ISPAs are in a continual state of flux. As older problems are solved or overtaken by events, some people question the continued usefulness of ISPAs formed to aid in the solution of those problems, for example, the Pugwash group that sought to provide a neutral forum for scientists from the United States and the Soviet Union. In a sense, when such ISPAs effectively carry out the tasks they set themselves (however difficult this may be to demonstrate conclusively), they work themselves out of business.

Alexander King, a cofounder of the Club of Rome, has noted the special relevance to this question of the Club's activities and deliberations. He argues that the Club of Rome has had considerable (though mostly indirect) political influence, especially in comparison with other nongovernmental organizations. However, he goes on to note that at most meetings of the Club's Executive Committee the question is raised, Has the time come yet for us to disappear or can we still have some influence as a pinprick to complacency?

The Club of Rome is particularly interesting in this regard, because it was initially designed as an essentially temporary organization. There is no formal Secretariat, nor is there a budget. The Executive Committee is composed of only eight people who meet rather frequently. The Club seeks to serve as a catalyst, stimulating research in selected areas and bringing the research findings to the attention of decision makers. The dilemmas involved in determining when to terminate the activites of an ISPA are real. Should one proceed to new, perhaps less appropriate, problem areas as the organization's functions in older ones are completed?

Another consequence of the activities of certain ISPAs is that they open new channels for communication, information exchange, and expert evaluation, which then exist independently. As new problems gain recognition at the international level, new ISPAs are formed. This took place, for example, as interest increased in deep-sea research and in the implications of such research. As a result the Scientific Committee on Oceanic Research (SCOR) was formed.

The experience of SCOR is interesting inasmuch as its concerns have been relevant to the U.N. Conference on the Law-of-the-Sea. The first issues with which SCOR concerned itself when it was established in 1957 were the use of the deep sea for waste disposal, the ocean as a source of protein, and the role of the ocean in climate change. SCOR has been closely associated with UNESCO and its affiliated Intergovernmental Oceanographic Commission (IOC), both of which request advice from SCOR, thus providing a closely linked governmental/intergovernmental/nongovernmental arrangement.

However, the developing states in the Law-of-the-Sea Conference have been resistant to the wishes of IOC and SCOR for a significant expansion of oceanographic research. It is thought that this attitude may have been caused in part by the fact that states with large-scale maritime research programs have failed to provide significant resources for technical assistance, training, and education in maritime science in the developing states. In addition, most members of SCOR, with the exception of the U.S. national committee and U.S. scientists, were reluctant to become involved in preparations for the Law-of-the-Sea Conference and did not accept various suggestions to this end, including a proposal that SCOR should offer its services to the United Nations Secretariat for the Conference in order to provide scientific advice on issues affecting marine science. The experience of SCOR is therefore something of an object lesson to ISPAs that may have a role to play at the international level in the future.

Some ISPAs have consultative status with the U.N. Economic and Social Council; some do not. Provision has also been made for consultative status with most of the specialized agencies of the U.N. system. In addition, there have been specific resolutions and other efforts to insure that those in this consultative status are in a position to contribute constructively to the preparation and proceedings of various U.N. conferences.

ISPAs played a role in connection with the U.N. Conference on Water and Desertification that took place in 1977; they have had a role in the activities of the U.N. Decade for Women (1976–85); and their cooperation was sought in the preparations for the 1979 U.N. Conference on Science and Technology for Development. It is in the preparatory phases of such conferences that ISPAs can exert influence because international conferences are of short duration and delegations are extremely busy throughout the conferences. ISPA influence in the implementation of decisions is also likely to be greater than their influence at the conference itself.

A new development has been the effort by the Secretariat of the U.N. Conference on Technical Cooperation Among Developing Countries (TCDC) to ensure participation by Professional, Technical and Voluntary Associations (PTVAs) from the developing states in the Conference, which was held in 1978. The distinct terminology is being used to separate PTVAs from INGOs and ISPAs, which are commonly based and centered in developed states. Plans were made for a parallel conference of PTVAs and for some preparation of discussion papers, in connection with TCDC.

A number of ISPAs have continuing relationships with the specialized agencies. SCOR, for example, does work under contract for UNESCO and its IOC, and the Advisory Committee for Marine Resources Research does work for FAO. ICSU's Scientific Committee on Problems of the Environment (SCOPE) and the International Union for the Conservation of Nature and Natural Resources have close working relationships with the Secretariat the U.N. Environment Program (UNEP), and perform contract services for

UNEP programs such as Earthwatch and the International Referral System that, respectively, conduct environmental research and evaluation, and information exchange.

Indeed, it is the ISPAs in the hard sciences that seem to have played the greatest role at the international level thus far, although others have also been active. It was at an international meeting of biologists at Asilomar, California, in February 1975 that warnings were sounded that led to stringent precautions in connection with recombinant-DNA research.

It may be noted that the scientific and technically oriented ISPAs also appear to have shown the most interest in international conferences. Of the 85 ISPAs that sent observers to either the U.N. Environment or Human Settlements Conferences, or to both, 19 were scientific and 15 technological associations. In each of the other categories of ISPAs, not more than 13 associations were represented. It is particularly interesting that only two organizations that were classified as economic or financial ISPAs (the European League for Economic Cooperation and the International Union of Building Societies and Savings Associations) sent observers to Stockholm, and only one of them sent an observer to Vancouver. There would seem to be a greater role for ISPAs representing disciplines other than the hard sciences. However, it will not be easy, as the experience of SCOR with the Law-of-the-Sea Conference has shown. In this connection it may be worth noting that it was ISPAs with specialized expertise that were particularly helpful in maintaining some East-West dialogue during the cold war.

The problem areas of the immediate future are likely to be on questions related to the so-called North-South negotiations over the establishment of a new international economic order based on equity, social justice, and meeting the requirements of the most needy. If, as seems generally agreed, some ISPAs, such as the Pugwash group and COSPAR, were extremely useful points of contact between the superpowers at a time of political tension between the two, do ISPAs have the same potential in the North-South dialogue between the industrially developed and the developing states?

The editor of the *Bulletin of the Atomic Scientists*, Eugene Rabinowitch, once said "The Pugwash 'movement' is much weaker than some people outside may think—but it is the only international movement trying to change national opinion and political leadership everywhere toward better understanding of the challenges of the scientific revolution and of policies adequate to cope with these challenges."[17] Is there, in the world today, a similar role for natural and social scientists through ISPAs, particularly those whose membership includes persons from developing states?

The Role of INGOs in Advancing the Cause of Human Rights[18]

During the more than 35 years that have elapsed since World War II ended, INGOs have proliferated as we have noted in Chapter 1. These have not only challenged the power of govermental elites to control international events, but they have also challenged their right to define international issues.

Indeed, one major explanation for the emergence of human rights as a global issue during the past decades lies in the increasing number and influence of INGOs acting transnationally for the promotion and defense of human rights. Simultaneous with this has been the diffusion of literacy and education, with more and more people at the base of society becoming conscious of the fact that poverty and repression are not immutable facts of nature. As people on all continents have begun to demand social justice, their voices have been amplified by INGOs in solidarity with their aspirations. The communications revolution—and the role that has consequently been played by the mass media—has meant that gross violations of human rights, even in a remote area, cannot be long covered up or locally contained, for those fighting oppression internationalize their struggles by appeals to international forums or to international public opinion. Thus, IGOs are frequently the arenas in which global issues come to be defined and INGOs are frequently the instrumentality through which demands for change are expressed.

It was the gas chambers of the Third Reich, and a very intensive lobbying effort by INGOs, that got human rights inscribed into the Charter of the United Nations. As Theo van Boven, former Director of the Division of Human Rights, observed at the opening of the thirty-sixth session of the Commission of Human Rights (1980), the human rights provisions of the U.N. Charter, and the express mention of the Commission in Article 68 thereof

> . . . was the result of the insistent pleas of nongovernmental organizations and individuals at the San Francisco Conference. It is a matter of record that had it not been for the determined role played by these organizations and individuals, the place assigned to human rights in the Charter might have been less pronounced.

With respect to promotion, the record of the last 35 years has been impressive. Human rights law is highly developed at the universal level and is evolving at the regional level. Many states have incorporated whole sections of the Universal Declaration into their national constitutions and some have made the effort to bring national law into line with international standards. IGOs have been particularly instrumental in this process, although credit must also be given to INGOs that have often stimulated or encouraged the process as with Amnesty International's role in the elaboration of the U.N. Declaration on the Protection of All Persons Against Torture and other Cruel, Inhuman, and Degrading Treatment or Punishment, 1979; the role of the International Committee of the Red Cross in developing the 1977 Protocols to the Geneva Conventions; or the role of the antiapartheid movement in drafting the Convention on the Suppression and Punishment of the Crime of Apartheid, 1973. Yet, if international human-rights law now exists, implementing a human-rights regime is still a distant objective.

By and large, those actors that have been in the forefront of monitoring the status of human rights have been INGOs: international human-rights INGOs like Amnesty International, the International Committee of the Red Cross, the International Commission of Jurists, or the Anti-Slavery Society; church organizations such as the Human Rights Office of the National Council of Churches in the United States or Vicariate of Solidarity in Chile; professional associations such as the Clearinghouse on Science and Human Rights of the American Association for the Advancement of Science or the Committee to Review the Abuse of Psychiatry for Political Purposes of the World Psychiatric Association; numerous national civil-liberties organizations, such as the Scottish Council Liberties; a myriad of support groups, such as the Argentine Human Rights Committee, TAPOL, or the Friends of the Filipino People; and, occasionally, ad hoc special peoples' tribunals such as the Bertrand Russell Tribunals on U.S. war crimes in Vietnam, human-rights violations in Latin America and West Germany, and the projected tribunal on genocide against indigenous peoples. Perhaps the most important function that these NGOs have performed has been the informational function of gathering, evaluating, and disseminating information on human-rights violations. For, without information on the status of human-rights observance, and the nature and context of human-rights violations, there is little hope for the protection of human rights.

With respect to human-rights enforcement, both INGOs and IGOs, as well as governments, have also performed some additional and vital functions. They have, through statements and other action expressed solidarity with the oppressed; they have, through a wide variety of different mechanisms, performed an advocacy function, actively taking up the case of the oppressed, in the mass media, in international forums, and through bilateral diplomatic channels. For INGOs, this has frequently involved lobbying, either of their own government or of other governments. For governmental authorities, this has frequently involved attempts at conciliation and mediation and, sometimes, the application of economic or political sanctions. The various policy options open to INGOs concerned with the promotion and protection of human rights depends, of course, on the nature and source of threats that are perceived and there exist very different perceptions concerning the causes of human-rights violations.

In summary, there has been a flowering of NGOs dedicated to the promotion and protection of internationally-recognized human rights and these have succeeded in attracting cointerest groups (labor unions, professional associations, and churches) into the struggle. Amnesty International, which was born only in 1961, not only received the Nobel Peace Prize in 1977 but has become a virtual worldwide movement of individuals and groups dedicated to the abolition of torture, prolonged political detention without trial, and the abolition of the death penalty. Thus, if there has been regional collaboration between dictatorial regimes to quell opposition (as in the Southern Cone or in Southern Africa), there has also been increasing regional cooperation between those dedicated to the protection of human rights. It seems hard to imagine that anything, short of nuclear disaster, can stem the tide of longing for a better future, or sever the ties of solidarity that are being forged in the common struggle of oppressed peoples throughout the world.

THE EXPANDING ROLE OF INGOs
IN THE U.N. DISARMAMENT DEBATE[19]

Even before the United Nations was organized, during the League of Nations, INGOs were active in disarmament affairs. INGOs had a large role in the disarmament conference during the 1930s in Geneva. In the 1950s some INGOs in ECOSOC went beyond economic and human-rights issues and tried to relate to the disarmament deliberations in the General Assembly and related organs. In the late 1960s Quakers and others formed the Special NGO Committee on Disarmament at Geneva. This brought together INGOs in Western and Eastern Europe who were concerned with problems of war and peace, especially arms limitation in the Eighteen Nation Disarmament Committee (ENDC) meeting in Geneva. In 1973 a sister INGO Committee on Disarmament was formed at U.N. Headquarters in New York. Here INGOs observed the work of the first committee on disarmament issues and also other General Assembly bodies devoted to disarmament.

General Assembly resolutions on disarmament have occasionally referred to INGOs, but mostly to distribute disarmament studies or information. Yet these resolutions indirectly recognized a role for INGOs in disarmament. On the other hand, an ad hoc committee on the review of the role of the United Nations in the field of disarmament convened in 1976 could have been an occasion for 42 member-states to explore the role of INGOs in this area. Despite a sympathetic chairperson, Mrs. Inga Thorsson of Sweden, the committee soon realized that the climate was not favorable for any real discussion of the role of INGOs, let along any recommendation. One reason for this lack of action was that some Third World and socialist states were critical of INGOs within ECOSOC for speaking out against human-rights violations, and thus they tended at the time to be against INGOs.

The first significant opportunity for INGOs within the U.N. system in the field of disarmament came at the Special Session on Disarmament of the General Assembly in 1978, and its preparations. The status that event gave INGOs in the field of disarmament provided for a higher level of subsequent involvement.

When the preparatory committee for the first special session on disarmament met in March 1977, INGOs were active in working with some friendly governments to assure an INGO role in the preparatory work as well as in the special session itself. In May 1977, the second session of the preparatory committee formally welcomed INGOs to observe and participate in its work. A table was provided for the distribution of INGO statements and the U.N. Secretariat issued a periodic index of such statements.

INGOs around the world in 1977 and 1978 prepared for the special session. Some worked educationally within their organizations. Some INGOs formed national coalitions to urge their foreign offices to prepare initiatives for the special session. A great number of national, regional, and even international seminars and conferences were held, some involving diplomats.

Early in 1978 the preparatory committee decided to allow INGOs and peace and disarmament research organizations to give oral interventions at the special session itself. The committee was hesitant to screen such organizations and institutions and gave the task to the INGOs. This was a difficult—and political—process and, finally with the help of the preparatory committee, 25 INGOs and six research institutions were invited to give addresses before the ad hoc committee of the special session on INGO Day, June 12, 1978. Ambassador Carlos Ortiz de Rozas, chairman of the committee (and the principal negotiator with INGOs) opened the day by asserting that "disarmament is not the province of governments alone" and that INGOs would be "a positive factor in cementing a climate of confidence and understanding [for] real progress to curb the arms race."

The informal activities of INGOs during the five-week special session were intensive. Several thousand representatives of INGOs from all continents converged on U.N. Headquarters. The INGO Committee on Disarmament (at U.N. Headquarters) organized a Disarmament Information Center, a storefront opposite the U.N. The Committee also published 31 issues of *Disarmament Times*, an independent newspaper in an edition of 5,000 copies. There were also major demonstrations, rallies, vigils, sit-ins, and forums.

While efforts were made to institutionalize the future role of INGOs in the final document of the special session, this largely failed. The final wording was contained in two sentences in paragraph 123: "The [UN] Centre [for] Disarmament should also increase contact with non-governmental organizations and research institutions in view of the valuable role they play in the field of disarmament. This role could be encouraged also in other ways that may be considered as appropriate." The penultimate paragraph of the final document also noted that "spokesmen of 25 INGOs and six research institutions also made valuable contributions to the proceedings of the session."

At the thirty-third regular session of the U.N. General Assembly in September-December 1978, there was a review of the work of the special session. One resolution requested the U.N. Center for Disarmament to increase contacts with INGOs and research institutions, in accordance with paragraph 123 and to report to the next session of the General Assembly on other ways to encourage the role of INGOs in the field of disarmament. Nothing tangible came from this initiative, although the U.N. Center soon acquired funds to employ a full-time INGO liaison officer.

As a result of the enhancement of the role of INGOs at the special session, various U.N. bodies welcomed INGOs as observers and, in some cases, their written statements were indexed (for example, the Disarmament Commission). The new Committee on Disarmament (CD) at Geneva, like its several predecessors since 1962, opened its galleries to INGOs. Ad hoc committees of the General Assembly on disarmament continued to be open to INGOs. Also the second review conference of the non-proliferation treaty in 1980, as the first in 1975, was open to INGOs.

Despite this followup of the first special session, an increased role for INGOs in disarmament, more precise than that given in paragraph 123, has not yet been elaborated by the General Assembly.

When the preparatory committee for the second special session was formed in 1980, and even before, INGOs began consulting to ascertain how they could again play a role, if possible, an increased one. At the first meeting of the committee, the chairman, Ambassador Alu Adeniji of Nigeria, declared: "The Committee might follow the practice of the first Special Session on disarmament, which had decided that such representatives [INGOs] should be present at meetings of the Committee and that they should provide the Secretariat with lists of communications received [on] research in the field of disarmament."[20]

The ad hoc INGO liaison group in a written statement to the second session of the preparatory committee asked for specific prerogatives during the preparatory process: oral statements by INGOs and research institutions in the preparatory committee itself; use of a uniform cover sheet, with documentation symbols, for written INGO statements; and admission of INGOs to working groups. The second session of the committee accepted the first of the three proposals and scheduled the oral statements for its third session in October 1981, again placing on the INGOs themselves the political problem of sifting the applications. It was believed that the committee would again suggest that INGOs be accorded in the second special session itself at least those privileges they were given in the first.

INGOs worked, worldwide, to help make the second special session on disarmament the success that it must be, despite the bleak political climate. The session was scheduled for up to five weeks beginning in May 1982 at U.N. Headquarters. Already, months before that event, there was much more international, regional, national, and even local activity directed toward the special session than at the same time before the first special session. Also cooperative relations among INGOs appear better.

There has long been a need for better coordination between the INGO disarmament committees in Geneva and New York. Even though they are sister committees, and have the same general objectives, they are sufficiently different to make cooperation difficult. The older Geneva committee has many members not resident in Geneva and consequently does not consider that its primary role is to be a watchdog for the several disarmament meetings occurring in Geneva. Containing representatives primarily of international (and not national) organizations in both Eastern and Western Europe, the results of its deliberations tend to be ideological. The newer New York committee, on the other hand, is open to both national and international INGOs. Most of its members are resident in the greater New York City area and consequently can in theory have a watchdog role for the many disarmament meetings at headquarters if they desire to do so. The New York committee contains representatives who tend to be nonideological or, at least, in disarmament policies, nonaligned. Most are not supportive of the foreign and disarmament policies of either Washington or Moscow.

Thus it has been difficult to bring the leadership of the committees together. After two years of effort, a three-day meeting was held at U.N. Headquarters in New York in April 1981 consisting of ten officers from each of the committees. Calling itself the ad hoc INGO Liaison Group, it was cochaired by the chairmen of both committees. The group spent most time working out plans for the INGO role at the second special session and its preparations. It agreed to (and has) met periodically.

INGOs reacted favorably to the proposal of then U.N. Secretary-General Kurt Waldheim at the first special session when he asked that "we devote to national and international disarmament efforts $1 million for every $1,000 million currently spent on arms." Unfortunately, not a single state took up his suggestion and it was not reflected in the final document of the first special session. However, the idea of millions of dollars to be spent on disarmament education and research—presumably by INGOs and other educational institutions—was not forgotten.

The creation of the proposed World Disarmament Campaign and Fund, with some relationship to the United Nations could have a catalytic effect in bringing INGOs together. Attempts to make even a loose coalition of INGOs have faltered over two decades for many reasons, both ideological and financial. Perhaps the need to monitor the U.N.'s campaign could stimulate a cross section of INGOs to cooperate. Some such cooperation is needed if indeed there is to be a world campaign and if indeed there is to be political pressure for significant disarmament in time.

INGOs persist in finding a role for themselves in all deliberative and negotiating forums on disarmament associated with the United Nations. Whatever roles they have attained have been the direct result of their pressures—and those of only a few member-states. There has never been an eagerness to involve INGOs despite the universal admission that it is political will that holds back disarmament and INGOs can be an important element in achieving political will for disarmament in some states.

If governments have often not been cooperative, the INGOs themselves have often not taken advantage of the opportunities that some of their leaders have eked out for them.

INGOs consist not only of organizations that specialize in disarmament, but general purpose organizations—religious, vocational, national, and so forth. Some of the latter also want to do their share to enhance disarmament. Yet both kinds of INGOs have not been particularly active in observing, or lobbying, at the United Nations those issues where disarmament and development coincide. For some years the disarmament deliberative bodies have been concerned about these twin subjects, culminating in the large expert study begun in 1978. This study, chaired by Mrs. Thorsson and released in the autumn of 1981, would make possible a whole new level of INGO study and activity. Yet even without this study, it has been obvious for years that adequate funds for world development cannot be available without a major reduction of world military expenditures—meaning world disarmament. Thus the second disarmament decade coincides with the third development decade. Yet, unless the second disarmament decade succeeds, it is unlikely that there will be a fourth development decade. This presents an important challenge to INGOs and considering the seriousness of continuing military confrontations in many parts of the world including the two superpowers, meeting this challenge successfully might well be the highest test for the viability of INGOs.

NOTES

1. Werner J. Feld, "The Impact of Nongovernmental Organizations on the Formulation of Transnational Policies," *The Jerusalem Journal of International Relations* 2 (Fall 1976), pp. 70ff.

2. Robert Fenaux, "The Transnational Family of Associations (INGOs) and the New World Order," *Transnational Associations* 4 (1978), p. 194.

3. For a fuller description see Ylter Turkmen, "The Role of the Non-Governmental Organization within the United Nations System," *Transnational Associations* 2 (1978), pp. 81–83. See also the UNITAR Conference Report by Berhanykun Andemicael and Elfan Rees, *Non-Governmental Organizations in Economic and Social Development*, 1975.

4. This section is drawn from Johan Kaufmann, *United Nations Decision Making* (Rockville, Md.: Sijthoff and Noordhoff, 1980), p. 93.

5. See, for background, Robert S. Jordan, "Why a NIEO? The View from the Third World," in *The Emerging International Economic Order: Dynamic Processes, Constraints, and Opportunities*, eds. Harold Jacobson and Dusan Sidjanski (Beverly Hills, Calif.: Sage, 1982). See also John P. Renniger, *ECOSOC: Options for Reform*, Policy and Efficacy Studies, No. 4 (New York: United Nations Institute for Training and Research, 1981).

6. Quoted in Walter R. Sharp, *The United Nations Economic and Social Council* (New York: Columbia University Press, 1969), p. 205.

7. For a summary of the varieties of impact of INGOs and IGOs, see Anthony J. N. Judge, "Assessing the Impact of International Associations," in *Transnational Associations*, October 1978, pp. 435–40. For a definition and basic discussion of INGOs, see Werner Feld, *Nongovernmental Forces and World Politics* (New York: Praeger, 1972), pp. 175–209.

8. This section is drawn from the UNITAR Conference Report, *Non-Governmental Organizations in Economic and Social Development*, op. cit., Appendix III.

9. For an example of INGO-IGO cooperation, see the Report from the INGO Forum on the World Economic Order,*Scanning Our Future* (New York: Carnegie Endowment for International Peace, 1975).

10. The following paragraphs were drawn from Werner Feld, "The Impact of Nongovernmental Organizations on the Formulation of Transnational Policies," *The Jerusalem Journal of International Relations* 2 (Fall 1976), pp. 87–89.

11. *Development Forum*, June 1981, p. 9.

12. Quoted in "A Chance to Sow," *Pan* (WCARRD's INGO newspaper), Issue 1, July 12, 1979, p. 1.

13. Statement made by Mr. Maxime Rafransoa of the World Council of Churches on behalf of the consortium of INGOs attending WCARRD.

14. Thierry Lemaresquier, "Back to Office Report," Non-Governmental Liaison Service (Geneva), undated office memorandum, p. 4.

15. Thierry Lemaresquier, letter to Robert S. Jordan, dated September 8, 1980, unpublished, p. 4.

16. The following is drawn from Robert S. Jordan, "Commentary on the Political Impact of ISPAs," in *Knowledge and Power in a Global Society*, ed. William M. Evan (Beverly Hills, Calif.: Sage, 1981), pp. 229–34.

17. *Bulletin of the Atomic Scientists* 21 (1965), p. 14.

18. This case study is drawn from Laurie S. Wiseberg, Arthur W. Blasor, and Betty A. Reardon, *Global Issues: Human Rights* (Columbus, Ohio: Consortium for International Studies Education, 1980).

19. This is excerpted from the article by Homer A. Jack, "The Expanding Role of NGOs in the UN Disarmament Debate," *Development* 1 (1982), pp. 62–64.

20. Ibid., p. 64.

Chapter 7

International Regimes

In Chapter 1 we discussed briefly the concept of international regimes and suggested that this could be a useful concept in gaining an understanding of the manifold interactions that are found in the international arena. We also stated that while both IGOs and regimes can pursue common goals through various cooperation management arrangements, those addressed by regimes typically are more narrow, often dealing only with an important single issue. Furthermore, regime structures are less formal and more fluid than those of IGOs and they are more likely to adjust to new or changing conditions.

IGOs can provide the legal setting for international regimes. For example, the ICAO, in cooperation with an international NGO, the International Air Transport Association (IATA), has established regimes for international flights. (We examined the IATA in Chapter 3.) A regional IGO, the Andean Common Market, set up an international investment regime through the well-known Decision 24. (This was discussed in Chapter 4.) Thus, at times IGOs may attempt to establish regimes, but often major difficulties arise because of disagreements among the member-states. Since 1975 the United Nations has endeavored to develop a code of conduct for transnational corporations (TNCs)—also known as multinational corporations (MNCs). A U.N. commission on TNCs and its subordinate working groups have held a large number of negotiating sessions on this subject, but so far success has been elusive. Nevertheless, even if this U.N. effort should fail, it is conceivable that, based on the partial agreements reached during the years of negotiations, an international regime may evolve. We will examine this case in detail later in this chapter. Meanwhile let us take a more systematic look at the characteristics of international regimes.

ORIGINS[1]

One path to the establishment of an international regime is the contractarian track. Actors interested in cooperating on a particular task or activity meet for the explicit purpose of negotiating a contract or convention setting forth the details of a regime to accomplish the task or to perform the activity in question. The best example of the creation of such a regime is the Antarctica Treaty of 1959, whose original signatory states numbered only 12. A much larger effort, yet following basically the same pattern, are the drawn-out negotiations for a Law-of-the-Sea Treaty that, inter alia, seeks to set up a regime on the mining of the deep seabed. Our first illustrative case will deal with this ambitious global undertaking. The inspection system of the International Atomic Energy Agency (IAEA), created in the late 1960s as a consequence of the conclusion of the Nuclear Nonproliferation Treaty (NPT) may also fall into this category.

A second type of regime origin is the evolutionary approach. Under this concept, regimes evolve from widespread practice over time, through which international institutions may develop, and rules that were temporary or provisional take on the character of customary law. Regimes concentrating on the exploration of marine resources have often followed this pattern. Regimes evolve as a consequence of a dramatic unilateral action taken by a state that subsequently is accepted by other states on a de facto, and (perhaps later) on a de jure basis. The post-1945 regime for the outer continental shelves is an example of such a pattern.

A third possibility for the creation of a regime can be characterized as the piecemeal process. States may reach agreement on one or more components of a regime, but for a variety of reasons they might not be able to obtain comprehensive consensus. Alternatively, they may hope that such a consensus will be found later as a consequence of task expansion or spillover. An example of the piecemeal approach may be the slow and arduous creation of a European Monetary System (EMS), which we will discuss in detail later in this chapter. The United Nations Code of Conduct for TNCs might also fall into this category. Other examples of the piecemeal approach include the regional fisheries regimes in the North Atlantic and Pacific (ICNAF and INPFC). In some cases the piecemeal approach may be transformed into the evolutionary approach. This might be the case, for example, with the code of conduct for TNCs. On the other hand, even agreement on a contractual basis for a regime might not always yield the benefits promised. The text of the contract or a convention may be cast in ambiguous language that is designed to obscure the basic conflicts of the parties to the agreement. Obligations may have been accepted by one or the other party without a true intention to comply. In all cases issues and issue areas may be linked, or package deals might be proposed and accepted that were reflections of coalitional and bargaining dynamics rather than in terms of an agreement on the integrated objectives to be attained. Additions or amendments to the agreements establishing a regime may be made over a period of time without the parties always keeping in mind their subordinate conception of shared objectives.[2] In summary, problems may be built into regimes, the extent of which will only emerge as the regime enters into sustained operation. The EMS case is illustrative of such a development.

During the period of regime formation, the capabilities of the participating states as well as the specific functions attributed to the regime are likely to determine the nature of the regime's activities. However, once the regime becomes relatively well organized, constraints on the regime become increasingly important. As Robert Keohane and Joseph Nye point out: "Regimes are established and organized in conformity with distributions of capabilities, but subsequently the relevant networks, monies, and institutions will themselves influence actors' abilities to use these capabilities."[3] Control over outcomes will then depend on voting power, ability to form coalitions, and influence in elite networks.

RIGHTS, RULES, AND COHERENCE

As pointed out in Chapter 1, regime participants have rights and obligations regardless whether they are governmental or nongovernmental actors. How the rights can be exercised and how the obligations must be carried out is stipulated by the rules of the regime. Some regimes emphasize central planning and provide detailed rules governing the actions of individual member-states. The deep-seabed mining regime as proposed in the U.N. Conference on the Law-of-the-Sea (UNCLOS) falls into this category. Other regimes tend to follow a laissez-faire philosophy and their rules are less restrictive, leaving the participants a measure of discretion as to cooperation and goal attainment, as illustrated in the OECD Guidelines for MNCs.

Coherence refers to the degree to which elements of an international regime are internally consistent.[4] Especially when regimes have several goals, the rights and obligations of the participants must show a high degree of coherence, with a careful determination of the trade-offs between the goals and expectations of the regime members. Otherwise, conflicts and contradictions arise, as exemplified between general use rights for marine resources and the specific right vested in adjacent coastal states to exclude outsiders from offshore activities that could impinge on their rights. It is highly desirable, therefore, that a state's sovereign interest and the obligations imposed by the rules of an international regime need to be carefully weighed and the relationship spelled out as precisely as possible.

ORGANIZATIONAL FEATURES

Although international regimes characteristically have fewer organizational arrangements and institutional features than IGOs, effective task achievement is usually enhanced by explicit organization, especially concerning budgetary requirements, physical facilities, and personnel staffing. Of course, considerable variations in organizational arrangements exist; the proposed seabed mining organization is highly complex, whereas the EMS structure is relatively limited. As Oran Young points out, even where a need for explicit organization is apparent, instead of creating their own autonomous arrangements, international regimes may make use of international institutional structures that were created for other purposes or were associated with a more comprehensive authority.[5] For example, the EMS relies heavily on the institutions and personnel of the EC to attain its goals; the NPT regime could not achieve its purposes without the use of the U.N.'s IAEA; and a future regime on the code of conduct for TNCs could not carry out its monitoring task without the U.N. Center for Transnational Corporations. On the other hand, if deep-seabed mining is to become a regime as proposed by the majority of the UNCLOS negotiating states, a vast new institutional and organizational framework will be a necessity.

Some of the reasons for endowing international regimes with rather extensive organizational arrangements include the collection and distribution of revenues, the need to conduct continuous research, the monitoring of activities to ensure compliance with regime rules, and the settlement of disputes.[6] Again, the proposed seabed regime provides a good example of all these organizational aspects, but less complex regimes, such as the various regimes regulating fisheries, also show the need for some of the actions enumerated.

Organizational arrangements also help in setting forth the clearly-defined procedures that would be required to assure the appropriate regime performance and the attainment of regime goals. Carefully thought-out procedures can avoid much of the conflict potential inherent in all regimes, can assure more effective collaboration with respect to the issue or issue areas for which the regime has been created, and can guide the task performance of the bureaucracy of the regime and its member-states.

When such organizational and institutional arrangements are devised, some critical questions, shared with IGOs, must be answered. How much authority should be conferred upon the organizational structure? What should be the extent of discretion given the institutional leadership? How much autonomy should the organization have vis-à-vis other centers of authority within the global or regional international system? How is the organization to be financed and staffed? The answers to all these questions are likely to affect the quality of task performance and the benefits of, or losses to, the members or participants of the regime. Some expectations will be disappointed as a direct result of the nature and shape of the organizational arrangements, and therefore certain organizational features may well be hotly contested throughout the operation of the regime. This will become quite apparent in the cases.

POLICY INSTRUMENTS

As in all organizations, policy instruments must be chosen carefully to attain intended regime goals. Examples of such instruments are: the introduction or relaxation of restrictive business practices in TNC operations depending on the overall goal of the code-of-conduct regime; the nondiscriminatory treatment on the transfer of technology by members of a regime; the introduction of stringent accounting standards for TNCs; the regulation for the issuance of mining licenses or permits in a deep-seabed regime; and the conditions under which the EMS can make currency exchange-rate adjustments.

If regimes lack explicit organizational arrangements, new policies may not be adopted unless all members agree. However, it is conceivable that some powerful government, supported by nongovernmental entities, may take unilateral actions to force an issue, to which other members of the regime subsequently conform.[7] This can happen in TNC codes of conduct, and has occurred in ICAO/IATA air-fare regimes. Such actions may also be taken to redefine the contents of regime rights and rules in order to adjust the regime operations to new conditions. For example, if important EMS members should experience serious currency problems, unilateral actions to force the EMS regime to change the currency relationships may be a way to proceed and obtain the modification of the rules.

REGIME TRANSFORMATION

Even after international regimes have fully developed, they are unlikely to become static structures. Since all regimes are created to attain goals that benefit their members politically, economically, or in terms of their perceived security needs, they tend to undergo transformation in response to changes in these environments. Hence, the content of rights and rules may be changed and procedures altered with respect to choice and compliance mechanisms.

Young distinguishes three types of pressure for regime transformation.[8] First, there can be fundamental changes in the nature of the activity for which an international regime was set up. Examples would be a change in the consumption pattern of a particular species of fish that would require modifying the content of marine fisheries regimes, or a major breakthrough in technology for a transfer of technology regime. Second, pressures for change may be generated because of dissatisfaction with the benefits and costs of a particular regime by one or more regime members or secondary participants. The various changes in the Law-of-the-Sea Treaty and especially the introduction of the 200-mile economic zone, have not pleased all the negotiating states and pressures for further changes are inevitable as witness the refusal in 1982 of the United States to agree to sign the draft treaty. The third kind of pressure is to rationalize a regime that has grown ambiguous or contradictory in the course of evolution.

If regime rules contain procedures for amendment, adjustments may be made, but the ease with which amendments may be carried out depends to some extent on the stringency of the amendment procedures and the willingness of the dissatisfied regime members to abide by them. If vital national interests are perceived to be at stake, and the concerned government disposes of sufficient political power or economic resources, it may withdraw from the regime unless its wishes are accommodated. In such a case, the whole regime may be threatened with collapse unless some relevant organizational and/or substantive adjustments are accepted by the other regime participants.

To offer greater insights into the creation and operation of regimes and especially the often difficult circumstances surrounding these processes, we have selected four cases: the establishment of the deep-seabed mining regime in connection with the deliberations of UNCLOS III, the operation of the European Monetary System (EMS), the NPT Nonproliferation Regime, and the possibilities for a U.N. TNC regime.

ILLUSTRATIVE CASES

The Deep-Seabed Mining Regime

The concept of freedom of the high seas is traced to Hugo Grotius in his *Mare Liberum* (1609), in which he enunciated his belief in the common use of the sea. During the next three centuries, the maritime states of the world plied the seas for the benefit of trade and commerce. Technology was not available for the exploration of the seabed beyond the depth at which an unequipped diver could be sustained.

Then on September 28, 1945, concerned about the exploitation of the U.S. continental shelf, President Harry Truman proclaimed that a "coastal state has sovereign rights for the purpose of the exploration and exploitation of the seabed mineral resources of the continental shelf area."[9] This right to explore and recover resources from the continental shelf—for example offshore oil and gas—has since been embraced by most of the coastal states of the world.

A further move for the development of a comprehensive Law-of-the-Sea was first pronounced on November 1, 1967, by the U.N. ambassador from Malta, Arvid Pardo. His statement to the secretary-general of the United Nations argued "the seabed and the ocean floor are a common heritage of mankind and should be used and exploited for peaceful purposes and for the exclusive benefits of mankind as a whole." Then in December 1967, Ambassador Pardo called for a "study of the peaceful uses of the seabed and the ocean floor beyond the limits of national jurisdiction."[10] Prior to this date, the United States had not announced any policy concerning the seabed beyond the limits of national jurisdiction, specifically beyond the continental shelf area. However, by the late 1960s, private mining companies had begun to develop the technology to explore the seabed beyond the continental shelf. But, these private interests carried little weight with the formulation of U.N. policy and the United States continued to embrace the concept of freedom of the high seas. At the same time, the developing states became alarmed that deep-seabed exploration would have an impact on their economic well-being.

United Nations Initiatives

In Geneva in 1958, the United Nations had held its first Conference on the Law-of-the-Sea, known as UNCLOS I. This Conference produced agreement only on the Convention of the Continental Shelf that after ratification, entered into force on June 10, 1964. A second Conference in Geneva in 1960, UNCLOS II, failed to produce any significant areas of agreement and was considered to have been a failure.

Under the international concept of freedom of the high seas still embraced in the late 1960s by most maritime states, ownership of seabed resources belonged to the first possessor, who would have no obligation to indemnify any coastal state as long as these resources were recovered beyond the limits of national jurisdiction. Then on December 15, 1969, the U.N. General Assembly passed Resolution No. 2574 (XXIV).[11] The major points of this resolution were that the General Assembly:

1. . . . acknowledged developing technology was making the seabed accessible for economic exploration and exploitation.

2. . . . affirmed that the seabed is to be used only for peaceful purposes and its resources used for the benefit of all mankind (concept of common heritage of mankind).

3. . . . requested the secretary general to prepare a study on establishing an international regime to regulate the exploration and exploitation of the seabed. It also declared that all states should refrain from all activities of exploiting the seabed beyond

the limits of national jurisdiction and that no claims to the seabed and its resources will be recognized.

The exploration and exploitation of mineral resources in the deep seabed beyond a depth of 10,000 feet requires an enormous expenditure of capital along with the development of the appropriate technology. When industrial corporations in the United States and elsewhere began to develop such mining technology, the issue of exclusive rights to seabed claims became relevant. Nevertheless, these corporations and the coastal states preferred to defer exploration and exploitation until the protection of their claims to do so would be internationally recognized. Thus, it should not be surprising that the United States voted against Resolution 2574, stating among other reasons, that the technology was still embryonic and unless it moved forward to the point where exploitation on a significant scale was commercially viable, no state could benefit from it. Hence, the United Nations should not prohibit the development of the technology and deep-seabed exploitation.

On December 17, 1970, the General Assembly passed Resolution 2749 (XXV), Declaration of Principles Governing the Seabed and the Ocean Floor and the Sub-Soil Thereof Beyond the Limits of National Jurisdiction. More important, however, was General Assembly Resolution 2750 (XXV), also passed on the same date.[12] The first part of this resolution requested the secretary-general to study the problems arising from the extraction of certain minerals from the seabed and their impact on the economic well-being of the developing states, particularly the fluctuations of mineral export prices. Section B of this resolution asked that there be a study of the special problems of landlocked states relating to the exploration and exploitation of seabed resources. Section C set forth the basic policy of the Group of 77 on seabed resources. It declared the seabed and its resources to be the common heritage of mankind. The exploration and exploitation of these resources should benefit mankind as a whole and should not be subject to appropriation by any state. Moreover, such exploration and exploitation should be governed by an international regime to be established by a so-called Conference on the Law-of-the-Sea. Finally, the seabed should be open for peaceful uses by all states.[13]

The UNCLOS III Results

The Law-of-the-Sea Treaty was passed by UNCLOS in late April 1982 after a protracted series of negotiations spanning a nine-year period.[14] The major features of the treaty are the establishment of an International Seabed Authority (ISA) modeled generally on the U.N. structure; the establishment of a mining company called the Enterprise, which would compete with private companies; a set of licensing, production, and price controls; and a mandatory transfer of technology. A Seabed Authority Assembly would operate on the basis of one-state/one-vote, resulting in a permanent developing states' majority. The Assembly would control the issuance of licenses, would set limits on production and marketing, and have the power to tax companies engaged in seabed mining. A limited membership Council was also envisioned that would have 36 members with the Soviet-bloc states guaranteed at least three seats. In contrast, the United States was not guaranteed any seat on this Council.

The Enterprise would compete with private mining companies and would possess the right to share in their technology. The Enterprise would also have the right to acquire mining sites that had been discovered by other companies in exchange for less profitable sites. The revenues from licenses and fees could well run into the millions of dollars, with production and prices controlled by the Assembly to benefit the developing states.

But the requirement of the mandatory transfer of technology has generated the strongest opposition from private sectors in the United States. Not surprisingly as mentioned previously, the United States voted against the Draft Convention.

Scope of Deep-Seabed Resources

The Pacific Ocean alone may contain over 15 billion tons of manganese nodules. As shown in Table 7.1, in 1979 the United States was dependent on foreign exports for 98 percent of its consumption of manganese, 94 percent for cobalt, and lesser amounts of nickel and copper. By 1985 the deep-seabed production of manganese and nickel would supply 85 percent of the U.S. demand, with the mining of cobalt from the deep seabed far exceeding United States demand. By the year 2000, exploitation of the deep seabed would provide all of the U.S. demand for manganese, cobalt, and nickel. Thus, by the year 2000 the United States would no longer be dependent upon any state or any group of states for its supplies of these minerals.

TABLE 7.1: U.S. Minerals Dependency, 1979

Minerals and Metals	Percent of Apparent Consumption	Sources (1975–78)
Manganese	98	South Africa, Gabon. France, Brazil
Copper	19	Canada, Chile, Zambia, Peru
Cobalt	94	Zaire, Belgium, Luxembourg, Zambia, Finland
Nickel	73	Canada, Norway, New Caledonia, Dominican Republic

Source: U.S. Department of State *Bulletin* LXXXI (April 24, 1981).

As of 1979, eight different mining consortia had been formed to develop the technology for and to begin exploration of the deep seabed. These consortia are identified in Table 7.2, along with the name and percent interest of some noteworthy corporations. Companies in the United Kingdom, Canada, Japan, Belgium, the Federal Republic of Germany, France, and Australia have varying interests in certain of these consortia. These mining companies have developed effective methods of deep-seabed mineral recovery: the vacuum dredge method and the continuous-line bucket system. However, both of these methods require multimillion dollar investments. It is for these reasons that the United States responded negatively to the initiatives of the United Nations, and formulated and implemented its own deep-seabed policy.

Supporting continued licensing of United States companies pursuant to the Deep Seabed Hard Minerals Resources Act, passed in 1980, the Reagan administration undertook a review of the entire treaty draft that had been approved earlier by the U.S. delegation appointed by President Carter and opposed any attempt to conclude negotiations or to formalize a text of the treaty.[15] This position was relayed to the Conference, the delegates of which voted to permit the United States to take time to complete its review. The review most likely was at the behest of those U.S. mining companies who were critical of the treaty text, especially the proposed mining-regime rules; the sections dealing with free right of passage through straits, and so forth, were supported by the Department of Defense.[16]

The Group of 77 was reluctant to consider any further amendments to the treaty text. In late April 1982 the Draft Convention was approved by 130 states and opposed by 4 with 17 abstentions. Joining the United States in opposing the draft treaty were Turkey, Venezuela, and Israel.

What are the details of the seabed regime bargained out under the auspices of UNCLOS, but so far rejected by the United States? As noted earlier, the major institutions of the regime, called the International Seabed

TABLE 7.2: Deepsea Mining Consortia, 1979

1. Kennecott Exploration Corporation (Kennecott Copper Corporation = 50 percent)
2. Ocean Mining Associates (successor to Deepsea Ventures, Inc.; U.S. Steel = 33.33 percent)
3. Ocean Management, Inc. (International Nickel Co., Ltd. = 25 percent)
4. Association Française pour l'Étude et la Recherche des Nodules
5. Ocean Minerals Company (Lockheed Missiles and Space Co.)
6. Continuous Line Bucket Syndicate (U.S. Steel)
7. Deep Ocean Minerals Association (Japan)
8. Eurocean — noncommercial

Source: U.S. Congress, House, Committee on Merchant Marine and Fisheries, *Law of the Sea*, Hearings before the Subcommittee on Oceanography, May-June 1979, pp. 156–58.

Authority, are the Assembly, the Council, and the Secretariat. Reporting to the Council is the Enterprise, the operational tool for the regime, and several commissions. One of these units deals with rules and regulations, another one with economic planning, and the third with legal and technical matters. These institutions are illustrated in Figure 7.3.

Analysis of Seabed Provisions

At the foundation of the proposed seabed regime lies, of course, the principle that the international area and its resources are considered to be the common heritage of mankind. Development of deep-seabed minerals is to be carried out "for the benefit of mankind . . . taking into consideration the particular interests and needs of the developing States and peoples who have not attained full independence or other self-governing status. . . ."[17] The policies of the International Seabed Authority are to assure that ocean mining shall be carried out so as to "foster the healthy development of the world economy and balanced growth of international trade, and to promote international cooperation for the over-all development of all countries, especially the developing States. . . ."[18]

FIGURE 7.1

Seabed Exploitation Regime Map

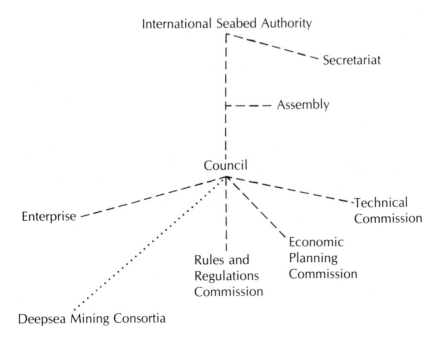

Within the Authority, the Assembly, composed of all states party to the treaty, is to be responsible for general policies and can make decisions on the basis of one-state, one-vote, with questions of substance to be resolved on a two-thirds vote. The Council, composed of 36 states reflecting equitable geographical distribution and representing various interest groups, is to deal with specific policies, provisionally apply rules and regulations pending final Assembly approval, and act upon applications for contracts to mine the seabed. The membership of the Council is to be chosen periodically by the Assembly from nominations by the regional and other specified interests groups. Eighteen seats are provided for geographical representation. Four seats are to be provided for those chosen from the eight states with the largest investments in seabed mining; four seats are to be given to states that have consumed or imported established high levels of the categories of minerals to be extracted from the seabed (including at least one Soviet-bloc state); four from among the group of major net exporters of such minerals (with at least two developing states); and six to be developing states representative of particular interests, including large populations, landlocked or geographically disadvantaged, major importers of the relevant minerals, major producers of those minerals, and the least developed.[19] There is to be no Great Power veto such as exists in the U.N. Security Council and has long been resented by the Third World, and there is to be no system of weighted voting based on economic interests of individual states, such as is found in international commodity arrangements and often looked upon by the Group of 77 as an undesirable model.

The voting system in the Council is to be extremely complex, with decisions on questions of substance being by two-thirds or three-fourths votes, or by a qualified or unqualified consensus, depending on the category of issue concerned. Consensus decisions would relate to rules and regulations of the Authority, amendments of the treaty, the protection of developing states from injury to their economies or export earnings by seabed-mining matters not specified in the treaty expressly, and certain questions regarding applications to mine the seabed. All other matters, including the budget of the Authority, would be handled by voting.[20]

A Legal and Technical Commission, composed of qualified personnel, but reflecting equitable geographical distribution, is to make recommendations to the Council concerning decisions on seabed-mining contract applications. If the recommendation with respect to any application is for approval, it may be rejected by the Council only by consensus—with the sponsoring state not participating and, therefore, unable to block. If, however, the recommendation is for disapproval, the Council may approve the application on a three-fourths vote.[21]

Under the envisaged access system, the small minority of Western industrialized states would have to rely on the Legal and Technical Commission being essentially nonpolitical and thus disposed to approve qualified applications on the basis of objective, technical criteria. Plainly, it would be hazardous for those states to proceed on the assumption that they could assemble the votes to override a Commission decision to disapprove of a qualified application. This is particularly significant to the United States, as it is likely to have the greatest number of qualified applicants, but will encounter in the Council a probable coalition of land-based minerals producers, Soviet-bloc states, Western ocean mining competitors, and developing states each of which would have its own reasons for wishing to prevent the approval of qualified U.S. contract applications. Under such circumstances, the United States could not have confidence that it could find even a single state willing to block consensus.

On the other hand, with the limitations on production provided by the treaty, the United States and other states with advanced ocean-mining capabilities or potential would need to be assured that unqualified applicants would not receive contracts on the basis of political decisions of the Commission. The Western industrial states could not reasonably expect to be able to achieve a consensus Council decision to override a Commission recommendation for approval of an unqualified application. The reason for these conclusions is the same in each scenario. Both the Council and Commission would probably be highly political: there is little likelihood that either of the bodies would depart from established political behavior in other international organs, notwithstanding treaty strictures to the contrary.

In light of these facts, it is clear that, in the envisaged seabed regime, there would not be assured access to deep-seabed minerals. The system would be quite discretionary, a result sought by the Group of 77 from the outset, yet the fact that the Commission's rules and regulations on voting procedures are yet to be established is of no practical significance in terms of the ultimate outcome. In the opinion of the U.S. government the Western industrial states have failed to achieve in the Draft Convention their fundamental negotiating goal on seabed mining, and the developing states have won theirs.

Still another serious problem for the Western industrial states lies in the provisions relating to amendments to the seabed regime. Fifteen years after the commencement of commercial recovery of seabed minerals, there would be a review conference and after five years of negotiations without reaching consensus, there could be a vote on amending the regime. Two-thirds of the states party to the treaty could vote through any changes whatsoever and, if the same number ratified, the revised regime would enter into force for all parties to the treaty. In other words, the developing states could determine the course of seabed mining, just when the industrial states would need access to the resources as world-wide, land-based supplies declined. The developing states would have enormous leverage on the industrial states in the negotiations for amendments and could dictate the final result, if the need arose.[22] Only previously existing contracts, if any, would be protected from this amendment procedure.

Seabed mineral production would be limited by the treaty. Such policies of the Authority as a production ceiling and antidensity and antimonopoly provisions, as well as commodity arrangements in which the Authority could represent all seabed production, would together serve to restrict production overall or with respect to any state or group of states. Market distortions and injury to consumer states—as well as lost revenues for industrial and developing states—would likely result.[23]

The Enterprise would carry out deep-seabed mining for the benefit of the developing states. Its initial, fully integrated operation would be funded by national contributions essentially on the U.N. scale (the minimum U.S. share would be approximately $125 million in long-term, interest-free loans and $125 million in loan guarantees), assuming a total project cost of $1 billion. The Enterprise would have the privilege of an initial share of the limited overall production permitted by the treaty, would be exempted from antidensity and antimonopoly restrictions applicable to other operators, and would receive priority consideration by the Authority in the process of selecting among applicants when the production ceiling was encountered. The Enterprise also could be temporarily exempted from making revenue-sharing payments and could be granted tax immunity by any state.[24]

Mining operators would have to submit two fully-prospected mine sites to the Authority for its selection of one to be reserved for development by the Enterprise, or by developing states in association with the Authority. The Enterprise and developing states could also operate in other seabed areas.[25]

The Enterprise would receive technology on a mandatory basis (if determined by the Enterprise to be otherwise unavailable on the open market "on fair and reasonable commercial terms and conditions") from state and private ocean mining operators and, in the last instance, from states that had ocean mining operations or access to the necessary technology. While the exposure of mining operators would exist until ten years after the Enterprise achieved commercial recovery, the obligations of states would extend at least throughout the first Enterprise operation. Mining operators would be obligated to transfer mining technology, but states would be obligated to ensure the availability of not only mining technology, but also processing technology.[26]

It is difficult to perceive how states would go about fulfilling their obligations to transfer technology, given its highly proprietary nature. As for companies interested in ocean mining, the obligation to transfer technology to their competitors would have to be highly objectionable. Third-party technology suppliers might well refuse to agree to the transfer requirements, thus depriving potential mining operators of important or even essential technology.

Another severe difficulty is that the Draft Convention falls far short of fully protecting the right to maintain technology transfer controls under existing U.S. law. Only technology essential to national security would be exempt from transfer obligations.[27]

Finally, a system of revenue sharing by mining operators would contribute to funding the Authority and financing the Enterprise, compensating those developing states whose economies were injured by seabed mining, and assisting developing states in general and national liberation groups recognized in U.N. General Assembly resolutions. The levels of financial obligations of contractors would range from $527 million to $1.3 billion over the life of each project, depending on profitability.[28]

The Participants in the Negotiations

It is noteworthy that in the negotiations for the seabed-regime rules and procedures, governmental delegations were not the only actors. Nongovernmental actors also participated although formal decisions were of course reserved to governmental officials. As a consequence, individuals representing numerous IGOs, private profit-making corporate enterprises, and nonprofit nongovernmental organizations were also actively involved. Among the most active of such participants was the Neptune Group coalition of nongovernmental organizations.[29] Among numerous other activities, this coalition hosted seven seminars requested by governmental delegates. For example, on July 21, 1979, a hundred delegates and experts attended three all-day seminars in New York. These discussions focused on the financial aspects, availability and transfer of technology, and decision making in the International Seabed Authority.[30]

Another segment of the negotiations involved political interactions within national governmental bureaucracies, most particularly the United States government. Ann Hollick has provided a detailed example of such governmental bureaucratic politics with respect to the seabed issue. In her analysis she demonstrates the various alignments and cleavages that emerged within the executive branch concerning the development of a so-called U.S. seabed policy.[31] She carefully examines the influence activities of numerous nongovernmental and governmental entities. She identifies the petroleum industry, the hard minerals industry, the marine science community, the Advisory Committee on the Law-of-the-Sea, and numerous units of the executive branch as participants in the policy-formulation process. Governmental bodies included the Departments of Defense, Interior, State, Commerce, Transportation, Justice, and Treasury, the National Petroleum Council, Bureau of the Budget (later the Office of Management and Budget), the White House Staff, the National Science Foundation, and the National Security Council Staff.

It should be noted here again that concerned U.S.-based corporate and other nongovernmental entities applied substantial pressures both in Congress and in executive bureaus and departments. A popular theme with industry groups, such as the American Mining Congress (AMC), was advocacy for the passage of unilateral U.S. legislation that would provide investment security for corporations' seabed-mining activities (in lieu of an UNCLOS Treaty or after such a treaty might come into force). An international authority under the auspices of the United Nations that would control the exploitation of the seabed was generally opposed.

Regime Characteristics

Without doubt, the seabed regime as envisioned by UNCLOS III is a most explicit organization, with institutions and their powers carefully delineated, the rights and obligations spelled out in detail, and regime transformation painstakingly circumscribed by specific amendment rules. There is also little doubt, as emerges from our description of the regime, that the specifics of the decision-making process ensure an appreciable tilt toward the interests of the Third World. Yet the technological and financial capabilities and resources for the exploitation of the seabed clearly lie with the Western industrial states and large corporations headquartered in the United States, Western Europe, and Japan. Is it reasonable to expect that these capabilities and resources will be used without definite assurance that their investment in deep-sea mining ventures are protected and that adequate yields from these investments can be anticipated in the event of successful exploitation? Or is it more likely that the necessary capabilities and resources will be withheld with the prospect that, in terms of regime goal attainment, the whole extensive and expensive structure will be a dismal failure?

Although the negotiators for most industrial states accepted the scheme set out in the Draft Convention, the TNCs that have invested in seabed-mining technology and have formed mining consortia have rejected the regime and maintain that they will abandon the field, rather than submit. The simple reason is that the treaty encourages a highly adverse investment climate. The amount of money that would be spent on this regime by the United States and other Western industrial states will be enormous. As the regime is presently contemplated, it would build up a new extensive international bureaucracy subsidized to an appreciable degree by the United States and other Western states—a bureaucracy which, by itself, could not mine the first nodule of seabed materials.

Under these circumstances, is it possible that efforts will be made by the United States and some other Western industrial states to create a counterregime for mining manganese nodules and other minerals? As we have seen from Table 7.2, most of the consortia of private companies that have the necessary technological capabilities and financial resources are headquartered in the United States, but some members of the consortia are also in West Germany, France, and Japan. With Great Britain, West Germany, Italy, Belgium, the Netherlands, and Spain having abstained in the vote on the Draft Convention, organizational arrangements for deep-seabed mining outside this Convention cannot be excluded. West Germany has already expressed its official disappointment with the seabed regime as stipulated in the Draft Convention.[32] France and Japan may hesitate to ratify the Convention under these circumstances.

However, this would not stop the Convention from going into force, because for this, only 61 ratifications are needed and the Group of 77 can easily assure this number of ratifications. In the United States, Senate approval of the Law-of-the-Sea Draft Treaty would have been most unlikely even if the new Convention had been signed, and in West Germany national legislation already exists for the promotion of deep-seabed mining by private companies. Therefore, organizational arrangements outside the Draft Treaty's seabed-mining regime would clearly be consistent with that legislation. The creation of such a counterregime appears to be feasible at present although unlikely because of other international political considerations such as issue linkage including concern with energy supply on the part of some of the Western industrial states. Meanwhile, 117 states signed the Law-of-the-Sea Treaty on November 10, 1982. On December 30 of that year President Reagan announced that the United States will not pay a U.N. assessment of about $1 million a year for implementing the treaty's sea-bed mining provisions because this very aspect of the treaty is unacceptable to the United States.

The European Monetary System (EMS)

While in our preceding case a very explicit organizational framework for an international regime had been devised to become effective once the new Law-of-the-Sea Treaty is ratified, the EMS regime is already in place. It does not have the detailed organizational structure of the prospective seabed regime and makes use of the existing institutions and bureaucracy of the EC to achieve its goals of monetary cooperation and stability among EC member-states. To appreciate the operation of this regime, a brief background description is necessary.

EMS Background

Monetary cooperation and integration was on the agenda of the Hague Summit of the EC governmental leaders in December 1969 and was dealt with in the final communique. In paragraph eight the EC Commission was called upon to draw up a plan for a phased development of an Economic and Monetary Union.[33] In March 1971 the EC Council decided that the first stage toward such a union would begin retroactively on January 1, 1971, and would last three years. The decision called for increased consultation among members and urged member-states to adopt common standpoints in international negotiations regarding monetary policy and within IGOs. It encouraged parallel progress in the alignment of monetary and economic policies, rather than one preceding the other. A part of the trade-off between France and West Germany, medium-term financial assistance was initiated for a period of five years. A Committee of Governors of Central Banks was created to guide the narrowing of exchange rates and draw up a proposal for a European Monetary Cooperation Fund (EMCF).

The central mechanism for achieving convergence among member-states' currencies was a system establishing a permissible fluctuation of ± 1.125 percent on either side of official exchange rates for the member currencies (one-half the range permitted by the IMF). Member-states would also limit fluctuation vis-à-vis the dollar to ± 0.75 percent on either side of the official exchange rates of member currencies with the dollar. The result of this arrangement was to create monetary stability by severely limiting the amount of exchange rate fluctuation among the currencies of the Six. The maximum possible range of fluctuation would be 3 percent when two of the member currencies shifted to opposite sides of the dollar.[34]

No coordination features were built into the system. The only exception was a telephone link among the five central banks of France, West Germany, Belgium, The Netherlands, and Italy, which was to become operative a month prior to the exchange rate system.[35] According to this system, when a member currency, such as the lira, would reach the outermost limit of fluctuation, the individual central banks would buy or sell dollars (in exchange for the affected currency) on the private exchange market as necessary to return it to the system's limits.[36]

Although well intentioned, the EC Council decision of March 1971 never became operational. An important reason was the official devaluation of the U.S. dollar in August 1971 (the so-called Smithsonian Agreement), formalizing a continued weakness of the dollar on world currency markets. Another reason was the inability of the Six to impose some kind of discipline on their currencies in the face of the turbulent climate of the financial markets everywhere.

The Snake

In anticipation of the Community's enlargement by three (Great Britain, Denmark, Ireland), the EC Council passed a resolution in March 1972 that introduced a somewhat broader currency coordination system, with an exchange rate limit of ±2.25 percent.[37] Based upon this resolution, the Committee of Governors of the Central Banks, meeting in Basel, agreed upon the arrangements for the snake in the tunnel, designed to stabilize exchange rates of the member-states, especially in regard to cross-rates with the dollar.

Two important differences characterized the new plan. First, the wider variation of ±2.25 percent on either side of the dollar exchange rate formed the walls of a tunnel. The snake was formed by the strongest and weakest currencies in the EC vis-à-vis the dollar (see Figure 7.2). In a sense, the EC currencies formed a joint float or snake, which stayed within the walls of a tunnel formed by the maximum fluctuation around the par value of the dollar. Second, the use of the dollar as an intervention currency was minimal. Primary intervention in exchange markets was to take place with the currencies of the member-states. Theoretically, the stronger currency states would purchase the weaker currencies in the EC to maintain the integrity of the snake. The dollar was to be used as an intervention currency only when it was needed to keep the joint float of EC currencies stable against

FIGURE 7.2

Operation of the Snake in the Tunnel

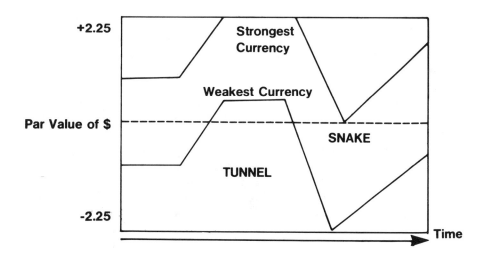

Source: Wittich and Shiratori, "The Snake in the Tunnel," *Finance and Development* 10 (June 1973), p.12.

the fluctuations of the dollar.[38] Not only did this lessen the impact of the dollar on the economies of the member-states but it effectively established a stable snake-to-dollar parity.[39]

The snake in the tunnel did not fare much better than its predecessor. Before actual accession to the EC, Great Britain had agreed, as had Ireland and Denmark, to join the snake arrangement. However, under intense speculative pressure, on June 23, 1972, Great Britain took the pound out, followed by the Irish pound. Four days later, Denmark also opted out of the arrangement, but was able to rejoin the snake in October 1972 after speculation on the kroner relaxed. The lira, the other chronically weak currency in the EC, was withdrawn by Italy following the second devaluation of the dollar in February 1973.[40] The attitude of France toward the snake varied. The franc remained in the snake until January 1974, but from then through July 1975 it dropped out of the snake because the French government came to prefer a fixed exchange rate. France briefly reentered the snake from July 1975 to March 1976 and then withdrew for good.

Following the withdrawal of Italy, and more so after the January 1974 French departure, the snake in the tunnel arrangement began to change in form and substance. The devaluation of the dollar in February 1973, and continued speculation thereafter, forced the abandonment of the tunnel, even though the snake continued as a joint float of European currencies. On January 8, 1974, France withdrew from the arrangement despite the offer of $3 billion in credit from West Germany to remain a snake participant.[41] West Germany also offered reserve assets to the smaller states (Benelux and Denmark) that continued in the snake in order to maintain the joint float.

It is important to note that the new minisnake effectively removed monetary integration from the purview of the EC institutions. The minisnake agreement of January 1974 was formed independently of the Council of Ministers or of the EC Monetary Committee. Representatives of the five member-states (the Club of Five) met on a monthly basis independently of the Council and the Commission. Only the first meeting of the minisnake in March 1974 was attended by an EC representative. Afterwards, the only official contact between the Club of Five in the minisnake and the EC came in 1976 and 1977, when they informed the Commission of changes in the alignment of exchange rates within the minisnake.[42] The minisnake arrangements continued until the 1978 Bremen Summit of EC governmental leaders (now called the European Council) that gave birth to the EMS.

Transition to the EMS

It was obvious by 1978 that the monetary coordination arrangements, as reflected by the snake devices, were insufficient to satisfy the economic needs and goals of the major participants, and that a different organizational and functional framework was required to attain some measure of monetary stability within the EC. West Germany wanted to eliminate recurring upward pressures on the deutsche mark (DM) that tended to damage its export business, and France was eager to assure as much as possible fixed currency exchange rates. Hence, French and German proposals called for the creation of a new system of monetary cooperation in Europe.[43] At the next meeting of the European Council in Brussels in December 1978 a resolution was introduced that called for the creation of the EMS. The EC Commission, acting on this resolution, "confirmed that the EMS had been set up as a Community instrument, and that it would be fully involved in operating the new scheme."[44] The EMS began operations on March 13, 1979. As conceived, the EMS has two main components: the European Currency Unit (ECU) and the credit mechanisms.

The ECU is a multifunctional device for EC monetary transactions. Primarily, the ECU serves as the common denominator for member currencies. That is, the exchange rates of member-states' currencies are pegged to fluctuation margins of ± 2.25 percent vis-à-vis the ECU, with the exception of the lira and the Irish pound that, because of structural weaknesses in the economies of Italy and Ireland, are allowed a fluctuation of ± 6.00 percent.

Besides its role as the common denominator, the ECU has another important purpose in the EMS, namely to serve as the threshold of divergence. When a currency's exchange rate with the ECU reaches 75 percent of its maximum deviation in either direction from par (± 1.6875 percent from par), it is a signal for consultation among the Central Banks of member-states and intervention in exchange markets to stem revaluative or devaluative tendencies.

The second major component of the EMS consists of two credit mechanisms. A short-term credit mechanism of 14 billion ECUs and a medium-term facility of 11 billion ECUs were created as a part of the EMS for maintaining values of member currencies experiencing balance-of-payments difficulties and experiencing speculation in exchange markets. Funding for these mechanisms have come from the member-states, who have deposited 20 percent of their gold reserves and 20 percent of their dollar reserves with the EMS in exchange for equivalent amounts of ECUs. The short-term credit is available for up to three months to remedy short-term deficits in the balance of payments. The medium-term assistance is available for periods of two to five years. Both forms of aid become available when a member-state's currency reaches its threshold of divergence away from the ECU. However, following the IMF practice, aid is not extended unless and until the recipient agrees to implement monetary reforms that are developed through consultations with the EC monetary authorities or central banks. According to the

Council's decision implementing the EMS, the credit mechanisms will eventually be transferred from the control of the EMCF to a new Community institution, the European Monetary Fund (EMF) in the 1980s.

Beside the short-run goal of minimizing exchange rate fluctuations on a day-to-day basis, the EMS is perceived by many Europeans as having favorable long-term implications for greater integration within the EC. In terms of the policies of member-states, it is hoped that the EMS, especially through its consultative arrangements, will lead to increased convergence among the economic policies of member-states, especially through its use as an instrument to ease inflation and unemployment.[45] Further down the road, the ECU is cast as a possible reserve currency to replace the fluctuating dollar as a means of maintaining international liquidity, not just for the EC, but for the rest of the world.[46]

EMS Problems

The short- and long-range projections for the role of the ECU are hampered by the progress of the EMS to date. Great Britain, despite the same offer as extended to Ireland and Italy of a wider threshold of divergence, declined to join the EMS. Instead, it preferred an associate membership that allowed it to tap into the medium-term credit facilities after depositing reserves with the EMCF.[47] The ECU also has failed to stem monetary divergence within the Community. In November 1979 the Danish kroner was devalued by 4.63 percent against the ECU and the other currencies were revalued by 0.14 percent. A month later, the kroner was again devalued by 3.80 percent, the deutsche mark was revalued by 1.01 percent and other member currencies were devalued by 0.97 percent against the ECU. Most recently, the DM and the guilder were revalued by 5.5 percent and the French franc and the lira were devalued by 3.0 percent against the other member currencies and the ECU.[48] Moreover, the European Monetary Fund, the institution designated to control the EMS and to replace the intergovernmental EMCF as the central bank of the EC in 1981, has yet to be implemented.

Although the EMS was greeted with great enthusiasm in 1979 as a step toward economic and monetary union of the EC member-states, and its implementation seemed to be assured because it reflected strong converging interests of two prominent actors in the EC—France and West Germany— the future of EMS may not be assured. France's President François Mitterrand threatened in 1982 to take the French franc out of the EMS and the West German central bank, the *Bundesbank*, has complained that France's expansionist economic course was creating increased disparities in inflation rates among the EC states, while at the same time restricting the transnational flow of capital and foreign currency exchange. According to the *Bundesbank* a better harmonization of economic policies by EC member-states seems more remote than ever and it is therefore extremely wary of any further institutionalization of the EMS.[49]

The regime institutions for the EMS lack the specificity and comprehensiveness of the prospective seabed regime. The major institutional roles are divided between the EC and the member-states. The Commission plays the most important managerial part in the EC structure; a much lesser role is assigned currently to the EMCF, although with the successful operation of the EMS, the credit mechanisms under the control of the EMCF can become very significant. Whenever the EMF is installed, it is likely to have greater authority than is exercised presently by the EMCF. In the member-states, the central banks have most of the influence on the operation of the EMS and their power is likely to exceed that of the Commission if conflicts between member-states should arise. The national finance ministries also have a voice in the EMS operation. Thus, there is an institutional division of labor that may create problems for EMS goal attainment. But even then, the rules and the procedures of the regime accepted by the participants may be jettisoned if new turmoil in the EC financial markets should break out.

As far as the future task performance of the EMS is concerned, we should note that some of the current problems of the EMS were not foreseen in 1978, when the rules and obligations of the regime members were negotiated. Nor was it possible then to recognize impediments to the creation of the EMF, although the history of the EC during the last 15 years should have been a warning that the pursuit of perceived national interests by member governments tends to outweigh the recognition or attainment of the common interest. Of course, the change in political leadership in France was not anticipated in 1977 and 1978, when President Giscard d'Estaing's government considered the benefits and costs of EMS. Clearly, since then the economic and political capabilities of some of the regime members have changed, and the EC institutions themselves, as far as they participated in EMS operations, may have influenced the regime members' attitudes and perhaps the use of their capabilities in the economic and political arenas. What kind of EMS changes in membership and rules will be forthcoming is unclear at this writing, but the *Bundesbank* concerns do not augur too well for the future of EMS and for progress in further monetary integration.

The Nuclear Nonproliferation Regime

The purpose of the nuclear nonproliferation regime is to enhance global security by preventing the spread of nuclear weapon capabilities to states not possessing such capabilities. At present only the United States, the Soviet Union, Great Britain, France, the People's Republic of China, and India have demonstrated the ability to build nuclear arms. But other states such as Israel, Pakistan, and South Africa may master the necessary technologies for the manufacture of these weapons and indeed may have actually produced them.

The regime is based on two pillars: the Treaty on the Nonproliferation of Nuclear Weapons (NPT) of 1968, and the establishment of the International Atomic Energy Agency (IAEA) in 1957. This institution grew out of President Dwight Eisenhower's Atoms for Peace Program and has been entrusted with the administration of a system of international safeguards. The aim of the safeguards is to prevent the diversion of fissionable materials from civilian to military purposes.

The negotiations for the creation of the IAEA and the safeguards system were long and difficult because it involved important political, economic, and strategic considerations.[50] The basic trade-off in the regime is the provision of assistance in the application of peaceful nuclear energy by states having the necessary resources and technological capabilites to those in need of this form of energy in return for which the latter are required to accept the intrusion of national safeguards and international inspection. Nonweapons states must agree to file with IAEA regular detailed reports on their nonmilitary nuclear activities, and to permit international inspectors to visit their nuclear facilities in order to verify these reports. The initial acceptance of IAEA safeguards was slow and halting, but gradually the program has been implemented to a considerable degree.

The NPT was negotiated within the framework of the U.N. disarmament effort, but obviously the main actors were the United States and the Soviet Union, and bilateral negotiating procedures were also used in order to reach agreement.[51] The basic aim of the short treaty was to obligate states not to develop or to aid in the development of nuclear weapons or explosives. In addition, nonweapon states were to agree to put all their peaceful nuclear facilities under safeguards, including those set up through domestically-generated technology. On the other hand, nonweapon states were promised access to the technology they needed for peaceful nuclear purposes as well as information on the potential benefits of peaceful nuclear explosions.

A complement to the NPT is its regional counterpart in Latin America, the Treaty of Tlatelolco. It seeks to set up an atom-free zone in that region and thereby helps to strengthen the international regime by emphasizing the same interest as symbolized by the NPT.

The regime has now 111 adherents, but eight important states have refused to sign the NPT, arguing that it is discriminatory. Nevertheless, the NPT and the IAEA safeguards system has made a significant contribution to international stability by establishing a normative presumption against proliferation, and by creating procedures for verifying national intentions. This has helped to increase confidence and to bring about a deeper sense of predictability in the behavior of states.[52]

The effectiveness of the regime was thrown into doubt when in 1974

India exploded a peaceful nuclear device using plutonium derived from a Canadian-supplied research reactor with U.S.-supplied heavy water. Another event adversely affecting regime effectiveness has been the gradual exhaustion of world-wide oil reserves and the fourfold increase of oil prices following the 1973 embargo on oil deliveries after the outbreak of the Arab-Israel war in October of that year. The consequences was a rush by many of the world's governments to build nuclear facilities for the generation of electricity and to increase the use of plutonium in many reactors. The IAEA predicted that by the end of the 1980s, 40 states would be using plutonium to fuel electricity producing plants.[53] Finally, during the mid-1970s West Germany and France contracted for the sale of reprocessing plants to Brazil and Pakistan through which weapons-usable fissionable materials could be produced. Under these circumstances it became questionable whether the safeguards system could cope with the necessary expansion of inspection activities.

In order to maintain the nonproliferation regime as best as possible, the United States began to embark on a more cautious policy toward the use of plutonium, focusing especially against the recycle of plutonium in thermal reactors as an obvious danger to nonproliferation. This policy approach, initiated under the Ford Administration, was officially announced in 1977 by President Jimmy Carter. In addition, the U.S. government proposed the establishment of a Nuclear Suppliers Group in London in which the major suppliers (15 states) would come together to discuss guidelines for nuclear commerce that would reduce competition that might undermine safeguards obligations.

Although West Germany and France initially objected strongly to the new policy approach to nonproliferation because it endangered their exports of nuclear plants and reprocessing facilities, the resulting frictions were gradually overcome when West Germany modified its sales contract with Brazil on these items, and France eventually cancelled its contract with Pakistan. Assisting in the elimination of cross-Atlantic frictions on the nonproliferation issue was a program suggested by the United States, called the International Nuclear Fuel Cycle Evaluation (INFCE), which brought together in Vienna over a period of two years 66 states and organizations from East and West including suppliers and consumers and a number of states that had not signed the NPT. In the Communique of the Final Plenary Conference of INFCE it was stressed that effective measures can and should be taken to minimize the danger of the proliferation of nuclear weapons without jeopardizing energy for peaceful purposes.[54]

It appears, then, that with the slight broadening of its institutions through INFCE the regime has adjusted itself to new conditions, the need for safeguards has received new justification, and the obligation of regime members under the NPT system have obtained greater legitimacy. On the other hand, the discrimination issue between nuclear weapon states and nonweapon states remains a continuing dilemma of the nonproliferation regime even if safeguards may be regarded as "beneficial necessities."[55] Indeed, for most states, national security concerns constitute the major rationale to preserve and strengthen the nonproliferation regime, although a desire for prestige or for a weak or unpopular regime to maintain itself in power could well tip some states such as Iraq or Argentina toward acquiring the capacity to produce nuclear weapons.

The U.N. Code of Conduct for the TNCs: A Future Regime?

Up to now, our cases have dealt with regimes whose institutions, procedures, and rules regarding rights and obligations have been bargained-out (seabed mining) or that are and have been operational. We will now briefly discuss a possible international regime that is still in the negotiating stage: the U.N. code of conduct for transnational corporations (TNCs).

Better known until a few years ago as multinational corporations or simply multinationals, TNCs have evoked sharply different reactions to their operations, which may span a few states or may be carried out worldwide. Many observers in the Western industrial states look at TNCs as good fairies, enhancing the standards of living in states where they establish subsidiaries by providing greater opportunities for employment, promoting the building of infrastructure facilities including schools and hospitals, and strengthening the host government's balance-of-payments. On the other hand, most Third World leaders look upon TNCs as "devils" exploiting natural resources and labor in their states, engaging in restrictive business practices, imposing their will on host governments through the sheer magnitude of their economic and financial activities, and seeking to influence the governments of the states where they are headquartered to the disadvantage of host-country interests.

Whatever the correct view of TNCs—and, of course, nothing in the world is either entirely white or black—the United Nations became involved in TNC activities in 1972 when the Economic and Social Council appointed a group of eminent persons to study the role of TNCs and their impact on development.[56] Following the delivery of the study group's report, U.N. Secretary-General Kurt Waldheim established in the fall of 1974 a unit named the Commission on Transnational Corporations, whose tasks included the elaboration of a code of conduct for TNCs. The Commission was to be assisted by a U.N. Center on Transnational Corporations (CTC), which was set up in 1975.

The first Commission meeting was held in March 1975, during which the first organizational steps toward the formulation of a code were taken. Other Commission meetings were held at least once a year; meanwhile, the substantive work on the code was carried out by working groups that met much more frequently. As of this writing, the code has not been completed because deep disagreements on major points of principle were unable to be bridged.

Initial Positions

The enormity of the working group's task can best be seen by the intitial positions taken by the Group of 77 and the five leading industrial states (the United States, Great Britain, France, West Germany, and Italy) during the commission meeting in 1976. There were 21 main areas of concern with respect to TNCs that were listed by the Group of 77 and that included:

- Lack of adjustment by TNCs to the legislation of the host states in the matters, inter alia, of foreign investment and policies concerning credit exchange, fiscal matters, prices and commercial matters, industrial property, and labor policies.
- The negative attitude of TNCs towards the renegotiation of original concessions when this is considered necessary by the government of the state.
- The refusal of the TNCs to accept the exclusive jurisdiction of domestic law in cases of litigation.
- Direct or indirect interference in the internal affairs of host states by TNCs.
- Requests by TNCs to governments of the home state to intercede with the host government, by means of political or economic initiatives in support of their private interests.
- Obstruction by TNCs of the efforts of the host state to assume its rightful responsibility and exercise effective control over the development and management of its resources, in contravention of the accepted principle of permanent sovereignty of states over their natural resources.
- Imposition of excessively high prices for imported technology without any adaptation to local conditions.
- Failure by TNCs to promote research and development in host states.
- Imposition of restrictive business practices, inter alia, on affiliates in developing states as a price for technical know-how.

The industrial states listed 23 areas of concern that they wanted to be taken into consideration in the formulation of the code and that included:

- The extent to which host state legislation and regulations may discriminate, either in favor of TNCs or against TNCs as compared to domestic enterprises, in the treatment of enterprises on the basis of whether or not such enterprises are under foreign control.
- The extent to which expropriation of properties undertaken for public purposes related to internal requirements of the countries concerned are

nondiscriminatory in application and are accompanied by prompt, adequate, and effective compensation.

- The effects of TNC operations and activities on employment and job creation, and whether these give rise to benefits, for example, job creation, or nonbenefits, for example, strain on indigenous resources of host states.
- The role played by TNCs and governments in the transfer of technology to host states, including the types of technology involved and the conditions that may be imposed by TNCs and governments in connection with such transfers.
- The extent to which TNCs take host-states' interests into account in the repatriation of capital, remittance of profits, payments of dividends, royalties, and management fees, and the extent to which the levels at which these are made are constrained by governments.[57]

Negotiation Problems

It was decided early in the deliberations that the code would consist of six chapters: 1) Preamble and Objectives; 2) Definitions; 3) Major Principles and/ or Issues Related to the Activities of Transnational Corporations; 4) Principles and/or Issues Relating to the Treatment of Transnational Corporations; 5) Legal Nature and Scope of the Code; and 6) Implementation. To overcome the differences in positions, the group turned its attention first to Chapters 1, 3, and 4, whose subject matters contained more common elements and appeared to have greater prospects for compromises than Chapter 2 and especially Chapter 5, where the gap between opposing positions was very wide.

The basic method of operation in the group's deliberations was to set forth the principle and/or issue involved with respect to each item for the code, identify the elements in which agreement existed, list other points raised by some group members, and add commentaries of a legal or organizational nature, for example whether a particular code provision should be in one or another chapter. The discussion of issues that had been dealt with in other forums, such as transfer of technology (UNCTAD), employment and labor (ILO), and corrupt practices (ad hoc working group), was initially postponed. Without doubt, this approach, although slow, was systematic, useful, and effective.

The first major attempt in producing an annotated code elaborated by the Commission staff was published in January 1978. It showed a beginning, although modest, convergence of viewpoints between the developed and developing countries.

A further significant step was taken by the working group at its September 1978 meeting, when it authorized its chairman to draft formulations for a future code that would attempt to consolidate the discussions of the working group so far. These formulations were a tremendous step forward toward agreement on the actual articles. However, it should be noted that the formulations did not commit the delegations in any way. Since the legal nature of the code had not been agreed upon and, therefore, specific commands to the parties involved would have been inappropriate, the word "should" instead of "shall" was used throughout the formulations. This suggested that the formulations were primarily a basis for deliberations rather than a definitive draft for a code.

After 17 sessions of the working group, each lasting a minimum of two weeks, considerable progress had been made by early in 1982 in narrowing the conceptual, legal, and factional gaps between the Western developed states and the Group of 77. On restrictive business practices a separate agreement was reached within UNCTAD in 1980 and on employment and labor issues a tripartite declaration acceptable to all parties was formulated within the framework of the ILO. However, in some issue areas agreement remained very difficult and quite elusive.

With respect to jurisdiction and sovereignty, including the concept of permanent sovereignty over natural resources, the Group of 77 delegates have taken a hard stand. Moreover, they have displayed a high level of solidarity on all issues despite the fact that their interests have begun to diverge. The reason is that such states as Mexico, Brazil, and Singapore have reached a more advanced level of economic development and sophistication than many of the very poor states in Africa and Central America.

The legal nature of the code or codes is most likely to be the most contested matter. For the Group of 77 states supported by the communist-bloc states, only a mandatory code can be effective in assuring that TNCs will contribute to the attainment of national policy goals and the objectives enshrined in the New International Economic Order. For TNC managements—backed by the Western industrial states—a compulsory code is anathema. Of course, even in the unlikely event that agreement could be reached on a mandatory code, the question of enforcement would prove to be very difficult indeed.

If the code were adopted in the form of a multilateral treaty, it would entail ratification by each U.N. member-state according to that state's constitution and could be a long process. The provisions of the code addressed to TNCs and their subsidiaries would most likely be incorporated into the national legal systems of those states adhering to the multilateral treaty. The provisions, therefore, could be enforced in the national courts. For situations in which the codes are embodied in international instruments other than a treaty (for example, a declaration passed by the U.N. General Assembly) enforcement would be through appeals to fairness and justice as well as sanctions such as unfavorable public opinion (black lists), or some other type of adverse measures by other states or even TNCs. Consultation mechanisms among governments, conducted within the United Nations framework, may also be useful to ensure adherence to the code.

It appears then that regardless of whether the code would be obligatory or voluntary, an extensive international regime would be created with clearly-defined rights and obligations for all participants—governments and TNCs—as well as the appropriate rules and procedures. Institutionally, and organizationally, the Center for Transnational Corporations would play a key role. Other U.N. bodies such as ECOSOC, the ILO, the UNCTAD (for the transfer of technology) may also be given specific managerial and supervisory tasks even if adherence by the regime is voluntary for TNCs. National governments would also perform significant organizational tasks within the regime framework; regional IGOs such as OECD and the EC, as well as economic and commercial INGOs may also be drawn into the regime network. For TNCs, compliance with the regime rules—the code—may flow from self-interest. Public declarations to this effect, or tacit acquiescence if generally known, could bolster the public image of TNCs so inclined, and may then enhance their negotiation potential when a TNC seeks to hammer out an access agreement with a prospective host government or attempts later to renegotiate such an agreement.

There have been recurring indications that some parties to the U.N. code of conduct negotiations have become rather apathetic about the outcome of the continuing deliberations. Indeed, in 1982 one or two delegations wanted to review the status of work accomplished so far before reaching a decision about future participation in the negotiations.[58] This raises the question about regime possibilities in the event of failure of the negotiations.

The code of conduct exercise in the United Nations has shown that some common interests between TNC and host states exist even if the latter are part of the Third World. It is not inconceivable that those articles of the code where agreement has been possible would constitute a basis for the rules of a regime. In addition, efforts to enact parallel legislation dealing with relations between governments and TNCs may supplement the initial rules of the regime. The foreign investment laws of the member-states of the Andean Common Market constitute the most comprehensive endeavor to regulate investment policy and incentives, taxation, exchange of information, and the regional protection of industrial policy. Other regional organizations, such as the African and Malagasy Common Organization (OCAM) and the Caribbean Community and Common Market (CARICOM), have attempted to enact common rules on a few selected TNC activities, but the effectiveness of these regulations is open to doubt, and some lack ratification by the member-states. The OAS has been pondering the problem as well as the possible development of a code of conduct of its own.[59]

Even if a formal treaty for a code of conduct is not forthcoming, the

CTC and the ILO may be assigned organizational tasks in support of the regime. What we might be witnessing then, would be an example of an evolutionary regime that might not be satisfactory to every interested party, but in the long run be better than the complete absence of rules and procedures in the international investment field.

SUMMARY AND CONCLUSIONS

Looking over the cases on international regimes, several commonalities and differences can be noted. All of the regimes have an organizational framework for task performance, but the specificity of functions assigned to the various organs and their size varies considerably. Indeed, only the seabed regime has organs specifically designed for the seabed mining undertaking and all rules and procedures are carefully delineated. In the EMS regime, the main IGO organ used for task performance has many other functions that, in the overall context of the EC, are more important than the EMS management task. Only EMCF is especially designed to support the EMS. Similarly, the national organs—the central banks and financial institutions—are borrowed for the EMS task performance. Nonetheless, the rules and procedures for the EMS seem to be quite clear.

In the NPT regime, the main institution, the IAEA, although not specifically designed for the regime, and in fact part of the U.N. structure, does expend many of its resources on task performance, that is, inspection activities. INFCE plays mainly a supporting role. The regime rules are clear, but since the regime activities are deeply involved in high-stake international politics and can affect critically the vital interests of the participating states, pressure may develop from a number of middle powers that are close to the nuclear-weapon threshhold for modifications in the regime to accomodate national aspirations.

The prospective TNC regime also will need to borrow heavily from the existing United Nations structure for its task performance, although regional IGOs and some INGOs such as the International Chamber of Commerce can aid in the complex management of this regime. This means that only the Center for Transnational Corporations at present possesses special capabilities to perform the regime tasks; other institutions will have to acquire full familiarity and expertise with the code of conduct before the overall management can become truly effective. If agreement on the code of conduct is reached, the rules will be explicit, though of course subject to interpretation considering the vast field that the operation of the world's TNCs constitute. Pressures for future rule changes will be exerted and, depending on the political and economic power of the units desiring such changes, the rules are likely to be modified.

The preceding discussion highlights the usefulness of the regime concept as an important construct for both defining and managing the attainment of objectives in the international arena by governmental and nongovernmental actors. At the same time, it also makes understandable the search for new conceptualizations in the international regime area that is pursued by many international relations scholars, and is reflected in the scholarly literature.[60] Some scholars feel that the notion of regime is useless; others present new, elaborate definitions and paradigms. Clearly, the last word has not been written on international regimes; perhaps, more studies need to be undertaken from which more solid conclusions about the concept of regimes can be drawn.

NOTES

1. The typology of regime origins in these paragraphs follows Oran Young, "International Regimes: Problems of Concept Formation," *World Politics* 32 (April 1980), pp. 349–51.

2. See Ernst B. Hass, "Why Collaborate? Issue Linkage and International Regimes," *World Politics* 32 (April 1980) pp. 357–405, especially p. 382.

3. Robert O. Keohane and Joseph S. Nye, *Power and Interdependence: World Politics in Transition* (Boston: Little Brown, 1977), p.55.

4. Young, op. cit., p. 343.

5. Ibid., p. 344.

6. Regimes would perhaps benefit from direct taxing authority. In addition to the proposals for revenue sharing in the proposed LOS Treaty, see Eleanor B. Steinberg and Joseph A. Yager, *New Means of Financing International Needs* (Washington, D.C.: The Brookings Institution, 1978).

7. Young, op. cit., pp. 246–47.

8. Ibid., pp. 351–52.

9. Presidential Proclamation, no. 2667, September 28, 1945.

10. U.N. Document A/6695 (1967).

11. U.N. Document A/7834 (1969).

12. U.N. Document A/8097 (1970).

13. VIII U.N. *Monthly Chronicle* (January 1971), pp. 37–39.

14. For a brief analysis of UNCLOS III, see Mohamed El Baradei and Chloe Garvin, *Crowded Agendas, Crowded Rooms, International Arrangements at UNCLOS III: Some Lessons in Global Negotiations* (New York: United Nations Institute for Training and Research, 1981).

15. Public Law No 96–283, 94 Statute 553, 30 U.S.C. 1401–1605.

16. See Doug Bandow, "UNCLOS III: A Flawed Treaty," *San Diego Law Review* 19 (1982), pp. 475 ff.

17. Draft Convention on the Law-of-the-Sea (Informal Text), U.N. Document A/CONF. 62/WP. 10/Rev. 3/Add. 1, Articles 136, 140. The description of the Seabed Regime can be found in Theodore G. Kronmiller, *The Lawfulness of Deep Seabed Mining* (New York: Oceana Publications, 1980), chapter 1.

18. Ibid., Article 150.

19. Ibid., Articles 151, 150, 161, 162.

20. Ibid., Article 161, para. 7.

21. Ibid., Articles 161, para. 7, 165.

22. Ibid., Article 151.

23. Ibid., Article 150.

24. Ibid., Articles 151, para. 2(c), 170, Annex III, Article 6, Annex IV, Articles II, 13.

25. Ibid., Annex III, Article 8.

26. Ibid., Annex III, Articles 5, 14, 15.

27. Ibid., Article 302.

28. Ibid., Articles 150, 162, Annex III, Article. 13.

29. The Neptune Group included The Ocean Education Project, Quaker Office at the United Nations, United Methodist Law of the Sea Project, and Global Interdependence Center at Philadelphia. The group got its name from the NGO newspaper, the *Neptune*, which was published jointly by The Ocean Education Project and United Methodist Law of the Sea Project for distribution at UNCLOS III sessions.

30. For a more detailed discussion of these activities see *Soundings: Law of the Sea News and Comments* IV (September–October 1979), pp. 1–4.

31. Ann Hollick, "Seabeds Make Strange Bedfellows," *Foreign Policy* 9 (Winter 1972–73), pp. 148–70 and "Bureaucrats at Sea," in *New Era of Ocean Politics*, eds. Ann L. Hollick and Robert E. Osgood (Baltimore: The Johns Hopkins University Press, 1974).

32. *Frankfurter Allgemeine Zeitung*, May 3, 1982.

33. "The Final Communique of the Conference of the Heads of State and of Government on 1 and 2 December 1969 at the Hague," in *Compendium of Community Monetary Texts* (Brussels: European Communities, Monetary Committee, 1974), pp. 14–15.

34. Marie Henriette Lambert and Patrick B. de Fontenay, "Implications of Proposals for Narrowing the Margins of Exchange Rate Fluctuations Between the EEC Currencies," *IMF Staff Papers* 18 (November 1971), p. 648.

35. Rainer Hellmann, *Gold, The Dollar, and the European Community: The Seven Year Monetary War* (New York: Praeger, 1979), p. 22.

36. Geoffrey Denton, "European Monetary Co-operation; The Bremen Proposals," *World Today* 34 (1978), p. 436; and Robert W. Russell, "Snakes and Sheiks: Managing Europe's Money," in *Policy-Making in the European Communities*, eds. Helen Wallace, William Wallace, and Carole Webb (New York: Wiley, 1977), pp. 70–71.

37. "Resolution of the Council and of the Representatives of the Governments of the Member States of 21 March 1972 on the Application of the Resolution of 22 March 1971 on the Attainment by Stages of Economic and Monetary Union in the Community," (OJ No C 38/3 of 18.4.1972) in *Compendium*, op. cit., pp. 33–34.

38. Gunter Wittich and Masaki Shiratori, "The Snake in the Tunnel," *Finance and Development* 10 (June 1973), pp. 10–12; also Hellmann, op. cit., pp. 24–26.

39. Joanne Salop, "Dollar Intervention Within the Snake," *IMF Staff Papers* 24 (1977), pp. 64, 76.

40. Hellmann, op. cit., pp. 26–29; Loukas Tsoukalis, "Is the Relaunching of Economic and Monetary Union a Feasible Proposal?" *Journal of Common Market Studies* Vol. 15 (June 1977), pp. 26–29.

41. Hellmann, op. cit., pp. 44–45.

42. Ibid., pp. 46–47.

43. EC *Bulletin* (6–1978), pt. 1.5.2.

44. EC *Bulletin* (12–1978), pt. 1.1.3.

45. Denton, op. cit., p. 445.

46. This view is already evident since the *Bulletin* of the EC, besides quoting exchange rates for member-state currencies, also quotes exchange rates for the ECU with other major currencies. See, for example, *EC Bulletin* (5-1980), pt. 3.1.4.

47. K. Johnson and C. Painter, "British Governments and the EMS," *Political Quarterly* Vol. 15, (July 1980) p. 322.

48. The official view is that these devaluations and revaluations were not the result of the inoperability of the EMS but a result of structural problems and divergences, especially inflation, among the member economies. See *EC Bulletin* (9-1981), pt. 2.1.4. The *Economist* (October 10, 1981) credits the success of the EMS in its early years with the fact that the members with high inflation rates were able to maintain exchange rates because of a strong trade surplus and the low inflation countries had small external deficits. And (p. 74) this made it look as if the EMS was working well. In fact, the currency harmony did little to promote any convergence of policies.

49. *Saarbruecker Zeitung*, April 29, 1982.

50. For a detailed discussion of these negotiations see Lawrence Scheinman and Richard W. Butler, "International Safeguarding as Rationalized Collective Behavior," *International Organization* 35 (Spring 1981).

51. Ibid., pp. 605–10.

52. Joseph S. Nye, "Maintaining a Nonproliferation Regime," *International Organization* 35 (Winter 1981), pp. 15–38.

53. Ibid., p. 19.

54. Ibid., p. 25.

55. Ibid., p. 29.

56. For details see Werner J. Feld, *Multinational Corporations and U.N. Politics* (New York: Pergamon Press, 1980) pp. 35–48.

57. Ibid., pp. 60–64.

58. U.N. ECOSOC Document E/C. 10/1982, May 28, 1982, p. 8.

59. See Feld, op. cit., pp. 122–24.

60. See especially the essays in the special issue on international regimes by Stephen D. Krasner, in *International Organization* 36 (Spring 1982).

Chapter 8

The Quality of IGO Task Performance: Past, Present, and Future

It seems to be self-evident that the quality of an IGO's task performance determines its success or failure in terms of the expectations that the founding fathers of the organization had in mind and that led to its establishment in the first place. It is also obvious that the circumstances, national and international, that prevailed at the time when creation of the IGO was considered, are likely to have changed with time. If we only look at the period since the end of World War II, we can appreciate the tremendous changes that have taken place in the political, economic, and physical environment of the world arena, and these changes are reflected in relations within nation-states as well as in relations among these states. No wonder then that the turbulence of global and national changes has also affected IGOs and their task performance, and indeed has also produced new conditions, sometimes better and sometimes worse, for the activities and effectiveness of INGOs in the pursuit of their particular interests.

It has been a characteristic of practically every IGO that the initial enthusiasm associated with its creation starts to diminish within a relatively short time, and with this development its task performance begins to suffer. In many cases, this initial enthusiasm was fed by ideological fervor; in the case of the United Nations it was primarily the vista of a world without devastating war, then self-government for colonial peoples and territories accompanied by economic and social improvement, followed in the 1970s by concern over human rights. Perhaps most significantly, the prospects of a world community, and perhaps eventually a world government evolving through the United Nations, has captivated large numbers of people the world over. Similarly, in Western Europe, it was a united Western Europe, avoiding the recurring hostilities of the past, that captivated the people in that region and made them strive for European union, a United States of Europe. It was in this climate of opinion that the European Coal and Steel

Community was born, although as we have seen in Chapter 3, other, more narrowly short-range motivations also played a role. These motivations had their origins in various foreign policy considerations of prospective member-states, including indirect control over a Germany that might seek revenge for its defeat and dismemberment. Finally, various sources of ideological support couched in economic terms, was stimulated by ECLA for the genesis of LAFTA and the CACM.

Foreign policy goals were also in the back of the minds of the statesmen who laid the groundwork for the United Nations. This new IGO was clearly seen as a potential instrument of national policy and indeed, national interests have played a significant part in the creation of all IGOs, as we have made clear in Chapter 3. It is largely for this reason that task performance begins to lag in almost all IGOs except perhaps in certain security-oriented organizations such as NATO and the Warsaw Treaty Organization, and those IGOs whose major functions were primarily technical, for example the UPU or ICAO. This does not mean that all security IGOs perform well; the demise of SEATO (the Southeast Asia Treaty Organization) and CENTO (the Central Treaty Organization, formerly the Baghdad Pact), makes this clear, and, as we have seen in Chapter 2, the OAU had its share of problems. But it appears that the more technical the nature of IGOs, the greater is the likelihood that their task performance will remain adequate and, moreover, will adapt itself to changing conditions. ICAO appears to be a prime example in support of this assertion.

What are the major reasons for the stagnation, or lag in task performance, of IGOs that have mainly economic and/or political objectives?

One important cause for declining quality of IGO task performance is essentially political. Member-states that showed a propensity for international organization in order to shore up or to supplement their national capabilities and resources militarily, economically, or politically (see Chapter 2) became apprehensive about the gradual loss or dilution of their national prerogatives. Especially during periods of economic stress, governments look for national solutions for economic problems that often have serious political implications for the governmental leadership. National solutions are sought in spite of the fact that from purely national points of view common IGO-administered policies might be not only desirable but also essential. In the Third World, newly-independent states usually are faced with the enormous effort of nation building and this is one of the reasons that the task performance of regional IGOs has up to now rarely been consistently successful.

Another cause for lagging task performance, also political in nature, is disappointment of IGO member governments that the hoped-for utilization of the IGO structure for the promotion of their foreign-policy goals either did not materialize or became increasingly difficult and frustrating. The latter is one reason for the growing U.S. disenchantment with the United Nations and this has had a negative impact on U.N. task performance. French disillusionment with the EC and NATO increased in the 1960s when it became clear that France's leadership in these organizations was eroding, and this has adversely affected their task performance over many years. The cases in Chapter 4 provide illustrations of this cause.

A third cause for undermining and perhaps completely destroying the task performance of an IGO is the perception of member governments and the people in the member-states that the distributions of benefits received through the IGO and the costs incurred is inequitable. In most cases this perception refects reality and as a consequence regional IGOs such as LAFTA, the CACM, and other IGOs in the Third World are now operating on a very limited basis. As we have seen in Chapter 4, the issue of disparity of benefits and costs among the member-states was a major reason for the collapse of the East African Community.

Obviously, cost-benefit calculations by member governments also have a bearing on IGOs in economically developed areas. Our case of the Regional Development Fund illustrates this problem in the EC. Increasing national economic egoism tends to aggravate this issue. But we should note that not only the task performance of the economic IGOs suffers from perceptions of unfavorable cost-benefit calculations by member-states. Security and political IGOs may also be regarded as imposing too heavy a burden on particular member-states; the OAU is a case in point and so is NATO where the question of financial-burden sharing has produced internal conflicts although it is not quite clear how far this issue has impeded task performance.

A fourth cause harming IGO task performance may be an increasing trend toward resorting to intergovernmentalisms that are apt to bypass the IGO decision-making process as laid out in the constituent treaties of particular IGOs. Under such circumstances cooperative activities between member-states are carried out and results achieved through national channels rather than through the IGO machinery. European Political Cooperation (EPC) is an excellent example of such intergovernmentalism among the EC states (see Chapter 5), but intergovernmentalism has invaded other issue areas for which the EC institutions were to be primarily responsible and has adversely affected task performance.

Intergovernmentalism is not only a problem for the EC, but for any IGO, except perhaps organizations exclusively dealing with technical matters. It tends to undermine the morale of IGO international civil servants, as discussed in Chapter 3, who see competing organizational arrangements blunting their own organizational arrangements and bureaucratic goals. All this is aggravated by frequently unfavorable perceptions of international bureaucracies that are not only prevalent among national civil servants who work with IGO officials, but also among the public, especially in the advanced industrial member-states.

Finally, the task performance of IGOs may be adversely affected by the waning enthusiasm for political and economic world organization in general. In the minds of most people, the nation-state remains the focus of their loyalty and support: the nation-state retains the highest level of legitimacy, and nationalism persists as a virtue, both morally and instrumentally. Under such emotional and ideological circumstances, IGOs, in spite of the continued growth in their numbers and in spite of the rational correctness of their existence, cannot produce the quality of task performance that may have been expected at their creation and of which they would be capable in a more favorable climate.

What does the future hold for IGO task performance? We do not see any indication that the factors and trends outlined in the preceding pages are likely to change radically. This does not mean that the creation of additional IGOs has ended. Since Third World leaders and UNCTAD officials consider South-South regional solidarity as an important strategy to improve the development levels in Third World states, new regional IGOs are likely to be established and the regional activities of existing IGOs will be strengthened. However, their task performances will probably suffer from the same problems besetting all IGOs. Whether there will be a further dramatic proliferation of specialized agencies or other IGOs in the U.N. family is difficult to predict. Certainly the United States and other Western states (and often the socialist bloc) will oppose further proliferation. On the other hand, as we have indicated in Chapter 7, international regimes to fulfill specific limited goals through cooperative ventures by nation states with the participation of transnational corporations, may well be formed as needs arise. INGOs will continue to play their useful roles as discussed in Chapter 6, probably focusing more on the national level as the more effective way into multinational conference decision making, and also continuing to pressure for more formal access to the political deliberative bodies of those IGOs of concern to their interests and goals. Networking among IGOs and INGOs will help to further both roles.

This somewhat pessimistic overlook, as far as the world community is concerned, is in our view realistic. While there may be more cooperation than conflict among international and transnational actors and worldwide conflagration may be avoided, the international arena will continue to be characterized by the pursuit of national interests and national egoisms, and the common interests of mankind are likely to be largely ignored. In such a scenario, IGOs, working at times with and through INGOs, can play a genteelizing role by fulfilling human needs wherever so allowed and will provide important functions primarily in the coordination of technical matters, without which this technologically complex world of ours could not continue to operate.

Appendixes

APPENDIX A: Membership of the United Nations and Its Specialized and Related Agencies

Organization [a]	UN [b]	FAO	GATT	IAEA	IBRD	ICAO	ICJ	IDA	IFAD	IFC	ILO	IMCO	IMF	ITU	UNESCO	UPU	WHO	WIPO	WMO
Members [c]	154	147 [d]	86 [e]	110 [f]	139 [g]	146 [b]	157 [i]	125 [j]	131 [k]	118 [l]	144 [m]	118 [n]	141 [o]	154 [p]	149 [q]	167 [r]	155 [s]	91 [t]	152 [u]
Countries																			
Afghanistan	1946	x		x	x	x	x	x	3	x	x		x	x	x	x	x		x
Albania	1955	x		x			x					x		x	x	x	x		x
Algeria	1962	x	(e)	x	x	x	x	x	2		x	x	x	x	x	x	x	x	x
Angola	1976	x	(e)			x	x				x	x		x	x	x	x		x
Argentina	1945	x	x	x	x	x	x	x	3	x	x	x	x	x	x	x	x	x	x
Australia	1945	x	x	x	x	x	x	x	1	x	x	x	x	x	x	x	x	x	x
Austria	1955	x	x	x	x	x	x	x	1	x	x	x	x	x	x	x	x	x	x
Bahamas	1973	x	(e)		x	x	x				x	x	x	x	x	x	x		
Bahrain	1971	x	(e)		x	x	x				x	x	x	x	x	x	x		
Bangladesh	1974	x	x	x	x	x	x	x	3	x	x	x	x	x	x	x	x		x
Barbados	1966	x	x		x	x	x		3	x	x		x	x	x	x	x	x	x
Belgium	1945	x	x	x	x	x	x	x	1	x	x	x	x	x	x	x	x	x	x
Benin	1960	x	x		x	x	x	x	3		x	x	x	x	x	x	x	x	x
Bhutan	1971						x		3							x			
Bolivia	1945	x		x	x	x	x	x	3	x	x		x	x	x	x	x	x	x
Botswana	1966	x	(e)		x	x	x	x	3	x	x		x	x	x	x	x		x
Brazil	1945	x	x	x	x	x	x	x	3	x	x	x	x	x	x	x	x	x	x
Bulgaria	1955	x		x		x	x				x	x		x	x	x	x	x	x
Burma	1948	x	x	x	x	x	x	x		x	x	x	x	x	x	x	x		x
Burundi	1962	x	x		x	x	x	x	3	x	x		x	x	x	x	x	x	x
Byelorussian Soviet Socialist Republic	1945			x			x				x			x	x	x	x	x	x
Cameroon	1960	x	x	x	x	x	x	x	3	x	x	x	x	x	x	x	x	x	x
Canada	1945	x	x	x	x	x	x	x	1	x	x	x	x	x	x	x	x	x	x
Cape Verde Islands	1975	x	(e)		x	x	x	x	3		x	x	x	x	x	x			x

Organization[a]	UN[b]	FAO	GATT	IAEA	IBRD	ICAO	ICJ	IDA	IFAD	IFC	ILO	IMCO	IMF	ITU	UNESCO	UPU	WHO	WIPO	WMO
Members[c] Countries	154	147[d]	86[e]	110[f]	139[g]	146[h]	157[i]	125[j]	131[k]	118[l]	144[m]	118[n]	141[o]	154[p]	149[q]	167[r]	155[s]	91[t]	152[u]
Central African Republic	1960	x			x	x	x	x	3		x		x	x	x	x	x	x	x
Chad	1960	x			x	x	x	x	3	x	x	x	x	x	x	x	x	x	x
Chile	1945	x		x	x	x	x	x	3	x	x	x	x	x	x	x	x	x	x
China, People's Republic of	1945						x		3	x		x		x	x	x	x		x
Colombia	1945	x	x	x	x	x	x	x	3	x	x	x	x	x	x	x	x	x	x
Comoro Islands	1975	x			x		x	x	3		x		x	x	x	x	x		x
Congo	1960	x			x	x	x	x	3	x	x	x	x	x	x	x	x	x	x
Costa Rica	1945	x		x	x	x	x	x	3	x	x	x	x	x	x	x	x		x
Cuba	1945	x		x	x	x	x	x	3		x	x	x	x	x	x	x	x	x
Cyprus	1960	x		x	x	x	x	x	3	x	x	x	x	x	x	x	x	x	x
Czechoslovakia	1945	x		x	x	x	x	x	3		x	x		x	x	x	x	x	x
Denmark	1945	x		x	x	x	x	x	1	x	x	x	x	x	x	x	x	x	x
Djibouti	1977	(e)			x		x	x	3	x	x	x	x	x	x	x	x		x
Dominica	1978	(e)			x		x	x	3	x	x	x	x	x	x	x			x
Dominican Republic	1945	x		x	x	x	x	x	3	x	x	x	x	x	x	x	x	x	x
Ecuador	1945	x		x	x	x	x	x	3	x	x	x	x	x	x	x	x	x	x
Egypt	1945	x	x	x	x	x	x	x	3	x	x	x	x	x	x	x	x	x	x
El Salvador	1945	x		x	x	x	x	x	3	x	x	x	x	x	x	x	x	x	x
Equatorial Guinea	1968	(e)			x	x	x	x	3		x	x	x	x	x	x	x		x
Ethiopia	1945	x		x	x	x	x	x	3	x	x		x	x	x	x	x	x	x
Fiji	1970	x	(e)		x	x	x	x	3	x	x	x	x	x	x	x	x	x	x
Finland	1955	x	x	x	x	x	x	x	1	x	x	x	x	x	x	x	x	x	x

Country	Year	1	2	3	4	5	6	7	8	9	#	10	11	12	13	14
France	1945	×	×	×	×	×	×	×	×	×	1	×	×	×	×	×
Gabon	1960	×	×	×	×	×	×	×	×	×	2	×	×	×	×	×
Gambia	1965	×		×	×	×	×	×	×		3	×	×	×		×
German Democratic Republic	1973															
Germany, Federal Republic of	1973	×	×	×	×	×	×	×	×	×		×	×	×	×	×
Ghana	1957	×	×	×	×	×	×	×	×	×	1	×	×	×	×	×
Greece	1945	×	×	×	×	×	×	×	×	×	3	×	×	×	×	×
Grenada	1974	×	×	×	×	×	×	×	×	×	3	×	×	×	×	(e)
Guatemala	1945	×		×	×	×	×	×	×	×	3	×	×	×		×
Guinea	1958	×		×	×	×	×	×	×	×	3	×	×	×		×
Guinea-Bissau	1974	×		×	×	×	×	×	×	×	3	×	×	×		(e)
Guyana	1966	×		×	×	×	×	×	×	×	3	×	×	×		×
Haiti	1945	×		×	×	×	×	×	×	×	3	×	×	×		×
Honduras	1945	×		×	×	×	×	×	×	×	3	×	×	×		×
Hungary	1955	×	×	×	×	×	×	×	×	×		×	×	×	×	×
Iceland	1946	×		×	×	×	×	×	×	×		×	×	×		×
India	1945	×	×	×	×	×	×	×	×	×	3	×	×	×	×	×
Indonesia	1950	×	×	×	×	×	×	×	×	×	2	×	×	×	×	×
Iran	1945	×		×	×	×	×	×	×	×	2	×	×	×		×
Iraq	1945	×		×	×	×	×	×	×	×	2	×	×	×		×
Ireland	1955	×	×	×	×	×	×	×	×	×	1	×	×	×	×	×
Israel	1949	×	×	×	×	×	×	×	×	×	3	×	×	×	×	×
Italy	1955	×	×	×	×	×	×	×	×	×	1	×	×	×	×	×
Ivory Coast	1960	×	×	×	×	×	×	×	×	×	3	×	×	×	×	×
Jamaica	1962	×	×	×	×	×	×	×	×	×	3	×	×	×	×	×
Japan	1956	×	×	×	×	×	×	×	×	×	1	×	×	×	×	×
Jordan	1955	×	×	×	×	×	×	×	×	×	3	×	×	×	×	×
Kampuchea	1955	×	×	×	×	×	×	×	×	×		×	×	×	×	(e)

Organization[a]		UN[b]	FAO	GATT	IAEA	IBRD	ICAO	ICJ	IDA	IFAD	IFC	ILO	IMCO	IMF	ITU	UNESCO	UPU	WHO	WIPO	WMO[u]
Members[c]		154	147[d]	86[e]	110[f]	139[g]	146[b]	157[i]	125[j]	131[k]	118[l]	144[m]	118[n]	141[o]	154[p]	149[q]	167[r]	155[s]	91[t]	152
Countries																				
Kenya	1963	x	x	x	x	x	x	x	x	3	x	x	x	x	x	x	x	x	x	x
Kuwait	1963	x	x		x	x	x	x	x	2	x	x	x	x	x	x	x	x	x	x
Laos	1955	x	x		x	x	x	x	x	3	x	x		x	x	x	x	x		x
Lebanon	1945	x	x	x	x	x	x	x	x	3	x	x	x	x	x	x	x	x		x
Lesotho	1966	x	x	(e)		x	x	x	x	3	x	x		x	x	x	x	x		x
Liberia	1945	x	x		x	x	x	x	x	3	x	x	x	x	x	x	x	x		x
Libya	1955	x	x		x	x	x	x	x	2	x	x	x	x	x	x	x	x	x	x
Luxembourg	1945	x	x	x	x	x	x	x	x	1	x	x		x	x	x	x	x	x	x
Madagascar	1960	x	x	x	x	x	x	x	x	3	x	x	x	x	x	x	x	x	x	x
Malawi	1964	x	x	x		x	x	x	x	3	x	x		x	x	x	x	x		x
Malaysia	1957	x	x	x	x	x	x	x	x		x	x	x	x	x	x	x	x	x	x
Maldives	1965	x	(e)	(e)		x	x	x	x				x	x	x		x	x		x
Mali	1960	x	x	(e)	x	x	x	x	x	3	x	x		x	x	x	x	x		x
Malta	1964	x	x	x		x	x	x		3		x	x	x	x	x	x	x	x	x
Mauritania	1961	x	x	x		x	x		x	3	x	x	x	x	x	x	x	x	x	x
Mauritius	1968	x	x	x	x	x	x		x	3	x	x	x	x	x	x	x	x	x	x
Mexico	1945	x	x		x	x	x	x	x	3	x	x	x	x	x	x	x	x	x	x
Mongolia	1961	x	x		x			x				x			x	x	x	x	x	x
Morocco	1956	x	x	x	x	x	x	x	x	3	x	x	x	x	x	x	x	x	x	x
Mozambique	1975	x	(e)				x		x	3	x	x	x	x	x	x	x	x		x
Nepal	1955	x	x			x	x	x	x	3	x	x	x	x	x	x	x	x		x
Netherlands	1945	x	x	x	x	x	x	x	x	1	x	x	x	x	x	x	x	x	x	x
New Zealand	1945	x	x	x	x	x	x	x	x	1	x	x	x	x	x	x	x	x	x	x
Nicaragua	1945	x	x	x	x	x	x	x	x	3	x	x		x	x	x	x	x		x

Country	Year									No.							(e)	
Niger	1960	x	x	x	x	x	x	x	x	3	x	x	x	x	x	x	x	x
Nigeria	1960	x	x	x	x	x	x	x	x	2	x	x	x	x	x	x	x	x
Norway	1945	x	x	x	x	x	x	x	x	1	x	x	x	x	x	x	x	x
Oman	1971	x	x		x	x	x	x	x	3	x		x	x	x	x		x
Pakistan	1947	x	x	x	x	x	x	x	x	3	x	x	x	x	x	x	x	x
Panama	1945	x	x	x	x	x	x	x	x	3	x	x	x	x	x	x	x	x
Papua New Guinea	1975	x	x	x	x	x	x	x		3	x		x	x	x	(e)	x
Paraguay	1945	x	x	x	x	x	x	x	x	3	x	x	x	x	x		x	x
Peru	1945	x	x	x	x	x	x	x	x	3	x	x	x	x	x	x	x	x
Philippines	1945	x	x	x	x	x	x	x	x	3	x	x	x	x	x	x	x	x
Poland	1945	x	x	x	x	x	x	x	x		x	x	x	x	x	x	x	x
Portugal	1955	x	x	x	x	x	x	x	x	3	x	x	x	x	x	x	x	x
Qatar	1971	x	x		x		x	x	x	2	x		x	x	x	(e)		x
Romania	1955	x	x	x	x	x	x	x	x	3	x	x	x	x	x	x	x	x
Rwanda	1962	x	x	x	x	x	x	x		3	x		x	x	x	x	x	x
St. Lucia	1979		x	x	x	x	x	x		3	x	x	x	x	x	(e)	x	x
St. Vincent	1980			x	x		x	x	x		x	x	x	x	x	(e)	x	
Sao Tome and Principe	1975															(e)		
Saudi Arabia	1945	x	x	x	x	x	x	x	x	3	x	x	x	x	x	(e)	x	x
Senegal	1960	x	x	x	x	x	x	x	x	2	x	x	x	x	x		x	x
Seychelles	1976	x	x	x	x	x	x	x	x	3	x	x	x	x	x	(e)	x	x
Sierra Leone	1961	x	x	x	x	x	x	x		3	x	x	x	x	x	x	x	x
Singapore	1965	x		x	x	x	x	x	x	3	x	x	x	x	x	x	x	x
Solomon Islands	1978	x								3	x	x	x	x	x	(e)	x	x
Somalia	1960	x	x	x	x	x	x	x	x	3	x	x	x	x	x		x	x
South Africa[v]	1945	x		x	x	x	x	x	x	3	x	x	x	x	x	x	x	x
Spain	1955	x	x	x	x	x	x	x	x	1	x	x	x	x	x	x	x	x
Sri Lanka	1955	x	x	x	x	x	x	x	x	3	x	x	x	x	x	x	x	x
Sudan	1956	x	x	x	x	x	x	x	x	3	x	x	x	x	x	x	x	x

Organization[a]	UN[b]	FAO	GATT	IAEA	IBRD	ICAO	ICJ	IDA	IFAD	IFC	ILO	IMCO	IMF	ITU	UNESCO	UPU	WHO	WIPO	WMO
Members[c]	154	147[d]	86[e]	110[f]	139[g]	146[b]	157[i]	125[j]	131[k]	118[l]	144[m]	118[n]	141[o]	154[p]	149[q]	167[r]	155[s]	91[t]	152[u]
Countries																			
Suriname	1975	x	x		x	x	x	x			x	x	x	x	x	x	x	x	x
Swaziland	1968	x	(e)		x	x	x	x	3	x	x		x	x	x	x	x	x	
Sweden	1946	x	x	x	x	x	x	x	1	x	x	x	x	x	x	x	x	x	x
Syria	1945	x		x	x	x	x	x	3	x	x	x	x	x	x	x	x		x
Tanzania	1961	x	x	x	x	x	x	x	3	x	x	x	x	x	x	x	x		x
Thailand	1946	x		x	x	x	x	x	3	x	x	x	x	x	x	x	x		x
Togo	1960	x	x		x	x	x	x	3	x	x	x	x	x	x	x	x	x	x
Trinidad and To-bago	1962	x			x	x	x	x			x	x	x	x	x	x	x		x
Tunisia	1956	x	(e)	x	x	x	x	x	3	x	x	x	x	x	x	x	x	x	x
Turkey	1945	x	x	x	x	x	x	x	3	x	x	x	x	x	x	x	x	x	x
Uganda	1962	x	x	x	x	x	x	x	3	x	x	x	x	x	x	x	x	x	x
Ukrainian Soviet Socialist Republic	1945			x			x				x			x	x	x	x	x	x
Union of Soviet Socialist Republics	1945					x	x				x	x		x	x	x	x	x	x
United Arab Emirates	1971	x	(e)	x	x	x	x		2	x	x	x		x	x	x	x	x	x
United Kingdom	1945	x	x	x	x	x	x	x	1	x	x	x	x	x	x	x	x	x	x
United States	1945	x	x	x	x	x	x	x	1	x	x	x	x	x	x	x	x	x	x
Upper Volta	1960	x	x		x	x	x	x	3	x	x		x	x	x	x	x	x	x
Uruguay	1945	x	x	x	x	x	x	x	3	x	x	x	x	x	x	x	x	x	x
Venezuela	1945	x		x	x	x	x	x	2	x	x	x	x	x	x	x	x	x	x

Country	Year	UN	FAO	GATT	IAEA	IBRD	ICAO	ICJ	IDA	IFAD	IFC	ILO	IMCO	IMF	ITU	UNESCO	UPU	WHO	WIPO	WMO
Vietnam	1977	x	x		x	x	x	3	x	x		x		x	x	x	x	x	x	x
Western Samoa	1976	x	x		x			3	x			x			x		x	x		x
Yemen Arab Republic	1947	x	x		x	x	x	3	x		x	x		x	x	x	x	x	x	x
Yemen, People's Democratic Republic of	1967	x	(e)		x	x	x	3	x		x	x		x	x	x	x	x	x	x
Yugoslavia	1945	x	x	x	x	x	x	3	x	x	x	x	x	x	x	x	x	x	x	x
Zaire	1960	x	x	x	x	x	x	3	x		x	x	x	x	x	x	x	x	x	x
Zambia	1964	x	(e)		x	x	x	3	x		x	x	x	x	x	x	x	x	x	x
Zimbabwe	1980	x	x		x	x	x					x		x	x	x	x	x		x

a The following abbreviations are used: UN-United Nations; FAO-Food and Agriculture Organization; GATT-General Agreement on Tariffs and Trade; IAEA-International Atomic Energy Agency; IBRD-International Bank for Reconstruction and Development; ICAO-International Civil Aviation Organization; ICJ-International Court of Justice; IDA-International Development Association; IFAD-International Fund for Agricultural Development; IFC-International Finance Corporation; ILO-International Labor Organization; IMCO-Inter-Governmental Maritime Consultative Organization; IMF-International Monetary Fund; ITU-International Telecommunication Union; UNESCO-United Nations Educational, Scientific and Cultural Organization; UPU-Universal Postal Union; WHO-World Health Organization; WIPO-World Intellectual Property Organization; WMO-World Meteorological Organization.

b Dates are those of each member's admission to the United Nations.

c Totals for all columns beginning with FAO include non-UN members.

d The 147 members of FAO include the following not listed in the table: Democratic People's Republic of Korea, Republic of Korea, Namibia (represented by the UN Council for Namibia), Switzerland.

e The 86 contracting parties to GATT include the following not listed in the table: Republic of Korea, Switzerland. Of the 29 states marked (e) in the table, Tunisia has acceded provisionally, while the remaining 28 (plus Kiribati, Tonga, and Tuvalu, which are not listed) are territories to which GATT applied before independence and which now as independent states maintain de facto application of the Agreement pending final decisions as to their commercial policies.

f The 110 members of IAEA include the following not listed in the table: Holy See (Vatican City State), Democratic People's Republic of Korea, Republic of Korea, Liechtenstein, Monaco, Switzerland.

g The 139 members of IBRD include the following not listed in the table: Republic of Korea.

h The 146 members of ICAO include the following not listed in the table: Democratic People's Republic of Korea, Republic of Korea, Monaco, Nauru, Switzerland. USSR membership includes the Byelorussian and Ukrainian SSRs.

[i] The 157 signatories to the statute of ICJ include the following not listed in the table: Liechtenstein, San Marino, Switzerland.

[j] The 125 members of IDA include the following not listed in the table: Republic of Korea.

[k] The 131 members of IFAD are divided into three categories: (1) developed states, (2) oil-producing states, and (3) developing states. Members include the following not listed in the table: Switzerland (1), Republic of Korea (3).

[l] The 118 members of IFC include the following not listed in the table: Republic of Korea.

[m] The 144 members of ILO include the following not listed in the table: Namibia, Switzerland.

[n] The 118 members of IMCO include the following not listed in the table: Republic of Korea, Switzerland. IMCO also has one associate member: Hong Kong.

[o] The 141 members of IMF include the following not listed in the table: Republic of Korea.

[p] The 154 members of ITU include the following not listed in the table: Holy See (Vatican City State), Democratic People's Republic of Korea, Republic of Korea, Liechtenstein, Monaco, Nauru, San Marino, Switzerland, Tonga.

[q] The 149 members of UNESCO include the following not listed in the table: Democratic People's Republic of Korea, Republic of Korea, Monaco, Namibia (represented by the UN Council for Namibia), San Marino, Switzerland. UNESCO also has one associate member: British Eastern Caribbean Group.

[r] The 167 members of UPU include the following not listed in the table: all territories represented by the French Overseas Posts and Telecommunication Agency, Holy See (Vatican City State), Democratic People's Republic of Korea, Republic of Korea, Liechtenstein, Monaco, Nauru, Netherlands Antilles, Overseas Territories of the United Kingdom, Portuguese Asia and Oceania, San Marino, Switzerland, Tonga.

[s] The 155 members of WHO include the following not listed in the table: Democratic People's Republic of Korea, Republic of Korea, Monaco, San Marino, Switzerland, Tonga. WHO also has one associate member: Namibia (represented by the UN Council for Namibia).

[t] The 91 members of WIPO include the following not listed in the table: Holy See (Vatican City State), Democratic People's Republic of Korea, Republic of Korea, Liechtenstein, Monaco, Switzerland.

[u] The 152 members of WMO include the following not listed in the table which maintain their own meteorological services: British Caribbean Territories, French Polynesia, Hong Kong, Democratic People's Republic of Korea, Republic of Korea, Netherlands Antilles, New Caledonia, Switzerland.

[v] Certain of South Africa's rights of membership in ICAO, IAEA, ITU, UPU, WHO, WIPO, and WMO have been suspended or restricted.

Source: Reproduced from *Political Handbook of the World, 1981* (New York: McGraw-Hill, 1981), pp. 673–76. © 1982 by SUNY Research Foundation.

APPENDIX B: Nonpermanent Members of the Security Council: January 1946–December 1980

(The permanent members of the Council are China, France, USSR, United Kingdom, and United States)

Member States	1946	47	48	49	50	51	52	53	54	55	56	57	58	59	60	61	62	63	64	65	66	67	68	69	70	71	72	73	74	75	76	77	78	79	80
Algeria																							X	X											
Argentina	X	X												X	X						X	X													
Australia											X	X																X	X						
Austria																												X	X						
Bangladesh																																	X	X	
Belgium		X	X						X	X																X	X								
Benin																															X	X			
Bolivia																			X	X													X	X	
Brazil	X	X				X	X		X	X								X	X			X	X												
Bulgaria																					X	X													
Burundi																									X	X									
Byelorussian Soviet Socialist Republic																																			
Canada			X	X									X	X							X	X										X	X		
Chile							X	X								X	X																		
Colombia		X	X					X	X			X	X											X	X										
Costa Rica																													X	X					
Cuba				X	X					X	X																								
Czechoslovakia																			X																
Denmark								X	X													X	X												
Ecuador					X	X									X	X																			
Egypt	X			X	X											X	X																X	X	
Ethiopia	X																					X	X												

Member States	1946	47	48	49	50	51	52	53	54	55	56	57	58	59	60	61	62	63	64	65	66	67	68	69	70	71	72	73	74	75	76	77	78	79	80
Finland																								X	X										
Gabon																																X	X		
German Democratic Republic																																			X
Germany, Federal Republic of																															X	X			
Ghana																	X	X																	
Greece						X	X																												
Guinea																										X	X								
Guyana																													X	X					
Hungary					X	X																													
India																						X	X					X	X		X	X			
Indonesia										X	X																								
Iran												X	X																						
Iraq																	X																		
Ireland																													X	X					
Italy														X	X											X	X		X	X					
Ivory Coast																			X	X															
Jamaica												X	X								X	X													
Japan																					X	X				X	X		X	X					
Jordan																					X	X													
Kenya																												X	X						
Kuwait																		X																	
Lebanon							X	X																											
Liberia																X																			

308

Libyan Arab
Jamahiriya
Malaysia
Mali
Mauritania
Mauritius
Mexico
Morocco
Nepal
Netherlands
New Zealand
Nicaragua
Niger
Nigeria
Norway
Pakistan
Panama
Paraguay
Peru
Philippines
Poland
Portugal
Romania
Senegal
Sierra Leone
Somalia
Spain
Sri Lanka
Sudan
Sweden

Member States	*Years* 1946	47	48	49	50	51	52	53	54	55	56	57	58	59	60	61	62	63	64	65	66	67	68	69	70	71	72	73	74	75	76	77	78	79	80
Syrian Arab Republic	X	X																																	
Tunisia														X	X																				X
Turkey						X	X		X	X						X																			
Uganda																					X														
Ukrainian Soviet Socialist Republic			X	X																															
United Republic of Cameroon																													X	X					
United Republic of Tanzania																														X	X				
Uruguay																				X	X														
Venezuela																	X	X														X			
Yugoslavia					X						X																X								
Zambia																								X	X									X	

Source: Davidson Nicol, *The United Nations Security Council: Towards Greater Effectiveness* (New York: United Nations Institute for Training and Research, 1982), pp. 295–99.

APPENDIX C: Status of Contributions to the United Nations Regular Budget as of December 31, 1980 (U.S. dollars)

Member States	1980 Scale of Assessments	Contributions Payable as of January 1, 1980			Collections in 1980	Contributions Outstanding as of December 31, 1980		
		Prior Years	Current Year	Total		Prior Years	Current Year	Total
Afghanistan	.01	–	51,206	51,206	–	–	51,206	51,206
Albania	.01	89,943	51,206	141,149	77,000	12,943	51,206	64,149
Algeria	.12	–	614,469	614,469	–	–	614,469	614,469
Angola	.01	–	47,206	47,206	–	–	47,206	47,206
Argentina	.78	–	3,970,045	3,970,045	3,970,045	–	–	–
Australia	1.83	115,266	9,370,645	9,485,911	9,485,911	–	–	–
Austria	.71	–	3,635,604	3,635,604	3,635,604	–	–	–
Bahamas	.01	–	51,206	51,206	51,206	–	–	–
Bahrain	.01	–	51,206	51,206	51,206	–	–	–
Bangladesh	.04	–	204,823	204,823	204,823	–	–	–
Barbados	.01	310	51,206	51,516	51,516	–	–	–
Belgium	1.22	–	6,247,096	6,247,096	5,480,490	–	766,606	766,606
Benin	.01	–	51,206	51,206	–	–	51,206	51,206
Bhutan	.01	47,614	51,206	98,820	98,820	–	–	–
Bolivia	.01	35,486	51,206	86,692	51,206	–	35,486	35,486
Botswana	.01	–	51,206	51,206	51,206	–	–	–
Brazil	1.27	2,371,851	6,503,126	8,874,977	3,724,204	–	5,150,773	5,150,773
Bulgaria	.16	1,336,318	819,292	2,155,610	529,414	806,904	819,292	1,626,196
Burma	.01	–	51,206	51,206	51,206	–	–	–
Burundi	.01	1,039	51,206	52,245	52,245	–	–	–

Member States	1980 Scale of Assessments	Contributions Payable as of January 1, 1980			Collections in 1980	Contributions Outstanding as of December 31, 1980		
		Prior Years	Current Year	Total		Prior Years	Current Year	Total
Byelorussian Soviet Socialist Republic	.39	1,457,269	1,989,021	3,446,290	1,878,038	–	1,568,252	1,568,252
Canada	3.28	–	16,796,711	16,796,711	16,796,711	–	–	–
Cape Verde	.01	47,614	51,206	98,820	47,614	–	51,206	51,206
Central African Republic	.01	152,780	51,206	203,986	55,860	96,920	51,206	148,126
Chad	.01	170,251	51,206	221,457	–	170,251	51,206	221,457
Chile	.07	–	350,440	350,440	350,440	–	–	–
China	1.62	3,687,531	6,743,325	10,430,856	6,605,171	–	3,825,685	3,825,685
Colombia	.11	80,478	563,263	643,741	637,581	–	6,160	6,160
Comoros	.01	181,468	51,206	232,674	71,343	110,126	51,206	161,332
Congo	.01	162,014	51,206	213,220	168,238	–	44,981	44,981
Costa Rica	.02	45,749	102,411	148,160	90,000	–	58,160	58,160
Cuba	.11	9,047	563,263	572,310	10,978	–	561,332	561,332
Cyprus	.01	–	51,206	51,206	51,206	–	–	–
Czechoslovakia	.83	3,497,988	4,246,073	7,744,061	1,989,049	1,508,939	4,246,073	5,755,012
Democratic Kampuchea	.01	164,868	51,206	216,074	118,348	46,520	51,206	97,726
Democratic Yemen	.01	–	51,206	51,206	51,206	–	–	–
Denmark	.74	–	3,789,222	3,789,222	3,789,222	–	–	–
Djibouti	.01	–	51,206	51,206	–	–	51,206	51,206
Dominica	.01	–	103,297	103,297	–	–	103,297	103,297
Dominican Republic	.03	262,278	153,617	415,895	83,000	179,278	153,617	332,895
Ecuador	.02	73,462	102,411	175,873	106,681	–	69,192	69,192
Egypt	.07	445,747	354,440	800,187	354,440	91,307	354,440	445,747

Country							
El Salvador	.01	–	51,206	51,206	51,206	–	51,206	51,206
Equatorial Guinea	.01	47,614	51,206	98,820	51,206	–	47,614	47,614
Ethiopia	.01	–	51,206	51,206	51,206	–	–	–
Fiji	.01	–	51,206	51,206	51,206	–	–	–
Finland	.48	–	2,457,874	2,457,874	2,457,874	–		
France	6.26	5,878,826	32,054,775	37,933,601	33,126,444	–	4,807,158	4,807,158
Gabon	.02	–	102,411	102,411	8,748	–	93,663	93,663
Gambia	.01	47,614	51,206	98,820	68,257	–	30,563	30,563
German Democratic Republic	1.39	1,527,457	7,117,594	8,645,051	6,758,136	–	1,886,915	1,886,915
Germany, Federal Republic of	8.31	–	42,551,947	42,551,947	42,551,947	–	–	–
Ghana	.03	–	153,617	153,617	153,617	–	–	–
Greece	.35	–	1,792,198	1,792,198	1,792,198	–	–	–
Grenada	.01	171,489	51,206	222,695	67,000	104,489	51,206	155,695
Guatemala	.02	31,853	102,411	134,264	112,722	–	21,542	21,542
Guinea	.01	19,369	51,206	70,575	1,015	18,354	51,206	69,560
Guinea-Bissau	.01	47,614	51,206	98,820	47,614	–	51,206	51,206
Guyana	.01	22,038	51,206	73,244	–	22,038	51,206	73,244
Haiti	.01	73,910	51,206	125,116	51,206	22,704	51,206	73,910
Honduras	.01	–	51,206	51,206	51,206	–		
Hungary	.33	746,850	1,689,788	2,436,638	1,500,000	–	936,638	936,638
Iceland	.03	–	153,617	153,617	153,617	–	–	–
India	.60	3,320,087	3,040,344	6,360,431	3,333,662	–	3,026,769	3,026,769
Indonesia	.16	–	819,292	819,292	10,304	–	808,988	808,988
Iran	.65	1,878,747	3,328,371	5,207,118	25,390	1,853,357	3,328,371	5,181,728
Iraq	.12	–	614,469	614,469	614,469	–	–	–
Ireland	.16	–	819,292	819,292	819,292	–	–	–
Israel	.25	2,014,500	1,280,143	3,294,643	919,379	1,095,121	1,280,143	2,375,264
Italy	3.45	–	17,665,970	17,665,970	17,665,970	–	–	–

Member States	1980 Scale of Assessments	Contributions Payable as of January 1, 1980			Collections in 1980	Contributions Outstanding as of December 31, 1980		
		Prior Years	Current Year	Total		Prior Years	Current Year	Total
Ivory Coast	.03	5,885	153,617	159,502	82,010	—	77,492	77,492
Jamaica	.02	—	102,411	102,411	102,411	—	—	—
Japan	9.58	—	49,055,072	49,055,072	49,055,072	—	—	—
Jordan	.01	36,296	51,206	87,502	87,502	—	—	—
Kenya	.01	—	51,206	51,206	50,684	—	522	522
Kuwait	.20	—	1,024,114	1,024,114	1,024,114	—	—	—
Lao People's Democratic Republic	.01	—	51,206	51,206	51,206	—	—	—
Lebanon	.03	365,140	153,617	518,757	214,723	150,417	153,617	304,034
Lesotho	.01	—	51,206	51,206	51,206	—	—	—
Liberia	.01	27,038	51,206	78,244	78,244	—	—	—
Libyan Arab Jamahiriya	.23	—	1,177,732	1,177,732	1,177,732	—	—	—
Luxembourg	.05	—	256,028	256,028	256,028	—	—	—
Madagascar	.01	3,106	51,206	54,312	54,312	—	—	—
Malawi	.01	—	51,206	51,206	51,206	—	—	—
Malaysia	.09	—	460,851	460,851	460,851	—	—	—
Maldives	.01	83,910	51,206	135,116	83,910	—	51,206	51,206
Mali	.01	115,648	51,206	166,854	166,854	—	—	—
Malta	.01	—	51,206	51,206	51,206	—	—	—
Mauritania	.01	147,185	51,206	198,391	—	147,185	51,206	198,391
Mauritius	.01	—	51,206	51,206	51,206	—	—	—
Mexico	.76	—	3,879,633	3,879,633	3,871,272	—	8,361	8,361
Mongolia	.01	51,670	51,206	102,876	50,353	1,317	51,206	52,523
Morocco	.05	—	256,028	256,028	256,028	—	—	—

	%							
Mozambique	.01	–	47,206	47,206	47,206	–	–	–
Nepal	.01	–	51,206	51,206	51,206	–	–	–
Netherlands	1.63	–	8,346,531	8,346,531	8,346,531	–	–	–
New Zealand	.27	–	1,382,555	1,382,555	1,382,555	–	–	–
Nicaragua	.01	180,084	51,206	231,290	67,869	112,215	51,206	163,421
Niger	.01	4,145	51,206	55,351	74,720	4,145	51,206	55,351
Nigeria	.16	558,621	819,292	1,377,913	–	483,901	819,292	1,303,193
Norway	.50	–	2,560,284	2,560,284	2,560,284	–	–	–
Oman	.01	–	51,206	51,206	51,206	–	–	–
Pakistan	.07	17,527	358,440	375,967	358,444	–	17,522	17,522
Panama	.02	55,925	102,411	158,336	70,000	–	88,336	88,336
Papua New Guinea	.01	47,614	51,206	98,820	98,820	–	–	–
Paraguay	.01	165,167	51,206	216,373	173,769	–	42,604	42,604
Peru	.06	288,909	307,234	596,143	–	288,909	307,234	596,143
Philippines	.10	67,940	512,057	579,997	579,997	–	–	–
Poland	1.24	4,240,015	6,289,508	10,529,523	3,001,460	1,238,555	6,289,508	7,528,063
Portugal	.19	1,126,697	972,908	2,099,605	430,000	696,697	972,908	1,669,605
Qatar	.03	–	153,617	153,617	153,617	–	–	–
Romania	.21	831,790	1,063,320	1,895,110	1,027,500	–	867,610	867,610
Rwanda	.01	–	51,206	51,206	51,206	–	–	–
Samoa	.00	–	51,206	51,206	47,641	–	3,565	3,565
Sao Tome and Principe	.01	–	51,206	51,206	51,206	–	–	–
Saudi Arabia	.58	–	2,969,930	2,969,930	2,969,930	–	–	–
Senegal	.01	77,313	51,206	128,519	–	77,313	51,206	128,519
Seychelles	.01	–	51,206	51,206	51,206	–	–	–
Sierra Leone	.01	83,910	51,206	135,116	–	83,910	51,206	135,116
Singapore	.08	–	409,646	409,646	409,646	–	–	–
Solomon Islands	.01	–	103,297	103,297	4,477	–	98,820	98,820
Somalia	.01	50,762	51,206	101,968	101,968	–	–	–
South Africa	.42	9,621,321	2,150,639	11,771,960	–	9,621,321	2,150,639	11,771,960

Member States	1980 Scale of Assessments	Contributions Payable as of January 1, 1980			Collections in 1980	Contributions Outstanding as of December 31, 1980		
		Prior Years	Current Year	Total		Prior Years	Current Year	Total
Spain	1.70	1,109,665	8,704,970	9,814,635	9,814,635	—	—	—
Sri Lanka	.02	—	102,411	102,411	102,411	—	—	—
Sudan	.01	173,505	51,206	224,711	175,412	—	49,299	49,299
Suriname	.01	—	51,206	51,206	51,206	—	—	—
Swaziland	.01	47,614	51,206	98,820	98,820	—	—	—
Sweden	1.31	907,442	6,707,948	7,615,390	6,707,948	—	907,442	907,442
Syrian Arab Republic	.03	—	153,617	153,617	153,617	—	—	—
Thailand	.10	476,140	512,057	988,197	988,197	—	—	—
Togo	.01	73,741	51,206	124,947	—	73,741	51,206	124,947
Trinidad and Tobago	.03	—	153,617	153,617	153,617	—	—	—
Tunisia	.03	12,256	153,617	165,873	153,617	—	12,256	12,256
Turkey	.30	2,018,465	1,547,841	3,566,306	2,044,367	—	1,521,940	1,521,940
Uganda	.01	47,614	51,528	99,142	47,614	—	51,528	51,528
Ukrainian Soviet Socialist Republic	1.46	4,438,919	7,448,034	11,886,953	7,032,563	—	4,854,390	4,854,390
Union of Soviet Socialist Republics	11.10	34,927,289	56,638,340	91,565,629	55,204,618	—	36,331,011	36,331,011
United Arab Emirates	.10	333,298	512,057	845,355	845,355	—	—	—
United Kingdom of Great Britain and Northern Ireland	4.46	—	22,813,748	22,813,748	22,813,748	—	—	—
United Republic of Cameroon	.01	—	51,206	51,206	51,206	—	—	—

Country								
United Republic of Tanzania	.01	33,307	52,334	85,641	21,012	12,296	52,334	64,630
United States of America	25.00	–	149,735,605	149,735,605	149,543,830	–	191,775	191,775
Upper Volta	.01	8,084	51,206	59,290	–	8,084	51,206	59,290
Uruguay	.04	190,456	204,823	395,279	395,279	–	–	–
Venezuela	.50	–	2,560,285	2,560,285	15,558	–	2,544,727	2,544,727
Vietnam	.03	–	153,617	153,617	–	–	153,617	153,617
Yemen	.01	36,296	51,206	87,502	51,206	–	36,296	36,296
Yugoslavia	.42	275,248	2,150,639	2,425,887	263,248	12,000	2,150,639	2,162,639
Zaire	.02	–	107,202	107,202	14,410	–	92,792	92,792
Zambia	.02	84,350	102,411	186,761	180,520	–	6,241	6,241
Total	99.99	93,711,646	531,925,776	625,637,422	509,679,521	19,151,257	96,776,646	115,927,903

Source: U.N. Secretariat, St/ADM/SER. B/252, March 12, 1982.

317

Index

About the Authors

WERNER J. FELD is UNO Distinguished Professor of Political Science at the University of New Orleans. During the 1968–69 academic year he was a Fulbright Lecturer at the College of Europe in Belgium where he held the George C. Marshall Chair. In 1977 he was Visiting Professor at the Free University of Berlin. He is the author of numerous publications, including *Transnational Business Collaboration Among Common Market Countries* (1970), *Nongovernmental Forces and World Politics* (1972), *The European Community in World Affairs* (1976), *Domestic Political Realities and European Unification* (with John K. Wildgen) (1976) *International Relations: A Transnational Approach* (1979), *Comparative Regional Systems* (with Gavin Boyd) (1980), *Western Germany and the European Community* (1981), and *NATO and the Atlantic Defense* (with John K. Wildgen) (1982). In addition, Dr. Feld is the author of more than 60 articles in various journals. He received a law degree (Referendar) after attending the University of Berlin, and a Ph.D. in Political Science from Tulane University.

ROBERT S. JORDAN, Professor of Political Science and former Dean of the Graduate School, University of New Orleans, received his Ph.D. from Princeton and his D. Phil. from Oxford University, where he was a member of St. Antony's College. Immediately prior to coming to New Orleans, he was Dag Hammarskjöld Professor of International Relations at the University of South Carolina; for much of the preceding ten years he served as a staff member of the United Nations Institute for Training and Research (UNITAR). He has served on the editorial boards of *Public Administration Review*, the *Atlantic Community Quarterly*, and the Section on International and Comparative Administration of the American Society for Public Administration. He is currently Chairman of the International Organization Section of the International Studies Association. Dr. Jordan's most recent publications include *Dag Hammarskjold Revisited: The UN Secretary-General as a Force in World Politics*, *The International Civil Service: Changing Role and Concepts* (with N. Graham), *Political Leadership in NATO: A Study in Multinational Diplomacy*, and *The World Food Conference and Global Problem-Solving* (with T. Weiss).

LEON HURWITZ is Professor of Political Science at Cleveland State University in Cleveland, Ohio. He received his A.B. from Bates College and

331

his Ph.D. from the Maxwell School of Syracuse University. He has published numerous articles in journals such as *Comparative Politics* and *Journal of Common Market Studies*. His previous books include *Introduction to Politics: Traditionalism to Postbehavioralism* (1979), *Contemporary Perspectives on European Integration: Attitudes, Non-Governmental Behavior, and Collective Decision-Making* (1980), *The State as Defendant: Governmental Accountability and the Redress of Individual Grievances* (1981), and *The Harmonization of European Public Policy: Regional Responses to Transnational Challenges* (1983).